Baedeker

Sri Lanka

www.baedeker.com

Verlag Karl Baedeker

TOP-REISEZIELE ✶✶

Sri Lanka's beauty spots are not just to be found in its landscape. An ancient cultural heritage has survived the ages to a greater or lesser extent and is just waiting to be visited. And not least, cities such as Galle and Colombo are bustling with modern urban life. Here we've compiled a list of Sri Lanka's main highlights.

1 ✶✶ **Mihintale**
Buddhism became established on Sri Lanka in Mihintale. The magnificent temples, caves and ruins of Mihintale's monastic complex are wonderfully embedded in the landscape.
▸ **page 301**

Sri Lanka's most impressive cave temple in Dambulla appears to grow out of the rock

2 ✶✶ **Anuradhapura**
More than 100 Singhalese kings decorated their ancient capital Anuradhapura with magnificent palaces, large gardens, artificial lakes and many religious buildings such as monasteries and dagobas.
▸ **page 188**

3 ✶✶ **Nillakgama excavations**
In this monastic complex an almost complete enclosure for a bodhi tree was found during excavations. It is the oldest found on the island of Sri Lanka so far.
▸ **page 200**

4 ✶✶ **Buddha statue of Aukana**
The monumental figure is a magnificent example of a standing Buddha in the blessing gesture.
▸ **page 201**

5 ✶✶ **Sigiriya**
On the summit of this rock rising up to the clouds was once a huge palace complex with gardens and pools. The climb is impressive and leads past the rock with the famous »cloud maidens«.
▸ **page 337**

6 ✶✶ **Polonnaruwa**
The medieval capital of the island has plenty of archaeological attractions, including a large network of canals and pools.
▸ **page 314**

7 ✶✶ **Dambulla**
The five cave temples in Dambulla stand side by side like pearls on a necklace.
▸ **page 227**

8 ✶✶ **Yapahuwa rock fort**
The remains of the 12th-century rock fort are still imposing. These days its location is remote, hidden in the jungle.
▸ **page 356**

9 ✶✶ **Aluvihara**
Here visitors can watch monks work on the library manuscripts. In days gone by the Buddhist canon was written on palm leaves here.
▸ **page 295**

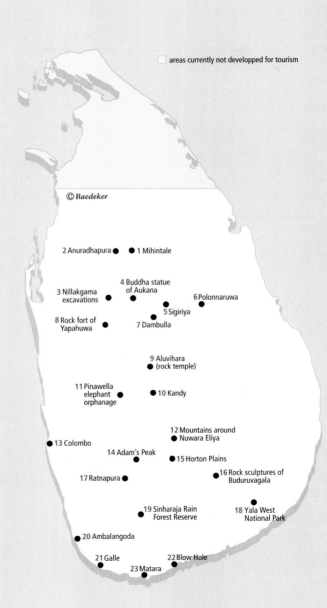

areas currently not developped for tourism

© Baedeker

2 Anuradhapura ● · ● 1 Mihintale

4 Buddha statue
of Aukana
3 Nillakgama · ● · ● 6 Polonnaruwa
excavations
● 5 Sigiriya
8 Rock fort of · ● · ● 7 Dambulla
Yapahuwa

9 Aluvihara
● (rock temple)

11 Pinawella
elephant · ● · ● 10 Kandy
orphanage

12 Mountains around
● Nuwara Eliya
● 13 Colombo
14 Adam's Peak
● · ● 15 Horton Plains
17 Ratnapura ● · ● 16 Rock sculptures of
Buduruvagala

19 Sinharaja Rain
● Forest Reserve · 18 Yala West
● National Park

20 Ambalangoda ●

21 Galle · 22 Blow Hole
23 Matara

10 ✳✳ **Kandy**
The former Singhalese royal city is not just worth a visit during the perahera in July/August. It is generally regarded as the most beautiful city in the country, its attractions including not only its cultural heritage but also a lake and a nature protection area within the city boundary.
▶ **page 260**

11 ✳✳ **Elephant orphanage of Pinawela**
Elephants so close you could reach out and touch them. An attraction for adults and children alike
▶ **page 286**

12 ✳✳ **Mountains around Nuwara Eliya**
The pleasant climate and beautiful landscape already made this town popular in British colonial times.
▶ **page 313**

13 ✳✳ **Colombo**
No visitor to Sri Lanka should come here without also visiting the country's capital.
▶ **page 213**

14 ✳✳ **Adam's Peak**
Nobody should miss the opportunity to watch sunrise from the summit of Sri Lanka's most sacred mountain.
▶ **page 182**

15 ✳✳ **Horton Plains**
This plateau at elevations of more than 2100m/6900 ft is quiet and perfect for hiking.
▶ **page 256**

16 ✳✳ **Rock sculptures of Buduruvagala**
In the middle of dense forest seven monumental Buddha statues rise from a rugged rock wall. They were created in the 9th and 10th centuries.
▶ **page 235**

17 ✳✳ **Ratnapura**
The city of gems is situated in the middle of Sri Lanka's lowlands. It is hard work to extract the treasures from the ground.
▶ **page 332**

Kandy nestles in a wide plain protected by a ring of mountains. The lake gives the town a mellow appeal

18 ✶✶ Yala West National Park
The park is one of the island's largest protected areas. It was founded as long ago as 1900.
► page 354

Yala National Park is home to more than 400 bird species. These waders can be seen in many of its lakes

19 ✶✶ Sinharaja Rain Forest Reserve
Real jungle adventures can still be experienced in Sri Lanka's oldest rainforest reserve.
► page 336

20 ✶✶ Ambalangoda
The town is known for its art of mask-carving. The maskmakers there use a centuries-old tradition.
► page 184

21 ✶✶ Galle
The heart of Galle is the fort built under the Dutch. The city is a good place to explore on foot and has relics of the colonial period.
► page 236

22 ✶✶ Blow hole
A natural phenomenon, of which this is one of just six in the world. On Sri Lanka it can be found close to Tangalla.
► page 345

23 ✶✶ Matara
The island's southernmost town was already an important trading port during the colonial period. While somewhat remote, it is nicely situated on a wide bay. Cinnamon and tea are cultivated in its hinterland.
► page 298

BAEDEKER'S BEST TIPS

Of all the Baedeker tips in this book, the most interesting have been collected in the list below. Experience and enjoy Sri Lanka from its best side!

▮ Journey of the butterflies
Watch thousands of these fragile insects on their flight to Adam's Peak.
► page 28

▮ Mask museum
An exhibition of precious historical masks and the way they were made can be seen in the museum of Ambalangoda.
► page 97

The island's masks are colourful and were originally made of wood

▮ Ayurveda cosmetics
Inexpensive and excellent: ayurveda products ►
page 144

▮ King coconut
The thirst-quenching and healthy milk of the king coconut is available on every street corner in Sri Lanka.
► page 206

▮ Jewellery, antiques and handicrafts
The Historical Museum in Galle has been designed in the style of historical manor houses and contains many treasures. It is housed in a famous fort.
► page 242

▮ Stroll on the Only Path
Temporary guests can meditate in the monastery on Polgasduwa, but only men are permitted.
► page 255

▮ To Kandy by rail
A one-of-a-kind experience through magnificent scenery. The train climbs 2000m/ 6560ft.
► page 269

▮ When babies get the bottle
One highlight at the elephant orphanage in Pinawela is the daily feeding time.
► page 284

▮ Growing pepper
Around Matale there are many spice plantations that also sell their produce.
► page 297

▮ Elephant safari
Watching elephants close-up
► page 328

Sri Lanka has always been known → as a spice island

Buddhism has shaped the island's culture for many centuries. The cave temple of Dambulla contains a large number of Buddha statues from different eras ► **page 227**

BACKGROUND

14 The Cradle of Buddhism

18 Facts

19 Natural Environment

24 *Special: The Great Flood in Paradise*

32 Population · Politics · Economy

36 *Special: The Story of a Conflict*

47 Religion

56 History

57 Prehistory

59 The Years of the First Visitors

61 The Colonial Era

63 Ceylon Becomes Independent

65 Building the New State

67 The Civil War Breaks Out

69 Since the New Millennium

Price Categories

► **Hotels**
Luxury: from 85 £
Mid-range: 40 – 85 £
Budget: under 40 £
For one overnight stay in a
double room

► **Restaurants**
Expensive: from 20 £
Moderate: 10 – 20 £
Inexpensive: under 4 £
For a three-course meal

72 Arts and Culture

73 Art Periods

79 Temple Architecture

84 Visual Arts

91 Literature

93 Dance and Music

94 Handicrafts

96 Customs

100 Famous People

PRACTICALITIES

108 Accomodation

109 Arrival · Before the Journey

112 Beaches

112 Children

113 Drugs

113 Electricity

113 Emergency

Colonial atmosphere lives on: the Galle Face Hotel in Colombo
► page 213

114 Etiquette and Customs
115 Festivals · Holidays · Events
118 Food and Drink
120 *Special: Four Pounds of Leaves, One Pound of Tea*
126 Health
128 *Special: Rediscovering Ancient Knowledge*
130 Information
132 Language
135 Literature
137 Media
138 Money

139 National Parks
142 Personal Safety
144 Post and Telecommunications
145 Prices · Discounts
146 Prostitution
147 Shopping
149 Sport and Outdoors
153 Time
153 Transport
156 Travellers with Disabilities
156 Weights and Measures
157 When to Go

TOURS

164 Travelling in Sri Lanka
166 Tour 1: Grand Tour of the Island
171 Tour 2: In Royal Footsteps
174 Tour 3: The Central Highlands
176 Tour 4: Combination with Tour 3

SIGHTS FROM A to Z

182 Adam's Peak
184 Ambalangoda
187 Ampara
188 Anuradhapura
201 Aukana
202 Avissawella
203 Bandarawela
205 Batticaloa

Laborious to harvest, but delectable: Sri Lankan tea

Chitals in Yala National Park
► **page 354**

208 Bentota
210 Beruwala
212 Chilaw
213 Colombo
227 Dambulla
230 *3 D: Cave Temple of Dambulla*
233 Dedigama
234 Ella
236 Galle
244 Gal Oya National Park
246 Giritale
248 Hambantota
250 Hatton · Dikoya
251 Hikkaduwa
256 Horton Plains
257 Jaffna
259 Kalutara
260 Kandy
270 *3 D: Dalada Maligawa*
281 Kataragama
284 Kegalla
285 Kelaniya
286 *Special: An Orphanage for Elephants*
289 Kurunegala
292 Mahiyangana
296 Matale
298 Matara
300 Medirigiriya
301 Mihintale
305 Monaragala
307 Negombo
309 Nuwara Eliya

314 Polonnaruwa
328 Pottuvil
329 Puttalam
331 Ratnapura
332 *Special: City of Gems*
336 Sigiriya
342 *3 D: Rock Fort of Sigiriya*
344 Tangalla
346 Tissamaharama
348 Trincomalee
351 Weligama
352 Yala National Park
354 Yapahuwa

358 Glossary
362 Index
366 Photo Creits
367 List of maps and illustrations
368 Publisher's information

Kalutara is home to the only dagoba on the island that can be entered
► **page 259**

Background

BRIEF AND TO THE POINT,
CLEARLY WRITTEN AND EASY TO
LOOK UP: INFORMATION ABOUT
THE PEOPLE, RELIGION, ECONOMY,
ART AND HISTORY AS WELL AS
EVERYDAY LIFE

THE CRADLE OF BUDDHISM

»When Buddha came to this land he wanted to fight the evil dragons …« wrote the Chinese monk Fa-Haein in his report after visiting the island of Sri Lanka in the 4th century AD. Whether dragons ever existed on the island off the coast of the Indian subcontinent is lost in the mists of myth and religion. What is certainly a fact is that Sri Lanka was hit by a tsunami on 26 December 2004, bringing the world's attention to the island.

There are many good reasons for visiting Sri Lanka: the turquoise water, palm trees gently swaying in the breeze, pleasant temperatures and an enchanting, lavish landscape. But are there not other islands in the world for which this is at least equally true? A trip to an island

that regularly makes headlines in the global media because of civil war or natural disasters? So why go to Sri Lanka? There are many reasons, first and foremost the almost proverbial hospitality of the population, which visitors will sense as soon as they set foot on the island. The smile with which people are welcomed here is warm; it does not come across as fake. Tourists here do not feel like they are only welcomed for their deep wallet. And it seems as if the island inhabitants, regardless of whether they are Singhalese or Tamil, want to put the ethnic conflict behind them. Those travelling through the country with open eyes will realize that most Singhalese and Tamil people co-exist quite peacefully.

A winning smile

It is difficult for holidaymakers to tell whether a person is Tamil or Singhalese

Magnificent Culture, Diverse Environment

Sri Lanka also has a great history, which goes back to the time before Christ. The country has unique artworks, august buildings and visible evidence of a deeply rooted religious attitude. The works of the Buddhist culture are equal in beauty to those of other civilizations. Anyone who walks past the dagobas, temples and palaces without paying attention to them and just spends the days on the admittedly outstanding beaches will have experienced, but not seen Sri Lanka. The country's true appeal is only revealed to those who venture into

Enchanting paintings
The cloud maidens of Sigiriya are both famous and mysterious. Their meaning is still unsolved

Living in paradise
Sri Lanka has accommodation in all price categories: from luxury resorts to basic guesthouses

Experiencing nature
Sri Lanka's national parks have a fantastic flora and fauna

Life's a beach
Sri Lanka's coast has miles of stunningly beautiful beaches to offer. Very lively and busy in some places, idyllic and lonely in others

City life
The cities, such as Colombo, Kandy and Galle, are always bustling

Magnificent architecture
The 200m/650ft rock was imaginatively incorporated into the architecture of Sigiriya's palace complex

the interior, into the highlands around Nuwara Eliya, to the old royal towns of Anuradhapura and Polonnaruwa. Pure culture rewards the active spirit and anyone who has ever stood at the foot of the famous rock fort of Sigiriya will fall silent in the face of this sheer unimaginable feat achieved so many centuries ago. Also unmissable are the traces that the Portuguese, Dutch and British colonial rulers left behind, such as imposing forts with which they tried to maintain their temporary power over Sri Lanka.

The diverse fauna also deserves mention: this island has endemic animals, meaning they can be found nowhere else on earth. Where else will visitors find an official orphanage for elephant children such as the one in Pinawela? However, Sri Lanka's natural beauties are also unique. In addition to palm-lined beaches that are amongst the most beautiful in the world and offer not just relaxation but also many sporting activities, there are the mountains, the thick jungle, waterfalls and a lavish flora and fauna.

Add to this the seemingly endless plantations on which the world-famous tea is grown.

Since the Buddhism practised in Sri Lanka is still very pure and unadulterated, the religious sites on the island are the destination of many pilgrimages all year round. The colourful religious festivals, full of mysticism, are also an unforgettable experience for tourists.

Pearl in the Indian Ocean

The mere fact that on such a small spot of this earth, which seems to have been casually dropped into the Indian Ocean, so much can be experienced that is beyond all post-

Shaped by Buddhism
Even today visitors see monks of all ages on Sri Lanka

card idylls makes a trip to this fascinating island state worthwhile. Sri Lanka has a lot more to offer than negative headlines. All that remains to be said by way of introduction is ayubovan, which means welcome.

Facts

Hundreds of miles of magnificent beaches and a diverse, evergreen mountain region with rugged peaks and gentle valleys characterize Sri Lanka's landscape. Unique cultural treasures are not just something to look at for archaeologists. They have also been venerated for millennia and are bound into the people's religious life.

Natural Environment

Once a part of India?

Until about 12 million years ago the island of Sri Lanka was connected to the Indian mainland; the separation took place as a result of intense tectonic activity during the Tertiary Period, when the current appearance of the earth largely took shape. Previously, around 250–150 million years before our time, the two supercontinents Gondwana and Laurasia had broken apart. India, which was originally part of the northern continent Laurasia, drifted south and reached Gondwana. Sri Lanka is **possibly a tiny detached fragment of the Indian subcontinent** that was formed during this process. The strait between the Indian mainland and the island of Sri Lanka, an Indian continental shelf, was formed as a result of a rise in sea levels. The land connection between the mainland and the island was immersed under water but Adam's Bridge, an approx. 86km/53mi connection consisting of coral reefs, sand dunes and small islands, remained.

Ancient rocks

From a geological perspective the island is part of the Deccan Plateau, which makes up the entire Indian peninsula south of the 25th parallel. The common factor both landscapes share is that they are characterized by pre-Cambrian crystalline rocks with an estimated age of up to 4.3 billion years, making them some of the oldest on earth. They were formed during a time when the earth's crust was gradually cooling. Younger rocks (highly karstified tertiary limestones) can only be found in the north and northwest of Sri Lanka on the Jaffna Peninsula as well as on a narrow seam on the west coast, which runs south all the way to around Puttalam. They lie on top of the old crystalline base, which forms a wide depression in this area.

Surface configuration

No less simple than the island's geological configuration is the structure of the surface, which can be divided into **just two large areas**. The island's core is dominated by a mountain range of up to 2500m/8200ft, known as the Central Highlands, which rises steeply from the plains in just a few steps. The range makes up around a fifth of the island's total area. Significantly larger are the extensive plains that surround the range. These plains are hard to classify and cover the largest section of the island. In the south and west they form a narrow strip 30–50km/20–30mi wide, while the north and the east are dominated almost entirely by lowlands.

Landscapes

Southwestern part of the island

The lowland strip in the southwest of the island, which is particularly affected by the rains brought by the summer monsoon, is Sri Lanka's

← *There are thundering waterfalls in the Central Highlands,
a range that reaches heights of 2500m/8200ft*

core area both regarding population density and economic significance. The year-round humid climate and the fertile soils are ideal conditions for diverse agriculture. Extensive coconut-palm plantations and intensively cultivated paddy fields are supplemented by large-scale fruit and vegetable plantations. The region's high population density also creates problems, mainly impacting on small-scale agricultural businesses.

Central Highlands

The western flanks of the Central Highlands have a tropical, year-round humid climate, and are also exposed to the moist air brought inland by the summer monsoon. However, as a result of the great differences in altitude, the landscape here is completely different. With increasing height the temperatures decrease. A noticeable feature of this part of the island are the extensive **rubber plantations, and even more so the tea plantations**. Both crops were until comparatively recently completely unknown in Sri Lanka; they were only introduced by the British colonial rulers, but since then they have fundamentally shaped the island's economic life.

Not least because of this **large-scale plantation agriculture**, the population density here is much lower than in the aforementioned lowland area. Although there are almost no economic problems here, in the past the region saw social tensions between Singhalese people and Tamils of Indian origin, since the latter are mainly employed on the plantations as low-paid labour.

Rice terraces shape Sri Lanka's landscape

The climate of the eastern side of the Central Highlands on the other hand is shaped by the winter monsoon. The low temperatures as well as an extended summertime dry period do still permit large tea plantations to exist here and naturally are accompanied by equally large **paddy fields and vegetable plantations**.

Southeastern lowlands

The southeastern lowlands lie in a rain shadow and are somewhat isolated from the rest of the island with regard to the road network, making them one of Sri Lanka's least densely populated regions. The five hot and dry months of October to February are a contributing factor, as they prevent profitable agriculture. This is said to have been different in the past. In the time of the ancient Singhalese kingdom this region was considered to be »Ceylon's granary« (the grain of course being rice).

Jaffna lowlands

Even though the conditions presented by the natural environment, particularly the bad soils, are less favourable than almost anywhere else in Sri Lanka, the inhabitants of the Jaffna lowlands in the north of the island knew how to produce fairly good agricultural yields here despite all of the factors working against them. An ingenious and well-thought-out **irrigation system** that channels water collected during the rainy season to the paddy fields and vegetable plantations helped to deliver the right conditions for this development. However, the civil war left unmistakable marks on the landscape, since the military conflicts between Tamils and Singhalese people were most severe in this region. They were also at least one of reasons why people continue to leave the rural areas for towns and cities, a phenomenon seen most strongly in the urban areas around the capital of Colombo.

Elevations

Of the many mountains in the Central Highlands, 15 are higher than 2000m/6500ft. The highest are Pidurutalagala (2524m/8281ft), Kirigalpotta (2395m/7858ft), Totapola (2359m/7740ft) and Kudahakgala (2351m/7713ft). Despite its height of »only« 2243m/7359ft **Sri Pada** (also known as Adam's Peak) is considered the most significant mountain; it is venerated as a holy mountain and is the destination of many thousands of pilgrims all year round.

Rivers

Five rivers ensure that Sri Lanka's lowlands are well irrigated. Mahaweli Ganga, which flows into the Gulf of Bengal near Mutur (south of Trincomalee), is the longest at 332km/206mi. Further important rivers are Aruvi Aru (length: 167km/104mi, flows into the Gulf of Mannar south of Mannar), Kala Oya (length: 155km/96mi, flows into the Gulf of Mannar north of Puttalam), Kelani Ganga (154km/96mi, flows into the Gulf of Mannar north of Colombo) and Kalu Ganga (110km/68mi, flows into the Gulf of Mannar south of Colombo near Kalutara). All rivers of significance have their source on the slopes of the Central Highlands.

Irrigation system

The Singhalese people achieved an almost unsurpassable feat when they constructed a carefully thought-through and practical irrigation system. As early as the 5th century AD **wewas, artificial lakes**, were constructed in which the rain of the monsoon season is collected and channelled. This irrigation system underwent its greatest expansion in the 12th century when King Parakramabahu I had the insight that »no drop of water should flow into the sea before benefiting the people first«. The dense network of tanks (as the British colonial rulers called the wewa system) allows the agricultural land to receive the necessary water, generally making two rice harvests a year possible. Some of these tanks are very large in area but are very shallow, having a maximum depth of only 5m/16ft. Nevertheless these artificial lakes are also significant for fishing, as they are home to **excellent edible fish** such as gourami and tilapia. Recently even carp have been farmed in them; these fish are an enrichment to the foods available to the rural population.

During the 1980s the centuries-old wewa system was **supplemented by artificial reservoirs**. Thus Mahaweli Ganga has been dammed east of Kandy by the construction of the Victoria Dam, 122m/400ft high and 520m/569 yd wide. It is part of the Mahaweli Project, which consists of a total of four dams. Today almost two thirds of the island's entire energy requirements are met by hydropower.

Flora and Fauna

The tropical rainforest

The extremely lavish vegetation on the island of Sri Lanka is primarily the result of the year-round hot and humid climate. However, what can be seen today is only a small percentage of the flora that once covered Sri Lanka. The pristine rainforest that grew over millions of years, was characterized by an overwhelming diversity and was home to countless plants and animals is now only a shadow of its former self. As a result of **excessive hardwood logging** as well as slash-and-burn only around a fifth of the rainforest, which still covered the majority of the island around two centuries ago, has remained.

The government in Colombo reacted far too late to this overexploitation of the natural environment. At last it began in the 1970s to put some of the remaining forests under **protection**. Some of the logged areas have been reforested, but usually with fast-growing woods which can only replace the tropical rainforest with regard to the wood's economic use. They are no substitute for the rainforest that is so significant for the intercontinental global climate.

Structure ▶

The tropical rainforest is structured into **five layers** that can easily be distinguished by their different heights. The average temperature, which remains relatively stable all year round at 24–30º C/75.2–86º F, and the plentiful precipitation of more than 2000 mm/79 inches per square metre, provide the ideal conditions for the forest to flourish. Its most imposing representatives are giants that can reach a height of up to 50m/165ft. They are the winners in the constant battle for the light of the sun. The forest floor, which forms a multi-layered, fertile foundation for the growth of new plants, only sees a fraction of the sunlight that hits the forest. This circumstance means the plants that want to survive must have abilities to adjust, which they have developed over millions of years. They

? DID YOU KNOW …?

■ … that the government of Sri Lanka hands out young trees to the population for free every year in September and October in order to compensate the decades of overexploitation of the native forests? However, this is nowhere near enough to repair the damage done in the past.

include many types of ferns, which try to capture even the faintest ray of light by having differently shaped leaves.

◄ Species diversity

The tropical rainforest is home to more species on a relatively small area than can be found on the entire American continent, for example. Botanists have counted more than 300 tree, shrub and flower species in just a single square kilometre. This extraordinary biodiversity means that there are often only a few specimen of each species present. Amongst the rainforest's typical trees are many Dipterocarpaceae, of which there are more than 250 different species. The number of different ferns is also remarkable.

Mountain rainforests

A subgroup of the tropical rainforests are the mountain rainforests, which are found in Sri Lanka mainly in the central part of the island. The elevated location and the resulting lower temperatures prevent this type of forest from growing so tall. Trees with a height of 22–25m/72–82ft are the giants here. However, the **diversity of flowers** such as orchids, of which there are around 125 different species in these regions alone, is remarkable.

Monsoon forest

The monsoon forests are secondary forests, that is forests that are the result of forestation or grew again by themselves after the primary forest was logged. In Sri Lanka they can be found in the island's humid regions, i.e. the lower lying regions in the north and east. Their determining characteristics are **savannah-like vegetation** and little biodiversity. The semi-arid climate means the plants have to be undemanding.

Tropical woods

Since the beginning of the 1990s the logging of tropical hardwoods, particularly teak, has been **strictly monitored**. Distributed throughout the entire island on strategically situated roads are »Timber Check Points« where passing wood transports are inspected. With this measure the government is trying to contribute to the conservation of the tropical forest, which are an important factor in maintaining the island's climate. Violations of logging restrictions are officially punished with high fines. In order to cover the demand for tropical hardwoods, these have been cultivated in big plantations since the 1970s.

It will be some time yet before the towns and villages destroyed by the tsunami are fully rebuilt

THE GREAT FLOOD IN PARADISE

On 26 December 2004 at 12.58am GMT (7.58am local time in Sumatra) the second-strongest earthquake ever registered, reaching 9.3 on the Richter scale, hit the sea floor at a depth of around 40 km/25mi just southwest of the northern tip of Sumatra. The energy unleashed was so enormous that the entire planet vibrated for a whole further day. The subsequent tsunami transformed large tracts of coastline in southeast Asia into a disaster zone. On Sri Lanka alone the tsunami claimed around 38,000 lives.

The tsunami (Japanese »tsu« = harbour, »nami« = wave), which reached a height of 30m/100ft, brought death on a huge scale. Hundreds of thousands of people suffered severe injuries and more than three million in the worst-affected coastal regions, northwest Sumatra, the Andaman and Nicobar Islands, Thailand, Sri Lanka and southeast India, were made homeless.

It began with the quake

Sumatra's west coast is well-known to seismologists. Two **tectonic plates** collide here. In this subduction zone the Indo-Australian Plate pushes eastwards under the Eurasian Plate, on which Sumatra is located, at a speed of 10cm/4in per year. This is not a smooth process: the plates get stuck and as a result the Eurasian Plate at the top is pulled down and forced eastwards. This compression zone on the sea floor is marked by the Sunda Trench. On the morning of 26 December 2004 the energy that had been building up for almost 200 years reached a critical threshold value. Over an area of 100,000 sq km/ 38,600 sq mi the contact area between the two plates suddenly tore open. In a huge burst, like a taut spring, the edge of the Eurasian Plate shot westwards by up to 13m/40ft over a length of around 500km/300mi, back to its original location. At the same time the ocean floor was heaved up by 23m/ 610ft, as was the column of water above it. Gigantic quantities of water were set in motion. An asymmetrical front of wave crests and wave troughs spread at a speed of around 700kmh/ 440mph in every direction. Over the next ten hours 15 further, powerful aftershocks struck the ocean floor, tearing the rupture zone open over a stretch of 1000km/600mi.

The waves followed

Just quarter of an hour after the big quake, wave fronts more than 10m/30ft high crashed down over the coast of the province of Aceh on northern tip of Sumatra and over the Indian Nicobar and Andaman Islands. Half an hour later the deadly waves struck Thailand's west coast, and after 23 hours they reached Sri Lanka and the Maldives. Only ten hours after they were triggered, the floods came to an end as they hit the African east coast.

Sri Lanka's affected areas

Sri Lanka's eastern, southern and southwestern coastal regions were affected particularly badly. Some places right on the coast were completely wiped out. Other holiday hotspots were at least severely ravaged. Locals and tourists alike lost their lives in the floods. The tsunami's destructive power varied greatly from bay to bay. **The reason** for this was the complex structure of the coastline and differences in offshore conditions, which either amplified or lessened the strength of the incoming mountains of water. The wave energy spread out at projecting headlands, while it became even more concentrated in the flat bays with their sandy beaches. Hotels built right on the high-tide line, the destruction of natural coastal defences such as pine forests, lagoons, dunes, mangroves and even coral reefs all made a significant contribution to the disastrous impact of the waves.

Trigger

Not every earthquake triggers a tsunami. It becomes critical when the earthquake reaches **7 or higher on the Richter scale**. The speed at which the waves spread depends on the depth of the water. In deep ocean trenches (5000m/16,500ft) the waves can reach speeds of up to 800kmh/500mph, in coastal regions only around 10kmh/6mph. This is because in shallow waters the oscillating water masses are braked in their forward motion. The wave crests are pushed closer and closer together, becoming steeper as a result.

There are now signs that indicate the direction away from the coast. The population can find safe areas within 2-7 km /1-4 mi

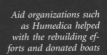

Aid organizations such as Humedica helped with the rebuilding efforts and donated boats

Early warning system

Had an early warning system been in place, like the one that has existed in the Pacific for many decades, the number of victims would have been significantly lower. However, even knowledge of the natural signs and the correct behaviour in the event of an impending tsunami would have helped. Just three weeks after the disaster Indonesia and Germany decided to set up an early warning system for tsunamis in the Indian Ocean. Since 2008 data have been gathered in the most vulnerable region, the Sunda Trench, and are made available to all surrounding states to allow timely and reliable tsunami warnings. A geological research station in Potsdam is responsible for the co-ordination and implementation of the project. Its globally acclaimed earthquake monitoring network is at the heart of this new warning system. The system is supplemented by regional measurement data from the land, the sea and from satellites as well as data about deformations on the ocean floor. In order to avoid false alarms any tsunami must also be registered at an oceanographic level. This is done by pressure gauges on the ocean floor and special GPS buoys anchored at strategically important locations. In addition the observations of new gauging stations on the surrounding island and mainland coastlines are taken into account. All of these data come together simultaneously in national and local warning centres. These centres apply computer simulations that use maps as well as tidal models and weather models that calculate the probable height and destructive power of a tsunami for the vulnerable coastlines. In the event of an emergency it only takes minutes to raise the alarm.

Natural signs

One sure sign that a tsunami is imminent is the fall of the water level by several metres in just a short space of time (510 minutes), uncovering large areas of the sea floor. The first wave front will then strike shortly afterwards, within a few minutes to a maximum of half an hour depending on the tsunami's wave period. A perceptible earthquake in the coastal area is equally alarming. If the epicentre, as was the case in Sumatra, is close to the coast, the waves can arrive within just minutes. It is then imperative to get to safety, either to secure reinforced concrete buildings or to higher ground.

Since tsunamis are very rare they should not stop anyone from enjoying the gorgeous beaches of Sri Lanka.

Considering that Sri Lanka is an island, the diversity of the fauna is remarkable. This has to do with the fact that the island was once connected to the Indian subcontinent via a **land bridge**. At this time many land animals found their way on to the island. They looked for and found their habitats in the tropical rainforests, which covered two thirds of Sri Lanka until just a few centuries ago. During the destruction of these forests by humans, birds, insects, mammals and reptiles were forced to retreat.

Development of the fauna

Of the officially registered 427 bird species, around 250 are permanently at home on the island, while the rest are migrating birds such as the different kinds of swallow that use Sri Lanka as a stopover or winter home. Of the birds that live on the island permanently, **21 are endemic**, which means they can only be found in Sri Lanka and especially in the humid regions. Amongst this group are a few parrot species and songbirds, Brahminy kites, fish owls, darters and the colourful kingfishers. The endemic species include Ceylon starlings, black-headed ibises, white-bellied sea eagles and red junglefowl. Plants that are considered symbols of beauty and elegance are also plentiful.

Impressive bird diversity

The nature reserves marked out by the government are ideal habitats for birds. Huge numbers can be watched during a visit to **Kumana National Park** in Eastern Province or in the national parks of Bundala, Kalametiya and Wirvila in the south of the island. Bundala is known for its many flamingos, Kitulgala for its large number of endemic birds.

! **Baedeker TIP**

Butterfly migration

A special event for fans of butterflies is the annual butterfly migration that takes place in March and April. The butterflies fly to Adam's Peak (which is why the mountain is also known as Samanale Kande, Butterfly Mountain).

The number of butterfly species living in Sri Lanka is also striking. **No fewer than 242 species** are registered, most of them living in the lower mountain regions up to an altitude of 1000m/3300ft. Only six butterfly species live higher up than that.

Butterflies

Mosquitoes are amongst the less appreciated insects. They can become a particular nuisance during the evening hours.

Mosquitoes

Flying foxes, or fruit bats, which hang in the trees as they sleep during the day and only become active in the evening and at night, are numerous. Then they come out to look for food, frequently surprising observers with their ghostly appearance. However, they are very shy and avoid contact with humans.

Flying foxes

Sri Lanka's monkeys can be quite bold at times; some of them are endemic, including leaf monkeys, which can be recognized by their

Monkeys

crimson faces, and purple-faced langur, which can now only be found in the mountainous regions. The most common representatives of this group are macaques and langurs as well as grey monkeys, which prefer living in trees. The grey monkeys are considered holy by Hindus since, according to the Indian epic Ramayana, a grey monkey in the form of the monkey god Hanuman is said to have saved the princess Sita, who had been kidnapped by the giant Ravana and brought to Sri Lanka.

Monkeys are generally vegetarians, but it is a good idea to refrain from feeding them peanuts, bananas and other fruit since the animals can **occasionally become quite aggressive** when their food stores are exhausted.

Bears and leopards
The opportunity to see bears and leopards in Sri Lanka now only exists in the nature reserves, but there chances are good. Their numbers have been **decimated**, since they are extremely unpopular with the local population and because they seek out agricultural areas, particularly at night.

Reptiles
A total of 75 different reptile species have been counted that live nowhere else but in Sri Lanka. Amongst them is a certain species of **mugger crocodile** that can reach a length of up to 5m/16ft and a weight of several hundred kilograms, making it the **largest reptile living in Sri Lanka**. However, it is usually quite shy and lives a very withdrawn life. It is rare for crocodiles to attack humans; this has usually occurred in the past because of carelessness while bathing. Monitor lizards, which can reach a length of up to 3m/10ft, are also nothing to worry about; like crocodiles they have a very sensitive sense of touch, which makes them run away even from the faintest vibrations on the ground. They mainly eat large insects, but also snakes, and during the hunt they develop a surprising agility.

Sri Lanka is also home to **five tortoise and terrapin species**, which are all under protection. They include the vegetarian Indian star tortoise, the only land tortoise. It reaches a length of 38cm/15in and can be recognized by the star-shaped pattern on its shell.

Snakes
Only a few of the total of 83 snake species are dangerous to humans; they include cobras, Indian Ceylon krait and two species of viper (one of them is the chain viper, which can grow up to 1.6m/5.2ft and whose bite leads to certain death). Burmese pythons are impressive for their size but in their behaviour they are harmless. However, all of the snake species tend to live in remote regions of the forests. They are rarely spotted in the vicinity of humans. Mongooses are considered to be their greatest enemy. They know how to kill even the most venomous snake with a single bite.

Geckos
One of Sri Lanka's useful animals is the gecko, a lizard with adhesive toes. Geckos are attracted to artificial light sources, particularly in

This sea turtle is only two days old

the evening. They make a cackling sound. They are popular because they love eating insects and will consume several dozen mosquitoes a night.

Although the lion is considered Sri Lanka's national animal, this **Elephants** honour should really be reserved for the elephant, not least because there have been no lions living in the wild on the island for decades. The number of Indian elephants has also been decimated; even at the start of the 20th century there were fewer than 12,000 elephants living in the wild, but today that number has dropped to **only around 2500**. Humans are largely to blame for this because of the ever more intensive agricultural use of the pristine forests, which cuts through the elephants' centuries-old routes. Like everywhere on earth where elephants exist, Sri Lanka's elephants are also hunted down by ruthless poachers for their precious ivory tusks, and countless elephants were injured or lost their lives in the upheavals of the civil war. There is an **Elephant Orphanage** in Pinawella near Kandy for orphaned young animals who would not manage to join other herds without their parents and would wander about helplessly (►Baedeker Special p. 286).

Elephants still play an important part in forestry where they are used as work animals. They also fulfil an important role during festive ceremonies such as in Kandy, where hundreds of them participate in the annual celebrations at the Temple of the Tooth, acting as colourfully decorated relic bearers.

Elephants are led by an **elephant driver (mahout)**; the animals obey only this one person and can remember around 100 words or commands. Elephants grow to a shoulder height of approx. 3m/10ft and a weight of around four tons. **They are generally considered good-natured animals.** They can become volatile during the winter months, the reason for which is a secretion produced by a small opening on the head during the mating season, which sometimes gets into their eyes. In addition their proverbial good memory (also for bad events) has surprised many a mahout and sometimes even cost his life.

Elephant cows are pregnant for 23 months. Once the calf is born they enjoy a **three-year »maternity leave«** during which they do nothing but look after the offspring. An elephant baby weighs around 100 kg/220 lbs and has a height of around 75cm/30in. Elephants can live for a maximum of 100 years and on average reach 80; their best years are between the ages of 25 and 60. During that time they can work eight hours a day, but only during the cooler months. During the hot season they cannot be motivated to work.

Elephant mothers look after their offspring intensively for three years

Amongst Sri Lanka's domesticated animals are first and foremost **water buffalo**, which have been used for hundreds of years to cultivate paddy fields and as reliable draught animals. **Cows and oxen** can also be found all over the island, grazing in a leisurely manner by the side of the road. Only recently have the people of Sri Lanka, with the practical support of Danish companies, learned about the use and preservation of cow's milk.

Domesticated animals

The marine fauna all around the island of Sri Lanka is no less impressive. The sea's larger inhabitants include sharks, dolphins, rays, moray eels, tuna and barracudas, while the smaller ones include tropical fish such as parrotfish, heniochus and marine angelfish, who prefer to live around coral reefs. The overfishing of the world's oceans is also having an effect around Sri Lanka. Dolphins in particular are being served as delicacies. At least 5000 a year are caught and some of them are exported to Japan. However, dolphin barbecues are also quite popular in Sri Lanka amongst those who can afford them.

Marine fauna

Other underwater creatures are **corals**; corals belong to the cnidaria phylum (polyps). They surround themselves with a coat of calcium carbonate for protection. Corals prefer to settle in large colonies; warm water with a good current and strong sunshine presents the most favourable conditions for their growth. Larger coral reefs can still be found off Hikkaduwa at the southwestern end of the island, but careless divers have caused grave damage here over the past few years. The coral reefs in the northeast off Trincomalee and along the east coast are still relatively untouched, but political circumstances make visits very difficult.

Many streams and inland lakes are home to fish. There are said to be a total of 54 different species. Some of them were brought to the island by the British – trout, for example, which are widespread in the clear streams of the Horton Plains.

Freshwater fish

Nature Conservation and Environmental Protection

The current government is serious about the idea of nature conservation. To date the island possesses **14 protected areas**, divided into three different categories: sanctuaries are protected areas in which agriculture is permitted but the animals who live in them may not be hunted. National parks are divided into two groups. One of the groups allows visitors to enter on foot or by vehicle, while the second group are designated Strict Nature Reserves. Visiting these is strictly prohibited, and any interference by humans is forbidden.

National parks

The best-known and most-visited nature reserve in Sri Lanka is **Yala National Park** in the south of the island; it is also known as Ruhunu National Park. Because of its exposed location it was, like the places

■ ... that the world's first nature reserve was probably set up in Sri Lanka? King Deva-nampiya Tissa declared a forest area close to his capital of Mihintale to be a refuge for animals of all kinds, forbidding anyone to hunt or kill them, as early as the 3rd century BC. In the 12th century AD King Nissanka Malla put a large area not far from Polonnaruwa under his personal protection.

along Sri Lanka's southern coast-line, affected severely by the tsuna-mi. The damage in the park has been rectified. The effects of the civil war between Singhalese and Tamils are particularly visible in Wilpattu National Park; large tracts of forest have been logged here, de-stroying a place of refuge for the once large number of animals liv-ing here in the wild.

In some nature reserves the De-partment of Wildlife Conservation maintains visitor accommodation, which does, however, need to be booked in advance. Yala National Park and Wilpattu both have ac-commodation.

Botanical gardens The three botanical gardens maintained by the government are also famous. The best-known botanical garden is in Peradeniya not far from Kandy. The others can be found in Hakgala and Gampaha.

Population · Politics · Economy

Vedda, the indigenous population The descendants of the aboriginal island inhabitants, called Yakshas (= demons) in the Mahavamsa legend, are ethnically quite mixed, making this group difficult to capture statistically. They are known as the Vedda people and belong to the Australoid or proto-Australoid races. Their roots probably lie in a prehistoric hunting people that al-ready existed during the Neolithic period. Today only an estimated **2500 Vedda live in Sri Lanka**. The government granted them places of refuge in the north of the island, where they can pursue their tradi-tions, some of which are animist in nature. Their settlements, which

■ When the legendary Vedda chief Tissahami died in 1998 aged 104, even President Kumaratunga paid her condolences and ordered a state funeral. Tissahami had worked as a mediator between the government and the Vedda people and managed to get some of their ancestral land restored to them.

are hard to find in the dense jungle anyway, may only be visited with a special permit from the authorities.

Singhalese people Of the approx. 20.2 million people living in Sri Lanka, the Singhalese represent the **largest group** with around 74 percent of the popula-tion. They are the descendants of people who are known to have come from northern India in the 5th century BC. The Singhalese ex-pelled large numbers of Tamils, who originated from southern India

National Parks   *Sri Lanka*

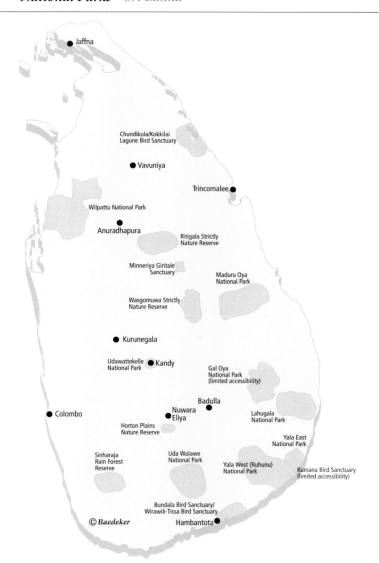

Jaffna

Chundikula/Kokkilai
Lagune Bird Sanctuary

Vavuniya

Trincomalee

Wilpattu National Park

Anuradhapura

Ritigala Strictly
Nature Reserve

Minneriya Giritale
Sanctuary

Maduru Oya
National Park

Wasgomuwa Strictly
Nature Reserve

Kurunegala

Udawattekelle
National Park   Kandy

Gal Oya
National Park
(limited accessibility)

Badulla

Colombo

Nuwara
Eliya

Lahugala
National Park

Horton Plains
Nature Reserve

Yala East
National Park

Sinharaja
Rain Forest
Reserve

Uda Walawe
National Park

Yala West (Ruhunu)
National Park

Kumana Bird Sanctuary
(limited accessibility)

Bundala Bird Sanctuary/
Wirawili-Tissa Bird Sanctuary

© *Baedeker*

Hambantota

and had come to Sri Lanka three centuries earlier, occupying the majority of the island. Today the Singhalese are the dominant social group, not least because of their better educational opportunities. Until 1977 the parliament in Colombo consisted almost exclusively of Singhalese, and until this date they also held all government offices. The Singhalese live mainly in the southwest and the south of the island as well as in the highlands of Kandy, a region that defied the attempts of the colonial powers to conquer it until 1815.

Tamil people The Tamil people make up around 18 percent of the population, 3.6 million people, making them the **second-largest population group** in Sri Lanka; however, this figure does include the Tamils from India as well as those from Sri Lanka. They are much more dark-skinned and shorter than the Singhalese and stocky rather than slim. The Tamils are mostly descendants of emigrants from Malaysia, Singapore, Burma and southern and eastern Africa.

However, here too there are subtle differences: only the Ceylon Tamils consider themselves native Sri Lankans. They see the Indian Tamils, the Tamil people who were mainly brought to Sri Lanka from India as cheap plantation workers during the British colonial period, to be foreigners, irrespective of the fact that these days most of them were born in Sri Lanka, meaning they have Sri Lankan citizenship. Since 1964 the Sri Lankan government has been implementing **repatriation programmes** whose goal is to send the Indian Tamils back to their original homeland. Since that time several hundred thousand have left the island. Some of them now live as refugees all around the world. The Tamils of Indian origin mainly inhabit the regions in the north of Sri Lanka and on the Jaffna Peninsula as well as along the east coast. They can also be found in other parts of the country too, however, such as in Kandy as well as in the highlands around Nuwara Ekiya, where they work as badly paid pickers on the tea plantations.

Moors From the 8th century AD onwards Arabs started settling in Sri Lanka. Most of them were seafarers, who initially worked as **spice exporters** and later also as **gemstone traders**. Some of their descendants, the Moors, still live as businesspeople in Colombo as well as on the southwest and south coasts. They make up the majority of the population in the district of Amparai, which stretches from the east coast far into the country's interior. They are either Sri Lankan Moors, who settled on the island before the 19th century, or Indian Moors, whose Arab ancestors only came to the island in the 19th and 20th centuries. Sri Lanka has a total of 1.2 million Moors, which is about four percent of the total population.

Burgher people The Burgher people, the descendants of the Dutch and Portuguese who came to Sri Lanka during the colonial period, number only around 45,000 now. Most of them left the island after 1948, when

Sri Lanka was granted independence. The majority chose to emigrate to Australia. Those still living in Sri Lanka are proud of their origin: in order to stand out from the large mass of Singhalese people they often use English as their language of choice.

Conflicts between the different population groups erupted even in early centuries. They usually emanated from members of the ruling families. Thus, Tamil mercenaries from southern India were at the centre of the conflicts between the rich Hindus in India and the Lambakanna and Moriya rulers in Sri Lanka.

Conflicts

Today it is mainly the Tamils living in the north and on the east coast who consider themselves second-class citizens. Their political representation, the **Tamil United Liberation Front** (TULF), has been de-

> **? DID YOU KNOW …?**
>
> ■ … that Sri Lanka has the highest suicide rate in the world? Every year an average of 9000 people kill themselves. Sociologists suspect a cry for help behind this suicide wave of mostly 14- to 30-year-olds, but the doctors and hospitals are not yet qualified enough to deal with it.

manding not just political equality since the 1980s, but also an independent Tamil state under the name of Eelam. While the TULF rejects violence to implement its political goals, another group that came into existence in the 1980s was the **Liberation Tigers of Tamil Eelam** (LTTE). The civil war in Sri Lanka that broke out in 1983 claimed more than 50,000 lives.

The **contacts between the Singhalese and Tamil populations** are closer than one might think. Even today, just like many centuries ago, marriages between Singhalese and Tamil people are no rarity.

The welfare system is well established considering Sri Lanka is a developing country. There are several state-organized Social Assistance Services that can be taken advantage of during emergencies and illnesses. Pregnant women also have the right to financial support; however, there is no unemployment pay. While civil servants have their own pensions system, widow's and orphan's pensions are not mandatory. Medical care is also good compared to other developing countries. It is free of charge. Hospitals and clinics are available in sufficient numbers. The traditional natural medicine of ayurveda (►Baedeker Special, p. 128) plays a special role in Sri Lanka.

Welfare system

Compared to other countries with a similar structure Sri Lanka has an outstanding position regarding education. Intense government efforts have contributed to a literacy rate of more than 90 percent.

In Sri Lanka education is compulsory for children for five years, between the ages of six and eleven; attendance at state schools and preparatory kindergartens is free. **The education system is based on the British model**; primary school is followed by junior secondary school and senior secondary school. In order to get into university

Education

THE STORY OF A CONFLICT

It was a fleeting scene outside the Bodhi Tree Temple in Anuradhapura: a young female soldier dressed in camouflage clothing, a machine gun casually slung over her shoulder, stood in front of one of the altars, completely in her own world, lighting a small oil lamp. Then she placed her hands together in front of her chest, bowed and left, as if she felt watched by her comrades, quickly returning to her guard post in front of the temple. An oil lamp for peace?

It is crazy. An island smaller than Scotland was devastated by a **civil war** that lasted more than 26 years and claimed the lives of many thousands of people.

Looking for signs

On a drive through the Central Highlands one of the reasons for the conflict between the **Singhalese** and **Tamil** people becomes clear. Young and old women are working on the countless tea plantations, even on Sundays. Up to their chests in the densely planted bushes they pick the leaves until one hand is full. Then they cast the leaves into the baskets on their backs with an expert throw. They are Tamil women, their skin burned by the sun, the red bindi revealing them to be Hindus on their foreheads. A quarter of an hour later the baskets are full and the women slowly make their way to the place where an overseer is waiting. Basket after basket is weighed and the pickers hold out tattered books in which the overseer records the quantity.

Suddenly it becomes quiet and although nothing can be seen yet the women silently form a wide alley. Seconds later a Jeep races over the sandy track, enveloping the women in thick dust. It is the plantation mana-

There have been victims on both sides: military cemetery of the Tamil Tigers in Killinochi

The Tamil Tigers demand an autonomous state. This can be seen on their flags but also on their number plates in their territory

ger, who has come up from his villa in the middle of the tea plantations, maybe for a Sunday outing with his family. The women close the gap again behind the Jeep and the weighing of the leaves continues.

Tamils are considered second-class citizens on Sri Lanka. They provide cheap labour and live largely under inhumane conditions. Not only do they have no right to vote, they are technically **stateless** because they are denied Singhalese citizenship to this day. They are paid a few rupees a day for their monotonous work; their children are only given the most basic education, meaning all they know is how to read and write their name.

Guest workers at first

When the British first brought this cheap labour to Sri Lanka from southern India, the Tamils were employed as seasonal workers. At the time the island still had many coffee plantations, which only required harvesting once or twice a year. During the second half of the 19th century coffee rust put an end to coffee plantations on Sri Lanka. They were replaced by tea plantations. Tea leaves can be harvested all year round, which meant that the Tamil workers left their homes forever. The concessions made to them socially and economically did not keep up with the profits

that were made with the tea plantations. Even today a picker earns little more than a dollar per day.

Second-class citizens

Tamils in the north of Sri Lanka were not satisfied with being second-class citizens. This mood festered for a long time and then turned into anger that expressed itself in attacks against the power of the Singhalese population. The Singhalese counter-reaction was not long in coming. **Terror was fought with terror**; the houses of rebellious Tamils were burned down and their inhabitants banished to the north. In response the LTTE, the radical Liberation Tigers of Tamil Eelam, was formed. They, and especially the group known as the Black Tigers that was prepared to carry out suicide attacks, were responsible for countless acts of terror that claimed many lives, including those of civilians.

After several attempts to end the civil war, the government in Colombo decided on a large-scale military offensive. It ended in May 2009 after weeks of bloody fighting with victory for the Singhalese, but also created tens of thousands of refugees, some of whom are still living in camps. It remains to be seen how this victory can result in long-lasting peace and reconciliation between Singhalese and Tamils.

students have to sit an entry exam. They are then selected by a quota system; as well as their attainment, the population and the level of development of the relevant district is taken into account. The University of Peradeniya near Kandy is considered to be the island's best.

Since a modern constitution was passed in 1972 there are **officially** **no more castes** in Sri Lanka; however, this separation of the social classes, based on the Indian model, is still ubiquitous. Even though the boundaries have become somewhat blurred, particularly amongst the smaller castes, members of a low caste have a hard time improving their professional position regardless of how much hard work they put. It is virtually impossible for the rural population to marry into a higher caste. This can be seen in the marriage advertisements in Sri Lanka's newspapers. Membership of a certain caste is an absolute must for the desired partner.

Caste system

While the term »varna« (= colours) for castes is customary in India, the word »caste« is of Portuguese origin (casta); **it means »pure« or** **»chaste«**. The term was coined by Portuguese seafarers, who also arrived on the Indian subcontinent, and was probably a reference to the fact that the members of the different classes of Hindu society had highly specific purity rules.

The basis of the caste system is the understanding that every Hindu is born into a very specific, closed religious and social group; upholding the rights and duties of this group is a lifelong requirement. Moving from one caste to another is generally only possible as a result of the process of **rebirth**, meaning only in the next life and after an existence full of good thoughts and deeds.

Originally there were only four castes in India: Brahmins (priests), Kshatriyas (warriors), Vaishyas (farmers and craftsmen) and Shudras (labourers). Over time around 3000 smaller castes were added, whose members were recruited from the different professions. The Brahmin caste naturally enjoy s the highest standing, due to the fact that princes, officials and intellectuals consider themselves as belonging to this caste.

Singhalese and Tamil people generally use different castes or give their castes different names. There are **four Tamil castes** in Sri Lanka, of which the Pujavis, the Hindu priests, have the highest standing. Below this caste are the people born into the Velalla caste (its main group of members are large landowners), the members of the Kovias caste (farmers in the service of the Velallas) and finally the Pallas and Nevalas (landless farm labourers). Anyone not belonging to a caste is largely ostracized by society, and in India the person is considered to be »dalit«, **»untouchable«**. In Sri Lanka the term for this social class is »paravas«; they are forbidden, for example, to enter certain Hindu temples.

← *There is no minimum age for monks*

The **Singhalese in Sri Lanka have 43 castes**, but more than half of them are part of the Goyigama caste, the caste of large landowners and free farmers. Below this is the Karava caste, which once included fishermen and seafarers, but is now made up of merchants and entrepreneurs. Amongst the lower castes, the Navamdama caste is worth mentioning. It is reserved to blacksmiths. The members of the Velli-duraya caste are the »guardians of the Bodhi tree«, the tree under which Buddha achieved enlightenment.

State and Administration

Official name

Since 1972 the island's official name has been Sri Lanka Prajathanthrika Samajavadi Janaraiaya (Democratic Socialist Republic of Sri Lanka). Until this time Ceylon was the standard name, but of course only since the period of the British colonial rule. The current short name, Sri Lanka, means **»venerable island«**.

Forms of government

Since 1972, when the constitution was passed, Sri Lanka has been a **democratic and at the same time socialist republic**. With this constitution, largely written by the United National Party (UNP), Ceylon became a republic and the governor general in place since 1948 was replaced by a president.

National emblems

The flag of Sri Lanka, which was hoisted for the first time on 7 September 1978, alludes to the former flag of the kings of Kandy. It has a yellow (sometimes golden) frame with two stripes in green and orange, which are symbolic of the Muslim and Hindu minorities. The larger field, whose colour was changed in 1985, is dominated by a **lion with a sword** and there is a leaf of the sacred fig tree in every corner.

The national coat of arms was assumed in 1972. Here too the **lion holding the sword of the kings of Kandy** is at the centre. It is crowned by the Dharma wheel that Buddha set in motion. The central field is surrounded by a wreath of lotus and ears of corn. Above the base are sun and moon and a punkalasa between them.

Government

Since 2005 Sri Lanka has been led by the **state president Mahinda Rajapaksa** and his **prime minister Ratnasiri Wickremanayake**. Rajapaksa succeeded Chandrika Kumaratunga, who was from the Bandaranaike family and was not allowed to stand for re-election again. The Bandaranaike family has been dominant in Sri Lankan politics for many years. The president and prime minister are elected by the population every six years.

Parliament

The parliament consists of 225 deputies, of whom 196 are elected by the population every six years. The remaining 29 are nominated on a national list. They are representatives of all classes of society, but also representatives of interest groups.

Facts and Figures Sri Lanka

Location
► Southern Asia in the Indian Ocean, east of the Indian subcontinent, approx. 880km/545mi north of the equator
► Latitude 6° – 10° N
► Longitude 80°– 82° E

Area
► 65,525 sq km/25,300 sq mi
► Also part of the state of Sri Lanka are 13 small islands northwest of the main island in the Gulf of Mannar and in Palk Strait.

Extent
► 225km/140mi east-west;432km/268mi north-south

Length of coastline
► approx. 1340km/830mi

Time Zone
► GMT + 5.5 hours (BST + 4.5 hours)

State and Administration
► Socialist presidential republic
► Präsident: Mahinda Rajapaksa (since 2005)
► Premierminister: Ratnasiri Wickremanayake (since 2005)
► Capitol: Colombo
► Seat of government: Sri Jayawardene-pura
► Largest cities: Colombo (approx. 650,000 inhabitants), Dehiwala Mount Lavinia (approx. 210,000 inhabitants), Negombo (approx. 123,000 inhabitants), Jaffna (approx. 110,000 inhabitants)

Population
► 20.9 million, of whom 74% are Singhalese, 18% are Tamils, 4% are Moors and 2% are Malays and Indians
► Population density: approx 310 people per sq km/800 per sq mi, population growth: approx. 0.9% p.a.
► Languages: Sinhala, Tamil, English
► Religions: Buddhism, Hinduism, Christianity, Islam

Economy
► Gross national product: about US$95.5 billion (approx. US$1160 per capita)
► GNP breakdown: agriculture 20%, industry 26%, services 54%
► Area used for agriculture: about 29%, of which one third is irrigated
► Products: tea, coconuts, rubber, textiles
► Raw materials: graphite, iron ore, uranium, gemstones
► Trading partners: India, the United States, Japan, Iran, Great Britain
► Tourism: 494,000 visitors, turnover: about US$410 million

Sri Lanka • Colombo
Equator
© Baedeker

The island of Sri Lanka is divided into **nine provinces** (Southern Province, Sabaragamuwa Province, Western Province, Uva Province, Eastern Province, Central Province, North Western Province, North Central Province und Northern Province), which are in turn divided into 24 districts.

Administrative structure

Political parties   The **United National Party** (UNP) was the dominant party in Sri Lanka at first but during the 1956 elections was beaten by the **Sri Lanka Freedom Party** (SLFP) of the former UNP prime minister S. W. R. D. Bandaranaike. After his assassination in 1959 the UNP came back into power, but lost again at the following elections. By using clever tactics such as bringing the election date forwards the Bandaranaike family succeeded in getting the UNP into government or keeping power time and again.

The **Tamil United Liberation Front** (TULF) , the political representation of Tamil interests, only played a subordinate role. Although it formed the largest opposition party with 18 members of parliament after the elections of 1977, it could not win the permanent support of the Tamil population of Sri Lanka.

Foreign policy   With regard to foreign policy the government has pursued the goals of the Non-Aligned Movement, but did maintain close relations with some eastern bloc states until the latter were reordered or dissolved.

International affiliations   As early as 1948, when the country's independence constitution came into force, Sri Lanka entered the **Commonwealth of Nations**, whose member states consider the British crown as the symbol of their voluntary association. In 1955 the island state joined the United Nations and has since sent representatives to the UN's many special and sub-organizations.

The **Colombo Plan** (in full Colombo Plan for Cooperative Economic and Social Development in Asia and the Pacific) was named after the place where it was ratified in 1950, initially by seven member states of the Commonwealth. The purpose of the alliance, which now has 28 member states, is the co-ordination and promotion of the economic development of its Asian and Pacific members.

Trade Unions   The many trade unions play an important role over and above their actual function, since they also pursue political goals and are associated with a party. This fact was particularly significant during the time when the United National Party (UNP) was in power (1977–94) and the unions formed an extension to the opposition parties. Traditionally unions are also represented in parliament. Wildcat strikes were made illegal in 1979 when a law to that effect was passed.

No compulsory military service   Sri Lanka does not have compulsory military service. Many social classes consider employment in the army as desirable, for women too, since it provides sufficient social security, including pensions.

Economy

Development   The location of the island of Sri Lanka as an »outpost« in the Indian Ocean allowed it to benefit from a **favourable economic develop-**

ment soon after the first settlers arrived. The first island inhabitants were farmers who cultivated paddy fields. They developed the method of artificial field irrigation using dams and reservoirs that is still in use today. This system, which was already highly developed in the 12th century, has allowed two rice harvests a year ever since.

The **period of colonization** of large parts of the Asian continent by Europeans brought the **Portuguese** to Sri Lanka in the 16th century. They wanted to created a trading post in Colombo and were helped by the fact that the largest part of the island, which they called Ceilao, had fallen apart into three kingdoms at this time and the kings were fighting for power. In around 1610 the Portuguese controlled almost the entire southwestern part of the island as well as some regions on the eastern end. Their area of influence ended below Kandy, however, whose king Senerath initially resisted the foreigners, but later (1617) came to contractual agreements with the Portuguese on trade. When the **Dutch** arrived in the mid-16th century Senarat's son Rajasimha II signed a pact whose goal was to put an end to Portuguese power in Sri Lanka. At this time trading in spices had reached

After the harvest the rice is spread out to dry

a first climax. The Dutch did not, however, stick to the agreements; although they helped the kings of Kandy oust the Portuguese from the strategically important ports of Galle and Negombo, they subsequently declared Galle to be their territory. The income from exporting spices subsequently formed the most important source of income for the state.

A good century later the **British** arrived, and their traces are still clearly visible today. After bringing the majority of the island under their control they set about restructuring the economy, basing it on the British model. During the first half of the 19th century they introduced coffee cultivation, which soon became so successful that it exceeded the profits from the spice trade, which had dominated until then. This development ended again however in around 1865 when the plants were affected by coffee rust. This disease spread from Sri Lanka all around the world. For the British the abrupt end of coffee cultivation was the reason why other profitable crops were brought to Ceylon. The plantation economy they had created was suitable for tea, rubber figs and coconut palms. These three plants still make up Sri Lanka's agricultural and economic backbone. More than a fifth of GNP comes from the agricultural sector.

The annual per capita income of just under US$ 2000 in 2009 (European Union: approx. US$ 33,000) means **Sri Lanka is still a developing country**, but in comparison with other south Asian states it has an outstanding position. According to the Human Development Index of the United Nations, in 2006 Sri Lanka held 99th place amongst the world's 173 states.

Tea cultivation The fact that Sri Lanka, after India and China, is now the world's third-biggest tea exporter with approx. 320,000 tons a year, is mainly owed to the British colonial rule. Around 14 percent of the entire agricultural area is used for tea crops, which corresponds to an area of around 260,000 ha/640,000 acres. In Sri Lanka tea grows at altitudes of around 1500–2000m/4900–6500ft. The young shoots are harvested and brought to factories where they are dried.

The cultivation of this land illustrates the division in the Sri Lankan population. Almost all plantation workers are Tamil people who were brought to the island from southern India; they are some of the worst-paid labourers in Sri Lanka.

Rice cultivation A further important role in Sri Lankan agriculture is played by rice, the vast majority of which is grown in watery fields or paddies. The foundation for this is the centuries-old irrigation system that brings sufficient water even to the most remote parts of the island. Visitors should not be fooled by the apparent large-scale nature of rice cultivation in Sri Lanka. It has no significance as an agricultural export. The quantities produced are not even enough for the country to cover its own demands. Sri Lanka has to import rice from, for example, the United States during difficult climatic years, which has a significant impact on the state budget. The government has been implementing targeted measures such as the **Mahaweli irrigation project** to make sure rice imports will soon be a thing of the past.

Coconut palms

Coconut palms are also cultivated on large plantations. Every year around 2.5 million coconuts are harvested. Copra, the flesh obtained from them, is an important export, most commonly used in the cosmetics industry. The great majority of coconut palm plantations are in private ownership.

Rubber figs

Even though Sri Lanka's rubber plantations take up eight percent of the country's agricultural land, the profits from exporting rubber are playing an ever decreasing role. Competition from other east Asian countries in particular, but also the devaluation of the currencies of Thailand and Malaysia, have led to a big drop in prices. Small farmers, whose rubber plantations often only consist of a few hundred square metres, are suffering the most. There has even been talk of

Toddy tappers climb like acrobats up to 30 m/100 ft from one coconut palm to the next to tap their sap, from which arrack, a rum-like drink, is made

planting tea between the rubber figs to compensate for the small profits. Nevertheless Sri Lanka still accounts for a good ten percent of the world's natural rubber production.

Forest areas Two thirds of the island of Sri Lanka was once covered by jungle, but human interference has left its mark. Unchecked logging for many decades means the island now only has around 1.7 million ha/4.2 million acres of forest left. The government has only recently begun making efforts to increase this percentage again by forestation measures. Around 90% of the wood from logging is used to supply the population with fuel.

Fishing Fishing in the waters around Sri Lanka is surprisingly underdeveloped; coastal fishing is not even capable of covering the country's own demands. Although 200,000 tons of fish was caught in 2003, the majority of that went into the nets of Japanese trawlers, whose owners have made quota agreements with the government. The large reservoirs in the country's interior are however of some significance to fishing; these tanks created centuries ago are now used to farm tasty freshwater fish.

Industry, mining, energy Sri Lanka does not have a noteworthy, mining and energy industry as the country is mainly focused on agricultural products. One reason for this is the **lack of natural resources and raw materials**. All around the capital, Colombo, an extensive free trade zone was set up causing dozens of **textile factories** to be opened, but the fabrics are imported from India and Europe rather than produced in Sri Lanka. As a result of the still exceptionally low wages for seamstresses (less than €100 a month), this method is nonetheless lucrative. As a result of the abolition of the internationally agreed textile quotas more than 25,000 people lost their jobs in 2005 alone.

More than two thirds of the country's energy requirements are now met from **hydropower**. The damming of Mahaweli Ganga east of Kandy and the construction of further dams in the country's interior were ambitious government projects to decrease dependence on expensive oil imports. They were the cause of many years of trade deficits, particularly during the 1970s.

Although Sri Lanka does not have any coal deposits, the search for **gemstones** is very significant for the island's economy. Rubies, sapphires and other gemstones are found, mainly in the south of the island around Ratnapura. The export of gemstones is worth €80 million annually (►Baedeker Special p. 332).

Tourism The civil war between the Singhalese and the Tamil population that flared up after 1983, and the tsunami, are both factors that have prevented a steady development of tourism. Sri Lanka is considered **one of the most popular Asian destinations**, maybe as a result of the fact that tourists have remained almost unaffected by the civil war. Sri

The Kalmunai women fish with their saris because they have no money for nets

Lanka is also an inexpensive destination, and the islanders' hospitality is almost proverbial.

The year 2004 saw record numbers; a total of around 566,000 visitors came to the island. Tourism, after the export of tea and textiles, is the **largest source of foreign exchange**, bringing in around US$ 410 million. It contributes more than a fifth of the national income. An estimated 52,000 people are employed in the tourism sector.

Religion

Strictly speaking Buddhism is more a philosophy than a religion. However even today it is still considered a counter-movement to Hinduism; Buddha wanted to reform the Brahmin culture of India, particularly the old caste system, and break the dominance of the Brahmins in society.

Buddha, meaning »the enlightened one«, was born as **Siddhartha Gautama** (▶Famous People), the son of a king in Nepal at the foot of the Himalayas. During his estimated 80-year life, which he largely

Buddhism

spent as an itinerant monk and hermit, he developed teachings that have spread around the world, and have significantly more followers in countries outside his own country of origin.

After Buddha's death, which took place in 480 BC according to historical sources, but is said by Buddhists to have occurred in 543 BC, the teachings of the Enlightened One quickly spread. During the reign of the Indian king Ashoka (approx. 272–236 BC), who was converted to Buddhism by a monk called Ugagupta, Buddhism **flourished for the first time**. It spread from India to Sri Lanka and far beyond to areas in modern-day Thailand, Burma and Cambodia. It is difficult to estimate how many people now live by the principles of Buddhism. The figure is thought to lie between 150 and 500 million people. It should be noted that Buddhists are allowed to be followers of other religions too.

Most Buddhists in Sri Lanka invoke the rules of the **Theravada school**, which was founded only shortly after Buddha entered nirvana. This school claims to follow the unadulterated teachings of the Enlightened One and cites as evidence three councils, of which one took place a few years after Buddha's death, the second 100 years later and the third in around 245 BC. While different schools formed at this time spread different teachings, the followers of the Theravada school held on to what they believe were Buddha's original teachings. Theravada monks can be recognized by their dark robes.

Buddhism took over many fundamental ideas and concepts from Hinduism as well as the term **karma**, the insurmountable cosmic law. According to tradition Buddha was only able to break free from this cycle after more than 500 life cycles in different incarnations. However, this does not mean the soul leaves one body for another. Instead, after the third step of the cycle, death, a new being comes into existence from the karma of the being that has just passed away. According to dominant opinion, those closest to breaking free from this cycle are the monks living in monasteries. They spend their entire life studying Buddha's teachings. That is the reason for the high standing monks enjoy in Sri Lanka.

Two different teachings ▶ The most important difference between **Mahayana Buddhism** (which has now become dominant in China, Korea, Japan and Vietnam) and **Hinayana Buddhism** (which has followers in Sri Lanka, Thailand, Cambodia and Laos) consists in the possibilities of breaking out of the cycle of birth, death and rebirth. While Hinayana Buddhism (the teaching of the »low vehicle«) starts with the idea that this has to be achieved by every single believer without any support, Mahayana Buddhism (»high vehicle«), which developed in the 1st and 2nd centuries AD, has bodhisattvas. These venerable people, who have already achieved the state of enlightenment, have chosen to remain on earth in order to help others find the way to enlightenment via the

A popular pose for depicting Buddha on Sri Lanka: →
the raised hand signals protection

»Eightfold Path«. Mahayana Buddhism has far more followers, presumably because it prescribes far less strict rules than Hinayana Buddhism and shows the path to breaking free from the eternal cycle to a much greater number of Buddhists.

The first country outside India in which the teachings of the Enlightened One became established was Sri Lanka. In around 250 BC King Ashoka sent his son (according to other sources his brother or his nephew) Mahindaals as a missionary to King Devanampiya Tissa of Sri Lanka, who was soon converted to Buddhism and had the new teachings spread through the entire country. He founded the island's Buddhist monastery in Anuradhapura and had the first dagoba, the Thuparama Dagoba, built to house a Buddha relic.

Spread of the new teachings ▶

After Ashoka's death his powerful empire fell apart into different individual states and a few centuries later Buddhism had almost disappeared entirely from India. It was only under the Gupta dynasty (around AD 310–500) that it flourished once more. The teachings suffered temporarily from the split that produced Hinayana and Mahayana Buddhism as well as the different schools. An important role was also played by Vishnu worship, which the Gupta rulers also participated in. Thus by just the 8th century Buddhism disappeared once more from the Indian subcontinent and was again replaced by Hinduism. Buddhism had nevertheless spread to other parts of Asia: to China since the second half of the 1st century, Korea since 372, to Japan, Burma, Java and Sumatra since the 5th century, to Siam since 720 (but possibly already during the reign of Ashoka) and to the Khmer Empire (whose core area roughly corresponds to modern Cambodia) since the year 800.

In Sri Lanka, in Burma and in Siam both types co-existed for a long time until the Theravada school, the most important school of Hinayana Buddhism, became dominant. It has remained dominant in these countries to this day.

The monks living in Sri Lanka have claimed to be the ones maintaining Buddha's original teachings but over the centuries they too have been exposed to attacks on a number of occasions. Already in the 1st century BC the monks split, and later Mahayana and Tantra Buddhism also became established in Sri Lanka. It was only under King Parakramabahu I (1153–86) that the Buddhist teachings were reunified.

More recently Buddhism in Sri Lanka has experienced a **multifaceted renewal**. Under the governments of Salomon and Sirimavo Bandaranaike it was employed to embed socialist values. They were able use monks for political ends and they were lucky in that Buddhism was still one of the country's most important social forces.

Buddhist monks Strictly speaking only monks (Bikkhu), novices (Samahera), nuns (Bikkhuni) and hermits are considered Buddhists because only they live in a world that is free from the pursuit of possessions and wealth. This is one of the most important conditions for **a life ac-**

cording to the teachings of Buddha, who said the Eightfold Path was the only way by which to break free from the eternal cycle of re-birth. Hinayana Buddhism, the more dominant type in Sri Lanka, only permitted this possibility to monks, not to lay people. This is the most important difference between this type of Buddhism and Mahayana Buddhism (the teaching of the »high vehicle«, which is very widespread in Thailand for example).

Monks, nuns, novices and hermits make up the monastic community (Sangha) or **monastic order**. At the head of every large monastery is an abbot, who also usually has jurisdiction over several small monasteries in the surrounding area. There are currently around 16,000 monks in Sri Lanka.

Every man can enter a monastery regardless of his caste and is also free to leave again if and when he chooses. In Sri Lanka the tradition that every man spends at least a few months in a monastery during his lifetime is less widespread than in Thailand for example. Most monks remain loyal to their decision to become a Bikkhu and spend their life in the monastery. There is no prescribed minimum age and there are even 12- to 14-year-old boy monks who wear a white novice robe until their ceremonial ordination amongst family, friends and acquaintances. when they enter the monastery or the order proper, they are given the saffron-coloured monk's robe and a new name (often one of a meritorious old monk). During the ceremony the young monk recites **the »Three Jewels« of the Buddhist teachings**: »I take refuge in Buddha«, »I take refuge in the Dharma«, »I take refuge in the Sangha«. Then the monk vows to adhere to the **five principles of the monks' rules**: no killing, no deception, no adultery, no stealing and no alcohol. Only over time does the monk learn the 227 detailed rules (Vinaya), of which the vows of poverty, celibacy and peaceableness are the most important.

A monk is not allowed to possess more than his robes, an alms bowl, a needle, a belt, razor and a filter to remove bugs from drinking water. He may not have **any other property** and he may not handle money (for that there are nuns, who generally take care of the monastic budget). When it comes to contact with women the monks in Sri Lanka are far more uncomplicated than the monks of Thailand, for example: in Thailand monks are not permitted to have direct contact with women, whereas those in Sri Lanka are generally quite willing to have a conversation and are also allowed to receive objects. Monks are not allowed to ingest any solid food after noon, but are restricted to drinks; after that they use their time to study the scriptures or to meditate. Monks gathering their food are a rare sight in Sri Lanka, by the way, because here the people living around the monastery are responsible for providing sufficient food for them. If you do see a monk going from door to door with an alms bowl, this should not be called begging: quite the opposite in fact, as it is a good opportunity for the population to gain more merit by aiding the monks. In order to achieve enlightenment and enter nirvana it is

◄ Property

◄ Daily routine

important to follow the **»Three Noble Disciplines «** which Buddha taught. The first prescribes sacrifices for gods and demons in their many different guises, the second consists of the pursuit of knowledge and insight, and veneration for others, particularly priests and old people. The third holds that self-contemplation (meditation) will bring about release from the clutches of the five elements, which is necessary in order to achieve unification with the divine principle.

Hinduism Hinduism is one of the four major world religions; it has a total of around 900 million followers. The expression Hinduism arose from

the translation of the Sanskrit word »Indu« into the Iranian language (»Hindu«). It was originally reserved for those people who lived along the Indian river Indus; the term Hinduism for their religious beliefs is a neologism of the Western world.

In contrast to monotheistic faith in a single personified divinity, Indian Hinduism is a **monistic religion** oriented to a de-personified principle (cf. Buddhism, Confucianism and Taoism).

The foundations of Hinduism have grown over the millennia; Hinduism is not a rigid religious principle. One of the basic elements of Hinduism today is Brahmanism, which only developed in the first millennium AD; it took its basic ideas from Vedism, a religion of ancient India.

According to Hindu beliefs all living beings (plants, animals, people) have a place on a **symbolic ladder** at the top of which is the pantheon. This highest rung is reserved for the gods and deities living on Mount Meru. On the rung below are saints, kings, spirits and demons, while human beings are located around half way up the ladder.

Hinduism has a **large number of gods and deities**, the most important of which are the trinity (Trimurti) of Brahma, Vishnu and Si-

Highly venerated by Hindus: Skanda, the god of war

va. They can, however, take on any guise they wish. They could, for example, enter the body of an object or a living being during a visit to earth and take possession of it for a certain amount of time.

The four-headed god Brahma is the personification of the supreme cosmic spirit Brahman. He is consider the creator of the world and was once the highest god of Hinduism. Today he is on the same rank as Vishnu (the preserver of the world, who, living on earth, is popularly depicted as the shepherd god Krishna) and Shiva (the destroyer of the world). In Sri Lanka the god of war Skanda, who appears in various incarnations (including Kataragama), is particularly highly venerated.

The most important foundation of Hinduism (as also of Buddhism) is the notion that every living being on earth is subjected to the eternal cycle of rebirth. This never-ending **cycle of birth, death and rebirth of the soul** (Samsara)is inescapable for all living things, unless they manage to enter nirvana after many lives filled with good thoughts and deeds. In what shell the soul of the Hindu is reborn is just as unpredictable as the number of lives. The cycle can be influenced, however, by good and bad deeds (karma) that are rewarded or punished in the next life as a better or worse existence. The goal of every Hindu is to escape from having to be reborn, thus breaking free from the cycle forever.

◄ Cycle of rebirth

Hindus also have a relatively fixed notion of the cosmos, which is based both on mythological and philosophical ideas and on the simple observation of natural processes. The world, put together from the essential constituent of the universe (prakriti), is thus in a constant **cycle of development and destruction**; between these two phases is a phase of rest separating the two. Human beings consider themselves as a small world (Buwana Alit) in a large world (Buwana Agung).

Around 7.5% of Sri Lanka's population follow the Islamic faith. They are largely found amongst the descendants of the Moors, who came to the island from the 8th century AD onwards as Arab seafarers and merchants.

Islam

Islam (translated »surrender« or »submission«) is a monotheistic religion. Its teachings go back to **Mohammed**, Allah's last prophet, who was probably born in Mecca in around AD 570.

Islam's most important sacred site is the Kaaba (cube) in Mecca, a cubical building on which the »Black Stone« can be found. By touching or kissing it the pilgrims show it the highest veneration during the hajj, the **pilgrimage to Mecca**. The Kaaba dates back to before Mohammed's time, when it was already a popular place of pilgrimage. According to a revelation made by Allah to Mohammed in the Koran it was built by Abraham and one of his sons at God's behest. Mohammed had the Kaaba freed from all images of gods.

The foundation of the Islamic faith written down by the followers of Mohammed is the **Koran** (= »that which is to be recited«). It consists of 114 suras (sections) in free verse and contains all the commandments and laws a devout Muslim has to obey. The most important part are the **»Five Pillars of Islam«** (»Arkan«): the affirmation that there is no other deity besides Allah and that Mohammed is His prophet; the ritual prayers (salat) that have to be performed; the giving of alms (zakat), the pilgrimage to Mecca (hajj), and the requirement to fast during the month of Ramadan (the 9th month of the Islamic calendar).

Even though almost all towns and villages in Sri Lanka have not just Buddhist and Hindu temples but also mosques, there is little evidence of Islamic missionary work on the island. Few women wear veils.

Christianity A further 7.5% of the Singhalese population are of Christian faith, most of them Roman Catholics. In contrast to other Asian countries where missionaries from Europe arrived very early on, Christianity

Sacrificial gifts are part of Hinduism:
here coconuts are being smashed in front of the temple

only became established in Sri Lanka from the 16th century, when the Portuguese, then the Dutch and finally the British came to the island. Missionary activity in Sri Lanka was never particularly strong.

History

The island's history was influenced throughout the centuries by Buddhism. Even when the various colonial rulers came and took control of the country's riches, the people did not stray from their faith. In the 20th century a civil war broke out which has claimed thousands of victims so far. And then the island was hit by the tsunami …

Sri Lanka had Many Names

Sri Lanka has had a large number of different names. The current one has only been the island's official name since 1972, when a new democratic constitution came into effect.

The Singhalese term Lanka goes back to a Sanskrit word and means »luminous«. This name already appears in some ancient Indian sources such as the Ramayana epic. The addition of the word Sri is a Singhalese honorary title and means something like divine, royal or holy. If the current official name is translated it means **the royal, luminous land**. During the time of the Romans and Greeks Sri Lanka was also known by the name Taprobane (**copper island**), or at least the Egyptian Ptolemy called it thus in his geographical work of the 2nd century. The island chronicle Mahavamsa penned by the Buddhist monk Mahanama in Pali at the start of the 6th century knew modern-day Sri Lanka by the name of Tambapanni (copper-coloured land). In the 8th century the Arabs called the island Serendib (**the enchanting one**).

In later times the Singhalese who had migrated to the island gave it a name that befitted their high self-confidence: Singhala Dvipa (**lion island**); it was named thus after the sons of the lion who came from southern India. Finally, the Tamil people had and have their own names for Sri Lanka: Singhalam, Singhala-divu and Ilankai (the latter stands for jewel island).

Last but not least the colonial rulers left their marks; the name of Ceilao introduced by the Portuguese later became **Ceylon** during the Dutch occupation and remained in place until 1972. The British also used the name Ceylon.

Prehistory

1st millennium BC	Farmers come to Sri Lanka from southern India.
250 BC	The first irrigation system is built.
80 BC	The First Buddhist Council is held.

Until the 1960s historians had assumed that it could not be proved whether settlers had come to the island in prehistory. However, then **stone tools** were found and dated to around 500,000 years ago. Further discoveries in the form of clay tableware presumably date to the Iron Age; their shapes and appearance resemble those found in

Around 500,000 years ago

← *Dagobas, like Ruwanweli Dagoba in Anuradhapura, are a reminder of Buddha and the right path to enlightenment*

southern India. The discoveries indicate that there may even have been trade relations between India and Sri Lanka. There is no certain knowledge about the ancestry of the people who lived in Sri Lanka during this time.

Balangaloda culture During the period of the Balangaloda culture tools were made of stone. They were probably made by people who came to the island from southern India.

Settlement The first parts of the Indian chronicle Mahavamsa contain clues about a settlement of Sri Lanka. In verse this reputed mix of legend and reality describes the arrival of the Singhalese, probably people of Indo-Aryan ancestry. They were followed three centuries later by the first Tamils, who were most likely merchants.

Vedda The Vedda, members of a Caucasian race who are related to different Vedic tribes of the Indian subcontinent, some of which live in the jungle, are still considered to be the island's aboriginal inhabitants. However, the Mahavamsa does not provide information about whether the beings identified with them were really human. They are rather described as yakshas and nagas, ghost-like beings.

The first settlers During the first half of the 1st millennium BC farmers came to the island of Lanka (the old name of Sri Lanka in Sanskrit) from southern India. They are now known as Ancient Singhalese. While many aboriginals, robbed of their lands, were pushed back ever further into the jungle regions where they led a hunter-gatherer existence, many others assimilated with other, more recent arrivals. Many sites dating from the prehistory of the first settlement in Sri Lanka have been discovered, such as the caves around Bandarawela near Badulla.

Irrigation system Long before channels were built to irrigate the paddy fields on the island of Bali, for example, Sri Lanka already had such a system. Archaeologists have found man-made structures that were in place as early as 250 BC; they captured the water running off from the mountains and stored it artificially for distribution on the fields.

Anuradhapura During this time the city of Anuradhapura became the island's first flourishing capital and a centre of Buddhist teaching, which had spread here from the Indian subcontinent. The king in power there, Ashoka, sent Mahinda, presumably his son, to Sri Lanka to spread the Buddhist teachings. King Devanampiya Tissa readily accepted them and soon declared Buddhism the universal religion. The town of Anuradhapura itself was extended. The basis of the wealth of its population primarily came from the irrigation system, which had been built long before but had since undergone comprehensive extensions. Many sacred buildings were constructed within the town. Travellers reported »golden stupas that could be seen from far away«.

The most imposing was the stupa of Jetavaranama with a height of 120m/394ft. It was followed by the stupa of Abhayagiri, which had a height of 70m/230ft.

Indian Tamils

In around 200 BC Tamil people from southern India occupied the majority of the island. This episode did not last long, however. The invaders were soon ousted by King Dutthagamani (161–137 BC). To this day Dutthagamani is considered a national hero amongst the Singhalese population for this reason.

First Buddhist Council

Around 500 Buddhist monks gathered in the monastery of Alu Vihara near Matala (north of Kandy) in 80 BC in order to write down those sermons of Buddha that were considered authentic. They were given the name »Tripitaka« (three baskets) and became a fundamental and still valid component of Buddhist teaching.

The Years of the First Visitors

1st century	Greek seafarers come to Sri Lanka; Ptolemy describes more than 50 places on the island.
around 450	The rock fortress of Sigiriya is built; Fa Xian, a monk from China, travels around Ceylon.
993	The Chola dynasty conquers the entire island; Polonnaruwa becomes the capital.

Visit and return visit

Greek seafarers came to the island of Sri Lanka on their way to India at the start of the 1st century AD. They called it »Taprobane« (copper island). In the year 45 Sri Lankan merchants responded to a visit by Roman emissaries by visiting Rome themselves.
The astronomer, mathematician and geographer Claudius **Ptolemy** (around AD 100–160) described more than 50 places in Sri Lanka. However, he presumably got his knowledge from the reports made by the Greek seafarers. An early map of the island is also attributed to Ptolemy.

A father-son conflict

The **rock fortress of Sigiriya** was built under King Kashyapa, one of the two sons of King Dhatusena of Anuradhapura. He feared revenge by his half-brother Moggallana, Dhatusena's rightful son, since, according to tradition, he is said to have chained their father naked to a wall and immured him alive. When Moggallana approached with his troops in 495, Kashyapa left the fortress (located at an elevation of 200m/660ft and considered impregnable) in order to ride out towards his half-brother, but committed suicide before falling into his hands.

Fa Xian and Buddhaghosa

In the 5th century BC the Chinese traveller Fa Xian visited the island of Sri Lanka. He stayed for two years and during this time wrote incredibly accurate **descriptions of the situation there**, although he often referred to legends from the Mahavamsa. Fa Xian does seem to have travelled through large parts of the island himself. Thus he reported a temple in which a shrine contained one of Buddha's teeth. The town of Mihintale, which is still considered the birthplace of Buddhism in Sri Lanka, was also mentioned in his records.

Around the same time as Fa Xian and during the reign of King Manama (406–428) the Buddhist dogmatist Buddhaghosa was working in the monastery of Anuradhapura. Many commentaries on Buddhist teaching written in Pali are attributed to him.

A Chola province

King Rajaraja I, a ruler of the southern Indian Chola dynasty, invaded Sri Lanka with his troops in 993, thereby beating other powerful Pandya rulers to it. He conquered the entire island and made it a province of his empire. He declared Polonnaruwa to be his administrative capital and Hinduism to be the valid religion. Anuradhapura had been the most flourishing town in Sri Lanka until this point but then it was drawn into conflicts. King Mahinda V ascended the throne in 982, but just a few years later had to accept that King Rajaraja the Great was conquering not just large parts of southern India but also Sri Lanka. In 1017 Mahinda V was deposed, taken prisoner and brought to southern India. His capital, Anuradhapura, largely fell victim to destruction and the population was evicted.

Polonnaruwa

The period of occupation by the Chola rulers was to last into the 11th century. It was only in 1070 that the Singhalese king Vijaya Bahu I was able to push them back to the Indian mainland. This was naturally too late for Anuradhapura. Polonnaruwa not only had a strategically more favourable location than the old capital, but also better agricultural conditions as a result of its proximity to the Mahaweli River. Instead of Hinduism Vijaya Bahu I reintroduced Buddhism and made a name for himself as a reformer of the administration and public life. This was a relatively short-lived golden age. After his death the country was divided up.

Fighting and reunification

When King Parakrama Bahu I ascended the Singhalese throne in 1153 he found a country whose people were deeply at odds with each other. By ruling with an iron fist he nevertheless managed to unify the country into one Singhalese kingdom again within just a few years. The new state structure with its capital in Polonnaruwa subsequently flourished, a development that also expressed itself in increased political influence towards the Indian mainland. The irrigation system, which was already centuries old at this time, was also expanded. The biggest part of this project was the construction of the 24 sq km/9 sq mi **Parakrama Samudra Reservoir**, which allowed more than three times as much land to be cultivated as had been possible before.

Artistically speaking Parakrama Bahu's successor Nissanka Malla (1187–96) made a name for himself despite his short reign by commissioning several sacred works of art such as the monumental Buddha statues of Gal Vihara and the Vatadage of Polonnaruwa. Politically, however, he did not succeed in stabilizing the situation in the long term. Shortly after his death a new conflict erupted between the Singhalese dynasties. Mercenaries from southern India (amongst them also countless Cholas), who were called in to help by various members, marched across the island, plundering as they went. An Indian pirate by the name of Magha finally brought matters to a head. He took his band to Polonnaruwa, overran the city and sacked it. The inhabitants fled to the surrounding areas.

The Colonial Era

16th century	The Portuguese discover Ceylon.
Around 1640	The Dutch expel the Portuguese.
1815	The British conquer Kandy.

The 14th and 15th centuries were marked by uncertainty. It was only during the reign of King Parakrama Bahu V (1411–67), a ruler who knew how to bring fractured kingdoms back together again, that this period ended. His residence was located in Kotte, a fact unpopular with the rulers of Kandy. Confrontations occurred time and time again, and after his death Kotte fell into the hands of Kandy entirely, which thus succeeded in subjecting a large part of the island to its rule.

Years of uncertainty

Even though Sri Lanka had been known since ancient times, not just by seafarers, foreign powers, apart from the ruling dynasties of southern India of course, did not show much interest in the island. This was to change at the start of the 16th century, when the Portuguese began extending their colonial efforts to Asia.

The Portuguese

Initially they only tried to establish a **trading post** en route between Europe and Asia where ships could call in. As early as 1510 Goa in the west of India had been conquered by the seafarer and viceroy Alfonso de Albuquerque and declared a Portuguese colony. Macao near Hong Kong followed in 1557. Ceilao, as they called Sri Lanka, was ideal for the Portuguese because it helped them **secure their shipping routes**, and soon the trading post they had been granted became an area of influence that covered the entire southwest of Sri Lanka.

However, they had no luck with the rulers of Kandy. The Portuguese even left the island temporarily, only to return in 1610 at the express wish of King Senerath (1604–35). Senerath, too, soon had enough of the Portuguese attempts to gain control of the island, particularly the important ports of Trincomalee and Batticaloa. When Senerath died and his son Raja Sinha II came to power, the Dutch appeared on the scene.

The Dutch The Netherlands also had overseas territories such as modern-day Indonesia. The **Vereenigde Oost-Indische Compagnie** (VOC) was responsible for trading with them. They were primarily interested in spices and gemstones, two commodities the Singhalese had plenty of. Raja Sinha II offered them a treaty giving the Dutch the sole right to trade in both of them. This treaty was conditional on the Dutch assisting the Singhalese in their fight against the Portuguese.

Raja Sinha II had misjudged the Dutch. After winning the ports of Galle and Negombo back from the Portuguese they quickly declared them to be their own territory. They had recognized how valuable these two ports were and a few years later they added Jaffna on the island's north coast. While the Portuguese had been expelled from Sri Lanka, the Dutch had now taken their place. In 1656 they had the fortifications of Colombo demolished.

They showed almost no interest in **Kandy**, however, which at this point still had the Singhalese name Srivardhanapura. This allowed King Raja Sinha II to secure the continued existence of his kingdom. He was not able to prevent the colonial rulers from trying to impose their Christian faith on the island population. Nevertheless they proved tolerant enough towards the Buddhist and Muslim faiths too. The **trade in spices started to flourish**, and of course it was firmly in the hands of the Dutch. Some of the export profits went into the state coffers and thus contributed to the growing affluence of the Singhalese islanders.

The British After some unsuccessful attempts the British managed to become established on Ceilao. Bit by bit they took the most important ports, an endeavour they did not find difficult in view of their military superiority. They managed to achieve what the Dutch could not: in 1803 the rulers of Kandy were able to fend off a British attack but twelve years later their days were numbered. The British benefited from the fact that the rulers of Kandy were at odds with each other, which made them an easy target for attack.

Singhalese rebellion Nevertheless the British took several years to secure their power in Kandy and had to use force. A Singhalese rebellion that arose in 1817 and lasted almost two years, claiming hundreds of victims, was brutally put down. Kandy henceforth became the capital of the entire island of **Ceylon**, a name that was to remain until 1972.

In 1815 King Shirivikramarashasimha's days were also over; he was deposed by his own noblemen. In the Kandyan Convention that was passed by mutual agreement, the king acquiesced to his entire king-

Foreign Rulers on Sri Lanka

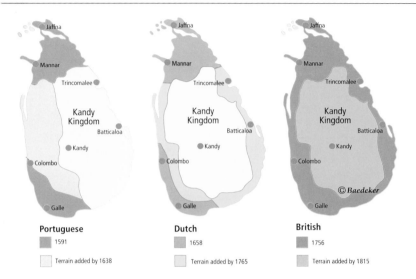

© Baedeker

Portuguese
■ 1591
□ Terrain added by 1638

Dutch
■ 1658
□ Terrain added by 1765

British
■ 1756
□ Terrain added by 1815

dom being made subject to the British crown. In return the British agreed to maintain the administrative system and protect the Buddhist religion.

The British soon began creating large coffee plantations, for which they needed more, and cheaper, labour than they could find on the island. Their solution was to recruit Tamil workers from southern India, who initially willingly followed the call of their new masters, but by 1848 realized their labour was being exploited. A rebellion broke out, which the British put down in a bloody confrontation. Adding to this problem the **coffee rust** disease began affecting the delicate coffee plants of Ceylon in 1865 and quickly spread to all the world's coffee-growing regions. The British had a solution, however: they quickly replaced the coffee plants with tea bushes.

Indian Tamils are recruited

Ceylon Becomes Independent

1931	Universal suffrage for all the island population.
4 February 1948	Ceylon gains its independence.

Elite and patriotism
The wealth that came to the island as a result of its coffee and tea plantations created an intellectual (and moneyed) elite amongst the Singhalese population. They succeeded in obtaining certain **rights of self-administration** from the British. However, even in the less well educated layers of society a certain patriotism was making itself felt, which had been a Singhalese characteristic since time immemorial. They started fighting their foreign rulers. Buddhist monks played an important role in this endeavour. However, the British had managed to obtain enough influence amongst the Singhalese early on for some of them even to have converted to Christianity. For this reason the efforts of individuals to escape from the rule of the British crown came to nothing.

In 1915, on the anniversary of Kandy's capitulation to the British, renewed **unrest** broke out. It had clear nationalistic tendencies and the refusal of the British to give at least the Singhalese elite a certain voice in government now came back to bite them. The violence was not aimed primarily at the British but rather at the Moors, the enterprising descendants of Arab seafarers who were living on the coast. However, when the British started to worry that the unrest would spread further and possibly bring about the end of their rule, they intervened and arrested the ringleaders.

Tamils against Singhalese
Although the Singhalese and Tamils were largely agreed in their desire to expel the British colonial power from the island in the not too distant future, some Tamils were worried as early as 1920 that the Singhalese were being given greater political power than themselves. Even a commission put in place by Sir Hugh Clifford, the governor at the time, could not change this. Its purpose was to advise on a new constitution and take the special ethnic needs of Ceylon into account.

Universal suffrage
Clifford had been in office for less than four years when the commission finally came to an agreement in 1931. It not only proposed a government that included Singhalese and Tamil politicians, but also permitted the introduction of universal suffrage for all island inhabitants from the age of 21. This made Ceylon the first British overseas territory that had such a suffrage.

Efforts to gain autonomy
The right to vote ignited more and more **nationalistic tendencies** amongst the population. The people became more self-confident in dealing with their British rulers; a labour movement developed and social conditions were improved. Don Stephen Senanayake earned himself particular merit in his efforts to improve the country's agriculture. It was also he with whom the British chose to negotiate about Ceylon's independence. Senanayake suggested handing over possession step by step. The British agreed to this proposal when Senanayake, whose parents had given him an English first name as a sign of their loyalty, said he would make sure this transition would be a peaceful one.

The Second World War put the efforts of the independence movement on hold. The ports of Colombo, Trincomalee and Batticaloa were important British bases between Europe and Asia. When the Japanese bombed these ports in 1942 more than 1200 Allied (mainly British) and Singhalese soldiers were killed, but the attacks ultimately remained unsuccessful. Maybe, historians suggest, Japanese control of Ceylon would have given the war a different direction.

Second World War

The years after the end of the Second World War were dominated by renewed efforts for independence. Britain once again set up a commission to draw up proposals. Although the draft would have allowed the Singhalese to govern themselves in the future, the British still wanted to determine foreign policy, but gave in surprisingly quickly when the Singhalese people were against this. On **4 February 1948** Britain granted the island of Ceylon independence and Don Stephen Senanayake became the country's first prime minister.

Independence

Building the New State

from 1948	Economic boom
1950	The Colombo Plan is born.
1972	Ceylon is renamed »Sri Lanka« and becomes a socialist republic.
1978	The presidential system is introduced.

Immediately after taking office Senanayake determinedly set about developing the young state of Ceylon. He aimed for a **strict separation of religion and state** and worked on building up the economy. His great skill in handling public opinion was a reason why the socialist-oriented opposition had little chance. The economy, severely weakened by the war years, underwent a boom. Profits from the export of tea and rubber filled the treasury; the government invested a large percentage of this money into improving welfare, but also into the first big irrigation project. Going back to the ideas of earlier kings, the **Gal Oya project** along with Senanayake Samudra came into existence. This reservoir is almost four times bigger than Parakrama Samudra.

Determined development

Senanayake must admittedly take some of the blame for the civil war that broke out in 1983. In 1948 he not only revoked the Indian Tamils' right to vote, he even took away their citizenship and thus clearly made them second-class citizens. Their **exploitation as cheap workers** was thus legitimized by the law. In addition he made Singhala the only official language.

Tamils lose their right to vote

Colombo Plan   The Commonwealth heads of government met in Colombo in 1950 in order to develop a mutual framework for their economic development. The resulting plan was named after the city in which this conference took place: the »Colombo Plan for Cooperative Economic and Social Development in Asia and the Pacific«, or »Colombo Plan« for short. It developed into an important instrument for co-ordinating development aid in Asia, which is paid for to this day by Great Britain, Australia, Canada, the United States and New Zealand. 19 further states joined the seven founding states over the years.

The Bandaranaike dynasty   When Don Senanayake suffered a fatal riding accident in 1952 his son Dudley (▶ Famous People) took over as prime minister, but could not build on his father's successes and had to step down just a year later. In the meantime the opposition had re-formed: with the participation of the minister Solomon West Ridgeway Dias Bandaranaike (▶ Famous People), who had left the United National Party, the **Sri Lanka Freedom Party** (SLFP) was formed. They won the elections of 1956 with Solomon Bandaranaike as the prime minister.

When he was assassinated three years later in September 1959 by a fanatical Buddhist monk, the UNP, led by Dudley Senanayake, managed to win the elections of March 1960. However, when they announced new elections just four months later, the UNP had to accept a heavy defeat in favour of a reinvigorated SLFP. Sirimavo Bandaranaike (▶ Famous People), the widow of the murdered prime minister, took over with the stated goal of continuing her late husband's policies, making her **the first female head of government in the world**. However, she was only partially successful in continuing these goals and met with particular resistance over her policy of nationalizing the tea and rubber plantations.

The UNP triumphed at the 1965 elections, and Don Stephen Senanayake became the head of government once again.

Since even his second attempt at solving the country's problems (increasing unemployment, rising costs of living) remained unsuccessful, he held office for only five years and in 1970 was in turn replaced by Mrs Bandaranaike. She had a **new constitution** drawn up that came into effect in 1972. Ceylon was henceforth the Democratic Socialist Republic of Sri Lanka.

Nationalizing the economy   Mrs Bandaranaike set about continuing her firm programme of nationalizing the economy, particularly the plantations. Possession of land was limited to 20ha/50 acres per family, monthly income to a maximum of 2000 rupees. In return she promised the people that »everyone would receive their rice for free«, which soon caused huge deficits in the state budget.

Just in time for the elections of 1977 **accusations of corruption** materialized, which helped the opposition win. Junius Richard Jayawardene of the UNP became president when one year later he introduced a presidential system based on the French model. Ranasinghe Premadasa (► Famous People) was elected prime minister. Both changed the policies of their predecessor in that they tried to reverse some of the nationalization programmes and win foreign investors for Sri Lanka. For this reason large **free trade zones** were set up north of Colombo, which were primarily used by the textile industry.

The Civil War Breaks Out

1976	The Tamil people demand their own state.
from 1983	Attacks on Singhalese institutions
1995	First ceasefire

Even though there were economic successes, Premadasa did not manage to keep the growing social tensions between the Singhalese and the Tamil people under control. More and more Tamils were demanding an independent state which they wanted to call »Eelam«. When these demands were rejected the military wing of the Tamil United Liberation Front (TULF), the »Liberation Tigers of Tamil Eelam« was formed. This **guerrilla organization** started attacking the Singhalese and their institutions.

When Premadasa's government lost control of the confrontations it called for help from **Indian soldiers** in 1987. They too were unable to solve the conflict and their presence on the island only lasted until March 1990. On 29 July 1987 Premadasa's government decided to implement an autonomy statute for the north and east of the island where the Tamil people live. The rights they were given were not enough for the LTTE, who continued to cause unrest under the leadership of their founder and self-proclaimed revolutionary Velupillai Prabhakaran (1954–2009).

Prabhakaran, who lived in the underground, succeeded in winning over young Tamils, who were even willing to commit suicide attacks. The LTTE did not even stop at recruiting women and children.

LTTE terrorism primarily targeted the Singhalese population, but Tamils who were considered moderates also became victims. At the heart of the confrontations was the Jaffna Peninsula in the north; acts of terrorism were also committed in Colombo and elsewhere. The LTTE is also considered responsible for the murder of the Indian prime minister Rajiv Gandhi on 21 May 1991. The targets of these attacks were initially people and buildings, but from the mid-1990s LTTE increasingly targeted the country's infrastructure (such as electricity substations).

Growing tensions

Peace talks

When prime minister Chandrika Kumaratunga (the daughter of S.W.R.D. and Sirimavo Bandaranaike) took office in 1994 she promised she would soon start peace talks with the LTTE. Later she even declared the »liberation tigers« to be negotiation partners, an offer which Prabhakaran firmly ignored, however. Although on 8 January 1995 a ceasefire was declared, it was broken again just three months later.

Pope John Paul II On 20 and 21 January 1995 Pope John Paul II visited Sri Lanka. Buddhist dignitaries boycotted the visit since derogatory statements about Buddhism from the Vatican were made public prior to the visit.

Wave of terrorism The country was affected by an unprecedented wave of terrorism in 1995. A bomb exploded in a commuter train in Colombo, killing 78 people. Further attacks followed, causing President Kumaratunga to extend the **state of emergency** to the entire country on 8 April 1996; up until this point it had been restricted to Colombo and the northern and eastern parts of the island. The army and police were thus given far-reaching powers, and from then on the freedom of assembly and the freedom of the press could be limited by the president.

Government soldiers are stationed in Tamil territory

In the opinion of the general population the LTTE committed a big mistake when it carried out a **bomb attack on the country's largest Buddhist temple**, the Temple of the Tooth in Kandy, on 25 January 1998. This suicide attack, which claimed eight lives and severely damaged part of the temple, gave the Singhalese population a new lease of solidarity. Although President Kumaratunga continued her policy of holding peace talks, a significant number of Singhalese people believed only military means could solve a conflict that had killed and injured more than 69,000 people since 1984.

Attack on Kandy

Since the New Millennium

Since 2002	Official peace negotiations
December 2004	The tsunami disaster kills around 36,000 and makes more than 500,000 homeless.

With Norway, which took over the UN mandate, as an intermediary, the Sri Lankan government and the LTTE agreed to a ceasefire and to hold peace talks. For the first time the LTTE foreswore its demand for a Tamil state and the government promised not just to work for a federal structure for the Tamil regions but also to lift the prohibition on the Tamil Tigers. Several peace conferences followed from September 2002 onwards, during which some decisive progress was made.

Peace negotiations

One problem was the fact that the government was led by different parties with different goals. President Kumaratunga had a sceptical attitude towards the peace talks, while the prime minister was committed to a policy of negotiation. Since they could not agree on a common strategy Kumaratunga dissolved the parliament ahead of time in 2004 and called for **new elections**, which she also won. After that the ceasefire entered on fragile ground, a state of affairs that continued when Kumaratunga's successor Mahinda Rajapaksa took office in 2005. Although it was not destroyed by spectacular violence, its sustainability was compromised as a result of several LTTE attacks. There were also disagreements among the LTTE leaders themselves, further compromising the peace talks.

The tsunami that struck the island on 26 December 2004 caused no change in the situation. While elsewhere (such as Sumatra) civil war parties put down their weapons and got to work helping the affected population, the government of Sri Lanka was faced with the accusation that it first helped the Singhalese population, leaving the Tamil people to make do with whatever was left. In addition, Sri Lanka's east coast, naturally the main Tamil settlement area, was the most af-

Accusation of partisan tsunami aid

fected. Help, including foreign aid, only reached these areas days and even weeks after the disaster. In June 2005 the two parties signed an agreement about the **equal distribution of aid money**, which was immediately declared invalid by the Supreme Court in Colombo. According to official figures the tsunami claimed more than 36,000 lives and more than half a million people lost their homes. Large parts of Sri Lanka's south and east coasts were flooded.

Economic strain

More than 25,000 textile workers have lost their jobs since the beginning of 2005; the reason, it is believed, being the **abolition of the textile quotas** in international trade. This is a serious economic strain for Sri Lanka since production has increasingly been moved to modern and even less expensive factories in the People's Republic of China.

Assassination of the foreign minister

In August 2005 the 73-year-old Sri Lankan foreign minister Lakshman Kadirgamar was murdered in his villa in Colombo; he was considered a hardliner on the Tamil issue. The **LTTE vehemently denied responsibility for the assassination**, which was a minor sensation in itself because the LTTE had not commented on any other assassination before this event. Many houses belonging to Tamils were searched, but the person or persons responsible have not yet been found.

New president

Mahinda Rajapakse won the presidential election in November 2005, but the people in the northeast of the country still continued to boycott the polling booths. Rajapakse was considered a strict opponent of autonomy for the largely Tamil regions. The former foreign minister Ratnasiri Wickremanayake became the new prime minister. The LTTE leader Prabhakaran then invited the government in Colombo to participate in talks about autonomy for the north of the island. The government immediately refused but did declare itself willing to negotiate on a »united Sri Lanka« with a special status for the Tamil regions.

In June 2006, the opposing parties met in Norway for peace talks, which however came to nothing. Just one month later the government started a first major offensive against the Tamils and thus definitively abandoned the ceasefire agreed in 2002, which was supposed to hold until January 2008. On 8 January 2009 government forces took the Jaffna Peninsula and hence were able to exercise a large degree of control over the area.

Once India started patrolling the Palk Strait between Sri Lanka and the mainland more closely, fewer and fewer weapons could get through to the insurgents, who were pushed back to a small area around their final stronghold of Mullaittivu. The flow of money from Tamils living abroad was also visibly drying up. When government forces took Mullaittivu on 23 January 2009, the end was already in sight, and after one last major offensive, on 16 May 2009

President Rajapaksa officially declared the LTTE defeated and the civil war to be at an end after 26 years. The revered leader and chief strategist of the LTTE, Velupillai Prabharakan, was shot dead two days later »while trying to escape«, and his body was put on public display. The fate of his deputy Pottu Amman, whom Interpol consider a master of disguise, is still uncertain, however. He is thought to be dangerous enough to step into Prabharakan's shoes.

The people who suffer, as usual, are the civilian population. Hundreds of thousands of Tamils were caught between the fronts and fled. Reception camps were set up for them. The government in Colombo categorically rejects foreign help, and refuses to allow aid organizations or journalists to the refugee camps.

In a speech to parliament President Rajapaksa promised the Tamil population a certain degree of autonomy in their ancestral territories. For the time being, however, all the Tamils in the camps will be interned until it is certain that there are no longer any LTTE members among them.

Arts and Culture

The island's most impressive cultural treasures are in an area known as the cultural triangle formed by Anuradhapura, Polonnaruwa and Kandy. The remains of old royal cities, some of which have been ripped from the jungle that covered them for centuries, can still be seen here. For many the highly visible rock fortress of Sigriya is the absolute highlight.

Art Periods

The Age of Classical Art

The **influence of the Indian Amaravathi style** is clearly recognizable during the first Anuradhapura period (250 BC–AD 432) in Sri Lanka. It is named after a place in southern India which was the cultural centre of south Indian Buddhism from the 2nd century BC to the 2nd century AD.

First Anuradhapura period

The characteristic features of the Buddha statues that were created during this time are majestic poses, a raised right arm that symbolized protection (abhaya mudra), a round face and a ushnisha or top-knot. This way of depicting Buddha continued until the end of the Polonnaruwa period, so that it is often difficult to say which standing Buddha statue came from which period.

Towards the end of the 4th century Buddha was no longer just represented in a standing pose but also seated. This period also saw the first **likenesses of bodhisattvas**, a development that went hand in hand with the spread of Mahayana Buddhism. They were mostly made of bronze. The preferred way of depicting the sitting Buddha was to show him meditating (Samadhi mudra), but contrary to the practice in northern India and many other Buddhist countries the legs in the hero pose (virasana) were placed on top of each other and not crossed.

Buddha poses

The round face was retained while the bodies were given softer shapes than the earlier examples. There is a fine difference in how the **facial features were modelled**; they are more hinted at than fully portrayed, giving them an air of inapproachability. This tendency for simplification and abstraction reveals the desire to depict the eternally valid rather than something with contemporary individuality.

While the artists of that time made use of Indian models for their Buddha statues, they deviated from these and created unique forms typical of Sri Lankan Buddha likenesses: the sitting Buddhas in particular were crowned by the splayed shield of the seven-headed naga.

Unique forms

While the period of monumental buildings and imposing dagobas was over in architecture, production began of **colossal stone sculptures**, either as free-standing statues or as high reliefs. Examples from this time can still be seen in Buduruvagala, Sasseruwa and Aukana, which has a beautiful, approx. 14m/46ft depiction of Buddha. It is the largest sculpture in Sri Lanka to survive from this period and was carved from a single boulder.

← *The Lion Gate marks the entrance to the rock fort in Sigiriya*

The Period of the Chola Kings

New perfection in sculpture The period of the Chola kings (996–1073) also brought a new kind of perfection to art. A large number of **bronze statues** were made, most of which depict Brahman deities; the artists' extraordinary feeling for depicting individual facial expressions and modelling elegant postures is remarkable. Statues from Indian Pallava art, which was characterized by exactly this style of representation, may have been used as models.

The **stone reliefs** from this period (such as the rock reliefs of Isurumuniya near Anuradhapura) and the depictions of figures on friezes and cornices were also rendered with a stronger design, giving them an impressive refinement. Moonstones, the sculpted thresholds at the base of staircases, guard stones and steles, as well as the makaras of the balustrades, were given their classical appearance. New motifs appeared on the steles serving as architectural ornamentation, such as the seven-headed naga under a parasol, the vase of abundance as well as mythical dwarfs with lotus blossoms on their heads.

Some impressive rock reliefs have managed to survive the ages in Anuradhapura

In architecture a new sense for proportions developed during this **Architecture** period. The dagobas were smaller and were crowned by a rounded cone structured by rings. One striking feature was that the boundary wall of the base was now also decorated (sparingly) with three-dimensional ornamentation. Fine examples of this can be seen on Ruvanveliseya Dagoba in Anuradhapura.

Amongst the rulers of this period the **desire for display** also grew. Palace complexes, such as those in Anuradhapura and Sigiriya, were given pleasure gardens and baths; the latter were often carved from the rock (such as the Lion Pond and Naga Pond in Mihintale). While few remains have survived from the palaces of this time, these artistically designed ponds can still be seen today.

The only evidence of Tamil architecture from the time of the Chola kings is the fairly plain Hindu temple in Dondra (in the district of Matara) dating from the 7th–8th century. It is probably the first purely stone building in Sri Lanka, replacing the wooden structures that had been customary up until then.

The paintings of this period reached extremely high artistic stand- **World-famous** ards. Well-preserved examples are the famous **Cloud Maidens** on the **paintings** walls of the gallery in the palace of Sigiriya. Their design is very graphic but their bodies, with their tumescent forms, elegant and graceful from head to toe, seem almost three-dimensional. The individual drawing style used in the design of the facial features is quite remarkable.

In Hindalga, not far from Kandy, cave paintings of impressive quality were made in the 6th century. They tell the story of the god Indra visiting Buddha; they captivate beholders with their loving attention to detail.

Polonnaruwa Period

The first king to choose Polonnaruwa as his permanent capital was **Only fragments** Vijaya Bahu I. After putting an end to the rule of the Chola kings in **survive** 1070 he began a programme of construction works. Of these buildings, which may have been very impressive, few remains are still extant today.

There is one building in Sri Lanka, the **Temple of the Tooth** in Kandy, that contains elements of this new stylistic direction. Thus, the cella, the temple's central room, was no longer round but rectangular in form. The ornamentation also became richer, as is demonstrated by the decorative bas-reliefs on the temple's 54 stone columns. They are characteristics of the Polonnaruwa style, which was much more showy than its predecessors. Under King Nissanka Malla the style reached its highest perfection, as can be seen on the Vatadage of Polonnaruwa, where an older sacred structure was fundamentally remodelled and to gain a far richer ornamentation than before. Another good example of the display-conscious Polonnaruwa style is the Missamkalata Mandapa, a hall where the sacred tooth relic was worshipped.

With the Polonnaruwa style Singhalese art departed almost completely from its Indian model and became **very independent**. No one worried about pulling down or altering a large number of Brahman buildings from the time of the Chola kings in such a way that they were only distantly reminiscent of the older days.

However, secular as well as sacred structures underwent changes to their exterior. The **palaces of the kings** of Nissanka Malla and Parakrama Bahu I were extensive complexes with large halls and many chambers, which according to ancient chronicles reached heights of up to seven storeys. King Parakrama Bahu's audience hall for example demonstrates a remarkable self-sufficiency of design. Substantial parts of this hall still exist today.

Monumental rock sculptures

Buddhist sculpture was enriched during the Polonnaruwa period through the introduction of the recumbent depiction of Buddha, symbolic of the moment in which the Enlightened One entered nirvana; the most famous example is the monumental rock sculpture of **Gal Vihara** near Polonnaruwa. The highest degree of solemnity, dignity, harmony and internalization was achieved with very sparing means. Amongst the masterpieces of this period is also the 3.5m/ 11.5ft rock sculpture of Potgul Vihara; it is not known, however, whom it depicts.

While stone was the main material used for making sculptures of Buddha, **bronze** was often used to depict Brahman deities. The works are characterized by sophisticated lines, elegant postures and a fine working of the details.

Lost painting

The painterly production of this period, which was so important for the development of Sri Lankan art, must also have been significant. According to old chronicles elaborately painted fabrics as well as high-quality wall paintings existed, but none of this has survived.

The Period of the Short-lived Capitals

Kingdoms

The period between 1235 and 1415 was characterized by the fragmentation of the Singhalese kingdom into several principalities. The capital also changed several times: Yapahuwa, Dambadeniya, Kurunegala and Gampola. Naturally not much remains, which is why information about any changes that may have taken place in art can only be obtained from written sources. One exception is the **rock fortress of Yapahuwa**; its still extant ruins allow an insight into the powerful will of the rulers to create buildings for display.

Of Gampola it is known that several significant temple complexes were constructed during this period in a mixed Brahman-Buddhist architectural style. The reason was probably that deities from both religions were worshipped within them. The depiction of figures and

A magnificent staircase marks the entrance to Yapahuwa rock fort

the floral ornamentation on the sculpted wooden pillars of Gadala-deniya Vihara and Embekke Devale are evidence of a high level of craftsmanship and also of great vitality. A certain Burmese influence is noticeable, particularly in Lankatilaka Vihara near Kandy.

The Kotte Period

Nor has much survived of the period from 1415 to 1597, when Kotte in the west of Sri Lanka was the capital of a small kingdom. The few artefacts from this time do not reveal whether any significant developments occurred on the artistic front. Several friezes, now in the National Museum in Colombo, are, however, evidence of a great creative power. **Few artefacts extant**

The Kandy Period

The few fragments of building still remaining from the early Kandy period (1597 to approx. 1650) show how the architecture of that period tied in with that of the Gampola period. **Simple, occasionally wide halls** with artistically sculpted and carved wooden pillars were built. During the heyday of the Kandy period, on the other hand, there were a few new developments, which are particularly obvious on the Temple of the Tooth in Kandy. More and more elements from the sacred art of other Buddhist countries, such as the Kingdom of Siam (modern-day Thailand), were incorporated. **Architecture**

Remarkable painting

The renaissance experienced by wall painting during this period, in a much more **vernacular form** however, was remarkable. The reason for this may have been that it was not so much artists as craftsman who worked in this area. At the centre of the paintings was the Jataka, tales from Buddha's life cycles, supplemented by scenes from Singhalese history. Generally speaking only the colours red and yellow were used, but because of the many different tints the paintings still seem very colourful.

From the Colonial Period to the Present

British and Dutch influences

The British also left unmistakable traces in Sri Lanka. As becomes obvious when visiting places such as Colombo, they introduced **European architectural features** that still shape large parts of the cityscape, even though much, such as parts of the old forts, has since been demolished. Colombo, still the island's economic centre, is aiming to treat the remains left by colonial rulers with more care than it has done to date.

This church in Galle was built by the Dutch in 1755 in the Baroque style

The Dutch, whose centre was in the south of the island, also left their mark, for example in Galle. Fortresses, churches and public buildings have typical features of **colonial architecture** such as homes and commercial buildings with arcades, ornamentation on the window-sills etc.

There are certain trends that aim to revive old building styles; one case in point being the Independence Memorial Hall built in Colombo during the 1980s. Nevertheless the city council is very much at pains to give Colombo a modern appearance on the Western model.

Contemporary architecture

Temple Architecture

Buddhist Temples

Despite the dependence of Singhalese art on India's Hindu art, a striking independence developed in Sri Lanka over the centuries. This is expressed in the incorporation of Buddhist artistic forms of expression and the conviction with which Buddhism was represented, believed in and lived amongst the Singhalese. For more than one and a half millennia the majority of all Singhalese art was Buddhist art, or, more precisely, the predominant art of Hinayana Buddhism.

Independently developed

Every town in Sri Lanka has a sacred complex that includes a temple, a bodhi tree and a monastery. Further buildings are the vihara (image gallery), the bana maduwa (preaching hall) and the pansala (house of the priest).

Temple complex

A dagoba is not a temple; rather it is an **inaccessible cult building** containing the relics of Buddha, his disciples or other sacred individuals. The dagoba's form and symbolism in Sri Lanka go back to the Indian stupa, which developed from burial mounds constructed over the relics of holy monks.

Dagoba

The oldest stupas are said to have been built under King Ashoka (273–231 BC), who made Buddhism the official religion. Examples include the five stupas in Pattan/Nepal. The Thuparama dagoba in Anuradhapura from the 3rd century is also one of the oldest. It is said to have contained a shrine with one of **Buddha's collarbones** that King Ashoka sent from India when the king of Anuradhapura converted to Buddhism.

Dagobas, also known as thupas in Sri Lanka, form the conspicuous centre of the monastery and usually consist of round, or, occasionally square or polygonal, stepped foundations, known as maluva or medhi, on which there is a terrace, which is in turn surrounded by a stone balustrade. Above this is the anda (egg), the usually hemispher-

? DID YOU KNOW ...?

■ According to tradition one of Buddha's sayings was responsible for the design of the stupa. »Build heaps of sand, like rice, which everybody needs«, the Enlightened One is said to have told his first disciples when they asked him for visible symbols with which they could express their devotion.

ical superstructure, which is symbolic of the firmament or also of the all-embracing principle of enlightenment. The anda is usually a brick structure coated in plaster or stucco. Above the anda is the harmika, which symbolizes the holy place above the world beyond all rebirths, nirvana. In the past it contained the actual relic, but later the preferred method was to immure the relic in the lower third of the anda. Above the harmika is the conical, ringed chattra, whose lower section is often surrounded by standing Buddha statues. The (mostly) eight rings of the chattra stand for the Eightfold Path that Buddha taught. The structure is completed by the tip, which is often coated in gold and sometimes decorated with precious stones. The **access to the base** of a stupa, which people always walk around in a clockwise direction during holy ceremonies, is designed using the arrangement for stairs that is typical in Sri Lanka. It consists of a moonstone in front of the steps, guard steles on both sides of the first step, the steps themselves as well as the stringers, which were often in the shape of a naga (a mythical snake).

Moonstone The moonstone has a special role: by walking across this symbolic stone slab a person leaves the world of material possessions and human weaknesses and enters a world of the senses, the world of the enlightened Buddha. **The best moonstone** in Sri Lanka is at the staircase to Mahasena Palace in Anuradhapura. It is composed of four semi-circular rings. The first, outer ring represents the flaming wreath as a symbol of human desire; the second ring depicts the sacred animals (elephant, lion, stag and horse). The third ring is decorated with plant ornaments, and the innermost ring with a half-open lotus blossom that symbolizes nirvana.

Four or five steps lead up from the moonstone to the sacred temple complex. They symbolize the stages of meditation.

Vatadage (stupa house) A further creation of sacred Singhalese architecture is the vatadage, the stupa house (also known as chetiya-ghara). It is a small stupa surrounded by concentric rings of stone columns that support a wooden beam ceiling. This stupa house **was used by monks and pilgrims as accommodation** and provided protection against the weather. The stupa itself, although it often did not contain an actual reliquary, was the object of a cult of veneration that took the form of a walking around it several times. Similar buildings can also be found in India but there they are known as chaitya halls and have a central nave and aisles and are built into the rock. In Sri Lanka the vatadage stood above ground and had a different, far simpler artistic design.

Moonstones symbolize areas of transition

The asana-ghara, the **temple of the (empty) throne**, a place commemorating Buddha's first sermon at Varanasi (Benares), was characteristic of Sri Lankan sacred architecture until well into the Middle Ages. The temple's focal point is a sculpted stone slab symbolizing Buddha's throne. Around it is a series of stone columns that supported a wooden beam ceiling. This building method also dates back to the early Buddhist period, during which there were no likenesses of Buddha; instead there were these asana-ghara as well as bodhi trees, stupas and symbolic footprints that referred to the teacher and his teachings.

The emergence of Buddha likenesses caused the asana-ghara to be replaced more and more by the statue house (patima-ghara)). This was often a high, narrow building with thick, often richly painted walls that housed the monumental statue of a sitting or standing Buddha. The Thuparama statue house in Polonnaruwa is considered to be the best example.

In addition to the stupa house, the patima-ghara and the bodhi-ghara, the uposatha-ghara (house of ordination), an often generously proportioned building with a trapezoidal floor plan, is also part of the monastic sacred complex. This is where ordinations take place, for which the members of the religious community assemble under their leader, the abbot. A Buddha image is obligatory here, while in a small room separate from the actual hall the holy scriptures are kept.

Living areas The temple complex also contains the monks' living cells (known as arama or pansala), the refectory and the baths as well as the bell-frame (ghantara). In monasteries of the Dhammarucika order, which claims to follow the teachings of Buddha particularly closely, the individual areas are clearly separated from each other by stone walls or ditches. Other monasteries do not have such divisions.

Cave temples Since the earliest times Buddhist monks have lived in caves, either alone or in groups; at first they were scantily equipped, for example with a pipe to catch and channel rainwater; later their interiors were decorated more lavishly with statues and frescoes. One excellent example of a cave temple, which are very plentiful in Sri Lanka, is the **temple complex of Dambulla**. Even before the birth of Christ it was inhabited by monks who founded a significant Buddhist monastery here in around 80 BC. The model for this cave temple came from the complexes in India (Bhaja, Karli and Ajanta), but it cannot be compared to them.

Bodhi tree The bodhi tree (*ficus religiosa*), also a standard component of every temple complex, is highly venerated by Buddhists because Buddha is said to have attained enlightenment while sitting under such a tree in India. Bodhi trees, which can be several hundred years old, usually stand on their own terrace (bodhi-ghara) surrounded by a wall decorated with reliefs or at least by a balustrade. They are decorated with colourful ribbons that reveal their sacred nature. The oldest known still extant bodhi-ghara was uncovered by archaeologists in the Kurunegala complex. It dates from around the 8th–10th centuries and is surrounded by nicely sculpted entrance gates.

Brahman Temples

Deities The main Brahman deities worshipped in Sri Lanka are Shiva, Isvara and Skanda, Vishnu, Ganesha and the goddesses Kali, Tara and Pattani. The largest numbers of Brahman temples are consecrated to them. However, it is not unusual for the abovementioned gods from the Hindu pantheon to be joined by beings from Mahayana Buddhism (such as bodhisattvas) and Vedic (ancient Indian) deities, since the devout Tamil population hoped to get special protection from them. This tendency to create a kind of synthesis has varied in strength over the centuries. It reached a peak at the start of the 13th century. This also explains the mixture of architectural styles from the Gampola and Kandy periods.

Models from India Pure Brahman architecture does not have any great past in Sri Lanka; no real creative impulses came from it. Hinduism had long become

This sculpture over an entrance to a Hindu temple is a symbol of the sacred Mt Meru

the popular religion in India, while in Sri Lanka Buddhism first had to establish itself and its architecture had to develop its own creative force. Elements were incorporated for this purpose, albeit only to a modest extent, from some of the art forms developed in India, particularly from the southern Indian Chola and Pandy styles. It is thought the northern ports of Jaffna and Trincomalee must have once had many sacred buildings modelled on Indian examples, but not much of them has survived.

Good examples of Brahman temple architecture can nevertheless be found in Polonnaruwa: a Shiva Devale, reminiscent of the Chola style, and another that has the characteristics of the Pandy style. They are difficult to distinguish, differing in just a few details such as the vertical and the horizontal structuring of the external façade. The biggest difference is on the crest, which is a modification of the basic shape of early Indian tower temple: at the base there is a stepped terrace, upon which is a cubic block with the main room, the cella, above which is a pyramidal, usually stepped tower. The highest point is often given a dome-shaped design. The cella's exterior wall was adorned with blind arcades, niches, small chapels and balconies, while the roof is divided into several storeys and small towers whose niches were decorated with statues of gods, people, animals and demons. These statues, sculpted in the round, emerge from the wall and at times even appear separated from it.

Temple architecture

Many Hindu temples in Sri Lanka are also based on **Chola architecture**, which reached its peak between the 8th and 10th centuries. Characteristic of this Dravidian style are the steep, multi-storeyed pyramid tower, whose angular tip is crowned by several lights, and also the secondary temples around the main temple, the processional corridors and the gates. Successful syntheses of Buddhist patima-ghara (picture house) and Hindu temple are Galadeniya Vihara and Vijayotpaya, both of which are in Galadeniya not far from Gampola. They were built in the mid-14th century.

The **Satmahal Prasada** in Polonnaruwa is quite unusual. It is a very high, simple stepped tower consisting of six elements roughly cubic in shape placed on top of each other, with the largest at the bottom and the smallest at the top. At the centre of each side of the cubes is a niche that may have contained a statue of a standing deity (possibly also Buddha statues). This building, in its atypical design, resembles the stupas built in the Mon architectural style that was widespread in Burma and Thailand. The only evidence of artists from those countries influencing Sri Lanka's architecture is that it is thought that Burmese or Siamese itinerant monks must have come to Sri Lanka for Buddhist congresses and donated funds for the construction of the Satmahal Prasada.

Secular Architecture

Victims of time The use of wood as a construction material must have been known about in Sri Lanka from very early on. One case in point is the eight wooden storeys of the Lohapasada (copper palace) in Anuradhapura. Most of these buildings, which must have once been very artistic, have fallen victim to the centuries so that much is very difficult to make out with certainty. The buildings that used other materials as well, such as those made of stone and wood, have survived.

They were primarily built during the Gampola and the Kandy periods, while hardly anything remains of those buildings that may have been constructed centuries earlier, such as in Anuradhapura. The employees of the Archaeological Survey of Sri Lanka, a government body that has the task of saving and preserving significant antiquities, have spent the past 25 years working very hard on uncovering the unique but overgrown **palace buildings of King Parakrama Bahu I in Anuradhapura** so that they at least give an impression of their former magnificence.

Visual Arts

Depictions of Buddha

Ban on images During the early Buddhist period there were no depictions of Buddha himself, and it seems they may even have been banned. In any case there is no proof of figural representations of Buddha having existed at this time. The reason was probably that it was neither possible nor desirable to capture the Enlightened One in an image. Instead symbols were used to give Buddha a physical presence: **lotus**

blossoms were symbols of the beautiful and the consummate harmony that appears to emerge from the nothing, or the **bodhi tree** (*Ficus religiosa*), the tree under which Siddharta Gautama reached the state of enlightenment. The symbolic and thus oversized **footprint** that is found in every country with a Buddhist following was also very popular at this time. All of these symbols were enough at first to bring to life Buddha's life-path and teachings to the hearts of Buddha's followers.

Since the first likenesses of Buddha appeared there have been hardly any changes to them. Buddhist artists strive not for individuality and artistic freedom but to follow the old canon. Of course the artist's individual expression of his personal religious experience is allowed. The artist, incidentally, always remains anonymous.

Early depictions of Buddha are known from around the 1st century AD. They were presumably made in the northern Indian kingdom of Kubhana in the reign of King Kanishka, who was devoted to art. Around the same time the Indian towns of Mathura and Ghandara, centres of art at the time, also already had depictions of Buddha. During this time an artistic style developed in Ghandara that was most likely influenced by **artists from Persia**, which was then part of Alexander the Great's empire. For this reason it is known as the Greco-Buddhist style.

Early depictions of Buddha

To this day the old canon is crucial for new likenesses of Buddha

These early depictions show Buddha Shakyami either standing or sitting; the fixed and still valid **canon of proportions, attributes and gestures** seems to have started to develop here. This iconographic canon emerged from the desire to create the »right« likeness and give it eternal validity. It is meant to point to the right path to enlightenment beyond worldliness and finiteness. Thus there are speculations about the existence of cosmic number relationships in the physical proportions.

Symbolism   Buddha's transfigured body exhibits 32 main characteristics, which were later supplemented by a further 80. One is the topknot on Buddha's head (ushnisha), which has the shape of a serpent with a flickering tongue (in other Buddhist countries such as Thailand it has the shape of a lotus bud). Other characteristics are the curl (uma) between the eyebrows, which is often shown as a mark or gem; Buddha's main head of hair, styled into small curls or waves; and the symbolized halo around Buddha's head or around the entire body as a symbol of energy.

Depictions of Buddha are always gender-neutral. The hands and soles of the feet always show religious symbols or Sanskrit words. The overly long earlobes are also remarkable; different interpretations have been given as to their significance. Some say they are symbols of Siddharta Gautama's noble origin, because only the rich were able to afford weighty jewellery to elongate the earlobes. Other scholars believe this form of representation is a further symbol of the Enlightened One's omniscience.

Movement is energy   The insights about the structure and movement of the human body, used in Greek sculptures for example, only play a subordinate role in the design of Buddhist sculptures. According to Hindu beliefs movement is the expression of the sensual and fertile energy that inhabits the body. On this interpretation it seems completely natural that Vishnu, for example, is depicted as a god with many arms and other gods (such as the elephant god Ganesha) are shown to have many heads.

Buddha's postures   Buddhism has four ways in which the first Enlightened One can be depicted: in standing, sitting, walking and recumbent positions. There are five different standing postures and five sitting ones, all with exactly prescribed hand positions, each of which has its own symbolic significance.

The **standing postures** include Buddha standing upright or sometimes bent at the hip . In another common posture one leg is stretched out, while the other is at a slight angle. Less common is the posture where one leg is bent and the other slightly pulled towards the body (dance posture).

The **recumbent posture** stands for the time when Siddharta Gautama reaches the state of enlightenment. Other scholars think, how-

Buddha's Poses and Gestures

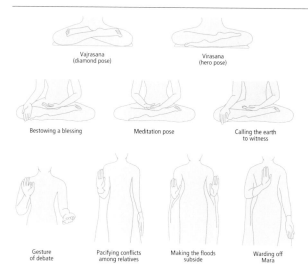

Vajrasana
(diamond pose)

Virasana
(hero pose)

Bestowing a blessing

Meditation pose

Calling the earth
to witness

Gesture
of debate

Pacifying conflicts
among relatives

Making the floods
subside

Warding off
Mara

ever, this is the moment when Buddha enters nirvana, i.e. dies. This latter opinion is strengthened by the particularly large number of depictions in Sri Lanka where Buddha is lying on a bed with his first disciples sitting in front of him in a semi-circle. This contradicts the first interpretation, because Siddharta Gautama is said to have been alone at the moment when he found enlightenment.

The classical **sitting postures** require a much larger number of interpretations. One well-known posture shows Buddha sitting with crossed legs with the feet over the knees, making the soles visible (lotus position, meditation position); others show Buddha with one crossed leg, while the other is dangling down, or sitting in the European fashion with both legs hanging down vertically (naturally a very rare depiction, which is typical of »the Buddha of the future« known as Maitreya). A very common depiction shows Buddha sitting under a serpent with five (sometimes seven) heads. It goes back to an event in Buddha's life: Muchalinda, one of the naga kings (serpent kings) protected the meditating Buddha from a torrential downpour by spreading out his heads like a fan.

Amongst the hand positions, the »seals« (mudra), which are possibly given the most attention by the sculptors, are the **gesture of fearlessness** or of protection (abhaya-mudra: the right hand is raised and the palm is facing forwards), and the gesture of **adoration or worship** (anjali-mudra: the palms of the hands are pressed together, the fingers are slightly angled and are pointing upwards). The latter

Hand positions

A good example of the gesture of granting a blessing can be found in Aukana

gesture is less common when depicting Buddha Shakyami himself; it tends to occur more in depictions of his followers and future Buddhas. A further gesture, known as asiva-mudra, is the **gesture of granting blessings** (a particularly good example of this is the monumental Buddha statue in Aukana).
The **gesture of calling the earth to witness** (bhumisparsa-mudra) goes back to a legend; in this mudra the right hand is resting on Buddha's crossed legs with the back of the hand facing upwards and the fingertips pointing downwards. Once, when Buddha was deep in meditation, Mara, evil, appeared in order to prevent enlightenment. Siddharta Gautama called the earth goddess Thorani to be a witness of his virtue by touching the earth with his fingertips. Thorani's hair was full of water because after every good deed Gautama made a sacrifice of water to the earth goddess, as was the custom. Thorani appeared and wrung her hair whereupon Mara and his helpers were washed away and Gautama became the »vanquisher of Mara« (maravijaya). This is one of the most common representations of Buddha in Sri Lanka.
The dhyana-mudra or samadhi-mudra, the gesture of meditation, involves Buddha's hands lying over each other on his lap with the palms facing upwards. Finally there is the gesture of fulfilment (karana-mudra), where the little finger and the index finger are pointing upwards, while the middle finger and the ring finger are bent downwards and are covered by the thumb. There are a few depictions of Buddha in a posture known as vajradhara or primordial Buddha. This is the mystical Buddha of the Vajarayana school (Adi Buddha), who stands for unification with the worldly principle (sakti): the arms are crossed in front of the chest, while the hands are enclosing a bell and thunderbolt.

Shiva Since the Shiva cult has a special significance in Sri Lanka the sculptural representation of the dancing Shiva (Nataraja) deserves special mention here. The statue is made exclusively of bronze and is almost one metre tall. **Every detail is filled with symbolism:** the lambent flames of the wreath surrounding Shiva symbolize the power of the Hindu religion. Shiva's face has three eyes; the central one is a symbol for omniscience. In his right earlobe the deity has a »male« earring and in his left a »female«, proof that he embodies both sexes.

The hair on his head is plaited until it forms a crown. The human skull at his feet symbolizes the principle of destruction Shiva that stands for. The lower plaits are following the whirling movements of the dance, the girl on the right is emblematic of the Indian river Ganges, the symbol of fertility, while the crescent in Shiva's left hand represents magnanimity and fame.

The best depiction of a dancing Shiva is to be found in the national museum in Colombo. There are, however, countless replicas of varying quality, including artificially aged ones that can be bought in every antique shop or even department store.

Buddha in the meditative pose

Painting

The oldest paintings and drawings, dating back to the Neolithic age, were found in caves in Central Province (in Tantrimalai, Madagala, Kadurupoluna and Mahalenama). The motifs include plant patterns and animals that were painted on the rock wall in red paint.

Early examples

During the Buddhist period many monks and hermits lived in caves, and there too the walls were painted. However, the painters could not have been the inhabitants themselves because the rules of Buddhism forbid monks to paint. It is much more likely that **donors** (maybe kings) commissioned the paintings. Amongst the various depictions, common ones are of Buddhas, bodhisattvas and worshippers. Characteristic of these paintings in Sri Lanka is the preliminary drawing in red. This tradition continued until the end of the Polonnaruwa period, thus differing from the Indian practice, where the outlines of figures and floral elements were drawn in black.

Famous examples of early Buddhist painting in Sri Lanka can be seen in the **caves of Kurandaka Lena** (2nd century BC) near Ambalantota and in **Karambagalla** (also 2nd century BC) as well as near Ridigama in Yala National Park. The figures are simple in their shapes, highly abstract and almost schematic, but the clear and confident lines and the lovingly worked details are striking.

Sri Lanka's paintings always emphasize the graphic aspect, but they lack perspective so that the people and scenes depicted are right in the foreground and come across directly to the beholder. The fresco technique seems to have been almost entirely unknown in Sri Lanka. The area to be painted was often covered in a layer of lime or clay but the paints, usually a **mixture of tempera and oil**, were only applied after this layer had dried. The range of colours was limited. The pigments were obtained from natural raw materials: white from lime or magnesia, black from coal, yellow and red from ochre, green from plants and blue from lapis lazuli.

Rock drawings of Sigiriya   Amongst the rock-painting masterpieces are undoubtedly the images on the gallery wall in the rock palace of Sigiriya, **the famous Cloud Maidens**. They date from the late 5th century, but experts are still debating who they represent. In 1897 the first archaeological commissioner of the government of Sri Lanka, the Englishman H. C. P. Bell, opined that it was a procession of queens, daughters or concubines living at the court of King Kassyapa, specifically a scene depicting an offering. This seems most likely, while other suggestions, such as that the women are mythical beings from the world of legend or that the painter was an Indian artist, are speculative.

The ceiling paintings in the second cave of Dambulla are remarkable.
They display an incredible wealth of details and an extremely lavish use of colour and form.

Even more significant than the quality of the colours are the confidence of the lines, the powerful desire to capture a great degree of individuality, and the depiction of the corporeal.

No less significant are the wall paintings in the cave temples of Dambulla, whose beginnings probably go back to the 1st century AD. They were only given their current appearance in the 12th century when King Nissanka Malla commissioned artists to renew the existing murals and to add some new ones. The paintings in the third cave temple date back to the 18th century, when King Kirti Sri Raja Sinha commissioned its decoration.

Wall paintings of Dambulla

The wall paintings of the Polonnaruwa period are predominantly to be found inside patima-ghara (picture houses). The number of motifs expanded to include **scenic depictions** that reveal the artists' evident joy in story-telling (such as the wall paintings in the cella of the Tivanka Pilimage in Polonnaruwa). They depict events from the Jataka, Buddha's previous lives, of which there were more than 500.

Polonnaruwa period

Some high-quality wall paintings from the Gampola period have survived, as in Gadaladeniya and in Lankatilaka Vihara in Polonnaruwa; their style however, ties in with tradition.

Gampola period

From around the 16th century the art of painting seems to have disappeared for some time, and when it reappeared two centuries later (including in Telwatta near Hikkaduwa and in Kathaluwa near Galle as well as around Kandy, in the Degaldoruwa cave temple) it had a fundamentally different character. From then on the paintings were **folksy, almost naïve**, filling up large sections of wall space. An unselfconscious enjoyment of narrative becomes clear, making the hand of the anonymous artist paint the worlds of people, animals and plants as well as scenes from the Jataka.
The 19th century saw the painting of further high-quality murals, such as in the temple of Kelaniya (not far from Colombo). They reveal a Burmese and sometimes even a European influence, which can be seen both in the hint of perspective and in the postures of the figures, as well as in the fall of the lavish robes.

18th century to modern times

Literature

The beginnings of Ceylonese literature lie in chronicles that go back to the 5th century BC and have been passed down through the ages under the names Dipavamsa and Mahavamsa. However, around a century earlier the Indian monk Buddhagosa, who had spent some years living in Sri Lanka, was credited with having translated Sanskrit

Beginnings before 5th century BC

Buddhist texts and commentaries and written them down in Pali. Maybe he is also a potential candidate for the authorship of a **Buddhist textbook**, the Visuddhimagga.

A little later, in around the 5th and 6th centuries, countless **biographical poems and novels** were written in Sanskrit. In the 12th century Singhalese-language literature finally emerged and immediately flourished during the reign of King Parakrama Bahu I (1153–86). He is also credited with having set up the first **public libraries** in order to allow the literate monks to read the texts that had been written down on palm leaves. The subjects of this time included religious, scientific and medical insights as well as countless stories (usually in verse) as well as poems. Parakrama Bahu's successor Nissanka Malla (1187–96) is believed to be the author of a **chronicle carved in stone** that reports on his (alleged) military campaigns, but also on his relations with other countries. The granite block, 8m/27ft long, 4.5m/ 15ft wide and richly ornamented all around, known as Gal Pota (»stone book«), is in Polonnaruwa.

In the 14th century literature also enjoyed a high standing under King Parakrama Bahu IV (1302–26). It was during this time that a **Singhalese grammar** was developed as well as a detailed description of the Jataka, Buddha's 500-plus previous lives.

Mahabharata and Ramayana

Two long literary works, the Mahabharata and the Ramayana, are of great significance to Buddhism, whose teachings spread from India to the rest of the Asian continent during the reign of King Ashoka (approx. 272–236 BC). While the former, consisting of 18 books with more than 90,000 verses, probably has a historical core that many »reporters« helped write, the Ramayana, consisting of seven books and around 24,000 verses, is more likely to be a collection of legends.

The Mahabharata largely consists of **descriptions of battles and festivals**. The connective elements between these episodes are elegies written in lyrical form, such as love poems, as well as mythological, fabulous and at times also instructive interspersions. Indian women, whose much-quoted qualities of purity and chastity play an important role in Indian literature, are often at the centre of these historically unverifiable stories. It is, on the other hand, considered certain that the Mahabharata was written between the 4th century BC and the 6th century AD. Rama, who is described as the divine incarnation of the Hindu god Vishnu in books I and VII, which may have been written at a later date, is at the centre of the Ramayana (»in honour of Rama«); its **poetry is more chivalric than priestly in nature**. It is believed the Ramayana was written between the 3rd century BC and the 3rd century AD.

The chronicle of the island of Sri Lanka

In around AD 320 Buddhist monks began writing the Dipavamsa, the great chronicle of events in Sri Lanka. This work still provides detailed information about this lively period, during which Bud-

The Gal Pota reports the (alleged) military campaigns of King Nissanka Malla

dhism became established on the island. It encompasses a period from pre-history to the year 303, the year King Mahasena died, describing life in prehistoric Sri Lanka and the arrival of the Aryans, following the development of Buddhism and also reporting on the three visits the Enlightened One is said to have made to the island. Furthermore it names the early Singhalese kings, describes their reigns and thus permits **conclusions about the social, economic and cultural conditions** of this period.

Dance and Music

Singhalese dance and the dance theatre that is based on it are a true popular art form, and although it is becoming more refined, it has never become separated from the popular soul. In some Sri Lankan dances Indian influences are unmistakable, but they now only play a very subordinate role.

Dance is popular art

Dances have always been the **main component of exorcist rituals**, where dialogues are not so much spoken as danced. Thus demons, a dramatic component of the mostly traditional stories, are integrated into the play in such a way that they embody their role through a highly fearsome appearance; this can be increased through commanding behaviour in the form of a dance.

There are two different types of Singhalese dances in Sri Lanka. While the **Up Country Dances** (also known as Kandy Dances) are

The drums provide the rhythm for dancing

performed in the highlands, the **Low Country Dances** are performed in the southwest of the island. They mainly differ in the nature of the dance performance, in the different dance rhythms and in the different use of instruments. The clearest difference lies in the dancers' appearance: the Kandy dancers wear headdresses and facial ornamentation but no masks; their transformation is mainly demonstrated by the dancers' expressive power. The dancers of the lowlands, on the other hand, do wear masks and thus complete their transformation into other beings, into gods and demons.

Music The classical Singhalese orchestra is made up of **three types of drums** in addition to cymbals, a small metal percussion instrument and a clarinet-like instrument. Drums are indispensable for accompanying dances and they are usually beaten directly with the hands. They are covered with one or two skins and there are also various types of flat drum. Drums set the rhythm for dances, but they can also emphasize the nature of a certain being through their pitch. Thus the Yak Bera (devil's drum), for example, is used exclusively for devils and demons. It accentuates their character because its sound resembles that of a deep human voice. The most-used drum is the rahana, which is available in many different sizes, from the large drums that stand on the floor to the small types that individual musicians can hold in their hands. The getaberaya is often used for religious ceremonies. This drum has one skin of cow leather and one of monkey hide, so that different sounds can be made on it. The getaberaya is carried around the neck so it can be played with both hands.

Religious ceremonies are opened with the hakgediya, a shell. When it is blown a deep, drawn-out sound is produced. A slightly modified version of this is the saksinnam; in this case a mouthpiece is attached to the shell. The wind instrument known as bata nawala is also popular. It consists of a bamboo pipe with seven holes. The brass horn known as kombu on the other hand has almost fallen into oblivion. It was once used as a signal horn.

Handicrafts

Handicrafts in Sri Lanka have a tradition going back many centuries, particularly in the manufacture of dance masks. The small town of Ambalangoda on the southwest coast, where the island's most famous carvers live, is considered the centre of mask carving. There is a good reason for this: the inhabitants of this fishing village on the southwest coast of Sri Lanka have held on to a variety of customs. The masked plays (kolam maduwa) play a significant role.

Mask carving

There are few certainties about the origins of the masked plays in Sri Lanka. It seems, however, that the participants incorporated political, historical and social elements over the years as well as myths that have been passed down across the centuries.

Kolam maduwa (masked plays)

Like so much in Sri Lanka the development of the masked plays is also connected to legend: a queen is said to have felt the insatiable desire for masked dances. However, nobody knew how to perform them, so in her need she appealed to the god Sakra, who in turn appealed to the god Visvakarma, the

> ! **Baedeker TIP**
>
> **Mask Museum**
> Ambalangoda has a Mask Museum displaying many old, valuable masks. In return for a small fee you get a small booklet that also describes some exemplary kolam performances (426 Patabendimulla, Sat – Wed 8am – 6pm; free admission).

god of the craftsmen, to ask him to make the required masks. The next day, according to the legend, not just the masks were found in the royal garden but also the right verses to make a play possible. After the plot had been studied, the kolam maduwa was produced and the queen was happy. By the way, this legend still plays a role in every kolam maduwa and is incorporated into the action.

A traditional kolam maduwa also uses current events from the lives of the village community; and since the characters actually exist in real life the plays often produce great amusement amongst the spectators. According to one story some kolam actors during the period of colonization represented the foreign arrivals as ridiculous characters.

Making the masks

Larger masks are carved from very light materials such as sandalwood and balsa wood, while the wood of the kaduru tree (Nux vomica) is used for smaller ones. In the old masks all facial features such as the nose, protruding eyes and oversized fangs were meticulously carved, whereas more recent masks tend to have some of these features merely drawn on.

The **purpose of the masks** is to be found in the dances in which they are used. Their colourful appearance is designed to produce as much tension and excitement as possible; when the dancer holding the mask in front of his face moves, the light of the oil lamps is reflected from the painted surface in the half-dark, giving the impression that supernatural forces are at work.

Amongst the particularly imaginative performances are the naga masks, which embody the snake god and often consist of several faces and upright cobras.

The centre of mask carving is Ambalangoda in the southwest.

Batik

The batik technique is not originally Singhalese, but a craft imported from Indonesia. Nevertheless, the batik items produced in Sri Lanka, mainly for tourists, are of exceptionally high quality, almost as good as the original, in fact. In this method of dyeing, certain areas of the fabric are sealed with wax, preventing them from taking up the dye when the fabric is dunked into the dye bath.

Metalwork

Among the few resources found in Sri Lanka that can be exploited are metals such as copper, which is used as the raw material for statues, containers of various sizes, and also vases. Silver is often used to make pretty pieces of jewellery.

Customs

Animism

Even though visitors are most likely to find out only by chance about the penchant of the people of Sri Lanka to believe in spirits, animism continues to play an important role in everyday life. Many temples throughout the country have cans for donations at which drivers stop and throw in a few rupees, while reciting a spell. They thereby hope to drive free from crashes.

The Sri Lankan belief in spirits also plays an important role when it comes to funerals. Small white flags that are hung on string over a street reveal that a person has died. They are hung all along the route between the home of the deceased and the burial site. Sometimes banners honouring the deceased's achievements are also hung up. The flags are meant to keep evil spirits away from the last journey of the body. If the small flags hanging across the street are yellow, it is a monk who has died.

The dead are only buried after four to five days in Sri Lanka, (members of certain castes as well as monks are cremated), but until then they are kept in their homes. Relatives, friends and acquaintances should have sufficient time to say goodbye and wish them a better existence in their next life.

The magical rituals to ward off evil spirits were developed as early as the 1st millennium BC. Details about them can be found in the earliest recorded written accounts. Together with the Singhalese invasion of the island, northern Indian influences were added. By the 17th century the ceremonies had already reached the level of development which characterizes them today.

Of the countless demons that, according to popular belief, have lost **Demons** their way in the mountains and forests, in rivers and lakes or linger on remote streets or three-way intersections, there are about 20 that have to be driven out and banished. The predominant group amongst these are the spirits that bring diseases (cholera, dysentery, fever etc.) and those that put evil curses on people.

The Singhalese believe the ceremony of the thovil to cast out spirits is the one most likely to be successful. It takes place in the relevant person's home and lasts from dusk till dawn. The ritual dances are performed by a kattadiya, an **exorcist**, in front of an altar-like set-up. The exorcist wears various colourful masks to prevent the spirit or demon from recognizing that a person is behind all of it. Different gifts such as betel leaves, blossoms, fruits or also linseed cake are placed on the altar. Since it is believed that the demon will slip into the betel leaves when it believes its harmful machinations to be over, they are wrapped in seven threads that are pulled tight as soon as the demon is in the leaves. Then the bunch is hung up on nails that were previously banged into a tree. At the end of the ceremony, which is particularly popular with the people of the southern part of the island, all the other gifts are taken to a remote location.

Since the people of Sri Lanka also imagine the planets to be deities **Planets** influencing the lives of the people on earth, they too need to be placated through certain rituals, particularly when a person has been affected by disease or misfortune. The most important of these rituals, called bali, is also held at night, and is conducted outside the home. Instead a spot in the garden is chosen and then cleaned with a mixture of fresh cow-dung, milk and pulverized sandalwood. Next an image of the planet deity, formed out of mud and covered in a white cloth, is set up in this spot.

The priest begins the **ceremony** by scattering rice kernels on the ground and putting down various sacrificial gifts. Then he takes a thread spun by a virgin, attaches one end to the statue, then draws it around the entire ceremony area and ties the other end to a branch, which he hands to the affected person. The dances, which now begin amidst intense drumming, can bring the participants to ecstasy. They are interrupted by songs and calls from the spectators. Once the ritual's climax has been reached, the afflicted person approaches the image (or is carried there), attaches the thread to it and throws the branch on to it. For safety's sake the statue stays in place for three days after the ceremony. Then it is placed under a tree and sprinkled with magic water.

Spells

The belief in the effectiveness of spells (mantras) is also widespread in Sri Lanka. They are very old; some were written down in Singhalese infused with Sanskrit words, others in the Dravidian languages. Before the magician (kattadiya) can put them into effect he has to fill them with life or supernatural power through incantations and certain rituals. For this purpose the kattadiya could use a cobra or scorpion, whom he would order to kill the enemies, by stinging them, strangling them or biting them.

Amulets

Amulets also have magic powers against all things evil. They are worn around the neck, waist or wrist. The complicated patterns that bring about the desired effect are drawn on copper or aluminium foil or onto a palm leaf that is rolled up and carried in a small gold or silver container.

Famous People

Sri Lanka was already a destination for globetrotters many centuries ago. Siddharta Gautama, who was later called Buddha, came from Nepal. Marco Polo came from Venice in the Middle Ages, and the Arabian traveller Ibn Battuta also visited the island in the mid-14th century.

Sirimavo Bandaranaike (1916–2000)

Politician

Sirimavo Ratwatte Bandaranaike was born in Balangoda near Ratna-pura as the daughter of a large landowner.

Her political career began after her marriage to the lawyer and politician ►Solomon Bandaranaike (1940). After his assassination in 1959 she took over the leadership of the Sri Lanka Freedom Party (SLFP), which was the opposition party at this time.

A year later she managed to be elected prime minister, not least because of her promise to hand out free rice for all the people of Sri Lanka. In order to achieve this goal she pursued a strict course of nationalization of many tea and rubber plantations as well as of banks and oil companies. Nevertheless the programme tore huge holes in the state budget with the consequence that she lost the general elections in 1965.

? DID YOU KNOW ...?

■ that Sirimavo Bandaranaike was the first female head of government in the world?

After five years in opposition Mrs Bandaranaike managed a political comeback in 1970, when she once again ran as the SLFP candidate and won. However, great resistance soon developed to her leadership: when a commission appointed by the government accused her of abusing her powers and of favouritism, she was deprived of the right to either vote or stand for office, which meant her only option was to withdraw from political life.

Her banishment from the political stage only lasted until 1986, and after her daughter Chandrika Kumaratunga became president when early elections were held (1994), she even managed to become prime minister the following year.

Solomon Bandaranaike (1899–1959)

Politician

Solomon West Ridgeway Dias Bandaranaike was born in Colombo. After studying law he first worked as a lawyer and then as a politician in the United National Party (UNP). After he left this party he founded the Sri Lanka Freedom Party (SLFP), whose leader he became in 1952. Four years later he managed to secure the election of the People's United Front led by the SLFP, and at the head of a four-party coalition he was elected prime minister. During his time in office, which only lasted three years, he implemented a first phase of introducing socialism to Sri Lanka (which his wife► Sirimavo Bandaranaike rigorously continued). In addition he made Singhala the official language in 1957. Politically he pursued a strictly nationalist course, while taking a neutral stance in foreign affairs.

← Marco Polo described Sri Lanka's inhabitants in his books as having dogs' heads. An illustrator (around 1412) shows them trading in spices

Solomon Bandaranaike was assassinated by a Buddhist monk on 26 September 1959. It is not clear whether the monk was acting on orders from anyone else.

Ibn Battuta (1304 to approx. 1368)

Arab globetrotter   If there is one man of the 14th century who can rightly be called a globetrotter, it must be the Islamic scholar Ibn Battuta. Thanks to his wanderlust there are relatively reliable accounts about the Islamic world and neighbouring regions at this time.

Ibn Battuta was born in Tangier (Morocco) as the son of a noble family. After training in law he left his home city when he was just 21 in order to go on his first pilgrimage to Mecca. It was not long, however, before he was off the beaten pilgrimage paths and without the protection of the pilgrims' caravans on much more dangerous routes.

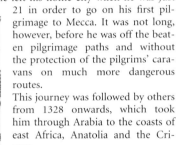

This journey was followed by others from 1328 onwards, which took him through Arabia to the coasts of east Africa, Anatolia and the Crimea.

After working as a judge for the sultan of Delhi, Ibn Battuta once again went on several trips that brought him to the Maldives and to Sri Lanka, where he stayed for two years. It is not proved whether he reached Beijing, but it can be deduced from Battuta's detailed travel accounts that he was in China.

He wrote down this travel account together with the scholar Ibn Juzayy in the form of a rihla. At this time this form of literature was a highly popular kind of travelogue; it super-

Ibn Battuta's travel routes

ficially dealt with religious subjects but also described the experiences of travellers in faraway countries as well as the idiosyncrasies of the landscapes, cultures and people.

Siddharta Gautama, Buddha (around 560 to 480 BC)

Buddha   Siddharta Gautama was probably born in Nepal at the foot of the Himalayas in around 560 BC. He was the son of a tribal leader who called himself a king. His children grew up as members of the noble

Sakya dynasty. At first he was shaped by the luxury of his parents' court, but on three trips he was confronted with human suffering, when he met an old man, a sick person and a deceased person, one after the other. His meeting with a hermit during his fourth trip was crucial for how he spent the rest of his life. It gave the 29-year-old the impetus to give up the life he had led so far and as a wandering ascetic to search for answers to questions about the purpose of human life.

After intense meditation and strict asceticism as well as many years spent wandering, Siddharta Gautama achieved the state of enlightenment under a fig tree (bodhi tree) by the Indian river Neraya, when he went through the »four stages of Jhana«. During this time he discovered the Four Noble Truths: »the nature of suffering«, »the cause of suffering«, »salvation from suffering« and »the way leading to the end of all human suffering«. Soon afterwards he gave his first sermon near the Indian town of Varanasi, which addressed these Four Noble Truths.

Just a few months later Buddha (which means »the enlightened one« or »the awakened one«) had a few dozen followers, whom he asked to teach his principles to the people. He himself spent 45 years as an itinerant preacher to proclaim his teaching of the »Wheel of Law«. While Buddhist tradition believes Buddha entered nirvana, a stage that releases every living thing on earth from the eternal cycle of birth, life and death, when he died in 543 BC at the age of 82, the historical account puts Buddha's death in the year 480 BC. Nevertheless, in the countries that have adopted Buddhism as their state religion the assumed year of death, 543 BC, is important for the calendar. The year 2010 thus becomes the year 2553 in these countries.

Marco Polo (1254–1324)

Marco Polo, whose name has become the epitome of travel, was born in Venice in 1254. His birth came at a time when Venice's trade relations were not just limited to well-known ports around the Mediterranean, but extended far beyond. There was particular interest in Asia.

Venetian merchant and traveller

Together with his father Nicolao and his uncle Matteo, Marco Polo, having just turned 17, travelled to what is now Pakistan via Iran and from there via the Hindu Kush to China, where the small group was warmly welcomed at the court of Kublai Khan. The khan liked the young, well-travelled Venetian so much he employed him as a diplomat and a special representative for trade with the Western world.

Marco Polo spent 17 years in China. During this time he went on many trips throughout Asia and wrote the first »travel guide«. His most famous book is called Il Milione (The Travels of Marco Polo), in which he wrote less about his routes than about his personal experiences when coming into contact with foreign cultures. When Marco Polo set off for home in 1292 he chose the sea route, which took him via Malaysia and Sumatra as well as the Andaman Islands and Sri Lanka. He spent a few months here, possibly in search of a precious ruby, which had allegedly been in the possession of the king of Lanka and had the diameter of a man's arm.

Marco Polo died in his home city of Venice in 1324, having married just a few years earlier and become the father of three children.

Ranasinghe Premadasa (1924–93)

Politician

Ranasinghe Premadasa was born the son of a labourer in Kehelwatte, a slum in Colombo. After working as a journalist he entered the Ceylon Labour Party (CLP) and in 1955 was elected vice-mayor of Colombo. Just a year later he left the CLP in order to become a member of the United National Party (UNP) and enter the House of Representatives. After the Sri Lanka Freedom Party (SLFP) lost the elections of 1965, Premadasa first became the parliamentary secretary of the minister of local government, whose office he took over in 1968.

Premadasa's political career was interrupted by a new election victory by ▶ Sirimavo Bandaranaike. It was only in 1977 that the UNP came into office again. Premadasa returned to the post he had held in 1965 and in 1978 became prime minister under President Junius Jayawardene.

During the course of the severe confrontations between the Singhalese and Tamil people, Premadasa played an important role. In 1987 he was given special powers when the rebels of the Liberation Tigers of Tamil Eelam (LTTE) threatened to violently take the control of government in their stronghold of Jaffna. Premadasa managed to prevent this with a large-scale military operation. In 1988 he won elections by a narrow margin, defeating the former prime minister Mrs Bandaranaike, and in the following year succeeded President Junius Jayawardene, who was already 82 at the time. He gave the Indian troops stationed in Sri Lanka since 1987 an ultimatum for their withdrawal; at the same time he also opened talks with the rebels. This led to a temporary truce.

Even though Premadasa was given a lot of credit, particularly for the many social measures he implemented for people of low income, his authoritarian leadership style was often criticized and caused one of the country's biggest governmental crises in August 1991. Even though the vote of no confidence directed at him was no more successful than the official impeachment proceedings, Premadasa's power declined. During a UNP election rally in Colombo on 1 May 1993 a young man armed with grenades blew himself up, killing the president and 23 others.

Dudley Shelton Senanayake (1911–73)

Politician

Dudley Shelton Senanayake was born in Colombo as the eldest son of the first prime minister of Ceylon, Don Stephen Senanayake. He

studied natural sciences and law in Cambridge, England. In 1934 he was given the right to practise as a lawyer in London but shortly afterwards he returned to his home, where he spent some time working as a lawyer. In 1936 Senanayake was elected to the Legislative Assembly for the UNP, from 1974 onwards he was also a member of parliament and the minister of agriculture.

When his father died on 22 March 1952, Senanayake was invited by the governor-general, Lord Soulbury, to form a government.

The many problems with which the Sri Lankan economy had to deal with during this time caused Senanayake to step down for health reasons. He subsequently dedicated himself to the study of Buddhist scripture, but in 1957 returned to the political stage and took over the leadership of the UNP. After ► Solomon Bandaranaike fell victim to an assassination he took Bandaranaike's place, but only for four months. Then he was replaced by ► Sirimavo Bandaranaike, whose socialist course he now attacked. During the parliamentary elections of 22 March 1965 the governing SLFP suffered heavy losses, while the UNP more than doubled its number of seats in parliament. Senanayake became prime minister for the third time. He reversed the socialist direction of his predecessor and worked at achieving a more balanced foreign policy.

He was no match for the growing agitation of the opposition under the leadership of Mrs Bandaranaike, however. In 1970 in another political landslide his party lost 55 seats. In May 1970 he stepped down to make way for Mrs Bandaranaike; a short while later he also resigned as party leader.

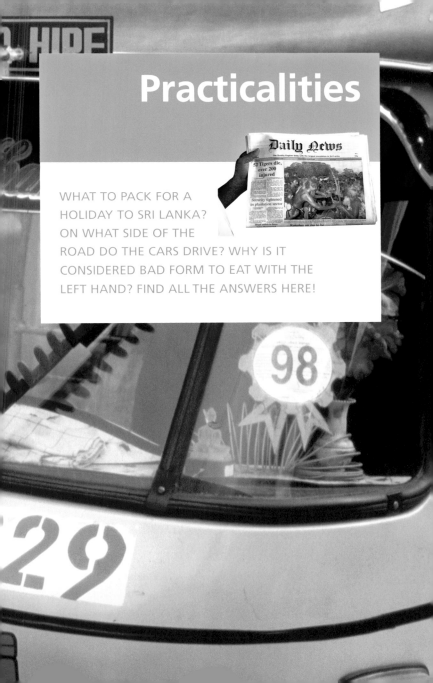

Practicalities

WHAT TO PACK FOR A
HOLIDAY TO SRI LANKA?
ON WHAT SIDE OF THE
ROAD DO THE CARS DRIVE? WHY IS IT
CONSIDERED BAD FORM TO EAT WITH THE
LEFT HAND? FIND ALL THE ANSWERS HERE!

Accommodation

Hotels

The hotels in Sri Lanka are, seen as a whole, less developed than those in some other Asian countries. The reason for this is the striking fluctuation in visitor numbers, which has stood in the way of steady development so far. Nevertheless countless new hotels have been built in recent years, whose owners are relying on the situation calming down.

The situation on the east coast is a difficult one at the moment, not just because of the confrontations between the LTTE and the Singhalese government, but also because the tsunami hit here particularly badly. Even so, some hotels have opened again here.

Rest houses

The Sri Lankan government maintains a number of rest houses, for example in Dambulla, Habarana, Sigiriya, Mihintale, Polonnaruwa and Ella. They are modest when it comes to creature comforts, but very cheap. Early reservations are vital.

Price categories

The hotels recommended in this travel guide in the chapter »Destinations from A to Z« are divided into the following categories (double room per night without breakfast): luxury from €80, mid-range €50–€80, budget up to €50. Breakfast is usually charged separately. Large hotels will take euros and US dollars, while smaller hotels generally accept only Sri Lankan rupees.

Ayurveda hotel

Stays that come with ayurveda treatments cost around €80–150 per person per day. Double rooms are not necessarily cheaper per person because the bulk of the cost is incurred for the treatments and doctors' consultations. The proper ayurvedic cuisine for all meals is, however, included.

Reservations

Reservations are recommended for the peak season from November to March. It is definitely necessary around Christmas and New Year. During the low season from April to October reservations are not necessary.

 INFORMATION AND RESERVATIONS

HOTELS

► **Sri Lanka Tourist Information**
►Information
A free directory of hotels and guesthouses
(accommodation guide) can be requested.

REST HOUSES

► **Ceylon Hotels Corporation**
411, Galle Road
Bambalapitiya
Colombo 4
Tel. 00 94 / 112 50 34 97
www.ceylonhotels.lk

One form of accommodation, homestays, allows visitors to stay with a Sri Lankan family and is usually including meals. It is an inexpensive option. Addresses can be found under: www.explorelanka.com.

Staying with the locals

There are **no youth hostels** in Sri Lanka. Travellers on a tight budget are best served staying at guesthouses.

Youth accommodation

There are no official campsites in Sri Lanka, but in theory camping is permitted outside the national parks if permission from the landowner is obtained first. However, staying in one of the many rest houses on the island is so inexpensive that it is hardly worth exploring Sri Lanka with a backpack and tent.

Camping

Arrival · Before the Journey

By Air

The distance between London and Sri Lanka is over 8000km/ 5000mi; the flying time is around nine hours. **Non-stop flights** are available with Sri Lankan Airlines. Routes run by Middle Eastern airlines or flights via India are worth considering.

Flying time

Ticket prices vary a great deal. Shopping around for the best deal is a good idea. It is important to book well in advance during the high season (Christmas–Easter). The weeks before and after this period are the cheapest.

Flight prices

Many tour operators have specialized in the sale of surplus or free tickets. Taking advantage of these money-saving deals requires flexibility regarding the departure date and the type of accommodation in Sri Lanka.

Low-budget tickets

The only airport open to international flights is Bandaranaike Airport around 35km/22mi north of Colombo. It has been undergoing modernization for years and there are plans to expand it and make it a modern hub for southern Asia. Flights come in from there as well as from all of the seaside resorts on the west coast. Meticulous security checks are performed in front of the airport building. Some hotels and the Sri Lanka Tourist Board have information stands in the arrivals hall. Transfer from or to the airport is generally organized by the booked hotel or the tour

Airport

? DID YOU KNOW ...?

■ that the abstract chariot drawn by peacocks on the tail fin of SriLankan Airlines planes goes back to the Hindu epic Ramayana? It is thought to be the oldest flying machine in world literature.

ARRIVAL INFORMATION

VISA

▶ **Department of Immigration and Emigration**
41 Ananda Rajakaruna, Mw
Colombo, 3rd floor
Tel. 11 / 532 93 00
Open: Mon–Fri 8.30am–noon

SRI LANKAN AIRLINES IN SRI LANKA

▶ **In Colombo**
Bandaranaike International Airport, Katunayake
Tel. 019 / 733 55 55
www.srilankan.aero

▶ **In Galle**
No 16 A, Gamini Mawatha
Tel. 091 / 224 69 42

▶ **In Kandy**
No 17, Temple Street
Tel. 081 / 223 24 95

SRI LANKAN AIRLINES: INTERNATIONAL OFFICES

▶ **In Canada**
Tel. 416 227 90 00
sales@srilankanca.com
www.srilankanca.com

▶ **In the United Kingdom**
Tel. 0208 538 20 01
www.srilankan.aero

▶ **In the USA**
Tel. 877 915 26 52
(nationwide toll-free)
E-mail: sales@srilankanusa.com
www.srilankanusa.com

operator. Individual travellers will find buses and trains and licensed taxis waiting outside.

Sri Lankan Airlines
The national airline company Sri Lankan Airlines is a renowned airline with a modern fleet mostly consisting of Airbuses. Sri Lankan Airlines has recently won several awards for its exceptional levels of quality and service. The airline flies to 44 destinations in 23 countries, most of which are in Asia (also including the Maldives, just one hour's flight away).

Travel Documents

Passports
Citizens of the UK, USA and most other English-speaking countries require a passport that has two months to run from the end of the visit and has one empty page.

Visa
Visitors from most English-speaking countries can spend 30 days in Sri Lanka without an advance visa. Trips lasting longer than this require travellers to be in possession of a visa, which are exclusively available from the Department of Immigration and Emigration. Upon arrival in Sri Lanka travellers also have to be able to produce a **valid return ticket**.

Entry and Exit Regulations

The Sri Lankan authorities do not require European visitors to have had any immunizations except when arriving from infected areas. It is still a good idea to get adequate **protection against tetanus and polio**.

Immunizations

Personal effects are exempt from duty. Visitors over the age of 18 can also bring in 200 cigarettes or 250g/9oz of tobacco or 50 cigars, 1 litre of wine or spirits, one camera and one video camera. Medication for personal use can also be brought in; in order to avoid misunderstandings it is best to carry medicine in the original packaging. Importing drugs and pornographic material is prohibited.

Entry to Sri Lanka

When returning to the EU, EU citizens have to pay third country duty and import tax (= VAT) on goods worth more than €300. Exempt from duty are all personal effects that were taken on the trip; it is a good idea to keep receipts for valuable items bought before the trip to avoid problems upon re-entry. Travellers over the age of 18 are also permitted to import 200 cigarettes or 100 small cigars or 250g/9oz of tobacco as well as 250ml of eau de toilet or 50g of perfume. Also exempt from customs are 1 litre of spirits at more than 22% or 2 litres of sparkling or fortified, as well as 2 litres of table wine. The import of food has been prohibited since 2005 to prevent the spread of infectious diseases.

Re-entry into the EU

> ### *i* Don't import!
>
> - In order to prevent the import of pests or the spread of animal diseases no food, fruit, vegetables, seeds, plants or animal products may be imported into Sri Lanka or into the EU. Luggage inspections are conducted. Violations are punishable with heavy fines.

The Convention on International Trade in Endangered Species of Wild Flora and Fauna, also known as the Washington Convention, prohibits the import of exotic animals, regardless of whether they are dead or alive. Even parts of these protected species may not be brought into the EU, and checks at airports could occur at any time. Anyone in violation of this convention faces heavy fines. When in doubt it is best to avoid buying protected animals or animal products, which include certain types of shell, corals, birds and reptiles (as well as crocodile-leather bags and shoes). Searches upon departure can occur at any time; every item of luggage is usually subjected to a manual inspection at the airport, both upon departure and arrival.

Washington Convention

The Sri Lankan authorities consider any objects of historical or artistic worth that are older than 50 years as antiques; for this reason their export is prohibited. The export of rare books (including palm leaf manuscripts) is also restricted. In cases of doubt or for questions assistance is available from the tourism authority in Colombo (▶Information). Visitors should expect inspections when they leave.

Antiques

Travel Insurance

Out-of-country insurance It is wise to take out medical insurance, which should include return flights for medical reasons.

Beaches

Inaccessible in places The best beaches for swimming are located on Sri Lanka's east coast. This area was not just affected by the civil war, but it was also severely hit by the tsunami, which is why these beaches should only be visited while taking every precaution. It will also not be easy to find accommodation since only few hotels and guesthouses are open to date.

It would be wrong, however, to talk down the quality of the beaches in the western and southwestern parts of the island. The lovely beaches of Unawatuna near Galle and of Hikkaduwa, Bentota and Negombo come to mind. Although all of these except Negombo were also hit by the tsunami, almost all of the hotels here have been rebuilt.

> ### ℹ The three best beaches
>
> - Unawatuna: One of the ten best beaches in the world, and almost all the hotels are new.
> - Beaches around Hikkaduwa: not necessarily the main beach but the long, palm-lined beaches somewhat further south are absolute insider tips.
> - Arugam Bay: this is where the world's surfing elite meet. It is also a wonderful place to go swimming.

Dangerous currents During the summer monsoon between the end of March and mid-November swimming can become a life-threatening »pleasure« along the southwestern and western coasts. There are warning signs about dangerous undercurrents, which, in contrast to high waves, cannot be seen at first glance, but in the interest of self-preservation should be taken seriously! A **red flag** on the beach means no swimming. During the other months swimming can be dangerous on the east coast.

Nudism Nudism is officially prohibited in Sri Lanka since it goes against the people's moral values. Bathing topless is quietly tolerated in some hotels.

Children

Child-friendly country A trip to Sri Lanka can also be a wonderful experience for children. Even though they do not generally have a strong interest in ruins and temples, riding on elephants and visiting national parks with their impressive fauna compensate for the long flight or visits to cultural sites. There are also lovely beaches that are great for swimming. Go to the family doctor in good time when travelling with children and make sure they have all the necessary **immunizations** (e.g. against tetanus). There are some special medications for children, such as anti-malarial drugs.

Baby food and nappies are available in the supermarkets of the larger towns. Bottles on the other hand are rare, so plenty should be brought from home.

Drugs

Like everywhere in Asia, the possession and consumption of recreational drugs is strictly prohibited, as is dealing in drugs. The Sri Lankan police are very tough on these offences, which in theory can even incur the death penalty.

Strictly prohibited

Electricity

The electricity grid in Sri Lanka operates on 230 V alternating current (50 hertz) almost everywhere. Fluctuations in electricity levels and short power cuts occasionally occur.

Electricity grid

Adapters are often needed. They can be obtained at hotel receptions and in shops.

Adapters

Emergency

► IMPORTANT NUMBERS

▶ **Tourist police**
Fort, Colombo 1
Tel. 22 69 41 or 242 11 11

▶ **Police in Colombo**
Tel. 43 33 33

Outside the capital there are no central emergency numbers.

▶ **Fire brigade**
Tel. 42 22 22
There is no central emergency number outside Colombo.

▶ **Accident recovery**
Tel. 222 22
Outside Colombo contact the
closest police station or locals.

▶ **Car accident service**
Ward Place, Colombo 7
Tel. 69 31 84 and 69 31 85

Etiquette and Customs

Never mind how tolerant Asians are towards Western travellers; there are some forms of behaviour that strain even the proverbial Sri Lankan equanimity. Even though tourists might not be aware of this, it causes them to lose face and they will subsequently be considered contemptible.

The people of Sri Lanka have a curious habit when asked a **yes or no** question: the answer yes is made by moving their head in such a way that resembles how Europeans shake their head. Upon closer inspection it can be seen that the head is swayed back and forth and this means something like affirmation.

Invitations Visitors who are invited to a Sri Lankan house should bring small gifts. The lady of the house will be pleased with a bunch of flowers, and if there are children sweets are a good idea. Shoes must be taken off before entering the house.

Dealing with the authorities When dealing with the authorities it is a good idea to wear a shirt and proper shoes. »Bohemian« clothes are frowned upon!

The left hand is impure The left hand is considered impure because the locals use it to clean themselves on the toilet, many of which are built in the French style. For that reason nothing should be handed over or accepted with the left hand.

Taboos Of course there are also taboos that should be observed in order to avoid hurting the feelings of the people of Sri Lanka. Monks do not always like having their picture taken; it should be common sense to allow people their privacy when practising their religion and not take photographs of them. The Sri Lankans really do not like it when religious objects are used as accessories for holiday snaps. Climbing up Buddha statues or any other temple statues is strictly forbidden and is punished with sizeable fines. Requests that no photographs be taken should be respected.

Smooching in public is improper and nude bathing not allowed.

Conversation During a conversation visitors should practise respectful restraint. Wild gesticulation and pointing at others is considered rude. Even amongst friends intimate subjects are unusual. It is best to answer questions about income or personal issues evasively. It is important never to forget the smile that is part of the conversation; the more non-committal the response, the friendlier the smile should be.

Respect for the Buddhist and Hindu religions means it is not allowed to enter sacred sites in clothing such as shorts and T-shirt. Women should keep their shoulders covered and men should (and sometimes must) put a sarong around the hips before entering a temple district. A sarong is available from any textile shop or dress maker. Sometimes they can be hired for a small fee at the entrances of the temple districts.

Visiting religious sites

? DID YOU KNOW …?

■ Visitors who see the notice »Reserved for Clergy« when travelling by bus or train are advised to not use this seat but stand. These seats are exclusively for monks.

Although the bill in most restaurants already contains a service fee of around 10% it is still customary to give an additional tip or to round up the bill when satisfied with the service. A small tip for room attendants at the beginning of a stay is recommended and guests who are still satisfied at the end can give a further tip then. Around 200 rupees per week is a good guideline. Taxi drivers will also be pleased if the amount owed is rounded up. But beware: giving less than five rupees could be considered an insult.

Tips

The people of Sri Lanka, regardless of whether they are Sinhalese or Tamil, generally do not mind having their picture taken. It is polite to ask for permission before taking a picture. It should be common sense to act with restraint at religious events. It is forbidden to photograph military facilities, harbours and stations. Photographs should also not be taken during traffic checks. To avoid losing face, which is just about the worst thing that can happen to a person in Asia, any promises made about sending photographs should be kept.

Taking pictures

Festivals · Holidays · Events

The people of Sri Lanka like to celebrate, and they have plenty of occasions to do just that. On the island on which Buddhism became widespread for the first time the events of the life of Siddharta Gautama are at the heart of the festivities. Full Moon Day (Poya Day) is a monthly holiday during which public life comes to a halt and, depending on the occasion, hundreds or even thousands of pilgrims travel to the historic sites of Buddhism. Serving alcohol is prohibited on Poya Days (in hotels alcohol is generally only available via room service).

Festivals during the year

An **up-to-date calendar** with the annually changing dates of all the important festivals and holidays in Sri Lanka is available from the Sri Lanka Tourist Board (►Information).

● FESTIVAL CALENDAR

HOLIDAYS

1 January (New Year's Day)
4 February (Independence Day in memory of 4 February 1948)
1 May (Day of Work)
22 May (Day of the Republic)
30 June (Bankers Holiday)
25 December (Christmas)
31 December (New Year's Eve)

Sri Lanka is home to many peoples, as can be seen in the large number of religious holidays celebrated on the island.

JANUARY

► **Duruthu Full Moon Poya Day**
All around the Buddhist temple of Raja Maha Vihara in Kelaniya one of Sri Lanka's most significant peraheras takes place; it commemorates the first visit of the enlightened Buddha to the island around 2500 years ago.

► **Thai Pongal (nationwide)**
Hindu harvest festival on the first day of the month of »Thai« (14 January) in honour of the sun god Duriye.

FEBRUARY

► **Nevam Maha Perahera (Colombo)**
This procession around Beira Lake is one of the most colourful and exuberant festivals on the island. The festival commemorates the sanctification of the monks Mahagollana and Sariputta, two of the enlightened Buddha's most significant pupils.

FEBRUARY/MARCH

► **Mahashivarithri festival (nationwide)**
Originally a purely Hindu festival, but Buddhists now also join in. After a strict day of fasting the symbolic union of the god Shiva and his wife Parvati is celebrated. The focal point is the lingam, a phallus-like symbol of the god that is adorned with flowers.

► **Miled-un-Nabi (nationwide)**
In memory of the birth of the prophet Mohammed, Muslims gather for common prayer in the mosques and a subsequent banquet. On this day the poor are given food and clothes.

► **Medin Poya (nationwide)**
On Full Moon Day in March the focus is on the return of the enlightened Buddha to convince his family about his new teachings.

APRIL

► **Singhalese and Tamil New Year Celebration**
Traditionally all open fires are put out in mid-April and the houses subjected to ritual cleaning ceremonies. Children ask their parents for forgiveness for the smaller and bigger sins, the rich give the poor food and clothes as well as betel leaves that have money rolled up in them.

► **Bak Poya (nationwide)**
On the Full Moon Day in April Bak Poya is celebrated in memory of the Buddha's second visit to Sri Lanka.

MAY

► **(Adi-)Wesak Poya (nationwide)**
A celebration to commemorate the day on which Buddha is said to have been born, achieved enlightenment and died. This is reason enough to undertake a pilgrimage to the island's sacred sites.

JUNE

► **Poson Poya (Mihintale)**
This Poya is celebrated in memory of the introduction of Buddhism to Sri Lanka; it is a particularly big event in Mihintale where television stations broadcast the religious ceremonies live.

JULY/AUGUST

► **Esala Poya (Kandy)**
The most spectacular festival in Sri Lanka. It begins in the second half of July and lasts eleven days. With hundreds of dancers, jugglers, acrobats and musicians the festival begins in Kandy around the Temple of the Tooth. For the first six days processions are held. The second part is exclusively in honour of the sacred tooth. Hundreds of decorated elephants take part in this ceremony.

► **Hikkaduwa Beach Festival**
The Hikkaduwa Beach Festival has been held since 2008. Locals and visitors from all over the world are attracted by numerous cultural events such as a jazz festival, beach markets, cinema nights, a street festival and a drum festival.

Decorated elephants participate in many festivals and processions

► **Perahera of Kataragama**
Impressive perahera in honour of the war god Skanda lasting nine days. All ceremonies begin with a bath in the Menik Ganga. The actual procession begins with festively decorated elephants; one of them carries the relics. On the final day believers flagellate themselves, fall into a trance or walk on hot coals.

AUGUST

► **Nikini Poya (nationwide)**
In contrast to the perahera of Kandy the Full Moon Day of August is a much more modest and quiet celebration. For the

monks who live in the monasteries the day centres on prayer and meditation.

SEPTEMBER

▸ **Binara Poya (nationwide)**
All over the country this Full Moon Day is celebrated in memory of the day Buddha entered the heaven of the gods in order to spread his teachings there.

OCTOBER

▸ **Wap Poya (nationwide)**
Two events from the life of the Enlightened One are at the heart of this event: the day he gave up his existence as a lay person and the day he returned from the heaven of the gods.

NOVEMBER

▸ **Dipavalee Festival (nationwide)**
This Hindu festival revolves around the gods Vishnu and Krishna and the victory of light over darkness. Thousands of small oil lamps are symbolically lit in temples on this day.

▸ **Il Poya (nationwide)**
Buddhists commemorate the sending out of the first 60 monks who spread the teachings of the enlightened Buddha.

NOVEMBER/DECEMBER

▸ **Haji Festival (nationwide)**
Moslems celebrate this festival in the country's mosques; some also go on pilgrimages to Mecca.

DECEMBER

▸ **Unduwap Poys (nationwide)**
The sacred bodhi tree in Anuradhapura is at the centre of the December full moon festival. Major celebrations take place all around the temple that houses the more than 2200 year-old tree, which was created from a cutting of the tree under which Buddha found enlightenment.

Around the middle of the month of December the pilgrimage season to Adam's Peak, Sri Lanka's sacred mountain, begins; it lasts until mid-May.

Food and Drink

Indian influences The influence on Sri Lanka's cuisine of the Indian subcontinent is obvious. Just as in India rice and curry are the staple foods and ingredients of the national dish. However, the term curry means something different from what it does in Europe.

Curry Curry is not a single spice, but a spicy **mix of up to 20 different ingredients**. The most important component of this mixture is turmeric; others include ginger, nutmeg, pepper, allspice, paprika, onions

In days gone by Sri Lanka's spices were a valuable trading commodity →

Diverse and multilingual: a guesthouse with restaurant

and chilli. All cooks and chefs who take a pride in their work use their own curry mixture. It is added to fish, meat or vegetables while they are frying. Coconut milk is then added to refine the dish.

Beware: very spicy!

Standard meals are often very spicy, and it is best to go easy on curries. One speciality is a simple curry that consists of chopped onions, green chilli and aromatic spices such as cloves, nutmeg, cinnamon, saffron and the leaves of the curry plant as well as coconut milk. Chicken, beef or pork is then marinated in this mixture. A tip for those who do not like their food so spicy: say **»without chilli!«** when ordering. Even like this the dish will still have plenty of bite.

Eating habits

Eating with cutlery is not really customary in Sri Lanka. The people **eat with their fingers**, or more precisely with the fingers of their right hand, since the left hand is considered impure. The fingertips are used to allow them to mix everything on the plate. A portion is then scooped up and eaten. Wet cloths are handed out for cleaning the fingers. Of course the usual eating utensils are made available to tourists.

Of course it is worth leaving the booked hotel complex to eat in restaurants, which are particularly plentiful in seaside resorts. The quality is generally good.

Higher-class restaurants require timely **reservations**. It is customary to enter the restaurant and then »wait to be seated«.

Menus are generally available in English.

Restaurants

Markets in particular have the cookshops that are so typical of Asia. They prepare their food using simple methods. Making a judgement about whether the hygienic conditions are good enough to order food from one of them is a personal matter. It should be emphasized that no food or drink should be accepted from strangers.

Cookshops

Typical Dishes

Sri Lankan cuisine does not end with the abovementioned specialities of rice and curry. It is much more diverse than generally believed, and fresh ingredients are an indispensable component. In addition the **spices** that grow in Sri Lanka in great diversity are also a must for every dish. This island has, after all, been considered **the** spice island since ancient times.

Fresh ingredients are a must

Dhal for example is a very nourishing dish consisting of red lentils cooked with dried fish as well as various spices in coconut milk.

Dhal

Sri Lankan cuisine is also known for its excellent fish dishes. Almost everything caught in the sea is also put on the plate: tuna (here the particularly tasty bonito), herring and goatfish. Fish curries are a delicious option.

Fish

Sri Lanka is a mecca for lovers of fresh seafood. The local chefs know how to prepare lobster, shrimps and mussels to make them just right. Whether boiled, fried or grilled, seafood only costs a fraction of what it does in Europe. Grilled king prawns in a garlic sauce are just one of the many delicacies on offer.

Shellfish and crustaceans

The way in which rice is prepared plays an important role here, just like everywhere else in Asia. It is not boiled, but steamed in special pots that cook it slowly and gently. This is the only way the valuable vitamins and minerals are preserved. White rice is customary for everyday cooking. The more expensive basmati rice or brown rice are reserved for holidays and special occasions.

Rice

Hoppers are a cross between muffins and teacakes. They have a

? DID YOU KNOW ...?

■ ... that there are 15 different types of rice in Sri Lanka? The best one is the reddish rice (kakuluhaal), which is in every main dish. Another tasty option is basmati rice, which is also exported.

crunchy exterior and are served with a freshly cooked egg on top. **String hoppers** are cooked rings of rice flour and coconut milk. They are a popular breakfast food. **Jaggery** is a type of caramel made from the crystallized sap of the kitul palm. One popular dessert is **wattala-pam**, a type of custard made from the sugar of the palm sap, coconut milk, eggs and various spices (including cinnamon). Another popular dessert is kiribath, a tasty rice pudding with spices.

Fruit

Bountiful orchard

Visitors from Europe will find Sri Lanka is a bountiful orchard with many tropical fruits unknown to the European market. Fresh fruit is offered in every restaurant, depending on the season. If buying fruit at a market do not forget to give it a thorough wash.

Types of fruit

Pineapples and bananas are available fresh all year round. Pineapples are rich in vitamin C and do not have many calories. Some varieties are customarily eaten after they have been slightly fermented, which can have a laxative effect. Bananas, which are a popular dessert, are dunked in sweet coconut milk and then grilled. A tip: the smaller the banana, the sweeter it will be.

Fruit vendors like to set up their stalls on the beach and in parks

The somewhat floury flesh of the **durian fruit**, which is also known for its strong and unpleasant odour, is considered a delicacy in Asia (April–June). The sweet, aromatic **jackfruit**, a round fruit weighing several kilograms, is sliced and served on ice (August–September). Another widely available treat is the yellowish-green to dark blue, oval **passion fruit** (up to 20cm/8in long). Its juicy, jelly-like flesh is spooned out and has a sour-sweet taste. The flesh of the hard-shelled **coconut** is removed with a spoon and enjoyed cold after the coconut milk (►drinks) is poured off.

Limes, small, green and round, are the local alternative to lemons. They grow all year round. The larger, yellow **lemons** have to be imported and are thus quite expensive. The light flesh of **lychees**, a reddish fruit, has a sweet and fresh taste (May–August). The small, red **rambutan**, which is covered in long hairs, is the fruit of a soapberry plant and has a taste not dissimilar to grapes.

Besides pineapples, **mangoes** are probably the most popular tropical fruit for tourists; only when they are fully ripe (yellow skin, limited lifespan) are they sweet, juicy and aromatic. They are cut open along the stone. The flesh is cut up or sucked out (March–June). **Oranges** have a thin green peel in Asia; they become particularly sweet when their peel turns yellow. **Grapefruits** generally have tasty pink flesh and are available fresh all year round. They are often eaten with a pinch of salt. **Papayas**, the fruit of the *Carica papaya*, are served in halves with half a lemon. It is the cheapest of all Asian fruits. Papayas are available at every market stall all year round. But beware: eat too many and they will have a laxative effect. The **Malabar plum** or rose apple often has the shape of a pear with a rust-coloured, wax-like peel and porous, light flesh, both of which are edible.

Drinks

As a result of the high temperatures in Sri Lanka, specialists for tropical medicine recommend drinking **at least two to three litres every day**. It does not matter how the fluids lost through perspiration are replenished.

It would be absolutely wrong, however, to do this with alcoholic beverages. The tropical heat increases the effect of alcohol. Good thirst quenchers for hot days are mineral water and juice. Tea is of course Sri Lanka's national drink. Every Sri Lankan pays great attention to preparing it carefully.

One popular alcoholic beverage is **Lions beer**, which is brewed in Sri Lanka and which has had some serious competition in recent years from the strong Bison beer. Hops and malted barley have to be imported since neither will grow in Sri Lanka. For this reason beer is a relatively expensive drink. Better restaurants serve **wine**, which also has to be imported. As a result wine, which comes from Europe and Australia, is one of the most expensive drinks.

Thirst quenchers

Alcoholic beverages

Workers in a tea factory near Nuwara Eliya

Tea production is often still d[one] with manual labour. Industri[al] hands are not just needed to pick [the] leaves, but also to roll th[em]

FOUR POUNDS OF LEAVES, ONE POUND OF TEA

Upon entering a tea factory visitors will see colourfully dressed tea pickers, picking the leaves from the bushes leaf by leaf. But what happens in these dark halls in which the leaves have been turned into a drink that has been popular for centuries?

Freshly picked tea leaves are put through five different processes, every one of which requires great care. In addition every tea factory has its own secret about how to produce its own special tea.

In the first of five stages four pounds of green, fresh leaves are turned into one pound of fragrant black tea. This is the wilting. The leaves are spread out on wire mesh on stacks of long racks. Hot air is then blown upwards from below at a precise temperature, while fans make sure the air is evenly distributed. This wilting process once took a day, but modern technology has shortened it to just a few hours. It has nonetheless remained the most important stage, because it determines the amount of enzymes that later release aromatic substances. Next, the leaves are rolled. They are fed between through two metal discs that rotate in opposite directions. This breaks up the cells of the wilted, still green leaves, allowing the cell sap to come into contact with the oxygen of the surrounding air. The subsequent stage is called fermentation. The essential oils in the tea leaves are released, as are the tannins. Something else happens during the rolling process that has a significant impact on the tea's flavour. Fine leaves and broken tips are sieved out and added directly to the final fermentation.

Quality

The higher the proportion of these sieved-out leaves, the better the quality of the finished tea. If the leaves sieved out during this stage known as 1st dhool make up around half of the total amount, the resulting tea is top quality. All the remaining leaves are processed again in the roller and broken down. It is only now that the full fermentation process unfolds, when the green tea leaf obtains its typical copper-red colour. This stage, during which the temperature has to be kept at exactly 40°C/104°F, takes around three hours. This activates the theine, which in tea is better bound to

the tannins than caffeine, so that it does not have the same stimulating and stressful effect on the heart and circulation as coffee.

To dry the leaves, the next step, the tea is put through a roaster on a long conveyor belt under a constant supply of heat. This procedure takes around 20 minutes. At the end, when the cell sap has thickened enough, the initially green tea leaf has turned into what is sold in shops: fragrant crumbs used to make an infusion that is drunk with pleasure.

Varieties

Broken Orange Pekoe, Orange Pekoe and Pekoe are the names of the different varieties of tea that set off on their journey around the world well packaged in boxes. These names refer less to the quality than to the flavour. Orange Pekoe is a pale, aromatic tea, while Pekoe is dark. It is a mistake to believe that only lesser quality tea is used for tea bags.

Reputable tea manufacturers in fact only use the best varieties for their bags, whose sole purpose is to facilitate preparation.

The history of tea

According to tradition the Chinese were the first to dry tea leaves and steep them in hot water. It was the 17th century before tea came to Europe, even though three centuries earlier Marco Polo had mentioned the drink.

It was not the British, who now consume a quarter of the world's tea production, but the Dutch who were the first Europeans to bring boxes of tea by boat from China with their Oostindien-Kompagnie. This was in around 1610, and at the time tea was still considered a medicinal drink. The Russian tsar's court was a step ahead: there tea had always been considered a delicacy. The tradition of drinking tea started at the English court in around 1662.

Top amongst the intoxicating beverages is **arrack**. It is made from the flowers of palm trees and processed into toddy, a kind of palm wine. Once distilled it is made into the cheap drink known as arrack, which is available everywhere. After enjoying a bit too much arrack you can obtain the cure from a pharmacy.

Non-alcoholic drinks

The **milk of coconuts** is very refreshing. Connoisseurs also spoon out the white flesh from the nut. A further popular drink is known as **curd**. It is a type of kefir made from buffalo's milk. Curd is served in a small clay bowl. If the curd doesn't run out when the bowl is turned upside down, it is fresh.

Drinking water is sold everywhere and bottled water is absolutely fine to drink. **Soft drinks** such as Coca Cola, Pepsi, Sprite and tonic water are imported and are available everywhere.

Health

Prior to departure

Going on holiday in the tropics requires preparations and certain precautions once there so that the trip has every chance of being a positive experience. The **family doctor** should be consulted in good time to eliminate health risks. Questions regarding vaccinations can be answered by institutes of tropical medicine.

Against the body clock

»Jet lag« is the name given to the state of physical exhaustion that regularly occurs after inter-continental long-haul flights. It takes some time for travellers to adjust their body clock after moving into a different time zone. Frequent fliers generally give their bodies the necessary **period of rest**. In addition it is a good idea to wear light, comfortable clothes and shoes during the flight. It is common sense that alcoholic drinks should be kept to a minimum since alcohol has a more potent effect in the lower pressure of the aeroplane cabin. It is a good idea to eat a light meal low in fat and calories before take-off and schedule at least one day of rest after arrival instead of plunging straight into major activities.

The **tropical climate** also requires a certain adjustment, for which the body needs time. It is wise to avoid physical exertion during the first few days and not stay out in the strong sun for too long. Sunscreens with a high protection factor are a must: Sri Lanka is not far from the equator!

! *Baedeker* TIP

Clothes

Light, breathable clothes made of cotton (not synthetic fibres) are a good idea all year round. Some warmer items (a pullover, cardigan or something of that nature) should be packed for the »cooler« months and excursions to the highlands and the evenings can also be quite chilly. Proper footwear is a must for trips to the mountains.

In tropical countries it is important to get plenty to drink

A feverish cold that is particularly common during the first few days is a notorious problem for people travelling to Asia. Often the cause is not an infection but the carelessness of the traveller. Such colds are associated with a high temperature (over 39ºC/37.4ºF), but there are not generally any other symptoms. Taking a medication for the fever and staying in bed for two days will be helpful. If your temperature remains high, it is best to consult a doctor.

When travelling to Asia a first-aid kit is far more important than when travelling in Europe. The risk of infection is higher and many medications in Asia are sold under different names or are not available at all. It is common sense to bring all medications needed on a regular basis in sufficient quantities from home. The first-aid kit should also include scissors, tweezers, cotton wool, gauze, bandages, first-aid dressing, plasters, adhesive tape, disinfectant solution, medications against fevers, pain, diarrhoea and constipation, travel sickness, circulation problems and infections. In addition to sunscreen an insect repellent that is applied to the skin is important.

It is a good idea to get a tetanus shot as well as one for hepatitis A, which is spread by the unhygienic preparation of food and drink (particularly ice). Sensitive tourists should get themselves immunized with a gamma globulin shot prior to departure.

Fevers

First-aid kit

Vaccinations

REDISCOVERING ANCIENT KNOWLEDGE

Ayurveda is »in«, and has been for quite some time in the West. Ayurvedic cookbooks and massage courses, natural cosmetics and tea mixtures are everywhere, demonstrating the popularity of this traditional medicine. In the home of ayurveda, India and Sri Lanka, where its methods have been used to heal for thousands of years, more and more hotels are attracting guests with ayurvedic stays and »wellness« offers.

Some of the insights of ayurveda are at least as old as the earliest literary works from India. Herbs and their healing powers were already praised in the Rigveda, the oldest collection of manuscripts dating from the time around 1200 BC.

Today it is known that the ayurvedic body of experience contains knowledge gathered over millennia. Most texts date from around 500 BC to AD 1000.

Knowledge of life

The translation of the Sanskrit term ayurveda is »knowledge of life«. It does not just encompass insights from the medical field, but also stands for a philosophy of the right way for human beings to treat themselves and their environment. Inner and outer harmony and balance are the fundamental goals. The teaching's holistic approach covers not just physical and mental aspects but also emotional and spiritual ones.

Doshas

According to ayurvedic teaching human beings are seen as the reflection of the cosmos. The same elements act in both: earth, water, fire, air and ether. They shape the human constitution and manifest themselves in the three doshas: Vata, Pitta and Kapha. Vata or wind/ether is associated with

It does more than feel and look good: a flower bath being prepared

Herbal medicines play a big role in ayurveda but proper diet and oil treatments are just as important. This way the body can heal itself

movement and in the body with the nervous system, the circulation, breathing and excretion processes. Pitta or fire is associated with the metabolism, digestive activities and the temperature balance. Kapha or water/earth relates to the body's fluid balance and its natural defences. A person is healthy when the three doshas are in equilibrium. Disease comes from them being out of kilter.

Diagnosis and treatment

Ayurvedic doctors diagnose their patients by examining their pulse, tongue and eyes as well as by taking their medical history into account. In doing so doctors can determine which dosha or doshas predominate. This gives them information about the patient's condition as well as about the origin of the complaint.

Ayurvedic treatment does not aim to cure symptoms. It looks at the person as a whole. Treatment is a diverse mixture of different methods with the goal of increasing the body's self-healing powers. Ayurvedic therapy includes oil massages, oil treatments, enemas, heat treatments and first and foremost correct nutrition.

Diet

One of the ayurvedic principles is »diet is medicine«. Depending on which dosha is dominant and what com-

plaints are present, different dishes are put on the menu. Those who have too much fire or Pitta must cut out chillies and peppers because their body temperature needs to be reduced. The right diet prevents many ills. Even the ancient Indians had recipes for diseases of civilization such as obesity and cardiovascular disease. Health through proper diet and sufficient exercise are old ayurvedic principles, and a correct lifestyle is fundamental. Emotional and spiritual equilibrium are part of the ayurvedic concept, and meditation and yoga are often part of the treatment plans.

Many patients from the West as well as an increasing number of conventional doctors now look to southern Asia's millennia-old body of knowledge with interest and hope. In many cases ayurvedic medicine can boast successes, particularly in the treatment of chronic illnesses. However, the new popularity of ayurveda does mean that the term »ayurvedic doctor«, which is not clearly defined or restricted in many countries, is abused. Anyone wanting legitimate treatment should check on the doctors' training. It takes at least six years and cannot be done on the weekend courses that are sometimes offered. Reputable hotels provide information about the training of their medical staff.

Malaria Malaria has recently been increasing again in Asia; precautionary medication is particularly advisable when travelling outside the centres of tourism.

AIDS The risk of becoming infected with AIDS (HIV) in Sri Lanka is relatively high. Only the known protective measures can help prevent infection: the use of condoms for heterosexual and homosexual intercourse and disposable syringes for injections are a must. Beware of blood transfusions as well as surgical and dental treatments.

Drinking water Water bottled in Sri Lanka is not a problem since it comes from the mountains and is clean. Sensitive travellers should also use this water to brush their teeth.

Sun protection It is very important to have adequate sun protection as the sun can cause severe burns. A hat or cap as well as a high SPF sunscreen (sun block) is absolutely essential.

Information

▶ USEFUL ADDRESSES

INFORMATION AT HOME

▶ **Australia: Department of Foreign Affairs**
The website www.dfat.gov.au provides up-to-date travel advice about Sri Lanka.

▶ **Canada: Department of Foreign Affairs**
See www.fco.gov.uk for up-to-date travel advice Sri Lanka.

▶ **Ireland: Department of Foreign Affairs**
See www.dfa.ie for up-to-date travel advice about Sri Lanka.

▶ **Sri Lanka Tourism Promotion Bureau in the UK**
No.1, 3rd Floor, Devonshire Square
London EC2M 4WD
Tel. 0845 880 63 33 (ext. 201)
www.srilankatourism.org

▶ **UK Foreign Office**
See www.fco.gov.uk for up-to-date travel advice about Sri Lanka.

▶ **Sri Lanka Tourism Promotion Bureau in the USA**
379 Thornall Street
6th Floor, Edison NJ 08837
Tel. 732 608 26 76
www.srilankatourism.org

▶ **U.S. Department of State**
See www.state.gov/travel for up-to-date travel advice about Sri Lanka.

INFORMATION IN SRI LANKA

▶ **Sri Lanka Tourist Board**
80, Galle Road, Colombo 03
Tel. 11 / 243 70 55, 243 70 55
E-mail: tourinfo@sri.lanka.net

▶ **Further branches**
Katunayake Airport
Colombo
(in arrivals)

▶ **In Kandy**
72, Victoria Drive, Kandyan Art
Association Building
Tel. 08 / 22 26 61
Open: Mon–Fri 8am–6pm, Sat,
Sun, holidays until 4pm

SRI LANKAN DIPLOMATIC REPRESENTATIONS

▶ **High Commission in Australia**
35 Empire Circuit
Forrest, ACT 2603
Tel. 02 62 39 70 41
www.slhcaust.org

▶ **High Commission in Canada**
333 Laurier Avenue West
Suite 1204
Ottawa, Ontario K1P 1C1
Tel. 613 233 84 49
www.srilankahcottawa.org

▶ **Consulate in Ireland**
59 Ranelagh Road
Dublin
Tel. 01 496 80 43
E-mail: aelred@ireland.com

▶ **High Commission in the United Kingdom**
No.13, Hyde Park Gardens
London W2 2LU
Tel. 020 72 62 18 41
www.slhc-london.co.uk

▶ **Embassy in the USA**
2148, Wyoming Avenue NW
Washington DC 20008
Tel. 202 483 40 25
http://slembassyusa.org/

DIPLOMATIC REPRESENTATIONS IN SRI LANKA

▶ **Australian Embassy**
21, Gregory's Road
Colombo 7
Tel. 011 246 32 00
www.srilanka.embassy.gov.au

▶ **British High Commission**
389 Bauddhaloka Mawatha
Colombo 7
Tel. 011 539 06 39
http://ukinsrilanka.fco.gov.uk/en

▶ **Canadian High Commission**
8, Gregory's Road
Colombo 7
Tel. 011 522 62
E-mail: clmbo@international.gc.ca

▶ **U. S. Embassy**
210 Galle Road
Colombo 3
Tel. 011 249 85 00
http:// srilanka.usembassy.gov/

INTERNET SOURCES

▶ **www.srilankatourism.org**
A wealth of information is
available in English on the Sri
Lankan Tourist Board website.

▶ **www.lankalibrary.com**
History, culture, wildlife: a highly
informative website.

▶ **www.artsrilanka.org**
Art history of the Buddhist and
other traditions and contemporary
art.

Language

Official languages

Sri Lanka's official languages are Sinhala and Tamil. The latter is spoken in several dialects. As a result of regular contact with tourists many Sri Lankans have also picked up basic English-language skills.

Sinhala

Sinhala belongs to the Indo-Aryan branch of the Indo-European language family but is actually an isolated dialect that developed from the languages spoken in central India. The first evidence of Sinhala dates back to the 3rd century BC. Over the following centuries words borrowed from Pali, Sanskrit and Tamil were incorporated into the language. The vocabulary and morphology maintained their resemblance to the Indo-Aryan languages spoken primarily on the Indian subcontinent, despite being isolated, while the syntax and style converged with the Dravidian dialects, the second-largest language family in India.

In addition to Sinhala, which is also sometimes called Elu, a literary language which developed between the 2nd century BC and the 2nd century AD also incorporated words from Pali and Sanskrit. While the probably oldest literary work from this period, a commentary on the Buddhist canon Tripitaka with historical elements, is believed to be lost, old Sinhala poems in the form of rock carvings made between the 6th and 10th centuries AD have survived.

Tamil

Tamil is one of the 16 official languages spoken in India, but also in Sri Lanka. With a more than 2000-year tradition, Tamil is one of the oldest of the Dravidian languages. Like Sinhala, Tamil is also an official language of Sri Lanka (since 1965), a concession by the government to the most significant minority on the island. Tamil also has a great literary past; in contrast to Sinhala, Tamil initially forwent Sanskrit models. It was only during the 11th century that Sanskrit words came into use. The extensive old Indian verse epics, the Mahabharata and the Ramayana, are seen as the most significant models.

Tamil has only taken on the status of a widely used language since the 19th century when the poet Subramanya Bharati (1882–1921), one of the most important representatives of Tamil literature, helped it achieve a breakthrough.

The »upper crust« speak English

It is noteworthy that members of the upper class use English to communicate with each other. This trend, which has been around for many years now, is countered by the fact that English is **not a compulsory subject** except in high school. The fact that many children, young people and adults still speak at least a few words of English, and are familiar with common turns of phrase, is the result of their contact with tourists on the island.

Class is all-pervasive in Sri Lankan society. This is reflected in the different forms of address for people of different social standing.

Forms of address

SINHALA PHRASE BOOK

Address

Numbe	Address amongst equals
Thamuse	Used by someone of higher standing to address someone of lower standing
Oya	Customary, informal address amongst friends and relatives
Tho	Insulting address made to people of a very low social standing (watch out!)
Umba	Form of address for domestic staff but also for one's own children (if it is used in the latter sense it is meant affectionately)
Thamunnaanse	Only people of higher standing are addressed this way, such as monks

Important expressions

Address (only men)	Mahatmaya
Address (only women)	Nona mahatmaya
Greeting	Ayubovan
How are you?	Kohomada sahpa sahneepa?
Fine, thanks!	Sanee-pen innava
Please	Karunakarala
Thank you	Istuti
Yes	Ou
No	Nä
No, thank you	Ehpa, istutiy
Excuse me!	Samavena
I don't understand!	Mate terenne na
No, I don't want to!	Mata epa!
What's your name?	Nama mokak da?
The bill please!	Karunakara bila génda!
How much is it?	Máka gána kiyada!

Out and about

Bus	Bas eka
Where is the bus station?	Bas pola koheda?

Station	Dumriyapala
I would like a taxi	Mata täksi-yak ona
Car	Kareken
Bicycle	Baisikalaya
Road	Mawatha
What is the name of this road?	Mé Páre nama mokakda?
To the left	Ren-na
Right	Da-ku-na-ta
Straight ahead!	Ke-lin yan-na!

Accommodation

Hotel	Hótelaya
Guesthouse	Thánayama
Where is there a hotel?	Hótalayak koheda thiyenne?
Do you have a room available?	Hiskamara ti ye navada?
How much does a room cost?	Ekamara ya kiyada

Geographical words

Mountain	Kandé
Beach	Werala
Waterfall	Diya ella
Hot Springs	Unu diya Ulpotha
River (small)	Oya
River (big)	Ganga
Place, town	Pura
Road	Mawatha

Days of the week

Monday	Sanduda
Tuesday	Angeharuvada
Wednesday	Badada
Thursday	Brahaspatinda
Friday	Sikurada
Saturday/Sunday	Senesurada/Irida

Months

January	Janavari
February	Pebaravari
March	Martu
April	Apprel

May	May
June	Juni
July	Juli
August	Agostu
September	Settembara
October	Oktombara
November	Novembara
December	Desembara

Time Words

Today	ada
Yesterday	iye
Tomorrow	heta

Numbers

1	eka	2	deka
3	thuna	4	hathara
5	paha	6	haya
7	hatha	8	ata
9	namaya	10	dahaya

Literature

David Robson: Geoffrey Bawa: *The Complete Works.* Thames and Hudson (2002)
Geoffrey Bawa (1919–2003) is Sri Lanka's most famous architect. This book, while devoted to his work, conjures up the atmosphere of the island.

? DID YOU KNOW …?

■ … that the British science fiction author Arthur C. Clarke lived in Sri Lanka from 1956? His most famous book, *2001 – A Space Odyssey,* was made into a film by Stanley Kubrick in 1968. Clarke died in Colombo on 19 March 2008.

Gehan De Silva Wijeyeratne: *Portrait of Sri Lanka.* New Holland (2007)   Travel and nature
Magnificent photographs of all aspects of the island.

Gehan De Silva Wijeyeratne: *A Photographic Guide to Birds of Sri Lanka.* New Holland Publisher (2000)
The island's birds.

Rory Spowers: *A Year in Green Tea and Tuk-Tuks: My Unlikely Adventure Creating an Eco Farm in Sri Lanka.* Harper Element (2007)
Sri Lanka from a different perspective, but perhaps not everyone's cup of tea

History/
politics

Rudolph Ludwig Carl Virchow: *The Veddas of Ceylon and their Relation to the Neighboring Tribes.* BiblioBazaar (2008)
A classic dating from 1888, but constantly (and recently) reprinted

Robert Knox: *An Historical Relation of the Island Ceylon* (2 vols). Tisara Prakasakayo Ltd.
Definitive historical work in English about Sri Lanka, written in 1681. After being shipwrecked Knox was held captive by the kings of Kandy for 19 years. During this time he recorded the habits, customs and political events from his perspective.

Nira Wickramasinghe: *Sri Lanka in the Modern Age: A History of Contested Identity.* Hurst (2005)
The title says it all: the Sri Lankans and their relationships with colonialists and each other.

Religion

Marvin Olasky: *The Religions Next Door: What We Need to Know about Judaism, Hinduism, Buddhism, and Islam – And What Reporters Are Missing.* B & H (2004)
An interesting read for those travelling to parts of the world where Christianity is not taken for granted, by a Jewish convert to Christianity

Cookbooks

Peter Kuruvita: *Serendip: My Sri Lankan Kitchen.* Murdoch Books (2009)
More than just a cookbook. The author draws deep on family experience.

Amadea Morningstar, Urmilla Desai: *The Ayurvedic Cookbook: A Personalized Guide to Good Nutrition and Health.* Motilal Banarsidass (2003)
This book is what it says: not just recipes, but it has them too of course.

Ayurveda

Mahatma Gandhi: *A Guide to Health.* BiblioBazaar (2009)
The great Indian statesman reveals his experiences with ayurveda and its effects on his life.

Vasant Lad: *Ayurveda, the Science of Self-healing: A Practical Guide.* Lotus (1987)
This book cannot replace an ayurveda cure in Sri Lanka but it gives many tips for a healthier life according to the rules of the ancient Indian medicine.

Michael Ondaatje: *Running in the Family*, Bloomsbury (2009)
Ondaatje made a name for himself with his bestseller »The English Patient«. In this book he tells the story of his family and their life in Sri Lanka during the colonial period. Charming and entertaining. A must read!

Shyan Selvadurai: *Cinnamon Gardens*. Anchor (1999)
Events from the lives of three generations, starting with the British colonial period in Sri Lanka. Gripping!

Nicolas Bouvier: *The Scorpion Fish*. Carcanet (2002)
Nicolas Bouvier moved to Ceylon temporarily in March 1955. Lonely, weakened and lethargic because of the hot and humid climate, his senses are heightened for the perception of the small things. A spiritual turnaround for a man who tried to capture the magic phenomena of Ceylon's shadow and insect world from a Western perspective that left him torn between fascination and terror.

Michael Ondaatje: *Anil's Ghost: A Novel*. Vintage International (2001)
A Sri Lankan woman, educated abroad, is sent back to her home country to invesitgate human rights violations. The intersection of the personal and the political against a backdrop of war

Media

Of the Singhalese daily newspapers that are published in English *The Island* and *The Times* are to be recommended. On Sundays much more extensive editions are published (such as the *Sunday Times*, the *Sunday Observer* and the *Sunday Leader*).
All newspapers sold in Sri Lanka are subject to censorship.

Newspapers and magazines

The state-owned Sri Lanka Broadcasting Corporation acts as the umbrella organization for all other broadcasters in Sri Lanka. The FM programme is broadcast in various languages, including English.
The English-language programmes of the **BBC World Service** get good reception in Sri Lanka with a suitable short-wave radio. Since the best frequencies depend on the time of day and the season, it is best to note all the alternatives. They can be found under http://www.bbc.co.uk, where you will also find a programme schedule. Satellite reception is much better, and many hotels provide it.

Radio

The television stations ITN, Rupavahini and MTV are also under state control. The programme consists of news, reports about local events as well as broadcasts of preferably Indian films.
Many hotels provide satellite reception of **BBC World**.

Television

Money

Currency
The currency is the Sri Lankan rupee (abbreviated Rs). The word rupee dates back to the British colonial period and comes from the Sanskrit word rupa, meaning silver.

One rupee breaks down into 100 cents. There are 2, 5, 10, 20, 50, 100, 500 and 1000-rupee notes, which can also be distinguished by their different sizes. There are 1, 2, 5, 10, 25 and 50-cent coins.

Exchange rates
100 Rs = approx. USD 0.90 or GBP 0.58.
GBP 1.00 = approx. 172.00 Rs.
USD 1.00 = approx. 110 Rs

Foreign currency regulations
When entering or leaving Sri Lanka a maximum of 1000 Rs may be brought in or taken out. The introduction of foreign currency (with the exception of Indian and Pakistani money) is not restricted, but larger sums have to be declared on a special form when entering Sri Lanka.

▶ CONTACT DETAILS FOR CREDIT CARDS

In the event of lost bank or credit cards you can contact the following numbers in UK and USA (phone numbers when dialling from Sri Lanka):

▶ **Eurocard/MasterCard**
Tel. 001 / 636 7227 111

▶ **Visa**
Tel. 001 / 410 581 336

▶ **American Express UK**
Tel. 0044 / 1273 696 933

▶ **American Express USA**
Tel. 001 / 800 528 4800

▶ **Diners Club UK**
Tel. 0044 / 1252 513 500

▶ **Diners Club USA**
Tel. 001 / 303 799 9000
Have the bank sort code, account number and card number as well as the expiry date ready.

The following numbers of UK banks (dialling from Sri Lanka) can be used to report and cancel lost or stolen bank and credit cards issued by those banks:

▶ **HSBC**
Tel. 0044 / 1442 422 929

▶ **Barclaycard**
Tel. 0044 / 1604 230 230

▶ **NatWest**
Tel. 0044 / 142 370 0545

▶ **Lloyds TSB**
Tel. 0044 / 1702 278 270

It is definitely more favourable to wait until arriving in Sri Lanka to change money because the exchange rate is significantly better. Money can be changed in the airport arrivals terminal. All banks will exchange foreign currency into Sri Lankan rupees. There are also private money changers, particularly in Colombo, who often only accept traveller's cheques and US dollars. When exchanging money, particularly larger sums, it is a good idea to shop around and compare the different rates offered by various money changers. Hotels generally have less favourable exchange rates than banks.

Banks and bureaux de change

The banks in Sri Lanka are open Mon 9am–1pm, Tue–Fri 9am–7pm and Sat 9am–1.30pm.

Cards with the Maestro symbol are accepted at many ATMs in Sri Lanka. The following credit cards are accepted: American Express, Visa, Mastercard/Eurocard; Diners Club currently only has a very limited acceptance. Travellers booking an all-inclusive trip will generally find the credit cards accepted at the destination listed in the tour operator's catalogue.

Means of payment

It is a good idea to compare the amounts invoiced on the original and the carbon copy. For security reasons it is also advisable to personally destroy the carbon paper between the two receipts that is sometimes still used. **Traveller's cheques**, preferably in pounds or dollars, work well. The insurance that comes with them provides fast help if they are lost or stolen, but only if they were well taken care of (it is a particularly good idea to keep receipts and traveller's cheques separate). In addition exchange rates for traveller's cheques are slightly more favourable than they are for cash.

National Parks

Sri Lanka currently has twelve national parks as well as 70 nature reserves, which can be divided into three categories. **Sanctuaries** are protected areas where hunting is prohibited. **Nature reserves** may be visited without obtaining permission first; human interference here only assumes a regulatory role. **Strict nature reserves** are areas where the flora and fauna are to be kept free from any human interference, which is why they may only be accessed with special permits. They are generally only issued to scientists from the Wildlife and Nature Protection Society.

Categories

The armed conflict between the Singhalese and Tamil populations affected some national parks in the north and east. The Sri Lanka Tourist Board in Colombo provides information on the extent to which the situation has improved since the end of the civil war. (► Information).

Access

Rules of conduct National parks may only be accessed **in the company of a ranger** as well as with a suitable vehicle. Rangers wait at the main entrances to the national parks. Their fee is already included in the entrance price. It is not allowed to leave the vehicle during the trip without the express permission of the ranger.

Spending the night in a national park The Wildlife and Nature Protection Society maintains bungalows for visitors in some national parks or just on their outskirts. Camping is not permitted in any of the island's national parks.

National Park tours In Colombo the organization known as the Eco Team stages tours of certain national parks (tel.: 11 583 08 33; fax: 11 583 59 83; www.sri-lankaecotourism.com). Tours are also on offer at certain hotels and guest-houses in the vicinity of national parks.

 ## NATIONAL PARKS

INFORMATION

▶ **Wildlife and Nature Protection Society**
86 Wajamalwatte Rd.
Battaramulla
Tel. 11 / 288 7390
Fax 11 / 288 7664
Information about Sri Lanka's national parks can also be found on the internet under www.wnpssl.org.

Information about national parks in Sri Lanka is available online at www.info.lk/srilanka/srilankana-ture/nationalparks.htm.

▶ **Bundula Bird Sanctuary**
Location: between Hambantota and Kataragama (southeast). Special features: relatively small protected area (approx. 62 sq km/ 24 sq mi) with many bird species. Visiting: unrestricted

▶ **Chundilaka and Kokkilai Lagoon Bird Sanctuary**
Location: on the northeast coast. Special features: the area lies on one of the main migration routes of large flocks of migratory birds, which is why it is a bird sanctuary. Visiting: enquire in Colombo first (Tamil settlement area)

▶ **Gal Oya National Park**
Location: north of Yale and southwest of Ampara. Special features: The Senanayake Reservoir in the approx. 63,000 ha/155,000-acre park is a refuge for many species of waterfowl and other birds; in addition there are elephants and fallow deer living in the wild. Visiting: unlimited

▶ **Horton Plains Nature Reserve**
Location: south of Nuwara Eliya (Central Highlands).

! *Baedeker* TIP

Bird books

The Oriental Bird Club, a group of interested ornithologists, is the main publisher of an extensive brochure with detailed descriptions of the most important national parks in Sri Lanka (available in the book store in Lake House in Colombo).

On trips to protected areas tourists are accompanied by wardens

Special features: high plain at approx. 2000m/6500ft with interesting vegetation; excellent for hiking and driving to the cliff called World's End.
Visiting: unlimited.

▶ **Kumana Bird Sanctuary**
Location: on the southern edge of Yala East National Park.
Special features: large bird sanctuary with remarkably numerous waterfowl.
Visiting: unlimited.

▶ **Lahugala National Park**
Location: west of Pottuvil.
Special features: many wild elephants, many bird species.
Visiting: unlimited; can be accessed by car.

▶ **Maduru Oya National Park**
Location: east of Mahiyangana.
Special features: many bird species as well as elephants living in the wild.
Visiting: enquire in Colombo first.

▶ **Minneriya Giritale Sanctuary**
Location: west of Polonnaruwa
Special features: small bird sanctuary, elephants and bears.
Visiting: unlimited.

▶ **Ritigala Strict Nature Reserve**
Location: southeast of Mihintale.
Special features: refuge of many mammals and birds.
Visiting: none.

▶ **Singharaja Rain Forest Reserve**
Location: near Ratnapura.
Special features: remaining tropical rainforests, protected by UNESCO since 1988; diverse flora, many animals.
Visiting: limited.

▶ **Uda Walawe National Park**
Location: approx. 200km/125mi southeast of Colombo, near Ratnapura.
Special features: the lake in the park is the preferred stopping-off place of many bird species; fallow deer.
Visiting: unlimited.

▶ **Udawattekelle National Park**
Location: in the middle of the town of Kandy
Special features: many bird species and monkeys.
Visiting: unlimited.

▶ **Wasgomuwa Strictly Nature Reserve**
Location: south of Polonnaruwa.
Special features: one of the main migratory routes of wild elephants leads through the park.
Visiting: none.

▶ **Wilpattu National Park**
Location: on the west coast.
Special features: one of the island's largest national parks; birds, reptiles, elephants, fallow deer.
Visiting: enquire in Colombo first.

▶ **Wirawila Tissa Bird Sanctuary**
Location: west of Tissamaharama.
Special features: very diverse bird world.
Visiting: unlimited.

▶ **Yala (Ruhunu-) National Park**
Location: on the southeast coast.
Special features: Yala East is a Strictly Nature Reserve. Yala West has elephants, leopards, bears, reptiles, fallow deer and countless birds.
Visiting: unlimited (western part).

Personal Safety

Sri Lanka is a safe destination

There is no more crime in Sri Lanka than elsewhere on earth. Often visitors' provocative behaviour makes them victims of theft. Often, for example, visitors carry more cash than Sri Lankans earn in an entire year. Sri Lanka is a developing country and when wealth is flaunted it can create envy.

Avoid areas of tension

The confrontations between Tamils and Singhalese people only marginally affected tourism in Sri Lanka. Even now that the war is over, it is best to avoid large gatherings of people until the situation settles down, and only visit the east and northeast if the tourist office in Colombo gives the go-ahead. Tour operators to this part of the country will in any case be aware of the current situation.

Beware of pickpockets!

Pickpockets are most common on markets. The best way to avoid becoming a victim is to carry cash and other valuables in a neck pouch or a special belt bag that cannot be seen from the outside.

Visitors should be particularly careful when dealing with strangers. In the past there have been cases in which locals robbed visitors by offering food or drink that at best made their victims lose consciousness temporarily. Refuse such offers in a friendly but firm manner if there is even the slightest doubt.

No food or drink from strangers

Every hotel has safes where guests can deposit their valuables for the duration of their stay. It is a good idea to take advantage of them, particularly for storing travel documents, cash, travellers' cheques and the like. Hotels never assume liability for items stolen from the rooms.
In addition it is a good idea to hand over the room key at the reception when leaving the hotel.

Valuables in the safe

Although Sri Lankan society is generally considered conservative and sometimes even prudish, sexual assaults do occur and European women can be victims too. For this reason it is best to forgo revealing clothes and flirtatious words. Night-time walks on the beach or in shady areas should be avoided.

Sexual assault

The mugger crocodile lies lethargically by the water, but do not annoy it – that could be dangerous

Animals living in the wild
There are several kinds of large animals that live in the wild in Sri Lanka (elephants, leopards, crocodiles etc.). In the interests of safety, do not approach them. They can be unpredictable in their behaviour, and if humans behave carelessly the animals could respond aggressively. It is also expressly forbidden for that reason to leave the vehicle within the boundary of a national park.

Post and Telecommunications

Post offices
Almost every town in Sri Lanka has a post office. They are open Mon–Fri, 8.30am–4.30pm as well as Sat 8.30am–1pm. The General Post Office in Colombo, opposite the President's House, is open around the clock; telephone calls to overseas numbers can only be made between 7am and 9pm.

Post boxes are everywhere, but it is best not to rely on the pick-up times stated on them. It is better to hand over any mail directly at post offices or at the hotel reception.

Mail delivery times
Letters and postcards take around eight to ten days from Sri Lanka to Europe. For safety's sake it is best to write »airmail« on all mail.

Stamps
Stamps can be bought in post offices and from hotel receptions. Places that sell postcards also usually sell stamps.

Telephone
The telephone network in Sri Lanka is good, even to European standards, but it is not yet possible to call overseas numbers directly from every hotel. In these cases an operator puts the call through and delays are likely. Local calls within Colombo cost one rupee but in most

▶ TELEPHONE CALLS

INFORMATION

National directory enquiry service: 161
International directory enquiry service: 141

DIALLING CODES IN SRI LANKA

Anuradhapura: 025
Bandarawela: 057
Colombo: 01
Galle: 09
Gampaha: 033
Kandy: 08

Negombo: 031
When making telephone calls to Sri Lanka from another country the zero in front of the local dialling code is dropped.

DIALLING CODES FROM AND TO SRI LANKA

Sri Lanka: 00 94
Australia: 00 51
Ireland: 00 353
New Zealand: 00 64
UK: 00 44
USA/Canada: 00 1

hotels more is charged. National calls cost at least eight rupees for the first two minutes and every further minute costs two rupees. Since IDD calls are not exactly cheap it is best to make calls to Europe from the offices of the Singhalese telephone company. The post office in Colombo (Duke Street near Colombo Fort) is open around the clock. **Payphones are widespread** and can be found in all larger towns. Phone cards worth 50, 100, 200 and 500 rupees can be bought in the main post office, amongst other places.

The cellphone network has been much expanded in Sri Lanka in recent years. Nowadays even places away from the main cities are well served. Calls on a mobile phone are still expensive, but the cost is reduced by obtaining a prepaid card on arrival, for example at the main post office in Colombo, but also in a number of shops. To avoid unpleasant surprises when the next bill arrives, it is best to ask your provider about roaming charges before you leave.

Mobile phones

Prices · Discounts

Sri Lanka is an inexpensive destination, which is not least the result of its population's low per capita income. Food is cheap, alcoholic drinks on the other hand are relatively expensive (except for arrak, which is made in Sri Lanka) because they or the ingredients have to be imported.

A collective ticket for the Cultural Triangle, which costs US$ 30, is recommended. It is available from the Central Cultural Fund (212/1 Bauddhaloka Mawatha, Colombo 7, tel. 25 78 912) or between 8.30am and 4.15pm from all cultural sites.

Collective ticket

3-course meal
from £5

Simple meal
from £2

Glass of beer
£2

Double room
from £25

Driver
from £25 per day

A curry is rarely served on its own.
They are available with fish, meat, poultry and as vegetarian options

Permission to take photographs Tourists wishing to take photographs in ancient ruins require permission from the Department of Archaeology in Colombo. The entrance fee of US$ 30 allows visitors to enter and take pictures of all of the country's historical sites for a month. This ticket is also available from the office of the Central Cultural Fund in Colombo.

Prostitution

Sex tourism on the increase Sri Lanka has been a destination of international sex tourism for many years. After Thailand and the Philippines, Sri Lanka takes third place. The sex tourists come from all around the world, particularly from Europe.

Sex tourism exploits the economic poverty of many young island inhabitants, without taking their psychological development into account. Many victims come from rural areas and there from the socially underprivileged classes. For them »selling« their body is often enough the last opportunity for survival. The often quoted opinion that prostitution is rooted in tradition in Asia is completely wrong, by the way.

Child and adolescent prostitution has grown alarmingly in Sri Lanka. The country's government, which initially responded timidly to this phenomenon, has signed a United Nations treaty, not least because of vigorous demands by European countries. This treaty guarantees every child and adolescent under the age of 18 protection from sexual exploitation. The punishment for child abuse has also been severely increased. British citizens and residents can be prosecuted in the UK for sexual offences committed against children abroad under the Sexual Offences Act 2003, and similar legislation exists elsewhere. Well-known European tour operators have also declared themselves willing to face up to sex tourism and particularly child and adolescent prostitution. Sri Lanka's law enforcement authorities have recently started passing on the details of offenders to their home police authorities and banned the people in question from the island for life.

Child and adolescent prostitution

Shopping

The long-standing tradition of Sri Lankan handicrafts makes it easier for visitors to find suitable souvenirs. Be it carved masks, batik fabrics or gemstones: the choice is diverse and inexpensive. It is none-theless worthwhile not to go for the first price that is given; **bartering is part of shopping almost everywhere** (except in department stores and up-market shops).
The Arts and Crafts Centers that can be found in every larger town offer a wide variety of goods and the state-owned Laksala shops are also a good place to look for souvenirs. They sell handicrafts made of wood, metal, silver, reed, natural fibres, buffalo horns, coconuts and bamboo as well as textiles, batik goods and silk. Laksala has many branches, while the main one is in Colombo (60 York Street, Fort, Colombo 1).

Souvenirs

! *Baedeker* TIP

Ayurveda cosmetics
Western toiletries are relatively expensive in Sri Lanka, but it is absolutely fine to use the local ayurveda products if anything runs out. They are both excellent and inexpensive.

Along the road between Colombo and Kandy a large number of small businesses laboriously make artistic batik goods by hand. It is often possible to watch how the colourful fabrics are made. Strictly speaking the art of batik is not originally Sri Lankan, but was imported from Indonesia. However, its quality is coming closer and closer to the original.

Fabrics, batik goods

The market for designer knock-offs is flourishing in Sri Lanka. However, since many designers also have their clothes made here, even the originals are cheaper in Sri Lanka than they are in Europe.

Clothes

Bobbin lace	In the south of the island all around the port of Galle the art of making bobbin lace, brought here by the Portuguese, has survived to this day. The main goods produced are tablecloths, handkerchiefs and similar items.
Woodworks, masks	The mask carvers of Ambalangoda, a small town on the south coast, are well-known for their traditional masks. As a result a large number of shops selling a wide variety of masks have opened up here. However, there is no place visited by tourists in Sri Lanka that does not also sell masks as souvenirs. Visitors will also find everything else that can be made of wood, such as elephants or Buddha figurines. It is wise, however, to avoid all **teak products** in favour of goods made from other types of wood. Amongst the larger souvenir items are complete furniture suites, for example made of rosewood. The stores that sell these also organize shipping to Europe.
Gemstones	The region around Ratnapura is a **Mecca for gemstone prospectors**. It has rubies, sapphires, topazes and many other precious and semi-

Coconuts are used for many things. This man is making a ladle from one.

precious stones. They can be found carefully cut and polished in jewellers' shops all over the island, where of course they are also sold as part of finished pieces of jewellery. However, the latter items can be disappointing in terms of quality. It is better to buy the stones in Sri Lanka and have them made into jewellery at home.

Like everywhere else in Asia Sri Lanka also has **mobile hawkers** who try to sell tourists »high-quality stones at exceptionally good prices« at places such as the beach. It should be obvious that these stones are either very poor quality or even imitations. It is also not advisable to buy gemstones directly from the mines around Ratnapura, because the dealers there can be very pushy at times. In general it is good to have some knowledge of gemstones in order to judge their quality. Many a purchase made without this knowledge has turned out an expensive mistake.

Brass goods

All over the island there are small companies that sell artistic brass goods. They are usually hand-made and the motifs are often of a religious nature, but can also be secular.

Tea

Those who leave Sri Lanka without a few packets of tea will probably be missing out on the best-tasting souvenir. Particularly in the highlands around Nuwara Eliya there are **many tea factories** that also have tea-tasting facilities and a shop. The prices even for the best varieties are low.

Spices

The highlands are also home to a number of **spice farms** that sell fresh spices such as nutmeg, vanilla, cardamom, cinnamon and many others straight from the producer, meaning they will be fresh and inexpensive. A further place to buy spices is at one of the markets that are held in every town.

Hours of operation

Since shop opening times are not regulated by law in Sri Lanka, there is no single time when shops close. Shops are generally open Mon–Fri 8.30am–7pm and often close for lunch between 1pm and 2pm. Many shops also open on Saturdays; most stay closed on Sundays.

Sport and Outdoors

Animal watching

Sri Lanka's rich bird world attracts ornithologists from all around the world, who can then combine ornithological excursions with cultural sightseeing in the company of qualified guides.

Cricket is the sport of the masses

Guests may find that they suddenly stop getting the familiar good service in hotels and restaurants from one minute to the next, and if almost all the staff have gathered around the television in the lobby or restaurant they will definitely be watching a crucial phase in a cricket match.

Cricket is the number one national sport, so this slip in service should not be judged too harshly. No other sporting event, not even the final of a soccer World Cup, will attract so many spectators. Even the smallest learn to play cricket in Sri Lanka, and every school in the country has its own team. Of course the national eleven is considered the nation's gem. It won the World Cup in 1996, which was the greatest sporting achievement in the country's history. In 2007 Sri Lanka took second place in the World Cup.

There are **two big cricket grounds in Sri Lanka**; one of them is in Colombo. Another was built in 1998 in Galle, where international matches are also held.

Golf   Sri Lanka currently has three golf courses of international standard. They are in Colombo, Rajawella and Nuwara Eliya. There are plans for setting up further golf courses in the next few years.

Mountain biking   The landscape of the Central Highlands is a paradise for mountain bikers. Bikes can be hired but it is best if passionate bikers bring their own.

Hiking   Sri Lanka is not a traditional destination for hikers but there are nonetheless some attractive regions that can be explored on foot. The Horton Plains, a unique natural landscape with an interesting flora, are just one example. There is a very well signposted hiking trail here. Hiking is also possible in the Sinharaja Rain Forest Sanctuary near Ratnapura but only in the company of a licensed guide. Climbing Adam's Peak could also be considered a hike.

Tennis   Tennis courts, some of which are floodlit, can be found all over the island, especially in the better hotels.

Water Sports

Sailing, surfing   Countless hotels along the west coast hire out sailing boats. These are small boats that belong to the dinghy class. Surf boards are even more common. Sometimes the first attempts to stand on a board can be made under the eye of an expert.

Canoeing   Canoeing is possible on the upper reaches of Kelani Ganga and Kalu Ganga, which flow through a superb mountain landscape. White-water rafters also get their thrills on some sections.

Rafting   The little village of Kitulgala on the banks of Kelani Ganga became widely known when it was used as a location in the film *The Bridge on the River Kwai*. Not far from the village is the Rafter's Retreat, a special kind of accommodation built as a tree house from the wood of the surrounding forests. It is a good base for many rafting tours, including for beginners and families. The 6km/3.5mi trip through gorges and rapids takes around two hours.

Off the coast of Sri Lanka the once magnificent coral reefs have been damaged by coral bleaching, while the tsunami by contrast caused little harm. Nevertheless diving trips are worthwhile for the varied **fish world** alone. Since the tsunami some diving schools have re-opened, and tour operators have also started running trips to diving areas once more. Between November and April there are good opportunities for encountering not only large fish but blue whales and sperm whales too.

Snorkelling, diving

The tsunami destroyed most of the diving schools in exposed locations along Sri Lanka's west coast. Amongst those that have been re-built, the one in Hikkaduwa can be recommended. It also trains beginners on the internationally recognized PADI principles.

Nurse sharks are part of Sri Lanka's underwater world

▶ INFORMATION; OPERATORS

ANIMAL WATCHING

▶ **Eco Adventure Travels**
58, Dudley Senanayaka Mawatha
Colombo 8
Tel. 011 / 268 56 01
E-mail: cdctrv@slt.lk

▶ **www.slwcs.org**
Homepage of the Sri Lanka Wildlife Conservation Society.

▶ **www.camacdonald.com/
birding/asiasrilanka.htm**
Many nice pictures of the island's
bird world as well as reports by
committed bird conservationists.

GOLF

▶ **Royal Colombo Golf Club
Colombo**
Model Farm Road, Colombo 8
Tel. 00 94 / 169 14 01
18 holes, total course length: 5770
m/6310 yd, par 71
Location: at sea level
This golf club was established in
1879 already, making it the oldest
in Sri Lanka. Special features:
many water obstacles, hole
number 5 is directly by some train
tracks. Equipment hire is possible.

▶ **Victoria International Golf and
Country Resort Kandy**
www.golfsrilanka.com
18 holes, total course length
6288m/6877yd, par 73
Tel. 00 94 / 81 23 76
Sri Lanka's newest golf course and
also one of the nicest, it was played
the first time in January 1999.

▶ **Nuwara Eliya Golf Club**
Tel. 052 / 52 28 35
18 holes, total course length
5550m/6070yd, par 70

Maybe the most attractive golf
course of Sri Lanka. It is situated
in a valley not far from Nuwara
Eliya and was founded in 1880.
Special features: long and narrow
fairways. Pro-shop for equipment
hire available.

SPORTS TRIP
OPERATORS

▶ **Lanka Sportreizen**
29-B, S.DES. Yayasinghe Mawatha
Kalubowila, Dehiwela
Tel. 00 94 / 11 / 282 45 00, 282 49 55
www.lsr-srilanka.com

CANOEING

▶ **Jetwing Eco Holidays**
Jetwing House
46/26 Navam Mawatha
Colombo 2
Tel. 011 / 234 57 00
www.jetwingeco.com

RAFTING

▶ **Rafters Retreat**
Hilland Estate, Kitugala
Tel. 036 / 228 75 98
E-mail: chnnap@jtmin.com

DIVING

▶ **Poseidon Diving Station**
Galle Road, Hikkaduwa
Tel. 00 94 / 9 12 27 72 94
www.divingsrilanka.com

▶ **Unawatuna
Diving Centre**
Matara Road
Peellagoda/Unawatunabei Galle
Tel. 00 94 / 912 24 46 93
E-mail:
info@unawatunadiving.com
www.srilankadiving.com

Time

Standard time is in place in Sri Lanka all year round. There is no summer time. The time in Sri Lanka is 5.5 hours ahead of Greenwich Mean Time (GMT) and 4.5 hours ahead of British Summer Time.

On Sri Lanka

Transport

By Car

Sri Lankans drive on the left.

Drive on the left!

The road network is good by the country's general standards, but its condition is in no way comparable to that of European roads. The roads on the southeastern side of the island are less good. Only around a fifth of the total road network of approx. 152,000km/ 94,400mi is surfaced.
The first road from Colombo to Kandy was built by the British in 1821. It primarily served as a transport route for coffee and later for tea and rubber. **There are still no motorways or fast roads**. Do not be fooled by the letter »A« in front of the road numbers. The road surfaces are in particularly bad condition in the remote parts of the island.

Road network

Roads have soft verges, there are potholes. The surface is generally rough and there are sudden changes of surface materials. Even on main roads **obstacles might turn up at any time**: grazing cows, sleeping dogs and pedestrians suddenly crossing the street require the driver's utmost concentration. During the monsoon lower-lying roads and streets can flood.

Road condition

Within towns the maximum speed limit is 56kmh/35mph. Outside towns vehicles may **not go faster than 72kmh/45mph**. The police carry out regular speed checks.
When planning a trip by car make calculations using an average speed of no more than 30kmh/20mph.

Maximum speed

After a break-down or accident drivers are dependent on the help of other drivers. There are no emergency telephones along the roads. In the event of a break-down it is best to gain the attention of other drivers by waving. Since the locals are very helpful drivers will not generally have to wait very long. Vehicles that are unfit to drive may be towed to the closest garage.

Break-down and accident service

The situation is more difficult at night, particularly far away from towns. This is a further reason why **driving at night should generally be avoided**.

Filling stations
Filling-station coverage is not dense and it is not customary for drivers to serve themselves. Diesel is very cheap because it is subsidized by the state.

Modes of Transport

By Rail
The trains in Sri Lanka are a relic from the time of the British colonial rule. The first line was opened in 1867. It ran between Colombo and Kandy. Over the decades a methodical expansion to a total of 1453 km/903 mi took place so that now every larger town can be reached by rail. The trains are run by Sri Lankan Railways. A trip by rail from Colombo to Kandy is one of the most impressive experiences a railway enthusiast can have.

There are **three classes**. First class must be booked in advance. Some long-distance trains have panorama carriages.

Although the trains run to **fixed timetables**, printed timetables for travellers are not always available. Trains **are one of the cheapest modes of transport** in Sri Lanka. A return trip between Colombo and Kandy (approx. 120km/75mi) only costs around €1.50, even in first class. Second class and third class are even cheaper but less advisable because they are overcrowded. Children up to the age of three travel free, between 3 and 12 they pay half price. It is possible to **reserve seats** for a fee, and for first-class seats (air-conditioned) in long-distance trains reservations are required. It is also wise to buy tickets in good time since trains are hopelessly overcrowded at all times of the day.

Sri Lanka's government railway occasionally organizes **round trips** including accommodation and meals. More information is available at Colombo Fort station.

The main railway lines in Sri Lanka are (the lines towards the north can currently only be taken to Vavuniya):

Colombo Fort – Anuradhapura: 206km/128mi, approx. 5 hrs.
Colombo Fort – Avissawella: 61km/38mi, approx. 1.5 hrs.
Colombo Fort – Badulla: 290km/180mi, approx. 10 – 11 hrs.
Colombo Fort – Batticaloa: 254km/158mi, approx. 8 – 10 hrs.
Colombo Fort – Bentota: 63km/39mi, approx. 1.5 – 2 hrs.
Colombo Fort – Galle: 112km/70mi, approx. 2 – 3 hrs.
Colombo Fort – Hikkaduwa: 92km/57mi, approx. 3 hrs.
Colombo Fort – Kandy: 116km/72mi, approx. 3 hrs.
Colombo Fort – Matara: 156km/97mi, approx. 3 – 4 hrs.
Colombo Fort – Polonnaruwa: 254km/158mi, approx. 6 – 7 hrs.
Colombo Fort – Puttalam, 133km/83mi, approx. 3 hrs.
Colombo Fort – Bentota, 63km/39mi, approx. 1.5 – 2 hrs.

Taxis are available in sufficient numbers in larger towns. Taximeters   Taxi
are not common outside Colombo, so the fare has to be negotiated
in advance. A general rule of
thumb is approx. 20–25 rupees per
kilometre, while fixed prices can be
agreed for longer trips (such as day
trips).

The **three-wheeler** (also known as
Bajaj after its manufacturer) is a typically Asian mode of transport. It
has three wheels, a two-stroke en-
gine and possesses an extraordinary cargo capacity. Three-wheelers
exist all over Sri Lanka; **the fare
has to be agreed in advance**. The
first kilometre of a trip should cost
around 30 rupees, but every further kilometre should not cost
more than ten rupees.

Buses are by far the most widespread and inexpensive mode of
transport in Sri Lanka. They can
also be used to reach remote parts
of the island. However, the buses
are often in a sorry state of repair
and even more often they are completely overcrowded. The sometimes reckless driving style of some
bus drivers is alarming. They occa-

*Taking the train to Kandy
is an experience*

sionally seem to confuse narrow roads littered with potholes with
racetracks.

There are regular buses and express buses. The latter mainly run between the larger towns. Every town in Sri Lanka, no matter how
small, has its own bus station, which is always located close to the
clock tower (the typical town-centre feature in Sri Lanka).
There is not necessarily a fixed bus timetable. Some drivers only
leave when enough passengers are on board. This is particularly true
of private buses, which can be recognized by their label »Intercity
Express«. Unlike the government buses run by the Sri Lanka Tourist
Board, they even have air-conditioning. **Bus fares** are very low. A trip
from Colombo to Kandy for example only costs around 30 rupees.

Some places popular with tourists (such as the ruins of Polonnaruwa   Bicycles
and Anuradhapura) have bicycle rental facilities. Some hotels also offer this service. The prices are low. A bicycle costs around 60–80 rupees per day.

Motorbikes The seaside resorts along the west coast have some motorbike rental places. This option should be avoided on principle. The unfamiliar traffic conditions (bad roads etc.) often lead to serious accidents.

Travellers with Disabilities

Trips are possible
in principle Trips to Sri Lanka are possible in principle for disabled people too. Tour operators provide information about how the island can be explored in a wheelchair for example. However, transportation in Sri Lanka does not cater for disabled individuals. The larger hotels are much better prepared for the needs of disabled travellers. Unfortunately there is no list of hotels deserving the title »disabled accessible«. On the plus side, the helpfulness of the Sri Lankan people helps to make up for the lack of facilities.

 INFORMATION FOR THE DISABLED

UNITED KINGDOM

► **Tourism for All**
c/o Vitalise, Shap Road Industrial Estate, Shap Road, Kendal
Cumbria LA9 6NZ
Tel. 08 45 124 99 71
www.tourismforall.org.uk

USA

► **SATH (Society for Accessible Travel and Hospitality)**
347 5th Ave., no. 605
New York, NY 10016:
Tel. (212) 4 47 72 84
www.sath.org

Weights and Measures

Imperial
system Even after Sri Lanka gained its independence it maintained the imperial system of weights and measures. The metric system is also in use, however.

 IMPERIAL MEASURES

LENGTHS, AREAS AND VOLUMES

1 inch = 2.45cm
1 foot = 0.305 m
1 acre = 0.405 ha
1 pound = 453 g
1 mile = 1,609 km
1 square mile = 2.59 km²

1 cubic foot = 0.028 m3
1 pound = 16 ounces

MEASURES OF CAPACITY

1 gallon = 4.54 l
1 quart = 1.135 l
1 gallon = 4 quarts
1 quart = 2 pints

When to Go

Sri Lanka has a tropical wet summer climate with little fluctuation in the high temperatures. The seasonal change in precipitation as a result of the Indian monsoon circulation is marked. Four precipitation seasons can be distinguished: the pre-monsoon season (March–mid-May), the summer monsoon season (mid-May–Sept), the post-monsoon season (Oct–Nov) and the winter monsoon season (Dec–Feb). The Central Highlands of Sri Lanka are an **effective climate barrier**. Its windward and leeward effects divide the island into a southwestern wet zone (around a third of the island's total area) and a relatively dry zone.

Monsoon period

With around 150cm/60in of rainfall per year, the Jaffna Peninsula and parts of the northwest coast are some of Sri Lanka's driest regions, closely followed by the northeast coast in the rain shadow of the mountains. Yala National Park also gets relatively little precipitation. In the humid southwest the average annual rainfall ranges from 240cm/100in in the plains to a maximum of 500cm/220in on the mountains' western slopes. The summer monsoon brings most of this rain and hits the island with storms and torrential downpours; it generally arrives around 24 May. From then on katabatic (descending) winds known as »kachan« blow down on the leeward side of the Highlands, increasing the aridity and summer heat in the northeast of the island even further. In the north and east the wet season lasts from the end of November to January as a result of the winter monsoon. The foehn wind then causes good weather on the southwest coast. During the pre- and post-monsoon periods (March–May, Oct–Nov) severe thunderstorms and torrential rainfall hit the island. They bring more precipitation to the southwest coast than the actual summer monsoon. The most humid months on the entire island, during which it rains for up to 20 days, are usually October and November, and in the southwest May and June as well, while on the northeast coast December is also very wet. **Continuous rain is the exception even during the wet season**, making it rare for the sun to shine for less than six hours a day. Tropical cyclones (Bay of Bengal cyclones) can only affect Sri Lanka in the northeast, if at all.

Rain, storms

The humid, clammy climate, only made more bearable by the occasional wind on the coast, is stressful for the human body. Constant daytime temperatures of 29–33°C/84–91°F and night-time temperatures of hardly below 25°C/77°F, coupled with high humidity levels of 70–90%, are **only bearable for longer periods of time if you are healthy**. The Highlands above altitudes of 1000m/3300ft are pleasant, as the temperatures here are 5–8°C/9–14°F degrees lower. Only the winter months are somewhat less sticky and marginally cooler, while the months of March and April before the arrival of the summer

Temperatures, heat problems

Sri Lanka *Three Typical Climates*

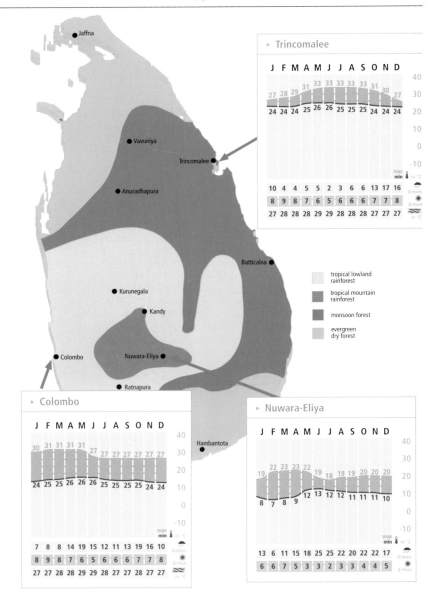

Trincomalee

J	F	M	A	M	J	J	A	S	O	N	D
27	28	29	31	33	33	33	33	31	30		27
24	24	24	25	26	25	25	25	24	24	24	

10	4	4	5	5	2	3	6	6	13	17	16
8	9	8	7	6	5	6	6	6	7	7	8
27	28	28	28	29	29	28	28	28	27	27	27

tropical lowland rainforest
tropical mountain rainforest
monsoon forest
evergreen dry forest

Colombo

J	F	M	A	M	J	J	A	S	O	N	D
30	31	31	31	31	27	27	27	27	27	27	27
24	25	25	26	26	26	25	25	25	24	24	

7	8	8	14	19	15	12	11	13	19	16	10
8	9	8	7	6	5	6	6	6	7	7	8
27	27	28	28	29	28	27	27	28	27	28	27

Nuwara-Eliya

J	F	M	A	M	J	J	A	S	O	N	D
19		22	23	23	22	19	18	19	19	20	20	20
8	7	8	9	12	13	12	11	11	11	10	

| 13 | 6 | 11 | 15 | 18 | 25 | 25 | 22 | 20 | 22 | 22 | 17 |
| 6 | 6 | 7 | 5 | 3 | 3 | 2 | 3 | 3 | 4 | 4 | 5 |

Jaffna
Vavuniya
Trincomalee
Anuradhapura
Batticaloa
Kurunegala
Kandy
Nuwara-Eliya
Colombo
Ratnapura
Hambantota

monsoon (»the burst of the monsoon«) are much hotter with maximum temperatures of almost 35ºC/95ºF, and 37ºC/99ºF on the northeast coast. The Indian Ocean is warm almost all year round with temperatures of 27ºC/81ºF to almost 30ºC/86ºF.

For beach holidays on the southwest coast with trips to the Highlands, January to March offer the best weather conditions, while February to March is the best time for the island as a whole (lowest risk of rain and lowest temperatures). The best weather on the northeast coasts (dry but very hot) lasts from February to September. **Absolutely avoid the wet months of October and November**. It is a general rule of thumb that it gets wetter with increasing altitude and drier further north and east. Watch out: protection from the strong tropical sun is a must. In addition to a broad-brimmed hat, light cotton clothes are also a good idea.

Travelling with the weather

> ! **Baedeker TIP**
>
> **Timing is everything**
> During the monsoon and inter-monsoon periods it is best to get going as soon as possible in the morning. The best weather conditions come between 10am and noon before new showers begin.

The monsoon (originally from the Arabic mausim = suitable for navigation) is a seasonally changing wind that mainly occurs as a southwest (summer) monsoon and a northeast (winter) monsoon in the Indian Ocean. The cause of this large-scale movement of air is the warming and cooling of the Asian landmass. During the summer months the strong sun over the Tibetan plateau produces a thermal low that is replaced in winter by the Asian cold-air high as a result of the high radiation. This change in atmospheric pressure, which affects large parts of the Indian Ocean on both sides of the equator, causes the seasonal change in direction of the monsoon current. Deflected by the Coriolis effect, the humid maritime summer monsoon blows over India and Sri Lanka from the southwest, the dry continental winter monsoon from the northeast. On its way over the Bay of Bengal the originally dry winter monsoon becomes wetter, causing the northeast side of Sri Lanka to have its rainfall maximum in the winter (Trincomalee).

Monsoon

Even the people of Sri Lanka need to cool down sometimes

Tours

50 km p.h.

THE TOURS IN THIS SECTION
HIGHLIGHT THE BEST AND MOST
HISTORIC PLACES ON THE ISLAND AS
WELL AS TO THE MOST SCENIC ONES.
OF COURSE WE ALSO PROVIDE
INFORMATION ON THE BEST ACCOMMODATION.

TOURS IN SRI LANKA

There is no need to complete all four tours to get an insight into life in Sri Lanka. That said, one tour will leave everyone wanting more and it is also possible to combine tours. Before setting off it is best to read through the following tips.

▬▬▬ **TOUR 1** **Grand Tour of the Island**
Even the Arabs called Sri Lanka »the serendipitous island«. This trip includes everything that makes it so attractive: old temples, lush green tea plantations, wonderful beaches and last but not least, friendly people. ▶ **page 168**

▬▬▬ **TOUR 2** **In Royal Footsteps**
This tour goes to Sri Lanka's royal cities, where many historic buildings reveal what a rich past this island has. In addition it takes you to attractive landscapes such as the Central Highlands. ▶ **page 173**

▬▬▬ **TOUR 3** **The Central Highlands**
Tea plantations as far as the eye can see. Tumbling waterfalls, one of Buddha's sacred teeth and the town that was visited by British colonial rulers in need of relaxation: this tour, which goes to the island's Central Highlands, delivers on all of this. ▶ **page 177**

▬▬▬ **TOUR 4** **Combination with Tour 3**
This round trip is based on the abovementioned Tour 3, but also makes room for experiencing Sri Lanka's fauna and the still extant tropical rainforest. ▶ **page 178**

Kelaniya
At full moon crowds of believers flock to the temple Raja Maha Vihara in order to celebrate Buddha's first visit to Sri Lanka

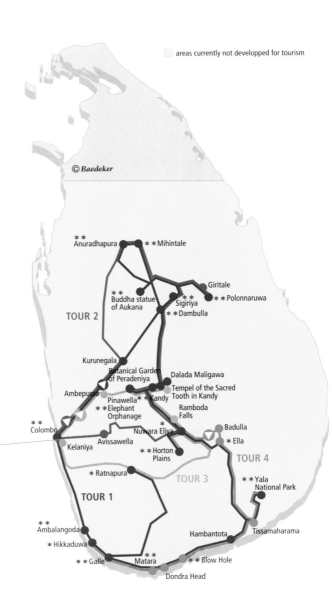

areas currently not developped for tourism

** Anuradhapura   ** Mihintale

Giritale

** Buddha statue   Sigiriya   ** Polonnaruwa
of Aukana

TOUR 2   ** Dambulla

Kurunegala

Botanical Garden   Dalada Maligawa
of Peradeniya

Ambepussa   Tempel of the Sacred
Tooth in Kandy

Pinawella ** * Kandy

* Elephant   Ramboda
Orphanage   Falls

** Badulla

** Colombo   * Nuwara Eliya

Kelaniya   Avissawella   * Ella

** Horton   TOUR 4
Plains

* Ratnapura   TOUR 3   ** Yala
National Park

TOUR 1

** Ambalangoda

* Hikkaduwa

Hambantota   Tissamaharama

** Galle   Matara   ** Blow Hole

Dondra Head

© Baedeker

Travelling in Sri Lanka

Allow for enough time

The island of Sri Lanka has so many sights that one week is just about enough to get a brief insight. Visits to the religious and historical sites of Anuradhapura and Polonnaruwa are a must. A drive through the Central Highlands, which, unlike the dry, almost arid lowlands, is covered in lush green vegetation as far the eye can see, should also not be missed. In the middle of the magnificent landscape is Kandy, with its Temple of the Sacred Tooth. The town has good accommodation, making it a good place to spend the night.

Sri Lanka's north remains difficult to explore, particularly Jaffna Peninsula. This is where the factions in the civil war fought particularly fiercely, as if their aim had been to destroy as much of the infrastruc-

Regardless of the time of year, the sea around Sri Lanka is always warm enough for swimming and the sandy beaches are almost velvety

ture of the enemy as they could. It will be decades, given a stable peace treaty, before the infrastructure is restored to any degree.

Animal lovers will get their money's worth in Sri Lanka's **national parks**. In addition to wild elephants there are many other animals, some of which can now only be found in Sri Lanka because they have long since died out elsewhere. Yala National Park is probably the best-known amongst Sri Lanka's protected regions, albeit not necessarily the most biodiverse.

The perfect Sri Lanka holiday could consist of part round trip, part beach holiday. A week to ten days should be allowed for the first part before enjoying some well deserved rest and relaxation while thinking about all the different experiences of the past few days. Sri Lanka's **best sandy beaches** are to be found on the east coast. Since they were hard to access during the civil war, this fact is not yet common knowledge. For that reason they are almost deserted and it is very easy to find a quiet place to go swimming and laze around. Attractive, well-tended beaches with fine sand can also be found on the southwest coast, near the seaside resort of Hikkaduwa, which became legendary in the 1970s. Although the tsunami destroyed most of the hotels along the coast, they have been rebuilt in a more attractive and comfortable manner. Alternatively there are a good number of seaside towns near Negombo north of the capital of Colombo.

Personal safety

Since the end of the civil war the east coast of Sri Lanka as far as Trincomalee has been open to travellers almost without restriction. New hotels are to be built, it is said, and tourist sites made accessible. Travel to the north of the country cannot yet be recommended, however, or only within certain limits, as the infrastructure has been almost totally destroyed.

Travelling through Sri Lanka

At first glance travelling through Sri Lanka by vehicle could look like an unproblematic undertaking, given the dense road network. The actual conditions make the express warning to visitors not to drive themselves but to hire a local driver a sensible suggestion. The round trips described in the following section have been put together taking this into account.

Having a **driver with knowledge of the country** also has the advantage that visitors do not have to concentrate on the occasionally anarchic traffic conditions and can instead pay attention to the beautiful scenery outside. Further information is available under »transport« in the section »Practical Information«.

Travelling by bus in Sri Lanka can be quite an experience, but not necessarily a positive one. The fares are cheap but the buses are usually hopelessly overcrowded. At times some drivers appear to have suicidal intentions, particularly in the interior and in the Central Highlands, where the roads are narrow and winding. **Official timetables are rare**; the buses leave when they are full.

Tour 1 Grand Tour of the Island

Start and End: Colombo   **Duration:** 12 – 14 days

The grand tour of Sri Lanka touches on almost all of the island's significant sites. Anyone visiting Sri Lanka for the first time will gain a comprehensive insight from this tour. The route has been designed in such a way that places away from the main route can also be visited.

Day 1:
Colombo –
Dambulla

Leave ❶ ＊＊ **Colombo** early in the morning northbound. Just a few kilometres outside of the city is Raja Maha Vihara in **Kelaniya**. Its oldest sections date from the 13th century; some of the stunning wall paintings are exceptionally well preserved. The landscape towards the island's interior now becomes very changeable. ❷**Kurunegala** can be reached by about noon. It is notable for strangely shaped rocks above the town that are named after animals. They can also be seen from the nicely situated **Lake Batalagoda**. Allow for plenty of time for the famous cave temples of ❸＊＊ **Dambulla**. They were already inhabited in prehistoric times, but the majority of their magnificent interiors date back to the 1st century BC (accommodation in Dambulla).

DON'T MISS

- Kelaniya: wonderful wall paintings
- Dambulla: magnificent cave paintings
- Kandy: a tooth attracts thousands of pilgrims.
- Horton Plains: a paradise for nature lovers

Day 2:
Mihintale –
Aukana

An early start is a good idea for this day too so as to have enough time to view the monastery of Mihintale and go on to Anuradhapura in the afternoon. The first stop is ❹＊＊ **Mihintale**, the birthplace of Buddhism in Sri Lanka. It is said King Ashoka sent the monk Mahinda here in around 250 BC to spread the teachings of the enlightened one. Every year on the day of the June full moon tens of thousands of pilgrims celebrate this event. ❺**The afternoon is devoted to** ＊＊ **Anuradhapura**. The exploration of the extensive ruins gives an insight into the architecture of earlier Singhalese kings. Next the ❻＊＊ **Buddha statue of Aukana** deserves a visit; it is a further masterpiece by an unfortunately unknown artist. (Accommodation in Dambulla)

Day 3:
Polonnaruwa –
Sigiriya

Two further highlights in the area known as the **cultural triangle** of Sri Lanka are on the agenda on day 3. The route first goes to ❼＊＊ **Polonnaruwa**, which replaced Anuradhapura as the capital in around 1073. Here too a large number of (in some cases) well preserved ruins are waiting. The highlight of this morning is viewing the famous **Buddha statues in the Gal Vihara**.

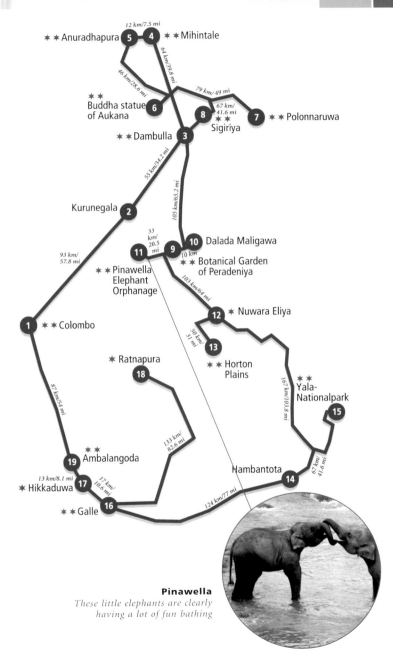

★★ Anuradhapura **5** **4** ★★ Mihintale

12 km/7.5 mi

64 km/39.8 mi

46 km/28.6 mi

79 km/49 mi

★★ Buddha statue **6**
of Aukana

8 **7** ★★ Polonnaruwa

67 km/41.6 mi

★★ Dambulla **3** ★★ Sigiriya

55 km/34.2 mi

105 km/65.2 mi

Kurunegala **2**

10 Dalada Maligawa

11 **9**

3.3 km/20.5 mi

10 km

★★ Botanical Garden
of Peradeniya

93 km/57.8 mi

★★ Pinawella
Elephant
Orphanage

103 km/64 mi

1 ★★ Colombo

12 ★ Nuwara Eliya

50 km/31 mi

13

★ Ratnapura

★★ Horton
Plains

18

167 km/103.8 mi

★★ Yala-
Nationalpark

15

87 km/54 mi

133 km/82.6 mi

19 ★★ Ambalangoda

Hambantota

13 km/8.1 mi   *17 km/10.6 mi*

14

★ Hikkaduwa **17**

16

67 km/41.6 mi

★★ Galle

124 km/77 mi

Pinawella
*These little elephants are clearly
having a lot of fun bathing*

Just a few kilometres from Polunnaruwa is the unique rock fort of **❽ ** ** Sigiriya**, the destination of the afternoon. After seeing the world-famous »**cloud maidens of Sigiriya**«, the somewhat laborious climb up to the actual rock fort is an absolute must. Just imagining how the workers under King Kassyapa brought the building materials up here takes your breath away (quite literally). A distant, magnificent view makes up for the tiring climb. (Accommodation in Dambulla)

Day 4:
Dambulla –
Kandy

What was already hinted at during the drive from Sigirya back to Dambulla is now at the focus of the days to come. The landscape becomes more lavish and the **Central Highlands** come into view. Around halfway to Kandy a detour to the Alu Vihara near **Matale** is a good idea. It draws visitors in for its impressive location in a fantastic rocky landscape. The temple also played a role for Buddhism; a council of around 500 monks is said to have taken place here and during this council Buddha's teachings were written down for the first time.

! **Baedeker TIP**

Kandyan Dance Show

Aim at getting evening tickets for the Kandyan Dance Show. Dances from all over the country are performed (Cultural Centre of the Kandyan Art Association, 72 Sangaraja Mawatha).

On the way to **Kandy**, which should be reached by around noon, it is a good idea to stop at one of the many **spice gardens** along the A 9 road. Visitors will learn a lot about the traditional naturopathic medicine known as **ayurveda**, which has been experiencing a revival for quite a while now.

Before visiting Kandy's Temple of the Tooth why not enjoy a short visit to the **❾ ** ** Botanical Gardens of Peradeniya** created in the 14th century as a royal pleasure garden. They are among the most beautiful gardens of their kind in the world.

Viewing Sri Lanka's most important temple is the culmination of this eventful day. The Sacred Tooth, which is said to have been one of the Buddha's own, and which went on an odyssey through the different parts of the country, attracts thousands of devout Buddhists every day to the **❿ ** ** Dalada Maligawa**, the »Temple of the Tooth«. (Accommodation in Kandy)

Day 5:
excursion

Once again an early morning start is rewarded by a very special experience. The **⓫ ** ** Elephant Orphanage of Pinawela** is located just a few kilometres west of Kandy near Kegalla. Start no later than 8.30am so as not to miss the feeding of the young animals. The elephant bath in the river afterwards is also very enjoyable. It is even possible to participate in it. (Accommodation in Kandy)

Day 6:
Kandy –
Nuwara Eliya

Day six of the round trip sees an increase in altitude, namely to the »city above the clouds« as **⓬ ** **Nuwara Eliya** is also called. The difference in temperature is quite noticeable and the air becomes fresh and clear. The landscape, which is densely vegetated with tea bushes, is one of the most beautiful in Sri Lanka, but it is also one that is most intensively farmed. Of course visiting a **tea factory** is an obvious choice and there are several here to choose from. The town of Nureliya, as the name is pronounced by the locals, has some sites of its own and also places to go shopping. (Accommodation in Nuwara Eliya)

Day 7:
Nuwara Eliya –
Bandarawela

Taking a Jeep to the ⑬ ＊ ＊ **Horton Plains** is one of the best experiences nature-lovers can have. Needless to labour the point, but once again an early start is advisable. The place known as **World's End** is covered by shreds of mist in the late morning, making the otherwise magnificent view from the steep rock almost invisible.
The route then goes back to Nuwara Eliya, but carries on immediately to Bandarawela. En route are the well-known **Botanical Gardens of Hakgala**, which developed from a coffee plantation. There are some fabulous views of an impressive landscape to be had during the onward drive to Bandarawela. In good weather they extend all the way down to Sri Lanka's south coast. Near **Bandarawela**, a further centre of tea growing, there is the opportunity to visit the caves in Istripura, time permitting. (Accommodation in Bandarawela)

Day 8:
Bandarawela –
Hambantota

The route on this day goes back again to the lowlands, which is noticeable from the higher temperatures alone. ⑭**Hambantota** was a very lively fishing town on the southeast coast of Sri Lanka until the tsunami on 26 December 2004. The destruction caused by the gigantic wave is still visible in some places, but much has been rebuilt. Hambantota is seen by the government as a model for the reconstruction process. The harbour is being enlarged with Chinese money to take bigger ships, and is due for completion by 2011. The former royal capital of **Tissamaharama**, in which the kings created an impressive irrigation system, has been largely destroyed. Rebuilding works are still going on. (Accommodation in Hambantota)

Day 9:
Yala National
Park

A trip through ⑮ ＊ ＊ **Yala National Park** can be done in two ways: either with an early morning start or an afternoon start. There is not much of a difference because at both times there are many animals to be seen, including wild elephants, water buffalo, crocodiles and plenty of birds. Renting an off-road vehicle with a knowledgeable guide is a good idea. (Accommodation in Hambantota)

Day 10:
Hambantota –
Galle

The route now runs along the coastal road through several **fishing villages**, or what is left of them after the tsunami. In some places the reality of what occurred here is really depressing. Thousands of families were made homeless and several thousand people died, leaving orphans behind. However, the impressive amount of aid from around the world is at least giving the people temporary homes. It is worth taking a detour to the **Blow Hole**, a gap in the rock where sea-water is compressed, making it shoot up as if from a fountain. This experience is at its most impressive during the monsoon season, when the waves are higher than at other times of the year. The town of ⑯ **✳✳ Galle** already had a significant harbour many centuries ago, but it long ago had to hand over its status to Colombo. A stroll through the **Fort** (which was completely spared by the tsunami because of its exposed location, while the town itself was largely flooded) is well worthwhile. The Fort provides a good impression of the typical architecture of the Dutch colonial period. The still extant, massive **fortifications** are particularly impressive, although they were unable to prevent the British from taking the city in 1796. (Accommodation in Galle)

Day 11:
Galle –
Hikkaduwa

It only takes around three quarters of an hour to drive from Galle to ⑰ **✳ Hikkaduwa**. This seaside resort, which became world famous in the 1970s, is appealing not so much because of its sights as because of its excellent beaches and diving opportunities. Hikkaduwa is also a good base for excursions. This is a further reason for the recommendation to plan several nights here and spend the eleventh evening in one of the excellent fish restaurants, for example.

Shell seekers can often be seen on Sri Lanka's beaches, such as here in Galle

A further day on the beach would be a relaxing option but another possibility would be to take a trip to ⑱ ✳ **Ratnapura**. The **City of Gems** is worthy of its name, because this is where most of Sri Lanka's sapphires, rubies and other gemstones are found. The entire town lives off searching for or trading in these precious stones; there are naturally many inexpensive **places to buy them**. The **mines** can be viewed, but they are not a good place to buy because the dealers there can be very pushy! (Accommodation in Hikkaduwa)

Day 12 or 13: Ratnapura

The final day of this round trip is spent travelling along the south-west coast back to the starting point of Colombo. Do not miss out on a break in ⑲ ✳✳ **Ambalangoda**, the centre of mask carving. **Kalutara**, with its imposing dagoba right on the road is also worth a quick stop. Taking both of these stops into account, visitors should get to **Colombo** in the early afternoon.

Day 14: Hikkaduwa – Colombo

Tour 2 In Royal Footsteps

Start and Destination: Colombo   **Duration:** 8 days

This round trip takes in all the former royal cities in Sri Lanka, and many ancient sites of significance await the visitor. The attractions of scenic interest such as the Central Highlands should not be neglected either.

The round trip begins in ❶ ✳✳ **Colombo**. On the first day there is plenty of time to visit the city's attractions. One recommendation for the morning is a walk through the oriental, colourful and lively quarter of **Pettah**. The afternoon could, for example, be spent in the **National Museum** of Colombo. An alternative could be to walk through the quarter known as **Cinnamon Garden**, which could also be done after visiting the museum. (Accommodation in Colombo)

Day 1: Colombo

The drive for day 2 covers 210 km/130 mi, so it is best to start early. On the way there are several attractions, such as the scenically located temple of **Kelaniya**. Driving on via **Kurunegala** taking a detour to the rock fortress of **Yapahuwa** is worthwhile. It takes you back to the 13th century and is an attraction for its remote location in the jungle if for nothing else. There is not much time because the road to Anuradhapura, the destination for this day, is narrow and busy.
In the olden days ❷ ✳✳ **Anuradhapura** was the capital of Sri Lanka. Now it is a huge ruin that is still being uncovered with the financial support of UNESCO. There is plenty to be seen: after all, a total of 119 kings ruled here, of whom many left their architectural mark. One of them even had a nine-storey building erected. (Accommodation in Anuradhapura)

Day 2: Colombo – Anuradhapura

Day 3:
Anuradhapura –
Giritale

Leaving Anuradhapura the route continues to ❸✳✳ **Mihintale**, the »cradle of Buddhism« in Sri Lanka. The view from the platform on which the gleaming white dagoba rises is magnificent.

The afternoon is earmarked for visiting ❹✳✳ **Polonnaruwa**, the second capital of the Singhalese kingdom. The many ruins possess countless valuable details deserving of attention. Of course a visit to the world-famous rock sculptures in **Gal Vihara** are a must. The drive then continues in the evening to ❺ **Giritale**. (Accommodation in Giritale)

Day 4:
Giritale – Kandy

Getting an early start today is important because the day starts off with a visit to the unique ❻✳✳ **rock fortress of Sigiriya**. King Kassyapa had it built to escape the revenge of his half-brother (which did not do him any good because he inexplicably left the fortress to face the battle. This virtual suicide is one of the biggest unsolved mysteries of Singhalese history). Also not to be missed on any account are the »**cloud maidens of Sigiriya**«, and the well-known nearby ❼✳✳ **cave temples of Dambulla** . The main cave with its 66 statues of Buddha and the unique wall paintings from different centuries is particularly beautiful.

Carrying on to Kandy (the road runs through ever more lavish landscape into the higher parts of the island) there is the monastery of **Alu Vihara** (► Matale) and the town itself can also be visited. Anyone who has the time should definitely look in on these historically very interesting sites. The next accommodation stop is Kandy.

❽✳✳ **Kandy**, the city in which the last king of a Singhalese kingdom reigned (before he was forced to capitulate by the British in 1815), is rich in different kinds of attractions. The morning is best spent visiting the most important Buddhist temple in Sri Lanka, namely the **Temple of the Tooth**. It was severely damaged in 1998 when it was bombed by the Tamil Tigers, the militant Tamil organization, but it has since been rebuilt. The attack hit the Singhalese people at their core and cost the Tamils a lot of the sympathy their particular problems had once brought them.

An afternoon activity could be visiting the **Botanical Gardens of Peradeniya** (► Kandy). This magnificent park, which is surrounded on three sides by Sri Lanka's longest river, Mahaweli Ganga, has a wealth of plants and trees that will be particularly interesting to those who enjoy botany. (Accommodation in Kandy)

✓ **DON'T MISS**

- Yapahuwa: rock fortress in the middle of the jungle.
- Anuradhapura: 119 kings ruled here, now impressive ruins remain.
- Polonnaruwa: masterfully crafted statues of Buddha in Gal Vihara
- Sigiriya: the cloud maidens alone make this place worth visiting.

Day 6:
Kandy –
Nuwara Eliya

From Kandy it is around a three-quarter of an hour drive to Pinawela, a town that at first glance seems inconspicuous. However, it has

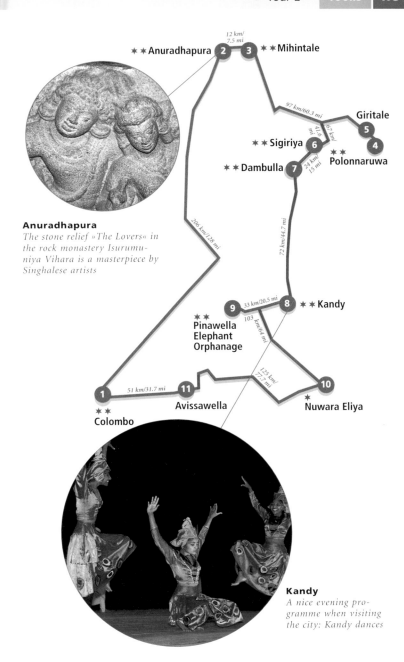

** Anuradhapura **2** **3** ** Mihintale

12 km/7.5 mi

97 km/60.3 mi   Giritale **5**

** Sigiriya **6**   67 km/   **4**
41.6 mi
** Dambulla **7**   24 km/15 mi   ** Polonnaruwa

206 km/128 mi

72 km/44.7 mi

9 33 km/20.5 mi **8** ** Kandy

** Pinawella Elephant Orphanage

103 km/64 mi

125 km/77.7 mi   **10**

1 51 km/31.7 mi **11**   ** Nuwara Eliya

** Colombo   Avissawella

Anuradhapura
The stone relief »The Lovers« in the rock monastery Isurumuniya Vihara is a masterpiece by Singhalese artists

Kandy
A nice evening pro-gramme when visiting the city: Kandy dances

an institution that is unique in the world, namely the **❾ ✳ ✳ Elephant Orphanage of Pinawela** (▶ Kegalla). It is unique because the state acts as the financial sponsor and pays for the upkeep of any elephant regardless of age, which, for whatever reason, requires special protection. The entrance fee only covers a fraction of the costs. It should be considered that a grown elephant requires around 250 kg/ 550 lbs of food a day and an elephant calf is raised with 60 litres (16 US gallons) of milk a day. The trip continues past tea plantations to **❿ ✳ Nuwara Eliya**, the highest town in Sri Lanka. That is the reason why it was so popular with the British, who ruled Sri Lanka for many years as a crown colony. The air here is clearer than in Colombo and the temperatures are nowhere near so high as they are in the lowlands. In the afternoon there should be enough time left to spot the traces of the British colonial rulers, which are still visible in many places. (Accommodation in Nuwara Eliya)

Day 7:
Nuwara Eliya –
Avissawella

Carrying on towards the west coast via the A 7 visitors will see many Tamil women working hard in their badly paid jobs as tea pickers on the vast **tea plantations**. Ignoring the turning to Hatton / Dikoya, a pretty double village in the midst of magnificent landscape, visitors will arrive at a place near **Kitulgala** (▶ Avissawella) that is particularly interesting to film fans. This is where part of the movie **The Bridge on the River Kwai** was filmed, since no suitable location was found in Thailand, where the actual bridge stood. There are two choices when it comes to accommodation: not far from the film location is a **guesthouse** and there is also accommodation in Avissawella.

Day 8:
Kitulgala or
Avissawella –
Colombo

If the second option is picked for the previous night's accommodation the drive to the ruins of the former **⓫ royal city of Sitavka** (▶ Avissawella) on the eighth and final day of this round trip is not too long. It is situated on a bend in the river of the same name and possessed Portuguese / Dutch fortifications. It is only another 60 km/ 35 mi to Colombo, the starting point of this round trip. The road to take is the A 4.

Tour 3 The Central Highlands

Start and Destination: Colombo	**Duration:** 4 or 5 days

The drive for this trip departs Colombo directly for the Central Highlands to the towns of Kandy and Nuwara Eliya. The focal point is less on visiting historically significant temple complexes and more on getting a good impression of the unique landscape of the island's interior.

Leave ❶ ✱ ✱ **Colombo** on the A 1 towards Kurunegala early in the morning. The first destination is ❷ **Kelaniya**. It is home to the remarkable temple of **Raja Maha Vihara**. The wall paintings in the older part to the right of the main temple are particularly interesting. They depict scenes from the Jataka, the tales that describe Buddha's previous lives. The trip continues onwards to ❸ **Ambepussa**. Although there are no particularly noteworthy sights here the landscape alone is interesting enough. **Kegalla**, one of the less significant capitals of the Singhalese kingdom, also reveals little of its former glory.

The actual attraction is a few kilometres to the north of Kegalla; it is the ❹ ✱ ✱ **Elephant Orphanage of Pinawela** (► Kegalla). Lucky visitors will be able to witness the baby elephants being fed, as there are always some calves around. Kandy is then reached in the evening. It was the final capital of the former kingdom. (Accommodation in Kandy)

Day 1:
Colombo – Kandy

✔ DON'T MISS

- Kelaniya: nice wall paintings and a magnificent Bodhi tree
- Kegalla: where elephant orphans are given a loving home
- Kandy: in search of nature? Find it in the Botanical Gardens of Peradeniya!
- Kandy: one tooth draws in thousands of pilgrims
- Nuwara Eliya: cooling off in the mountains
- Ratnapura: the place to look for gemstones.

Reserve the morning for visiting the ❺ ✱ ✱ **Temple of the Tooth** in ► Kandy. Thousands of believers assemble in front of the most significant temple of Buddhism every day to worship the Buddha relic.

Leave Kandy via the A 1 southwestbound, passing through Peradeniya with its famous **Botanical Gardens** (► Kandy). Only plan a short visit to the gardens.

Leave Peradeniya via the A 1 and carry on southbound on the A 5. Passing Gampola, the Sacred City on the River (i.e. the Siripura Ganga, on which the lovely town stands) the road has already reached the **Central Highlands**. This region is known for the cultivation of the best tea on the island. A short stop at the ❻ **Ramboda Falls** should be seized upon to enjoy the unique landscape. From here it is not far to ❼ ✱ **Nuwara Eliya**, the »town in the clouds«, the destination for the second day. (Accommodation in Nuwara Eliya)

Day 2:
Kandy –
Nuwara Eliya

The drive on day 3 is around 150 km/90 mi. It departs Nuwara Eliya on the A 5 eastbound, then, at Wellmade, it carries on southbound. Near Haputale the road turns west again and passes the ❽ ✱ ✱ **Horton Plains**. At first glance from the valley this landscape is not much different from that of the rest of the Central Highlands. However, the plateau on which the Horton Plains are located forms an interesting change to everything else around. Nature lovers and hikers may want to plan an extra day here. It is wise, however, to find accommodation in Ratnapura, since there is none in the area which can be recommended (the round trip in this case would also be extended by a

Day 3:
Nuwara Eliya –
Ratnapura

Kelaniya
The stone dwarfs at Raja Maha Vihara are dancing

day). Ratnapura is reached in the evening, which is the centre of prospecting for and trading in gemstones. (Accommodation in Ratnapura)

Day 4 or day 5:
Ratnapura –
Colombo

For those who choose to drive back from Ratnapura to visit the Horton Plains this tour will be extended by a day. In this case it is also a good idea to stay an extra night in Ratnapura.

It is only around 100 km/60 mi from Ratnapura to Colombo so there is plenty of time to take it easy on this day. One option would be to visit the gemstone museum in ⑨ ✶ **Ratnapura**, which is definitely worthwhile. During the drive back to Colombo the changing landscape from the lush green of the mountains to the dry areas of the west coast is very striking.

Tour 4 Combination with Tour 3

Duration: 4 or 5 additional days

This round trip is based on tour 3 described above for the first two days, but it also offers the chance to get to know the fauna of Sri Lanka in the famous Yala National Park.

Instead of driving from ❶ ✳ **Nuwara Eliya** towards Ratnapura take the A 5 to ❷ **Badulla**. The ❸ **Dunhinda Falls** deserve a brief visit before driving southbound via the A 5 and then the A 16 to Ella. Visiting the **rock sculptures of Buduruvagala** (► Ella), at the centre of which is a 15 m/50 ft statue of Buddha carved from the rock; it is not to be missed. It was created either in the 4th century or, according to other sources, not until 500 years later. Leaving Ella the trip carries on via the A 23, which turns into the A 2 that goes to ❹ **Tissamaharama** not far from Sri Lanka's southeast coast. (Accommodation in Tissamaharama)

Day 3:
Nuwara Eliya –
Tissamaharama

Not far from Tissamaharama is ❺ ✳ ✳ **Yala National Park**. It offers a good insight into Sri Lanka's diverse fauna. It is a good idea to start a trip to Yala National Park as early as possible, since the animals retreat to the cover of the bushes during the heat of the day. If Yala National Park is reached by 9am the probability of seeing even leopards in the large area is high. In addition the park is home to countless wild elephants, birds and reptiles.
The afternoon can be used for visiting the **Maha Devala** in ► Kataragama. This temple seems to have survived the times unchanged. (Accommodation in Tissamaharama)

Day 2:
excursion

The road from Tissamaharama to Galle runs along the south coast almost all the time, through the **fishing villages** and small towns that were largely destroyed by the tsunami, where the odd worthwhile market is beginning to appear again.
The ❻ ✳ ✳ **Blow Hole** is situated near Tagalle; it is a gap in the rock through which the sea water is compressed and pushed up into the air like water in a fountain.

Day 3:
Tissamaharama –
Galle

In the western part of Yala National Park there are countless birds

Nuwara Eliya
The Ramboda Falls near Nuwara Eliya plummet 100m/330ft

* Nuwara Eliya **1** — 55 km/34.2 mi — **2** Badulla

21 km/13 mi

3 * Ella

** Yala National Pa▶

182 km/113 mi

5

38 km/23.6 mi

Tissamaharama **4**

* Hikkaduwa

10

** Galle

9 — 45 km/28 mi — **8** — 7 km/4.3 mi — **7** — 20 km/12.4 mi — **6** ** Blow Hole

21 km/13 mi

79 km/49 mi

** Matara   Dondra Head

Galle
Galle was a significant port on Sri Lanka. The lighthouse once showed ships the way.

7 ✳ ✳ **Matara**, the day's next destination, is still known for its pleasant **beaches** even after the tsunami. They can be seen even before reaching the town. **8** **Dondra Head** is Sri Lanka's southernmost point. It is marked by a 64 m/210 ft **lighthouse**.

From Matara it is only a few miles to **9** ✳ ✳ **Galle**. Assuming that this city, which was so significant during the Portuguese and Dutch times, is reached in the afternoon, a pleasant option would be to stroll through the **Fort** district. The witnesses to colonial architecture, such as some of the churches as well as the largely excellently preserved fortifications, are impressive. (Accommodation in Galle)

Along the southwest coast the A 2 makes its way to the lively tourist town of **10** ✳ **Hikkaduwa**. It is only a few miles, so there is time to stop and relax on one of the **magnificent beaches** on the way.

From Hikkaduwa to Colombo it is another 100 km/60 mi. Given the time it is a good idea to find **accommodation in Hikkaduwa** or else in Bentota in order to be away from the noisy bustle of the city. This is also true for those who have booked (or want to book) a room in a hotel in Negombo north of Colombo for their remaining time in Sri Lanka. The drive from Hikkaduwa or Bentota to Negombo goes through Colombo, and so it will take up at least half a day.

**Day 4:
Hikkaduwa –
Colombo**

Sights from A to Z

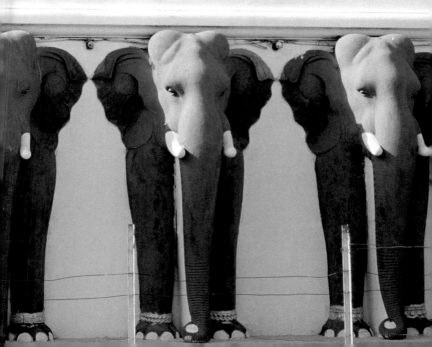

JUNGLE LANDSCAPES, TEA PLANTATIONS IN THE MOUNTAINS AND DREAM BEACHES AREN'T ALL THAT SRI LANKA HAS TO OFFER. AN ANCIENT CULTURE HAS ALSO LEFT ITS TRACES.

★ ★ Adam's Peak (Sri Pada)

B 8

| Province: Sabaragamuwa | Height at summit : 2243 m/7359ft |

Although Adam's Peak is only the fifth-highest mountain in Sri Lanka, it's regarded as the island's most important. Not only for Hindus, Buddhists and Muslims, but also for the country's Christian population, it is *the* place for pilgrims; for nature-lovers standing on its summit and watching the sun rise is an unforgettable experience.

Adam wept for 1000 years

The mountain probably owes its present name as a result of a tradition attributed to the Arab explorer lbn Battuta (▶Famous People). In one of his numerous travel accounts, he describes a holy mountain called Al Rohun, on which, following his expulsion from Paradise, Adam first set foot on earth and is said to have bemoaned his fate for no less than 1000 years. There is also a passage in the account of the Venetian explorer Marco Polo, who visited Sri Lanka in the 13th century, where he suggests that Adam lies buried on the mountain. While it is mainly Muslims who have adopted this tradition,

Although Adam's Peak is only the fifth-highest mountain in Sri Lanka, it is the most significant from a spiritual perspective. Buddha is said to have left a footprint here

▶ VISITING ADAM´S PEAK

GETTING THERE

By car:
from Colombo to Dalhousie via the A 4 to Avissawella, from there via the A 7 to Hatton
(app. 154km/95mi)

By train:
from Colombo to Kandy, from where there are daily connections to Hatton. From Hatton take a bus or taxi.

By bus:
no regular bus services to Dalhousie, only pilgrim buses

Alternative: from Colombo there are several connections each day to Maskeliya (journey takes app. six hours), from there take a taxi.

WHERE TO STAY

▶ **Budget**
In Dalhousie there are a number of guest houses and pilgrim hostels (e.g. the White House, open Dec – May). They are plain and simple but very cheap.

some of Sri Lanka's Christians base their belief in the significance of the mountain on it. Others however say that St Thomas, one of the apostles, climbed the mountain during his missions to India and Persia and left a footprint on the summit.

Buddhists and Hindus alike regard Adam's Peak as a holy site, in their case as the mountain of the god Saman, one of the four guardian deities. But for Buddhists the holiness resides first and foremost in **Buddha's footprint** (Sri Pada), a depression 1.6m/5ft 3in long and 75cm/2ft 6in wide, which the Buddha is said to have left on one of his three visits to Sri Lanka. The footprint is supposed to have been discovered by King Valagam Bahu in the 1st century AD. But Hindus too regard this depression as sacred, seeing in it a **footprint of their god Shiva**. They call Adam's Peak Shivanadi-padam. But ultimately they also give credence to the Buddhist interpretation, for in their eyes Buddha is an incarnation of the god Shiva.

A mountain for every faith

Climbing Adam's Peak

Of the two routes leading to Adam's Peak, the longer one winds its way up from the south, i.e. from the direction of Dalhousie. The other begins on the northern side near Maskeliya.

Two routes

Whichever way is chosen, **two days** should be allowed for the ascent. The path leading to the summit is some 6.5 km/4mi in length, includes about 5,200 steps, and is extremely strenuous; especially in the hot and tropically humid season, you need to be physically fit. Good equipment (stout shoes or boots, drinking-water supply and warm clothing) is a must. At a comfortable rate of progress, the climb takes between three and four hours.

When starting out from Dalhousie, the first day should be devoted to getting there. Stay in one of the simple hostels or in the nearby town of Dikoya (►Hatton · Dikoya). The actual climb to the summit should be started around midnight, in order to not to miss the fascinating sight of the sunrise. The route from the tea plantation in Dalhousie leads to the top of the mountain entirely via steps, so that no additional signposting is necessary. There are tea-houses along the way serving hot drinks.

On the summit On the summit is a platform about 300 sq m/360 sq yd in area, on which the footprint (evidently of a left foot), with a wall around it, is enclosed within a small temple. In the 12th century King Parakrama Bahu I had a first temple erected on the summit of Adam's Peak, dedicated to the Hindu god Saman. Later it was occupied by Buddhist monks, until King Raja Sinha I, who had converted to Brahmanism restored it to the Brahmins in the 16th century. It was only two centuries later, under King Kirti Sri, who brought Buddhism back to Sri Lanka, that Buddhist monks moved in once more. The Brahmin priests were however not expelled; they built themselves a smaller temple which is still extant. None of the other buildings are particularly interesting; they are all fairly recent.

> **!** **Baedeker TIP**
>
> **Not only at weekends!**
> If you want to climb Adam's Peak, you should choose a weekday. At weekends there are sometimes queues on the path to the summit that may be kilometres in length, and guest houses are likely to be full.

The **bells** which visitors can strike on reaching the summit have a symbolic significance for pilgrims: on their first ascent, they are permitted to strike one of them once, on their second visit twice, and so on.

Following the sunrise, which is celebrated by the faithful with wild cheering, there is a splendid panoramic view from the summit (in good weather) extending across the highlands as far as Colombo.

✶✶ Ambalangoda

B 9

Region: Southwest coast	**Province:** Southern
Altitude : 5 m/16 ft	**Population:** app. 60,000

This little town occupies a splendid location on the south-west coast of the island and has a swimming-pool made of rocks. Those seeking refuge from the crowds of tourists in Bentota or Hikkaduwa and looking for contact with the locals will like it here. Ambalangoda was severely affected by the tsunami.

Things to see in Ambalangoda

Ambalangoda is the home of Singhalese mask carving. Numerous workshops still produce masks based on traditional motifs, some of them thousands of years old. They are used for the various forms of Singhalese dance. The magnificent, colourful Kolam masks are carved for the popular dance theatre. Sanui (or Thovil) masks are used when exorcizing demons. Only three sorts of wood are permitted: sandalwood, kadura (a kind of mangrove) and the wood of the strychnine tree (nux vomica).

✳ ✳
Carved masks

Ambalangoda is the birthplace and home of the famous Wijesooriya mask-carving family, who have been practising this craft for generations. They run a small museum in the home of Wijesooriya's grandson, Ariyapala Gurunnanse. Here the history of the art of mask-carving and the significance of the various kinds of mask is explained in a lively and informative fashion. There is also a workshop in the building; a **brochure** is available at a small charge (426 Patabendimulla; opening times: daily 8am – 5pm; admission free).

Mask Museum

Also in the centre of town is the Dance School, where from time to time original lowland dances and sometimes Kandy dances too are performed.

Dance School

The mask carvers of Ambalangoda have been masters of their craft for centuries

▸ VISITING AMBALANGODA

GETTING THERE

By car:
From Colombo (85 km/53mi), Bento-
ta (28 km/17mi), Hikkaduwa (13 km/
8mi) and Galle (35 km/22mi) via the
A 2
By train:
Ambalangoda is a station on the route
Colombo – Matara
By bus:
there are regular bus services from the
above-named places.

WHERE TO STAY / ESSEN

▸ Mid-range

Sri Lanka Ayurveda Garden
95B Sea Beach Road
Patabendimulla, Ambalangoda
Tel. / Fax 0 91 / 2 25 98 88
Buchung in Deutschland:
Tel. 060 82 / 92 80 80
Fax 060 82 / 92 86 39
www.ayurveda-garden.de (with rea-
sonable English translation)
9 rooms and 1 apartment house
Nicely situated traditional hotel with a
cosy atmosphere.
Has its own Ayurveda herb-garden

Triton Hotel
Ahungalla
Tel. 09 / 640 41-4
Fax 09 / 640 46
www.aitkenspenceholidays.com
160 rooms, restaurant with local and
international cuisine, bar, pool, all
kinds of water-sports
Not for from Ambalangoda, the town
of the mask-carvers, this hotel is
situated not only on the sea-front but
on one of Sri Lanka's finest beaches.
All-inclusive bookings are possible,
and that means (almost) what it says.

▸ Budget

Piya Nivasa Guesthouse
Galle Road, Akurala
(5 km/3mi outside Ambalangoda)
Tel. 09 / 12 25 81 46
6 rooms
Simple guesthouse in the colonial style
with clean rooms.

The rooms in Sri Lanka Ayurveda Garden are furnished in the colonial style

5km/3mi from Ambalangoda in the direction of Hikkaduwa is Galagoda Temple, which houses Sri Lanka's longest recumbent Buddha statue, measuring 50 m/165ft.

Galagoda Temple

At the southern exit to the town there is also one of the largest temples in Sri Lanka, the Sunandaramaya Mahavihara. A noteworthy feature is the arch over the entrance, which not only displays Hindu elements, but also murals dating from the 18th/19th centuries depicting scenes from the Buddha's previous lives.

Sunandaramaya Mahavihara

✱ Ampara

E 7

Region: Southern section of the east coast
Altitude: app. 25 m/270ft

Province: Eastern

Population: app. 60,000

Ampara, the provincial capital, will be encountered by visitors exploring the Gal-Oya National Park and by those who have chosen the broad, quiet beaches of the east coast for a holiday. The town is largely inhabited by Muslims.

Here, as throughout the province, the tsunami caused huge damage; more than 10,000 people, about one third of the population, were killed. Reconstruction is under way, but it will be many years before Ampara is fully restored. Not far away one of five SOS Children's Villages was established, providing a home for traumatized children.

Tsunami damage

The town in the Gal-Oya valley was founded as long ago as the 10th century, but almost nothing has been preserved from this period or the following centuries. What little there is can be seen in the small archaeological museum.

Practically no historic remains

Ampara is the centre of the Gal Oya Development Scheme, the largest such project on the island. It was started in 1950. One result is the Senanayake Samudra, a **reservoir** covering 77sq km/30sq mi, forming the central feature of the Gal-Oya National Park. Exploration of this very attractive landscape generally starts from Juginiyagala, a town at the eastern end of the reservoir, about 16km/10mi from Ampara, to which it is linked by a good road.

Development project

Surroundings of Ampara

Near Digayapi, some 10 km/6mi east of Ampara between the town of Trakkamam and the coast, the ruins of a Buddhist temple were uncovered in the 1980s. It had been erected on a spot which according to legend had been visited by the Buddha in person.

Buddhist temple

▶ VISITING AMPARA

GETTING THERE

By car:
From Colombo there are two routes:
via Kandy – Mahiyangana – Maha Oya
(app. 270 km/170mi) or via Ratnapura
– Wellawya – Siyambalanduwa (app.
300 km/190mi). The former route is

recommended, as it leads through very
attractive mountain scenery.

WHERE TO STAY
In Ampara there are some reasonable
places, e.g. Monty's Guesthouse.

✳
**Hamangala
Caves/
Malayadi Temple**

The Hamangala Caves, some 20 km/12mi from Ampara, were inhabited very long ago by, among others, the Vedda. Some of the
caves contain inscriptions, while one has **ancient wall-paintings** by
them. The caves are accessible by driving north-west along the A 27,
turning left between the 8th and 9th milestones, taking the road as
far as Bandaraduwa, and then another 6 km/4mi or so along a jungle
track.
The Malayadi Temple , also known as the Raja Maha Vihara, consists
of several once inhabited caves, in one of which there are also Vedda
murals.

✳✳ Anuradhapura

B 5

Province: North Central
Population: 56,000

Altitude : app. 90 m/300ft

**Anuradhapura, one of the oldest and most interesting cities in Sri
Lanka, lies in the island's Dry Zone. The present-day town of Anuradhapura consists of an area of ruins plus a new centre, which
dates from the 20th century. The ruins of Anuradhapura have been
declared a World Heritage Site by UNESCO.**

**City of the
90 kings?**

The name of the town, Anuradhapura, used to be derived from the
Singhalese word anuva, which means ninety, and this was seen as an
allusion to the city of the 90 kings. However, since there were actually 119 kings who ruled from Anuradhapura, this derivation is
probably mistaken. It is more likely that the name of the town goes
back to an aristocratic family by the name of Anuradha. According
to other sources, the town was named after the star Anuradha, which
embodies the god of light in Indian astrology.

Royal capital

Anuradhapura, today an imposing ruin, was the capital of no fewer
than 119 kings across 13 centuries. While they were not always un-

disturbed in their possession, it was nevertheless one of the most important capitals of the Singhalese kingdom. It was here, (and in ► Mihintale) that the first Buddhist shrines were erected, and here too that a classical artistic style developed. Permeated by the Buddhist idea, the buildings bear witness to the high degree of self-assurance felt by the young kingdom. The literary and religious culture centred on the monasteries and royal palace.

While the town-planning looks modern, it dates from app. 500 BC. Three reservoirs (wewa in Singhalese) constructed in the 1st century BC and a **sophisticated canal system** allowed the very dry land to be irrigated while at the same time providing drinking water for the inhabitants, who in the city's heyday must have numbered several hundred thousand.

Modern town-planning

In about 380 BC the settlement of Anuradhagama (gama = settlement) was raised by King Pandukabhaya to the status of capital of

Anuradhapura was Sri Lanka's first capital and is venerated by the locals as a sacred place because of its bodhi tree

▶ VISITING ANURADHAPURA

GETTING THERE

By car:
from Kandy via the A 9 (138 km/90mi); from Puttalam via the A 12 (app. 70 km/45mi); from Polonnaruwa via the A 11 (app. 97 km/60mi)

By train:
Anuradhapura is a station on the line from Colombo to Jaffna

By bus: regular services from the above-named cities

WHERE TO STAY / WHERE TO EAT

▶ Mid-range

① *The Village*
Habarana
Tel. 066 / 2 27 00 47
Fax 066 / 2 27 00 46
www.johnkeellshotels.com
106 cottages, restaurant, bar, pool
Ideally situated hotel about halfway between Anuradhapura and Polonnaruwa with very comfortable rooms in the cottage style.

▶ Mid-rangeKomfortabel

② *Tissawewa Rest House*
Old Town, Anuradhapura
Tel. / Fax 025 / 2 22 22 99
20 rooms. This pretty rest house in the colonial style stands in the middle of a tropical garden not far from the ancient ruins of Anuradhapura. The rooms are very tastefully furnished. The veranda with a view of the garden is also a bar and in the evening after supper in the in-house restaurant it is a popular rendezvous for guests.

③ *Palm Garden Village*
Puttalam Road, Pandulegema
Tel. 025 / 51 32
Fax 025 / 32 48
www.palmgardenvillage.com
50 rooms, restaurant, bar, shopping arcade, large pool
The rooms (including 10 suites) are in small houses in an extensive and attractively laid-out complex.

the Singhalese kingdom. He called it Anuradhapura (pura = town, city). The actual history of the city, however, only started with the reign of King Devanampiya Tissa (250–210 BC), who adopted and supported the doctrine of Buddhism as preached by the monk Mahinda. It was during this period that the first substantial building activity took place, though the first buildings consisted of simple dwellings for the populace and the ruler, while those in honour of Buddha were more monumental. In 993 came the first disruption in the city's development, when it was occupied by the Chola invaders from southern India. However they also attacked the city of ▶Polonnaruwa, less than 100km/60mi away, which they made their capital, and it was from here that Anuradhapura was administered in the following period. In 1070 the former Prince of Ruhuna, King Vijaya Bahu I of Polonnaruwa, which he had already recaptured 15 years earlier, succeeded in snatching Anuradhapura too back from the Cholas. As Polonnaruwa occupied a more strategic location, though, he retained it as his capital, and confined the reconstruction of Anuradhapura to the restoration of the largely destroyed irrigation system and some Buddhist shrines.

Anuradhapura then fell into a Sleeping Beauty-like slumber and over the centuries became overgrown by the surrounding jungle. Until the beginning of the 19th century, all that was known of it was that a British civil servant, Ralph Backhaus, who came here by chance, gave an enthusiastic account of a magnificent ruined city in the north of the island. In about 1820 the British archaeologist H. P. Bell decided that these reports were worth investigating and discovered the city. It was 1890, however, before excavations began.
In 1980 UNESCO put the ruins under its protection, and since then the excavations (by no means complete) have been financially supported by the organization.

A sleeping beauty

> ### ! Baedeker TIP
>
> **By bicycle or with a driver**
> The ruined city covers some 50 sq km/20sq mi, making it not only very extensive, but also difficult to take in, as excavations are still going on in many places. Bicycles can be hired from hotels or at the entrance. Or else it's possible to hire a driver, who will also know something about the history of the sights.

Tour of the ruins

We recommend the Tissa Wewa Resthouse on New Road as the starting point for the sightseeing tour recommended here. It was built by a British governor as a summer residence and is surrounded by an attractively laid-out park. The building reflects the charm of the former colonial style. The reservoir which gave its name to the house was created by King Devanampiya Tissa in the 3rd century BC. The town of Anuradhapura still gets much of its drinking-water from here.

Starting point

To the right of New Road are the remains of the Mirisavati Dagoba, which King Duttha Gamani commissioned in about 100 BC in the place where he had once planted his spear and the royal standard in the ground. When he tried to pull the spear out again, he couldn't, and so ordered the dagoba to be built around it. The spear, it must be said, had a particular significance for the king: he had acquired it during a victorious battle with the Tamil king Elara (158 BC), and its shaft was said to contain a relic of the Buddha. Both the spear and the standard are still said to be in the shrine in the interior of the dagoba. The Mirisavati Dagoba was **once one of the largest dagobas**

Mirisavati Dagoba

✔ **DON'T MISS**

- Archaeological Museum: valuable finds
- Sri Maha Bodhi: oldest tree in the world
- Bronze Palace: the most imposing ruin in the city
- On the Queen's Pavilion: the most beautiful moonstone in Sri Lanka
- In the Rock Monastery: unique elephant relief

in Sri Lanka. When it was renovated in around 930 on the orders of King Kassyapa V, its height is said to have been reduced.

Of the surrounding monastic buildings, a few foundations and rows of columns still remain. Also still extant is a 3m/10ft-long stone trough in the refectory, where the faithful would place their daily offerings of food for the monks.

Basawak Kulam, Bulan Kulam

New Road leads to the banks of the Basawak Kulam Tank, an artificial lake, which, like the adjacent Bulan Kulam, is said to date from the period when Anuradhapura was founded.

Archaeological Museum

Along Arippu Road, turn right for the Archaeological Museum. Alongside a few dagoba models the collection includes several valuable Buddha statues, sculptures and frescoes as well as stone inscriptions. Particularly noteworthy are the **bronze statues** of Hindu deities, some of them of outstanding execution. The upper storey is devoted to craft objects, including some in ivory, and Chinese porcelain. The outdoor section of the museum includes urinating-stones decorated with reliefs; these originally stood in the forest monasteries to the west of Anuradhapura (opening times: daily 8am – 5pm, closed Tue and Fri, admission charge).

The world's oldest tree

Not far from the museum is the Sri Maha Bodhi, allegedly the world's oldest tree. It is said to have grown from a twig cut from the Indian bodhi tree (*Ficus religiosa*), beneath which Siddharta Gautama found enlightenment. After coming to Sri Lanka, legend has it that it was planted here in 230 BC by Sanghamitta, the sister of the Indian missionary Mahinda. The tree, which today because of its size has to be propped up, is the **destination of countless pilgrims** from the whole Buddhist world every day; they venerate it by making offerings (blossoms, incense sticks etc.). The bodhi tree is surrounded by a high wall erected in the 18th century, so that it is almost impossible to get any real idea of its actual size. The white façade of the entrance gate is decorated with numerous reliefs of Buddhist and Hindu deities and with floral elements. Before entering the sacred area, take a look at the finely carved moonstone flanked by the obligatory guardian steles. In the interior courtyard is a hall for devotions, surrounded by a number of shrines with statues of the Buddha. The terrace on which the bodhi tree stands was restored under Kirti Sri Raja Sinha, the last king of Kandy, in about 1800.

Lohapasada (bronze palace)

Among the most imposing ruins of Anuradhapura are the 1600 columns erected in rows of 40 which formerly bore the Lohapasada set

Anuradhapura Map

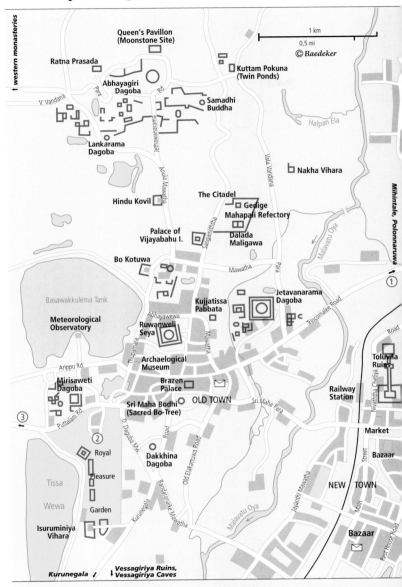

Queen's Pavillon
(Moonstone Site)

Ratna Prasada

Abhayagiri
Dagoba

V. Vandana

Lankarama
Dagoba

Kuttam Pokuna
(Twin Ponds)

© Baedeker

1 km

0,5 mi

Samadhi
Buddha

Halpan Ela

Nakha Vihara

Hindu Kovil

The Citadel

Gedige
Mahapali Refectory

Palace of
Vijayabahu I.

Dalada
Maligawa

Bo Kotuwa

Mawatha

Basawakkulema Tank

Kujjatissa
Pabbata

Jetavanarama
Dagoba

Meteorological
Observatory

Ruwanweli
Seya

Aripu Rd.

Archaeological
Museum

Mirisaweti
Dagoba

Brazen
Palace

OLD TOWN

Sri Maha Para

Railway
Station

Puttalam Rd.

Sri Maha Bodhi
(Sacred Bo-Tree)

Market

Royal

Bazaar

Tissa

Pleasure

Dakkhina
Dagoba

NEW TOWN

Wewa

Garden

Isuruminiya
Vihara

Bazaar

Kurunegala ✓

Vessagiriya Ruins,
↓ **Vessagiriya Caves**

Mihintale, Polonnaruwa

Toluvila
Ruins

Where to stay
① The Village

② Tissawewa Rest House
③ Palm Garden Village

up under King Duttha Gamani (161 – 137 BC). This was probably a nine-storey structure containing **more than 1000 rooms**, a masterpiece of Singhalese architecture at the time. Over the years it was destroyed and rebuilt on a number of occasions, most recently under King Parakrama Bahu I (AD 1153 – 1186). The first building is said to have been destroyed by fire just 15 years after its completion. According to tradition, there were only two similar buildings in the world: there is another in Bangkok. The Lohapasada probably got its name from a bronze roof, but the façades are also said to have been clad in copper plates. If the Mahavamsa chronicle is to be believed, the roof ridge and eaves were set with precious stones, silver ornaments and quartz crystals. In the great audience hall on the ground floor there was a richly carved throne, around which a thousand monks could gather. They lived in the palace, which was actually, then, a residential monastic building, in accordance with a certain order of rank: the simple monks lived in the lower storeys, the old monks and those regarded as holy on the upper floors.

> **? DID YOU KNOW …?**
>
> ■ …that the shape of the dagobas in Sri Lanka is supposed to go back to Buddha? When his disciples asked what they should build in his honour after his death, he replied »Build heaps of sand, like the rice that everyone needs.«

Ruwanweli Dagoba The Lohapasada also includes the Ruwanweli Dagoba, which was likewise erected during the reign of King Duttha Gamani in thanks for the victory over the Tamil king Elara. Maybe, though, he also had it built as a sign of his personal remorse for the war, which cost many thousands of lives.

The dagoba is the oldest of the monumental structures of this kind in Sri Lanka, measuring to no less than 90m/295ft to the tip of its golden pinnacle (which is said to have been a gift from Burma), and 91m/298ft in diameter at its base. Its shape was due to a desire of the king that the architect should build the dagoba so that it would look like a **a drop falling on to water** (in the succeeding period, more of these drop-shaped dagobas were constructed). The king himself is said not to have lived to see the completion of the dagoba. On his death-bed, though, his son covered the incomplete sections with cloth, in order to do his father one last favour.

The terrace of the dagoba is surrounded by a wall decorated on its outer surface by 338 stucco elephants. Today, though, the original sculptural quality can only be made out with difficulty, as the sculptures have been restored several times over the centuries. It is striking that the elephants are all different.

All four access routes lead across the square terrace to the altar, which is built against the side of the dagoba and is itself decorated with noteworthy **elephant friezes**. In the northern part of the terrace it is worth sparing a moment for the stones, some of them orna-

The original drip shape of the Ruwanweli Dagoba was changed in favour of the bell shape in 1893

mented with attractive **reliefs**, which have come to light during the excavations. Their original locations are not yet known with any certainty.

Leaving the dagoba area to the west, you will see a very attractive ancient bathing pool, with carefully carved stone steps leading down into it.

Thuparama-Dagoba further to the north is the oldest dagoba in Sri Lanka. King Devanampiya Tissa had it built in the 3rd century BC. It was intended to house a sacred relic, a splinter of Buddha's collar bone, a gift from King Ashoka. Whether it ever did, is lost in the mists of history. The dagoba was also once in the »heap of rice« form, but numerous restorations gave it its present bell-like appearance. The base was constructed of four blocks of gneiss, while the pillars surrounding the dagoba in for concentric circles date from the 1st century AD and once supported a round timber roof. It is thought that this structure may have been the first vatadage in Sri Lanka; they became more frequent from the 7th century on. The road leading northwards from this dagoba is lined on the right by a few small dagobas, and on the left by the ruins of a Hindu temple.

Thuparama Dagoba

Lankarama Dagoba The road now branches: the left-hand fork leads to the ruins of the smaller Lankarama Dagoba built in the reign of King Vattagamani in the 1st century BC. The pillars, whose capitals are decorated with reliefs, probably once supported a roof. To the left of the entrance is a stone slab with an attractive lion relief.

Ratna Prasada (Jewel Palace) Beneath the ruins, mainly huge stone pillars, of the Ratna Prasada, a 2nd-century building probably once belonging to the Abhayagiri monastery, there is what is **probably the most beautiful guardian stele in Sri Lanka**. It dates from the 8th and 9th centuries, .and is entirely in the classical style. 1.38m/4ft 6in in height, the stele depicts the snake king Naga with a pointed hood protected by the seven-headed Naga. In one hand he holds the Purnagheta, the vase of abundance, brimming over with magnificent lotus blossoms, in the other a blossoming lotus stalk: both are symbols of purity. On a pillar to the side kneels a guardian elephant.

Moonstone on the Queen's Pavilion The Queen's Pavilion was built at the end of the 3rd century and is famous for the most beautiful moonstone in Sri Lanka. As it was damaged several times in the past, it has been enclosed by an iron fence intended to prevent people stepping over the stone, which is supposed to symbolize the transition from the material to the spiritual world. Of the pavilion itself, though, nothing remains but a few stone pillars and surrounding walls.

Abhayagiri Dagoba Measuring 115m/377ft overall, Abhayagiri Dagoba is the second-highest in Sri Lanka. It was erected during the reign of King Vattagamani Abhaya at the end of the 1st century BC. Later, in the 3rd century AD, it became the centre of the Mahayana sect. Over the years it has become overgrown with grass, but is currently being restored.

Samadhi Buddha One of the most famous Buddha statues in Sri Lanka is the 2m/6ft 6in tall Samadhi Buddha, a stone sculpture dating from the 4th century. The artist has succeeded in using a minimum of means to achieve a maximum of expression. The face shows transcendental calm and the highest degree of internalization in equal measure (the nose however has had to be reconstructed, as it had been shattered). There is now no trace of the original paint. There is a roof to protect the statue from the weather, but at certain times of the day it prevents the fascinating effects of the sunlight; the statue comes across best in the early morning.

Kuttam Pokuna (pools) Round about the 7th century, the two classically beautiful Kuttam Pokuna cisterns formed the bathing facilities of a monastery that

The pools were used for cleaning the body as well as for ritual bathing

presumably stood where today the ruins known as the Kaparama are to be found. A Buddhist university was possibly also attached to the monastery. The pools measure 42m/138ft x 17m/56ft and 30m/ 98ft x 17m/56ft respectively, and the water for them is brought here by a 6km/4mi subterranean pipe; it flows through a filter complex first into the larger and then into the smaller pool. Considering when this pipe, which was only discovered a few years ago, was designed and constructed, it can only be described as a really extraordinary engineering achievement.

Both pools are clad with carefully shaped granite blocks arranged stepwise, the edges being decorated with a few reliefs (including a very beautiful Naga stone). The monks would have taken their baths not just to keep clean, but also for religious reasons.

Following the road southwards, we come to the ruins of the Dalada **Dalada Maligawa** Maligawa, the Temple of the Tooth, which was built under King Siri-meghavana in the 4th century. It is said to have housed the tooth relic of the Buddha when it first arrived in Sri Lanka in AD 313; it is now in ▶Kandy). This at least is the import of an inscription found in the ruin.

With a height of 122m/400ft, Jetavanarama Dagoba was once the **Jetavanarama** tallest building of its kind in Anuradhapura, but today it is only **Dagoba** about 75m/246ft tall and was covered in dense greenery. It was built at the beginning of the 4th century in the reign of King Mahasena, who preferred the doctrine of Mahayana Buddhism, to which the Jetavana school belongs, to the austere teaching of Hinayana Buddhism. This was, incidentally, the only period in which Mahayana Buddhism played any major role in Sri Lanka. Restoration work on the dagoba has been under way for several years.

Ranamasu Uyana (Royal Gardens)   The Royal Gardens (also known as the »Park of the Golden Fish«) are situated close to the Tissa Wewa, but were formerly much more extensive than they are today. It included artificial waterways, small lakes, bridges, pavilions and bathing facilities. The gardens were laid out as early as the 1st century BC and constantly enlarged thereafter. **The two well preserved baths are among the finest examples of rock-building.**; the more northerly, whose basin was largely carved out of the rock, is the older of the two. It got its water via a canal from the Tissa Wewa. A noteworthy feature is the low-relief elephant frieze carved directly into the rock.

Isurumuniya Vihara (rock monastery)   The rock monastery of Isurumuniya Vihara is worth a visit if only for its unique reliefs, but its picturesque location on the Tissa Wewa is also noteworthy. The conical and spherical rocks are integrated into what used to be a more extensive complex, dating from the 3rd century, while the temple is even built into the cliff. All the buildings visible today are later in date, however; all that is left from the original period being the hermit's cave in the centre of the cliff.

The baths on the right hand side, which belonged to the monastery, are edged by coarsely fitting blocks of stone; the steps are of the same material. On the cliffs to either side of a deep cleft behind the bath are **attractive low reliefs depicting almost jaunty-looking elephants**. On the way up the steps to the actual shrine, there is on the right-hand side a very fine relief of a "man with a horse", which should not be overlooked. It probably dates from the 7th century. It depicts a man in a relaxed pose while the head of a horse appears from the background and touches the man's arm. The purpose and meaning of the portrait, which resembles those of the India Pallava style, are unknown. Maybe an artist simply gave free rein to his imagination. The main shrine no longer houses all the statues, some of them having been moved to a small museum right next door. Kept here also is the **probably most important relief in this monastery**, which bears the title »The Lovers«. It is dated to the 5th or 6th century, and reveals a rare harmony in its depiction of a warrior with a woman. In the past it was thought it might depict two deities, but

A former cave of a hermit developed over time into the Isurumuniya rock monastery

the attributes (sword and shield) point rather to a couple belonging to this world.

On this topic there is also a legend in the Mahavamsa chronicle, according to which the couple are Prince Saliya, a son of King Duttha Gamani, and his wife Asokamala. She was actually the daughter of a blacksmith, whom the prince was only able to marry after renouncing all rights to the throne. But as it states in the Mahavamsa, nothing and nobody could separate them, as they had already been married to each other in a previous life. The princess was, it was said, reborn into a lower class because she had been disrespectful towards her mother.

Surroundings of Anuradhapura

The western suburb of Anuradhapura was not considered a desirable area to live in. It was the location of cremation sites and cemeteries, and the local inhabitants were all from low castes. Even so, a community of strictly ascetic monks settled here, possibly in protest at the worldly ideas of various city monasteries. They ate for example nothing but rice and the bitter oil of the margosaa tree, and sewed themselves robes from pieces of clothing which they found in the nearby morgue.

Western monasteries

They surrounded their precinct with high walls in order to protect themselves from the gaze of the curious. The buildings were without exception simple, but well-proportioned; each building had a roofed hall and an open terrace, but the monks renounced sculptures and other decoration entirely. There was one exception, though: the urination stones. These were decorated with reliefs, maybe to demonstrate the monks' contempt for all worldly wealth.

✷ ✷
Excavations of Nillakgama

The famous excavation site of Nillakgama lies some 45km/28mi from Anuradhapura in the direction of Maho. It is best accessed by car. An inscription on the western entrance gate, dating from the 8th or 9th century, indicates that the structure had the function of a bodhigara. It has still not been explained, however, who endowed it or what the place was called in Antiquity. In the late 19th century, under the supervision of H. P. C. Bell and Dr Paranavitana, the remains of an interesting monastic complex dating from the 8th to 10th centuries were uncovered. They include **an almost completely preserved bodhighara** with finely worked reliefs. This sacred bodhi tree enclosure is the oldest yet found in Sri Lanka. It consists of a square platform measuring 3.3m/4ft on each side, with the two opposite anterooms of a masonry wall. On this platform is another, smaller one measuring one metre (3ft 3in) on each side, on which the bodhi tree stood. On the outside of the masonry enclosure between two carefully carved cornices is an elephant frieze, with the individual animals separated by pilasters. A balustrade, convex towards the outside, whose underside in the vicinity of the entrance anterooms is decorated with geese, forms the top of the 2m/6ft 6in wall.

The moonstone in front of the two steps is undecorated, while the short balustrades are also simple, and lack the usual makara form. The anterooms are decorated with elaborate reliefs: the motifs are a flute-playing dwarf and the snake king Muchalinda beneath the spread hood of the Naga, with the vase of abundance in his hand along with a blossoming twig. In addition, they show an archer mounted on a rearing horse, an unusual motif in Sri Lanka. In his hand he is holding some indefinable objects, and there is a kneeling figure at the horse's feet. A flat slab of stone forms the roof of the anteroom.

The 2m/6ft 6in high stone base of the inner platform is surrounded by a frieze with geese, cornices with lotus leaves, and an elephant frieze, the last being unusual in that some of the elephants are shown from the front, others from the side. The small courtyard is paved with carved stones of various sizes. There are flower altars on each side. 16 pillars, of which some are still extant, once supported the wooden roof.

Ruins of Ranjangane

About 30km/19mi south of Anuradhapura (on the A 28) are the ruins of Ranjangane. They are the remains of a large forest monastery, which was probably founded in the 6th century. The monastic movement that preferred to live in isolation in the solitude of the forest also restricted itself to buildings without any architectural or artistic elaboration, and experienced its heyday in the 8th and 9th centuries. An interesting feature here is the vatadage, a round temple with a stupa beneath a wooden roof supported by several concentric rows of stone pillars.

Aukana

C 5/6

Province: North Central   **Altitude:** app. 90m/300ft

Aukana lies not far from the Kalawewa reservoir. This, along with the nearby Balaluwewa reservoir, was constructed in the context of an irrigation programme with a total of 18 reservoirs. The programme was initiated by King Dhatusena (AD 455–473). The reservoirs were mainly there to provide the capital with drinking water. ►Anuradhapura.

What to see in Aukana

In the middle of the mountain jungle near Aukana there rises the monumental statue of an app. 14m/45ft high standing Buddhas, which is regarded as a masterpiece of the Singhalese stonemason's art. It was carved out of a single rock and is one of the most important Buddhist shrines in Sri Lanka. The statue was probably made at the bidding of King Dhatusena. To be admired are its perfect proportions, the **transcendental effect of the face** and the working of the robe, which falls in regular folds, with the thick hem fold characteristic of the period, and held in the left hands in such a way that this end seems to float. The Buddha's right hand is raised in the gesture of blessing (asiva mudra). On his head is the flame of enlightenment (ketumala).

✷ ✷
The Buddha Statue of Aukana

The small monastery next to the statue is no longer home to many monks. From here there is a waymarked path to caves in the cliff, which were occupied by Buddhist anchorite monks in the 3rd century, when the scratches on the rock were also made.

Monastic complex

Surroundings of Aukana

About 6km/4mi south of Aukana is Vijithapura, one of the oldest towns in Sri Lanka. It was founded as long ago as the 6th century BC and has a (now derelict) dagoba, in which there is said to be a jawbone of Buddha.

Vijithapura

Some 12km/8mi to the west of Aukana, near Sasseruwa, there is a further Buddha statue, albeit only 12m/40ft tall, showing the Buddha in the gesture of "according protection". Artistically it is somewhat less

✷
Buddha Statue of Sasseruwa

▶ VISITING AUKANA

GETTING THERE

By car:
From Anuradhapura via the A 9 to Kekirawa, from there app. 6km/4mi to the north-west along the road to Talawa. Turn left in front of the railway track and drive about 5km/3mi along the Kalawewa reservoir before

turning right towards Aukana (4km/2mi). The final stretch from Kekirawa to Aukana is sometimes impassable during the monsoon season.

By train:
The nearest station is in Kalawewa (on the route from Colombo to Trincomalee).

important than the statue in Aukana, possibly having been made by a pupil of the man who sculpted the latter. According to other sources, though, it was only made in the 8th or 9th century. There were once a number of monasteries in the area, and more than 100 caves inhabited by monks. These can however only by reached via rough paths.

Avissawella

B 8

Province: Western   **Altitude:** app. 75m/250ft

Avissawella, surrounded by luxuriant tropical vegetation, is located on the banks of the River Sitavka, and is a centre of the rubber industry. Sitavka, as the city was formerly known, was a royal residence in the 16th century, capital of one of the Singhalese sub-kingdoms and during the Portuguese colonial period much fought over.

History   The name Sitavka is probably linked to Sita, the consort of Rama. According to the Ramayana, she was abducted by the demon king Ravana in India and kept hidden here. While this is one of the legends of the Ramayana, it accords with the fact that Sitavka played am important part when the kingdom of Kotte was divided in three and King Mayadunne set up his residence here. His son too, King Raja Sinha I, who converted from Buddhism to Brahmanism, lived here until his death in 1592. Both kings offered the Portuguese stout resistance, although the city changed hands several times. The Portuguese were followed by the Dutch, who built a fortress.

What to see in Avissawella

Old Sitavka   Old Sitavka lies on a bend in the river of the same name. Only a few ruins of the royal palace are still to be seen, and this goes for the Portuguese and Dutch fortresses too.

⏵ VISITING AVISSAWELLA

GETTING THERE

By car:
via the A 4 from Colombo (59km/ 37mi)

By train:
Avissawella is the terminus of the line from Colombo

By bus:
good, regular bus services from Colombo

RAFTING

The Kelani Ganga has plenty of water and is one of Sri Lanka's best rivers for rafting. An ideal place to get on is next to the tea factory near Pattewatta, from which the first few kilometres are very demanding. There are many places to get off, as the road runs more or less parallel to the river.

WHERE TO STAY

► Budget

Kitulgala Rest House
Kitulgala
Tel. 036 / 875 28
www.ceylonhotels.lk/kith.html
19 rooms (15 without air-conditioning)
In the middle of splendid landscape on the banks of the Kelani River, this guest-house is not far from the location where »The Bridge on the River Kwai« was filmed.

To the left of Talduwa Road (near the police station) a stone marks the burial place of King Raja Sinha I. It is the only grave of a Singhalese king whose location is known for certain.

Royal grave

Beneath the bridge, a path to the right of Ginigathena Road leads to the temple of Berende Kovil, which is dedicated to Shiva. It was started by command of King Raja Sinha I, but for reasons unknown it was never completed. Some of the stone sculptures are worthy of note.

Shiva Temple

Surroundings of Avissawella

From Avissawella a road leads eastwards via Talduwa to the village of Kitulgala in a landscape dominated by dense forest. Kitulgala achieved a measure of fame as **the location for the jungle scenes in the film »The Bridge on the River Kwai «** (1957) based on the novel of (almost) the same name by Pierre Boulle. The real bridge, during the building of which tens of thousands of Allied POWs lost their lives, was however in Kanchanaburi province in Thailand.

✷
Kitulgala

✶ Bandarawela

C 8

Province: Uva   **Altitude:** app. 1250 m/4100ft

Bandarawela is one of the centres of tea-growing in Sri Lanka. Its pleasant climate made it a kind of health resort in colonial times.

What to see in Bandarawela

Landscape
Typical of the landscape around Bandarawela are the undulating hills and conical mountains, on which, seemingly at least, every square centimetre is covered with tea plants. The climate also favours the growth of strawberries and other fruits, though.

Tea-factory viewing
In and around Bandarawela there are several tea factories, some of which are open to visitors (watch out for signs at the entrance). The guided tours provide much interesting information about the local tea plantations and tea production, and about the difference between the individual varieties. They also include tea tastings, and of course you can buy the products.

Surroundings of Bandarawela

✶ Caves of Istripura
Some 21km/13mi north-west of Bandarawela is the Welimada Rest House, which is a good starting point for exploring the caves of Istripura to the north. The caves contain the longest underground passages in Sri Lanka; nearby are the ruins of Fort MacDonald, built by the British.

Dowa Temple
The scenically attractive stretch northeastwards towards Badulla leads after 6.5km/4mi to the Dowa Temple, carved out of the rock. It is decorated with an 8m/26ft tall Buddhist statue, likewise carved from the rock. For reasons unknown, it was never completed, but probably dates from the 10th century and represents the bodhisattva Maitreya. Also worthy of note are a few smaller statues of Hindu deities and some fine murals, which have been carefully restored by monks.

✶ Drive over the Haputale Pass to Haputale
Particularly fine scenic views can be enjoyed on a drive across the 1600m/5300ft Haputale Pass, which leads through the nature conservation area of the same name. Some wild elephants still live in the dense jungle here. Haputale itself is a **popular resort**, lying at a height of about 1300m/4300ft and is built on a steep rocky ridge. On clear days the view stretches to the south coast of the island, and at night even the light from the Hambantota lighthouse is visible. Down on the plain is the Uda Walawe National Park with the lake of the same name, one of Sri Lanka's largest reservoirs.

● VISITING BANDARAWELA

GETTING THERE

By car:
from Badulla on the A 16 (30km/
19mi), from Nuwara Eliya on the A 5
(50km/30mi)
By train:
Bandarawela is a station on the line
from Kandy to Badulla
By bus:
good bus services from Kandy and
from Nuwara Eliya.

SHOPPING

A drive into the mountains around
Bandarawela will take you past numerous well-signposted tea factories,
where tea can be tasted and bought.

WHERE TO STAY

Baedeker recommendation

► **Mid-range**
Bandarawela Hotel
14, Welimada Road, Bandarawela
Tel. 057 / 222 25 01
Fax 057 / 22 22834
www.aitkenspencehotels.com
The first mountain hotel in Sri Lanka, it was
built in 1893 and offers the charm that
comes with a long tradition. The cosy
rooms are furnished in the British colonial
style, with much velvet and lace.

Bandarawela is a good place from which to visit the scenically very **Excursion tip**
attractive ►Horton Plains.

Batticaloa

E 6

Province: Eastern
Population: app. 78,000

Altitude: app. 3 – 8 m (10–26ft)

**Batticaloa, which lies half on a spit of land and half on an island
in the north of a 54km/90mi long lagoon, is a town of picturesque
charm, while excursions to the hinterland have much to offer in
the way of exotic experiences. Tracking down the phenomenon of
the »singing fishes« in the lagoon can turn into an exciting adventure.**

The main attraction on the east coast of Sri Lanka lies in the wonder-   **Lagoon location**
ful long and almost empty beaches in the immediate and less imme-
diate vicinity. The city's sheltered location on a lagoon largely protected it from the tsunami. However serious damage was caused by
the flood waves in the nearby fishing villages, where hardly one stone
was left upon another. Following the government's order that no
house may be built within 100m/110yd of the beach, many people
are still living in emergency accommodation.

History Tamils settled in the area around Batticaloa at an early date, calling the place Madakala puwa (»Marshy Lagoon«). Later Arab and Malay traders also settled. In 1602 the Dutch admiral Joris Spielbergen landed in Batticaloa, to be followed shortly afterwards by Admiral de Weert. He could however reach no agreement with King Vimela Dharma, who sought to expel the Portuguese colonial masters from the island with the help of the Dutch, and at a meal together there was a major diplomatic incident: when the king casually remarked that he had to get back to Kandy, as he could not leave the queen alone for so long, de Weert replied ambiguously that there must be enough men at court to entertain the queen, whereupon the admiral was struck dead by the king in person. In spite of this setback, an agreement was sealed in Kandy in 1612 with another Dutch admiral, de Boschouwer, which was aimed at removing the Portuguese and obliged the Dutch to take measures in this direction. In around 1620, though, the Portuguese managed to establish a small fort in Koddamunai (Tamil: »spit of land with the fort«), with which they hoped to ward off attacks by the Dutch.

Baedeker TIP

Coconuts

The milk of the king coconut not only quenches the thirst, but is good for the digestion. In Sri Lanka it is sold by the roadside almost everywhere, and costs very little.

In 1636 the Dutch returned under Admiral Coster, however, and in just two years had driven out the Portuguese and taken the fort. Together with the town of Batticaloa, they handed it over to the kings of Kandy. By around 1660, though, the Dutch East India Company had recognized the strategic importance of Batticaloa, and so it suited them well that the kings of Kandy still owed them promised payments for the war: they took the town as a lien and built a fort here too. When in 1795 the British started occupying increasingly large swathes of Sri Lanka, the little fort at Batticaloa was unable to offer resistance for very long. It held out, in fact, for just three weeks.

It was during the period of British colonial rule that the road between Batticaloa and Kandy was built. The development of Batticaloa, however, did not keep up with that of ▶ Trincomalee 145km/90mi to the north, as the latter had a far better natural harbour. The modesty prosperity of the inhabitants is primarily due to rich fisheries along with fruit and vegetable growing. The location, which before the civil war and the tsunami was well connected in regard to transport infrastructure, also allowed steady growth.

What to see in Batticaloa

Lagoon The 54km/33mi long saltwater lagoon between Chenkaladi in the north and Kalmunai in the south can be explored by boat, and the scenery, with its notable diversity of bird species, is very attractive. In

▶ VISITING BATTICALOA

GETTING THERE

By car:
from Colombo via the A 1 to Kandy, from there via the A 26 and then the A 5 to the east coast. From there, turn right on to the A 15 (app. 300km/190mi).

By train:
Batticaloa is the terminus of the line from Colombo via Polonnaruwa

WHERE TO STAY / WHERE TO EAT

▶ Budget

Co-Op Inn
Trinco Road

Tel. 065 / 226 13
Simple, but clean and cheap rooms in the middle of town. The restaurant serves excellent curries!

Riviera Resort
New Dutch Bar Road
Kallady
Tel. / Fax 065 / 2 34 47
www.riviera-online.com
7 rooms, 1 family villa, conference room, restaurant.
Very well kept establishment attractively situated on the lagoon, with lovingly furnished rooms.

---

two places, near Batticaloa and near Kallar, the lagoon is connected to the open sea by narrow channels. A bridge (near Batticaloa) and a causeway (near Kallar) connect the long narrow island with the mainland.

Dutch fort

The Kallada bridge links the small island of Batticaloa with the spit of land where, directly on the lagoon, the Dutch built their fort in the 17th century. The massive outer walls, now much overgrown with grass, are well preserved; at each corner there was once a defensive tower armed with cannon.

Lady Manning Bridge

The Lady Manning Bridge is made of iron and one of the longest bridges in Sri Lanka, connecting the spit of land with the island; it carries the A 4 road leading to the south.

Hindu temples

As Batticaloa is largely inhabited by Tamils and most of the Moors still left in Sri Lanka, almost all the religious buildings are Hindu temples. They are attractive enough to look at, but without exception of fairly recent date and of no great art-historical importance.

Singing Fishes

The phenomenon of the »Singing Fishes« has long been known in Batticaloa, even finding mention in the Encyclopædia Britannica. If a paddle is dipped into the water on moonlit nights in calm weather, by holding your ear to the other end you will hear (perhaps) about six different, very clear notes. There is still **no scientific explanation** for the sounds, and no one has ever seen the fish. The »singing« may perhaps emanate from the numerous molluscs in the waters here. The assumption is that the noise is caused when the rise and fall of the tides causes the water to flow through the empty shells. Others suggest that the noises may be produced by catfish, which are also very numerous here.

✳ Bentota

A/B 9

Province: Southern   **Altitude:** 2 – 5 m (6–18ft)

A very attractive palm-lined beach was the main reason why in the 1980s the fishing village of Bentota was developed into a world-famous tourist centre. But Bentota has paid for its colourful beach life with a loss of local colour. But there are still some good restaurants here, serving excellent fish dishes.

History   From 1644 to 1652 the Dutch/Portuguese border ran to the north of Bentota. The Dutch had advanced as far as here from the south, destroying the fort the Portuguese had built apart from one building, which they furnished as a Rest House for their officers. The British, who later replaced the Dutch as the colonial power, chose Bentota as a rest and recuperation resort for those seeking to escape the oppressive heat and humidity of the capital Colombo.

! **Baedeker TIP**

Bentota perahera
At the November/December full moon, Bentota is the venue for a colourful perahera, attended also by many visitors from the surrounding towns and villages.

What to see in Bentota

✳
Beach   The 4km/2.5mi long sandy beach is what people actually come to see in Bentota, although bathing can be dangerous during the monsoon season. There are also surfing and sailing opportunities.

✳
Galapatha Raja Maha Vihara   The Galapatha Raja Maha Vihara probably originated in the 2nd century BC and is said to have been built in the reign of King Duttha Gamani. Later, under King Parakrama Bahu I, a relic is said to have been placed here, which is why the temple was for a long time an important pilgrimage centre. It is also claimed that there was an important Buddhist university here too, but there is no evidence for that.

Excursion tips   Rewarding excursions from Bentota include the mask-carving town of ►Ambalangoda and the popular bathing resort of ►Hikkaduwa further to the south. To the north lies the district administrative centre ►Kalutara with its imposing dagoba.

▶ VISITING BENTOTA

GETTING THERE

By car:
from Colombo or Galle via the A 2 (42 and 74km (26 and 46mi) respectively)

By train:
Bentota is a station on the line from Colombo to Matara (several trains daily)

By bus:
regular services from the above places

DIVING

LSR Bentota Dive Center (CIS)
29B de S. Jayasinghe Mawatha Dehiwala
Tel. 011 / 282 49 55
Fax 011 / 282 61 25
lsrdive@sri.lanka.net
Diving school based on the international PADI guidelines with equipment hire. Daily excursions to interesting diving areas

WHERE TO STAY

▶ Luxury

Saman Villas
Aturuwella, Bentota
Tel. 034 / 227 54 35
Fax 034 / 227 54 33
www.samanvilla.com
27 rooms. Maybe the best address in Bentota, certainly one of the priciest. Outstanding service

Taj Exotica Bentota
Tel. 034 / 227 56 50
Fax 034 / 227 51 60
150 rooms. New luxury establishment belonging to the Indian Taj hotel chain. Splendid location on a spit of land

The Induruwa Beach Hotel has a lovely pool

► **Mid-range**
Ceysands
Aluthgama, Bentota
Tel. 034 / 227 50 73
www.ceysands.com
84 rooms. Also on a spit of land
between the Bentota river and the sea

► **Budget**
Induruwa Beach Hotel
Kaikawala Induruwa
Tel. / Fax 034 / 331 04
90 rooms plus 15 rooms for ayurveda
guests. Very nice hotel in location with
good views and comfortable rooms

Beruwala

A 9

Province: Western
Population: app. 33 000

Altitude: app. 7m/25ft

The small fishing town of Beruwala, idyllically situated in a broadly curving bay, is probably the oldest Muslim settlement in Sri Lanka and a place of pilgrimage for all Moors.

Lively bathing resort

The Moors probably landed in this sheltered bay in around AD 800, but the first documented evidence of settlement by Muslims dates from 1024. At that time the town was called Barberyn. Today Beruwala is a popular bathing resort with a few comfortable hotels by the beach. It's possible to observe the **toddy tappers** at their risky business on the ropes stretched between tall coconut palms. They use the palms as a source of the sap from which the spirit called arrack is made in a local distillery.

! *Baedeker* TIP

When Ramadan ends ...

...up to 60,000 Muslim pilgrims come to Beruwala in order to celebrate the end of the fast. It is also an occasion for markets and cultural performances.

What to see in Beruwala

Kachimalai Mosque

Kachimalai Mosque (13th/14th century.) still dominates the skyline with its slender minaret; it is **the oldest mosque in Sri Lanka**. There is a modern mosque in China Fort, the quarter inhabited by wealthy Arab gem dealers. The tomb of a Muslim saint, whose stone sarcophagus is supposed to have been washed ashore, is the destination for many Sri Lankan Muslim pilgrims.

Gemstone workshops

In Beruwala there are some workshops in which predominantly local stones are cut.

Islands

There are a number of offshore island with luxuriant vegetation and protected by a **coral reef**. This is however no less threatened than most of the others around Sri Lanka, as even strict prohibitions cannot stop the locals from plundering it.

▶ VISITING BERUWALA

GETTING THERE

By car:
from Colombo or Galle via the A 2 (55 and 61 km (34 and 38ni) respectively)

By train:
Beruwala is a station on the line from Colombo to Matara (several trains daily)

By bus:
a number of services daily from the above places

WHERE TO STAY / ESSEN

▶ Luxury

Ayurveda Villa Hotel Riverina
Kaluwamodara
Tel. 034 / 760 44 - 45
Fax 034 / 60 47
www.ayurveda-health-resorts.com
188 rooms, restaurant, coffee shop, 2 bars, pool (with children's area), discotheque, large range of sporting facilities. Guests seeking relaxation are no less welcome than ayurveda »patients«, for whom there are various programmes. Very good location on the Bentota River. The in-house diving station offers course and numerous excursions.

Lanka Princess
Kaluwamodara
Tel. 034 / 227 67 18
Fax 034 / 227 63 23
www.lankaprincess.com
110 rooms, restaurant, bar, pool. Much recommended hotel under German management

▶ Mid-range

Eden Resort and Spa
Kaluwamodera
Tel. 034 / 227 60 75
Fax 034 / 227 61 81
www.edenresortandspa.com
158 rooms, restaurant, coffee shop, pool, wellness centre, water sports. Holiday in a stylish ambience, the rooms are spacious.

▶ Budget

Barberyn Reef Ayurveda Resort
Morgolla
Tel. 034 / 227 60 36
Fax 034 / 227 60 37
www.barberynresorts.com
One of the first ayurveda hotels, cosy rooms. Cooking courses

The Lanka Princess Hotel is situated at the mouth of the Bentota River

✦ Chilaw

A 6

Province: Western
Population: app. 24,000

Altitude: app. 5m/16ft

The busy fishing port of Chilaw, one of the most important in the country, is situated at the northern end of a long lagoon on the west coast known as Chilaw Lake, which opens out into the sea some 2km/1.5mi further on. This is also the mouth of the Deduru Oya, marking the southern boundary of the hot dry zone of the island.

Jesuit missionary base
In the past Chilaw played an important role as the site of one of the larger Jesuit mission stations. This explains why more than a third of the local population are Roman Catholics.

What to see in Chilaw

✳ Fish market
The activities of the fishermen, the women and girls who carry fish around in baskets on their heads, can best be watched from the bridge connecting the town to a narrow spit of land to the west of Chilaw Lake.

Catholic church
Near the sea is the large Catholic church of St Mary, dating from the 19th century, which bears witness to the effectiveness of the Jesuit mission. Chilaw today is one of eight Catholic dioceses in Sri Lanka.

Surroundings of Chilaw

✳ Hindu Temple
A little outside the town (app. 3km/2mi to the east) near the village of Munneswaram is one of the oldest Hindu shrines in Sri Lanka. It is dedicated to the god Shiva and greatly venerated by the faithful.

▶ VISITING CHILAW

GETTING THERE

By car:
from Colombo on the A 1 northwards (81km/50mi)

By train:
Marawila is a station on the line from Colombo to Puttalam

By bus:
good services from Colombo (travel time app. 3 hours)

WHERE TO STAY / WHERE TO EAT

▶ **Mid-range**
Club Palm Bay Hotel
Morogolla
Tel. 034 / 227 60 39
Fax 034 / 227 60 38
Attractive mid-range beach hotel with comfortable rooms. The hotel has a large pool and a good restaurant.

The road to Marawila (app. 24km/15mi to the south) passes a little reservoir known as Lake Tinapitiya. To the left, next to the temple of Taniwella Devale is the figure of a rearing horse. The story goes that the horse, which to a wealthy merchant, shied when its rider tried to pass the temple in a hurry. The merchant fell to the ground badly hurt, and swore to endow the temple with an image of his horse when he recovered.

Lake Tinapitiya

Marawila is one of the centres of Sri Lankan batik production. It is of course possible to buy **batiks** here more cheaply than in the tourist centres.

Marawila

✳ ✳ Colombo

A 8

Province: Western
Population: 650,000

Altitude: app. 1–5m/3–18ft

Colombo is the capital of Sri Lanka and also the largest city on the island. Bustling and noisy today, it is an agglomeration of previously separate towns, each of which has retained its style and character.

1344	First mention of the port
1505	The Portuguese come ashore; in 1518 they build a fort.
1658	The Dutch take the town
1796	The British take the town
1869	The port gains greatly in significance following the opening of the Suez Canal.
Early 20th century	Development of the town into a metropolis; in 1948 Ceylon achieves independence from Britain; Colombo remains the capital.

The gulf becomes particularly clear after a visit to the Pettah and Cinnamon Garden districts. While Pettah still has hovels where the misery hits you in the face, Cinnamon Garden is dominated by the villas of the wealthy. And while Pettah comes across as noisily oriental, the traffic in Cinnamon Garden passes along broad avenues past neatly tended gardens.

Deprivation and affluence

The favourable location on the island's west coast along with the fact that this particular coastal strip is fertile, certainly favoured Colombo's rise to become an **economic centre** of Sri Lanka. But it was never a royal city, the Singhalese rulers preferring places like Anuradhapura, Polonnaruwa and Kandy, maybe on account of the more

Historical development

pleasant climate. Since 1982 Colombo has no longer been the seat of the parliament, which moved in that year to Sri Jayawardanapura, an artificial city that was once called Kotte. A suburb of Colombo, it got its present name only when it became the administrative capital. Even so, Colombo is still the seat of numerous ministries and other government agencies.

It is not known for certain where the name Colombo comes from. In the 4th century AD the Chinese traveller Fa-Hsien mentioned a small port, but failed to say what it was called. Later, in about the 8th century, the harbour had attained some importance as a result of Arab traders (the forebears of the Moors now living in Sri Lanka) settling here; they called in Calenbou. The Chinese merchant Wang Tai Yuan, who visited Colombo in about 1330, mentions in his notes a town called Kao-lan-pu. It was only under the Portuguese that Colombo got its present name, maybe in memory of the explorer Christopher Columbus. Other versions trace it back to the Singhalese words Cola-amba (= leaf of the mango tree). The simplest theory is also the most likely: the Singhalese always called the place Kolamba, which just means harbour. **Colombo has been known since Antiquity**, for example to King Solomon and the kings of Sheba, through whom it achieved great wealth as a result of worldwide trade as long ago as the 1st century BC. Fa-Hsien mentioned a small harbour which was becoming an important entrepôt for the trade in pepper, cinnamon, gemstones, ivory and peacock feathers. Ibn Battuta, the great Arab traveller (► Famous People), describes Calenbou, as he calls the place, in the 14th century as the »most beautiful town on the island of Serendib«, but he is likely to have been referring to its commercial importance and cosmopolitan flair rather than its physical attractiveness as a city.

In 1518 the **Portuguese**, with the consent of the kings of Kotte, built a massive fort just a few kilometres to the south of Colombo in the vicinity of the harbour. It watched over the actual town, which consisted mostly of wooden huts but also included some prestigious administrative buildings. In 1656 the Dutch succeeded in taking the fort following an act of treachery by one of the Portuguese, but he was not rewarded for his pains as promised, being immured alive instead. The **Dutch** extended the fortifications and founded the residential quarters of Wolfendahl and Hulftsdurp, the latter named after the Dutch governor Gerard Pieterszoon Hulft. They also laid out numerous canals, including the one from Kalutara, south of Colombo, to Puttalam; 174km/108mi long, it is still in use as a waterway for transporting freight. This period also saw the laying out of the Cinnamon Garden, today the best address in town.

In 1796 the **British** occupied Colombo and made the fort district the seat of their colonial administration. The cinnamon gardens disap-

← *At the weekends the locals meet to walk along the beach of Colombo*

Colombo Map

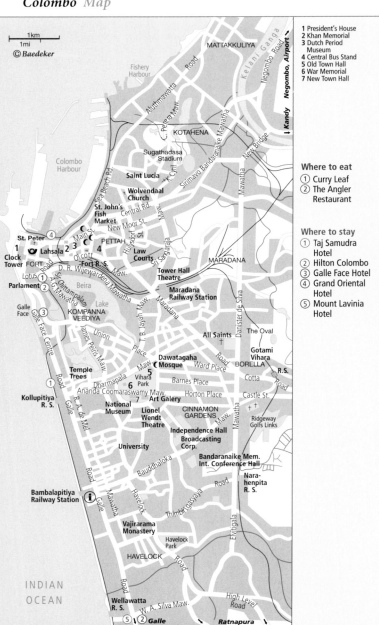

1 President's House
2 Khan Memorial
3 Dutch Period Museum
4 Central Bus Stand
5 Old Town Hall
6 War Memorial
7 New Town Hall

Where to eat
① Curry Leaf
② The Angler Restaurant

Where to stay
① Taj Samudra Hotel
② Hilton Colombo
③ Galle Face Hotel
④ Grand Oriental Hotel
⑤ Mount Lavinia Hotel

▶ VISITING COLOMBO

INFORMATION

Sri Lanka Tourist Board
80, Galle Road
Colombo 3
Tel. 011 / 243 70 55, 243 70 59
www.srilanka.travel

TRANSPORT

The best way to get around in
Colombo is by taxi or in a hired car
with a chauffeur. Numerous travel
agents, whose addresses can be obtained from the Sri Lanka Tourist
Board, offer these tours.
The public buses are mostly hopelessly overcrowded and strangers are
likely to find themselves more lost
than before.
The Pettah neighbourhood can however be explored on foot.

MARKETS

South of the entrance to the lagoon
there is a fish market every morning
until about 11am.
In the old fort, a Sunday market takes
place beneath trees with aerial roots.

SHOPPING

Odel Unlimited
704, Galle Road 5, Alexandra Place
Colombo 03
Large shopping centre with numerous
shops (fashion, leather goods, jewellery, books, tea, ayurveda cosmetics,
sports goods etc.) as well as »factory
outlets« of European designers, who
often have their clothes made up in
Sri Lanka.

Laksala
60, York Street, Colombo 1
Large selection at very low prices (no
haggling!). The range includes batiks,
wood carvings, basketwork and much
else besides.

Paradise Road
213 Dharmapala Maw 61, Ward Place
Colombo 07
One of the best shopping addresses in
Colombo. The rooms are packed with
goodies from ceiling to floor: hand-
painted porcelain, table decorations
made of palm branches, ayurvedic
oils, salad spoons made from coconut
shells, furnishing fabrics from the
bale, hand-knitted cushion covers.

Elephant Walk
61, Ward Place, Colombo 7
One of Colombo's new shopping
paradises. Not only household textiles
and kitchen utility ware, but also
original presents for the folks back
home can be picked up in its historic
ambience.

Victorian Charm Kalaya
No. 08 Palm Grove 116 Havelock
Road, Colombo 03
A real treasure trove for high-quality
textiles. The proprietor Praneela Fer-
nando-Kururuppu combines eastern
and western techniques of production, e.g. hand-made lace as well as
exquisite embroideries.

Hermitage Gallery Suriya
Home Décor Store
28 Gower Street 61, 5th Lane
Colombo 05

Antique chests, tables and other items of furniture as well as old household objects from birdcages and brass lamps to early pictures.

WHERE TO EAT
► Moderate
① *Curry Leaf*
(in the Hilton Hotel)
Tel. 01 / 254 46 44
Probably the best restaurant in Colombo for excellent curries. Splendid garden. Only open in the evenings, reservations advisable.

② *The Angler Restaurant*
71, Hotel Road, Mount Lavinia
Tel. 01 / 271 66 26
Not much choice, but what there is is really fresh and brilliantly prepared. The proprietor also has pleasant rooms to let at low cost.

WHERE TO STAY
► Luxury
① *Taj Samudra Hotel*
25, Galle Face Center Road
Tel. 011 / 244 65 39
Fax 011 / 262 42 55
www.tajhotels.com
350 rooms, 3 restaurants, coffee shop, pool, tennis, squash, gym.
5-star hotel with attentive service and very comfortable rooms situated directly on the Galle Face Road promenade in very nicely laid-out grounds.

② *Hilton Colombo*
2, Sir Chittampalam A. Gardiner Mawatha
Tel. 011 / 234 46 44, 249 24 92
Fax 011 / 254 46 57
www.hilton.com
384 rooms, 6 restaurants, shopping arcade, pool, discotheque.
Centrally situated hotel belonging to the Hilton chain with a large pleasant garden directly on the promenade.

Baedeker recommendation

► Luxury
⑤ *Mount Lavinia Hotel*
100, Hotel Road, Mount Lavinia
Tel. 011 / 271 17 11
Fax 011 / 273 07 26
www.mountlaviniahotel.com
275 rooms, 2 restaurants, pool.
Establishment with a long tradition, occupying a 200-year-old building in the colonial style. The British governor Sir Thomas Maitland, who commissioned it, certainly knew how to live. The winner of several awards, it is one of the best hotels in Asia.

► Mid-range
③ *Galle Face Hotel*
2, Galle Road, Colombo 3
Tel. 011 / 254 10 10 - 16, 254 35 65 - 77
Fax 011 / 254 10 72 - 74
www.gallefacehotel.com
65 rooms in the Classic Wing, 82 rooms in the Regency Wing, 9 restaurants, 4 bars, pool.
The Galle Face, built in 1864, is a solid hotel in the colonial style with a modern wing. The rooms are spacious but nothing special. The suites by contrast are very attractively furnished. The ambience breathes tradition. Afternoon tea is served on the splendid terrace. The hotel is right by the sea.

► Budget
④ *Grand Oriental Hotel*
2, York Street (by the docks)
Tel. 011 / 32 03 91
Fax 011 / 44 76 40
www.grandoriental.com
62 rooms, 2 restaurants, bar. Inexpensive, well-kept hotel with large rooms furnished in the colonial style.

peared, being replaced by houses. In 1872 most of the fortifications were demolished.

Until 1822 Galle had been Sri Lanka's leading port, before being replaced by Colombo. In 1877 the British governor Sir William Gregory had the open mooring developed into a sheltered harbour. Following independence, the government and parliament moved into the buildings erected by the British. In 1950 a Commonwealth foreign ministers' conference was held in Colombo, at which the » Colombo Plan for Co-operative Economic Development in South and South-East Asia« was decided upon.

✳ Fort (district)

The district, approximately triangular in shape, could be termed the germ-cell of the present-day city of Colombo. It is bounded by the docks, Marine Drive, Lotus Road and York Street; the latter was a canal during the Dutch period, but was filled in by the British. Nor is there now anything else in Fort to recall the presence of the Dutch, as only a few remains can now be seen of the once massive fortifications that once enclosed the district. Even the streets have lost their Dutch names, and now have English ones. The remains of the fortifications can be found behind Queen's House, where a bulwark dominates the rocky coast (known to the Singhalese as Gal Bokka, Rock Belly, corrupted by the English into Galle Buck). The **lighthouse** where Chaiytya Road becomes Marine Drive was built on a rocky promontory, but is fairly modern.

At the end of Marine Drive is the Neo-classical **Old Parliament Building**, erected in the typical style of the colonial period. Since Sri Jayawardanapura City became the seat of parliament, this building has served as an administrative centre only.

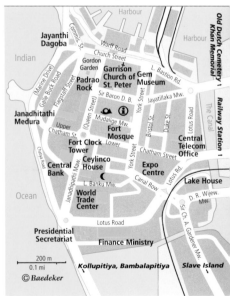

Colombo Fort Map

© Baedeker

Diagonally opposite the Old Parliament Building, Janadhipathi Mawatha (formerly Queen's Street) leads to the centre of the district, which is characterized by the Clock Tower. It was actually built as a

Clock Tower

Highlights Colombo

Fort
The former Dutch Fort is today a bustling business quarter with many shopping opportunities.
▶ page 221

Pettah
Lively bazaar quarter, with all kinds of acrobats and snake-charmers
▶ page 222

Galle Face Green
Popular recreation district right by the sea
▶ page 226

Cinnamon Garden
The posh quarter of Colombo also has a huge park with ancient trees, a good place to rest.
▶ page 227

lighthouse in 1850, but because it became crowded in by tall buildings all around, it could no longer serve its purpose, and was consequently converted in 1952.

Prime Minister's Residence
Going up the street to the north, we come to a white building the colonial style on the left. It was once the residence of the British governor, but today is the official residence of the prime minister. The long building is another piece of colonial prestige architecture, the General Post Office, which is open round the clock. The residence is adjoined by an attractive park, which however is inaccessible for security reasons.

Streets with formerly magnificent houses
After crossing Sir Baron Jayatillake Mawatha (formerly Prince Street), we come to a building on the right which houses the Cabinet Offices). The street itself was largely built during the British colonial period, as still evidenced by numerous buildings. However time is visibly doing its destructive work. Sir Baron Jayatillake Mawatha now joins the broad York Street, conspicuous for the red building of Miller's department store with its roof balustrades, gables and turrets. Not far away is the state-owned Laksala department store with a large selection of craft objects along with gemstones and textiles. The Grand Oriental Hotel on the corner of York and Church Streets likewise proclaims the charm of bygone days, but the glamour left by such celebrated visitors as the writer Somerset Maugham has now largely faded.

St Peter's Garrison Church
Also on Church Street is the old Garrison Church of St Peter (19th century), which today houses the offices of the Mission to Seamen.

✶ ✶ Pettah (District)

Traders and market quarter
The Pettah (Tamil: pettai, old town), which adjoins the Fort district to the east, used to be the quarter where the residential and business

district of the Portuguese, and later of the Dutch. The traces of the latter are still visible in many places. Today the Pettah is the noisy, frenetic bazaar quarter of Colombo, where all manner of goods are available for very low prices if you know how to haggle. The Pettah is still home to the Moors, the descendants of the Arab seafarers, but also to members of all the other ethnic groups in Sri Lanka. During the 1983 unrest, the Pettah was the target of looters and arsonists, the Moors being the main victims. The streets form an approximate grid pattern. **Each street is reserved for particular goods:** metal wares in one, textiles in another, while currently spices, herbs and tea, for example, are only sold on the 5th Cross Road, and jewellery along the 2nd Cross Road.

Hindu Temple

The 2nd Cross Road is also the location of one of the most important Hindu temples in Colombo. It is dedicated to the goddess Kali, the consort of Shiva. Its façade is decorated, perhaps too richly, with figures from the Hindu pantheon. Inside, the cruel and bloodthirsty, but courageous goddess is depicted by a statue; as usual she has a tiger skin around her black body, and is depicted with a necklet of human skulls, while in her hands she holds a sword and stick, a noose, and a man's head. Kali, the Black One, symbolizes all-consuming time.

Market stalls in Colombo: colourful, lively and inexpensive

On Sea Street, the street of goldsmiths, which leads uphill, there are three imaginatively decorated Hindu temples dating from the early 19th century, known respectively as the Ganeshan, the New Kathiresan and the Old Kathiresan Temples. The latter is dedicated to Skanda, the god of war. Every July it is the scene of a colourful ceremony in honour of the god.

Jami Ul-Afar Jumma Mosque
The Jami Ul-Afar Jumma Mosque (1908) in 2nd Cross Road is also known as the Great Mosque; the decorative use of red and white bricks gives it a magical appearance. The architectural elements, too, such as the domed clock-tower and the slender minarets, the seemingly »twisted« pillars, the pilasters and the gables, all exercise an incomparable charm.

Dutch Period Museum
This museum, set up with the support of the Dutch government, is housed in a 17th-century building. It provides an insight into the history of Sri Lanka during the Dutch colonial period (opening times: Tue–Thu, Sat & Sun 9am–5pm, closed on public holidays; admission charge).

Hulftsdorp

Former Dutch residential quarter
To the east of the Pettah lies the formerly Dutch Hulftsdorp, a residential and legal district named after the Dutch governor Gerard Pieterszoon Hulft. Beyond the Anglican All Saints' Church, a 19th-cen-

The Wolfendahl church is one of four Dutch churches in Sri Lanka

tury building, is the Supreme Court , built in the Dutch colonial style, and imposing with its colonnades. Along the narrow, hilly Hulftsdorp Street and in its side alleys there are still a few typically Dutch houses, albeit pretty dilapidated.

The Dutch Reformed Wolfendahl Church built in 1749 in the quarter of the same name is the oldest Christian church in Colombo still extant. It stands on the foundations of the Portuguese church of Aqua de Lupo. With its cruciform plan, the massive building dominates a hilltop, from which there is a **fine view** of the docks and the old parts of Colombo. Some of the attractive tombstones, decorated with reliefs, of Dutch governors and colonial officials and their families are older than the church; they were transferred here from the old Dutch cemetery in Gordons Garden in the Fort quarter. Noteworthy features inside the church are the pulpit, the pews and the registers.

✳ Wolfendahl Church

North of the Pettah

This district to the north of the Pettah is still largely inhabited by Christians; Kotahena, an 18th-century mission station, is home to many descendants of mixed marriages between Portuguese and Singhalese, known as Burghers. Some of the many churches in this district are worth a visit.

Burgher district

The splendid Roman Catholic church of **Santa Lucia**, built in the Baroque style in the 18th century, is crowned by a high dome. Also of note are the tombstones of a few French bishops. The attached monastery includes a school for young boys. The Anglican **Christ Church** was endowed in 1845 by the first Anglican bishop Dr James Chapman. The local residents still call the church by its old name of Stone Church.

Its alleged miraculous powers have given the statue of St Anthony in the Roman Catholic **St Anthony's Church** on Mahawatta Road a remarkable reputation, and not only among Christians. Attached to the church are St Anthony's Convent and St Anthony's School. Not far away are the little Buddhist temple of Sri Pushparamaya and the small Roman Catholic church of St James.

Churches

> **!** *Baedeker* TIP
>
> ### View of the docks
> For those interested in the activities in the docks, the best place to watch them is the restaurant of the Grand Oriental Hotel (2 York Street, Colombo 01).

Docks Area

Colombo docks, today the economic heart of the city, were expanded to create a harbour of world importance between 1875 and 1907. Three moles with lengths of 1580, 800 and 325m (1728, 880 and 355

Harbour of world importance

yd) enclose an area of 49sq km/19sq mi. At both Queen Elizabeth Quay in the west, and at Delft Quay, five ocean-going ships can berth at a time; at Prince Quay another two. The harbour includes a modern dry dock, efficient cranes, large warehouses and the English-colonial Port Authority building. For security reasons, most of the harbour is not open to the public.

To the south of Fort district

Beira Lake

To the south of the Old Parliament Building visitors will, as they will in many other parts of town, come upon a section of Beira Lake. Now divided up into different sections, the lake used to surround an island known as Slave Island; today, the district is officially known as Kompannaveediya. There are still some slums in the area of the island, a former convict settlement.

Galle Face Green

Stretching along the coast is a lawn, several kilometres long, known as Galle Face Green. The British used to stage horse races and other entertainments here, along with military parades. The lawn was laid out by the British governor Sir Edward Barnes in 1828; he dedicated it to the women of Colombo. Today, Galle Face Green is a **popular meeting place, especially in the evenings,** for the local people, who greatly appreciate the fresh breeze blowing in from the sea. There are a number of cookshops, whose cleanliness, however, sometimes leaves something to be desired.

Prestigious hotels

On the other side of Galle Face Center Road is the pretty **Samudrah House** with the luxury hotel of the same name, and at the rear, the Sri Lanka Tourist Board. The **Galle Face Hotel** at the south end of Galle Face Green, an imposing Victorian building with extensions dating from the 1970s, has the longest tradition of almost any hotel in Colombo. It was once the rendezvous of anyone who was anyone in commerce and the colonial administration, while its terrace was often termed the »most beautiful East of Suez«. Even today some of the magic and the exclusiveness of this venerable establishment can still be felt, even though the shine has faded somewhat. Attached to the hotel is a nicely laid-out garden with a pool.

! **Baedeker TIP**

Lunch with cricket

The Cricket Club in the hip Kollupitiya district is the lunchtime venue for a mostly young clientele who come for a light meal but more especially to watch cricket matches being played all over the world. There are five television screens in all (34 Queens Road).

Other sights

The street that branches off in front of the Galle Face Hotel to the city centre leads past the Holiday Inn, whose architecture is based on the Islamic style, to the interesting 19th-century Christ Church. Galle Road runs parallel to the coast through the districts of Kollupitiya, part of which is **enlivened by street markets** , Bambalapitiya, Wella-watta and leads eventually to Mount Lavinia, a popular bathing resort since time immemorial. This street is also the location of a number of other hotels in the luxury class, such as the Lanka Oberoi with an extensive garden and an imposing foyer, along with a number of embassies.

The Scots Presbyterian church of St Andrew is a Gothic-revival building dating from 1842. Among its characteristic features is the crenellated vestibule and the towers, which resemble castles. Two buildings in the best English colonial style are the United States Embassy and the Prime Minister's Residence in the middle of a magnificent park with frangipani trees.

Cinnamon Garden

The streets named Dharmapala Mawatha and Ananada Kumaraswamy Mawatha, which branches off the former, now lead to the leafy suburb of Cinnamon Garden. The British chose it as their preferred residential district, and today it is home mostly to wealthy Singhalese. Their attractive houses are largely hidden behind tall trees, ornamental shrubs and bushes. This opulent district got its name from the fact that there were once extensive cinnamon and other spice plantations here.

The posh district of Colombo

The heart of Cinnamon Garden is Viharamahadevi Park, which until 1958 was called Victoria Park. Its present name derives from the mother of King Dhutta Gamani, who liberated the city of Anuradhapura from Tamil rule in the 2nd century; there is a statue commemorating her in the park. At the northwestern end, opposite the Town Hall, is a fine statue of a seated Buddha, at the southwestern end a memorial to those killed in the two world wars. The park today is a **popular recreation area** for the people of Colombo, who flock here at weekends especially. At its north-east corner is the imposing Town Hall, whose dome is reminiscent of that of the Capitol in Washington. Also impressive is the massive portico with attractive decoration on the capitals of the pillars.

Viharamahadevi-Park

The modern Bandaranaike Memorial Conference Hall, an hexagonal building, was built in 1973 as a gift to Sri Lanka from the People's Republic of China. It bears the name of the assassinated Prime Minister Solomon Bandaranaike (► Famous People), who is memorialized in a small museum. It contains numerous mementoes and documents relating to the prime minister's life (opening times: Tue–Sat 9am–5pm; admission charge).

Bandaranaike Memorial Conference Hall

The shining white, stately building, which house the National Museum of Colombo, stands in the middle of an attractively laid-out park. The park and the building reflect the grace and dignity of the Victor-

✹ ✹ National Museum

*The National Museum of Colombo
documents a turbulent history*

ian colonial style. The architectural elements and the façade with its three pediments and projecting portico radiate an impressive harmony. The museum was built between 1873 and 1877 at the instigation of the Royal Asiatic Society under the auspices of the British governor Sir William Gregory. daily except public holidays 9am – 5pm; admission charge).

Surroundings of Colombo

Dehiwala Dehiwala forms a dual town together with Mount Lavinia, and is separated from Colombo's southernmost district, Wellawatte, by the Dehiwala Canal. The first street to the right after the traffic island leads to the Buddhist temple of Sri Subnadarama, whose interior walls are decorated with attractive paintings. The interior also houses the figure of a recumbent Buddha, whose sapphire eyes gleam in the light of an oil-lamp. In Dehiwala the Zoological Garden of Colombo

**✶
Zoological
Garden ▶** is also worth a visit, not only because of its large and varied collection of animals, but also because of its attractive grounds, with their many trees, shrubs and flowers. Near the entrance various species of parrot live in large aviaries; next comes a zone with all manner of

deer, and then the section for beasts of prey (lions, Bengal tigers, pumas, leopards, jaguars and bears). The aquarium has a particularly diverse stock. A further enclosure is home to crocodiles and snakes. The many other groups of animals in the zoo, famed as **one of the best in Asia**, whose beginnings go back to the German animal merchant and modern zoo pioneer Carl Hagenbeck (1844–1913), sealions, tortoises, monkeys, storks and a few specimens of kingfishers (opening times: daily 8.30am – 6pm; admission charge).

Some 3km/2mi south of Dehiwala is the famous seaside resort of Mount Lavinia, which can be reached by train or bus from Colombo. In 1819, on a cliff overlooking the sea, the British governor Sir Thomas Maitland had a **large, splendid residence** built, albeit only for weekend use. However his successor, Sir Edward Barnes (governor from 1824 to 1831) was instructed by the Colonial Office in London to sell it, because it had been built without government permission. Later the residence was converted into the Mount Lavinia Hotel, still a first-class establishment. From its terrace there is a view far out to sea and down to the kilometres of palm-lined beach. The name of the hotel does not go back to some girl called Lavinia, but rather to the plant of that name, or possibly to the Singhalese word Lihiniya-gala, which means bird-cliff. The Singhalese, who visit Mount Lavinia mainly at weekends, still call the place, which used to be a fishing village, by its old name of Gakkissa. Unfortunately the quality of the water has grown steadily worse in recent years as the sewage from Greater Colombo is largely piped into the sea untreated. During the monsoon season there are high waves and undercurrents that make it dangerous to bathe.

Mount Lavinia

✶ ✶ Dambulla

C 6

Province: Central Province   **Altitude:** app. 110m/340ft

Dambulla, a small town on the road between Matale and Anuradhapura, is best known for the five caves with numerous Buddha statues and unique wall and ceiling paintings, which are among the most beautiful things ever produced by Singhalese artists. The town itself has nothing worth seeing as such, but the large daily market is worth a visit.

Cave temples of Dambulla

Probably one or two of the caves of Dambulla were already holy places in prehistoric times. In the 1st century BC they were taken over by Buddhist monks. In 102 BC King Vatta Gamani Abhaya (also known as Valagam Bahu) hid here when he was driven out of Anu-

History

▶ VISITING DAMBULLA

GETTING THERE

By car:
from Kandy via the A 9 (72km/45mi);
from Anuradhapura via the A 13 and
A 9 (108km/68mi), from Kurunegala
via the A 6 (55km/33mi)
By train:
the nearest station is Habarana on the
line from Colombo to Trincomalee
(26km/15mi away)
By bus:
good services from Kandy and Kurunegala

WHERE TO STAY

▶ **Mid-range**
Amaya Lake Dambulla
Kandalama, Dambulla
Tel. 066 / 446 81 00
Fax 066 / 223 19 32
www.amayaresorts.com
92 rooms
Situated in a picturesque spot by a
lake, this hotel has very nice rooms
with all comforts. An extensive sports
programme is also provided.

radhapura by the Tamils; not until 85 BC did he succeed in regaining his kingdom. Out of gratitude to the monks who had offered him shelter, he transformed the caves into magnificent temples, making them a **destination for pilgrims**, and also founded a monastery. King Vijaya Bahu I (1055–1110) had the decoration of the caves restored, and in part redesigned. For this purpose he provided funds for several sculptures and donated land. It is also known that King Nissanka Malla (1187–1196) donated further statues. And finally the rulers of the Kandy kingdom, Senerat (1605–1635) and Kirti Sri Raja Sinha (1747–1778) were involved in further re-design of the caves.

Ascent to the temple
The black granite cliff called Dambula-gala rises some 34m/110 ft above sea level, while visitors have to manage 180m/600ft when ascending from the eastern side. The ascent leads first along a simple track, and then up about 250 steps cut into the rock. From the top platform, there is a fine view of the jungle landscape with its many reservoirs (including the Kandalama reservoir), while on clear days, the imposing cliffs of ▶ Sigiriya are visible in the distance. In the temple forecourt an inscription in memory of King Nissanka Malla can be seen directly to the right.

The entrances to the caves were created beneath the projecting cliff wall, and are marked by open structures built on to the cliff; the gable above the main entrance is shaped like a dagoba. The first three caves are the oldest, and in part date back to the 1st century BC; the other two caves are no older than the 18th century.

First cave temple
The first cave bears the name Devaraja-lena (cave of the gods) and contains the 14m/50ft long recumbent figure of a Buddha, carved out of the rock, with his favourite pupil Ananda sitting in front of

him. In addition to numerous other statues, there is one of the Hindu god Vishnu.

The second cave temple, known as Maharaja-lena (cave of the great kings), is **beyond doubt the most beautiful**. Inside, 66 juxtaposed Buddha statues of various dates surround a small dagoba. Some of them are carved out of the rock, while others were donated over the years. They used to be covered in gold, but today they are simply painted gold. The Buddhas, in the Kandy style, can be recognized by the red stole over the left shoulder and the red hem of their garment. Near to the more westerly of the two entrances is the statue of King Vatta Gamani Abnaya, and opposite him the statues of Vishnu and Rama.

Second cave temple

These days the temple complex is surrounded by an electric fence because the monkeys became altogether too tiresome

CAVE TEMPLE OF DAMBULLA

✳ ✳ **The paths to paradise are known to be laborious, and so a high, free-standing rock has to be climbed to reach the site of the wonderful cave temple of Dambulla. The difficult ascent is rewarded by a breathtaking view over a green plain framed by hills and by five temples with their exuberant interiors, whose oldest artworks date back to the pre-Christian era, while the most recent ones are 20th-century work.**

⏱ Open:
daily 8am-5pm

① **Devaraja-lena**
The first cave houses a 14m/45ft statue of a recumbent Buddha, who is just about to enter nirvana. His favourite student Ananda is sitting in front of him. The paintings on the wall and ceiling, some of which have been restored, date from the 1st century BC.

② **Magharaja-lena**
The second rock temple, 60m/200ft long, 30m/100ft wide and up to 15m/50ft high, is not just the largest, but also the most beautiful temple. It houses the most precious treasures.

③ **Maha Alut Viharaya**
The many Buddha statues in the third cave largely date from the 18th century. They include the main cult image showing Buddha under the makara arch, as well as a statue of the last Kandyan king,

Sri Kirti Raja Sinha. Here too the walls are richly adorned with bright materials; they depict Buddha and bodhisattvas of different sizes, poses and skin colours. Marble, sandalwood and ebony were used to make them.

④ **Pachima Viharaya** (not shown on 3D)
The small, fourth cave contains five statues in the popular Kandyan style. It is said the small dagoba once housed the crown jewels of the wife of King Valagamba.

⑤ **Devana Alut Viharaya** (not shown on 3D)
The most recent of the five caves possesses a recumbent Buddha from more modern times and many figures of the Hindu pantheon. The paintings date back to the late Kandy period.

⑥ **Museum**
The monastery houses a small museum that explains, amongst other things, how palm leaves are prepared for use.

Sri Lanka's most impressive cave temple: the Dambulla monastery

The large standing Buddha statue is surrounded by murals, whose theme is the temptation of Buddha by Mara the seducer: Mara, having been defeated by Buddha, is seen falling from his black elephant, with his army of snakes, demons and mythical beasts around him. Other paintings on the ceiling depict **episodes from Buddha's life**: the attack on Mara's army, while the elephant on which Mara sits indicates its submission to Buddha. Further scenes show the start of Siddharta Gautama's path to becoming the founder of a religion, preceded by some scenes of life at the parental court: he proves his mastery of the bow in the palace courtyard; he sets out to practise his use of weapons (his servants are carrying a sword and a discus, among other things) and finally his departure from the palace on his horse Kantaka.

Behind the statues at the end of the cave is a **frieze** depicting scenes from the battle of King Duttha Gamani against the Tamil ruler Elara. In the second half of the 2nd century BC Elara ruled the city of Anuradhapura. In paintings, some of them containing a multitude of figures, come across as very colourful and display compositional idiosyncrasies. These, along with the faces, have given rise to the idea that the artists may have been influenced by the Moghul paintings of the Deccan in India, or possibly even came from there.

Next to the entrance is a small **dagoba**, surrounded by seated Buddhas. Some of them are sitting on cobra plinths, symbolizing the snake-god.

The water, which at one place in the cave drips incessantly from the ceiling, is caught in a stone basin and is used for ritual ablutions. The constant source does not dry up even in the dry months, and is supposed to have given the place its name (»Dambulla« means »water« in Pali). According to legend, the **secret spring** is part of a subterranean river which is said to flow uphill.

Third cave temple

The third cave, Maha Alut Viharaya (great new temple) likewise contains numerous Buddha statues, most of them dating from the 18th century. They include the **main cult image**, which shows Buddha beneath the Makara arch, along with a statue of King Kirti Sri Raja Sinha (reigned 1747–1780). Here too the walls have a superabundance of murals; they show Buddhas and bodhisattvas of various sizes and in various attitudes, and with different skin colours.

Fourth and fifth cave temples

The small fourth cave (Pachima Viharaya, western cave) contains five statues and attractive, albeit inexpertly restored, wall paintings. The fifth cave (Devana Alut Viharaya, second new temple) is the most recent; along with a recumbent, relatively modern Buddha, it has figures from the Hindu pantheon. A noteworthy feature is the statue of Devata Bandara, a local deity. The paintings date back to the late Kandy period and were restored in the 1920s.

Dedigama

B 7

Province: Sabaragamuwa   **Altitude:** app. 64m/200ft

Dedigama, located in the foothills of the gentle Sabaragamuwa highlands, is important mainly because one of the most glorious of the rulers of the Singhalese kingdom, Parakrama Bahu I, was born here. He emerged as victor from the battles of the princes for the kingship. Later, in the 14th century, Dedigama became the residence of King Parakrama Bahu V, who ruled over one of the island's three independent kingdoms from here.

What to see in Dedigama

The Mahavamsa chronicle reports that King Parakrama Bahu I had a massive dagoba erected at the place where he first saw the light of day. However it was only recently that Dedigama could be positively identified as the Punkhagama mentioned un the Mahavamsa.

✳
Punkhagama (dagoba)

The dagoba called Kota Vihara was elaborately restored in the early 1980s. It is in the splendour of the Polonnaruwa style and has **relic chambers**. Some of the contents are to be seen in the small nearby archaeological museum, among them a very beautiful bronze oil-lamp decorated with dancing figures and an elephant. The museum also has some Buddha statues and other finds from the immediate vicinity.

Some 5km/3mi further south, in the strictly isolated forest hermitage of Salgala, Buddhist monks lead an ascetic life of meditation. The monastery has a long tradition, but was re-occupied only in 1931.

Kumarankanda Raja Maha Vihara (monastery)

 VISITING DEDIGAMA

GETTING THERE

By car:
from Colombo via the A 1 until shortly beyond Ambepussa, then turn right (68km/45mi); from Kandy via the A 1 until a few kilometres beyond Nelundeniya, then turn left (50km/30mi)

By train:
the nearest station is Alawwa (11km/7mi away).

By bus:
good bus services from Colombo and Kandy

★ Ella

D 8

Province: Uva **Altitude:** 1012m/3320ft

Ella lies in the enchanting jungle landscape of the Uva plateau. Caves, gorges and waterfalls are the hallmarks of the region. In many places, there are wonderful panoramas of the varied landscape. The town is a suitable base for walking as well as interesting drives, for example through the Ella Gap.

What to see in Ella

Legendary view From the Ella Rest House there are perhaps the most fantastic views that Sri Lanka has to offer, ranging across the amazing landscape all the way to the sea about 100km/60mi away. The large cave, now filled with water, in front of the Rest House is where the demon king Ravana is said to have kept Sita, the consort of Prince Rama, captive and hidden. In the Neolithic period, the cave was probably inhabited, as simple tools (mainly of quartz) of the Balangoda culture have been found in other caves in the vicinity.

 VISITING ELLA

GETTING THERE

By car:
from Bandarawela via the A 16 (12km/8mi); from Badulla via the A 16 (18km/12mi)
By train:
Ella is a station on the line from Colombo to Badulla
By bus:
good bus services from Bandarawela and Badulla

WHERE TO STAY / WHERE TO EAT

► Luxury
Country Comfort Inn
32, Police Station Road
Tel. 057 / 222 85 00
Fax 057 / 222 85 01
www.hotelcountrycomfort.lk
20 rooms, restaurant, bar, excursion programme

Of the total of 20 rooms, eight are in the old colonial-style building. Good restaurant, Sri Lankan cuisine, albeit limited views of the countryside.

► Mid-range
Grand Ella Motel
Wellawaya Road
Tel. / Fax 057 / 222 86 55
www.ceylonhotels.lk
14 rooms, restaurant
The drive to the Grand Ella Motel is an experience in itself; it goes through fascinating mountain scenery, past rice fields and tea plantations. The motel was once a government guest-house, before being renovated a few years back. Since then it has been of 3-star standard. Numerous attractive footpaths

Surroundings of Ella

The Dowa Temple, app. 6km/4mi south of Ella, is worth a visit. There are some steps leading into the interior of the temple, which is completely carved out of the rock. The wall paintings have been very carefully restored by the monks in recent years. Also worthy of note are the statues of various Hindu deities and an 8.1m/27ft tall image which probably dates from the 10th century and is said to represent the bodhisattva Maitreya.

✱ **Dowa Temple**

6km/4mi south-east of Ella a road leading downhill to Wellawaya passes the foaming **Ravana Ella waterfall**. 13km/9mi west of Wellawaya are the majestic **Diyaluma falls**, where the water plunges about 175m/575ft. This is the highest waterfall in Sri Lanka.

✱ **Waterfalls**

In the middle of the jungle near Buduruvagala is a group of important rock statues, carved according to some sources in the 8th or 9th century AD, according to others, though, as early as the 4th century BC. They can be accessed from Wellawaya (app. 7km/4mi) via the Tissamaharama Road leading south, then turn right and continue for 4km/2.5mi along the unmetalled road (during the monsoon season usually only possible in an off-road vehicle).

✱✱ **Rock statues of Buduruvagala**

The rock sculptures of Buduruvagala rise in the middle of the jungle

The centrepiece of the relief statues carved out of the rock is a 15m/50ft tall standing Buddha in the gesture of fearlessness (abhaya-mudra). He is flanked by two groups of three, whose 7.3m/24ft tall centre figures each represent a bodhisattva. The one on the left, probably the bodhisattva Avalokitesvara, is artistically the best of the seven. Alongside him in graceful tribhanga pose is the goddess Tara, holding a vase with a lotus in her hand. The figure on the other side probably represents Sudhana Kumara, the companion of Avalokitesvara.

The bodhisattva on the right may be Vajrapani, a »guardian of the doctrine«, who holds the Vajra (lightning, thunderbolt), but may represent the bodhisattva Maitreya. Legend has it that it is Upatissa, a son of King Silakala (523 – 535). This king was the first in Sri Lanka to forbid the killing of animals, in accordance with Buddhist teaching. The two other figures have not been identified.

★ ★ Galle

B 9

Province: Southern
Population: 91,000

Altitude: 7m/25ft

Visitors to Galle might be forgiven for thinking they were back in the 17th century, so well have the buildings from the Dutch colonial period been preserved. The main reason may well be that when the British took the town in 1798, not a shot was fired. Today Galle is under UNESCO protection as a World Heritage Site.

Industrial location
As a natural harbour, Galle was of great strategic importance for the Arabs and Chinese at an early date, and later for the colonial powers. Today Galle is **Sri Lanka's seventh-biggest city**, and is home to many Muslims and Christians, alongside the Buddhists, who form by far the largest faith group. The city is known too for its industry, primarily cement production and fisheries (in particular tuna). Galle is, in addition, a craft centre; its lace-making is well-known. In the hinterland are a few tea, rubber and coconut plantations. The harbour is mainly employed exporting tea all over the world.

i **Worst tsunami damage**

■ Galle was the scene of some of the worst damage caused by the tsunami of 26 December 2004. While the massive fort by the harbour withstood the wave, more than 1000 people were killed in the bus station behind it within a few minutes.

Name of the city
The name Galle derives from the Singhalese word Gala (cliff, mountain, but also place to rest). The Dutch incidentally confused Gala with the Latin gallus (cockerel), an error which explains **the cockerel**

on the coat-of-arms of the Dutch East India company. The Arabs. who probably ran a trading dock in Galle as long ago as the 9th century, called the city Kalahl.

14th century	First mention of the harbour in Galle
1505	The Portuguese land in Galle and build a fort in 1589.
1640	The Dutch take Galle, destroy the fort and build one of their own in 1663.
1796	The British take Galle without a fight.
1815	Galle's position as the most important harbour on the south-west coast is lost to Colombo.

Galle could be the place mentioned in the Bible as Tarsis, which King Solomon only knew from hearsay, but from where he got gemstones, silk and spices. The Chinese and Arabs conducted much of their trade via Galle, their goods being shipped from here as far afield as Genoa and Venice. In the 9th century Galle seems to have been a significant Arab trade settlement.

History

In 1505 Portuguese ships trying to capture Arab spice ships coming from Sumatra or the Malay peninsula chanced upon Galle when they were driven into the harbour by a storm. They soon departed, on to return in 1518 with the intention of getting a foothold on the island. The first Portuguese trading settlement and a small church date from 1543; in 1587 the Singhalese king was forced to hand over the town to the Portuguese, who built a fort they called Santa Cruz. Within a short time they had built a rampart and three bastions, and fortified the harbour.

After the Dutch under General Coster had landed with twelve ships at the future Sun Bastion in Galle harbour in 1640, they only needed 2000 men to take the city. In 1663 they surrounded the headland with fortifications, which were greatly reinforced under the Dutch governor Petrus Vuysr (1728/29). In addition the Dutch built kitchens, administrative buildings and houses. In 1796 the Dutch governor Dieterich Thomas Fretzsz handed over the Galle garrison keys to the British major general, Lachlan Macquarie.

The further development of the harbour suffered from the fact that offshore coral reefs made access difficult in stormy weather. As a result the British chose Colombo as their main port and developed that instead.

✳ ✳ **Tour of the Fort**

The Fort district, the old Dutch town centre, is located on a small peninsula and is separated from the Kaluwella district by the old Dutch Parana Ela canal, and from the Dharmapala Park district (formerly Victoria Park) and the Pettah to the east of the canal on

Old Dutch town centre

▶ VISITING GALLE

GETTING THERE

By car:
from Colombo, Kalutara and Hikkaduwa via the A 2 (from Colombo 115km/72mi); from Matara via the A 2 (45km/25mi)

By train:
Galle is a station on the line from Colombo to Matara

By bus:
good services from Colombo and all the other towns named above

SHOPPING

Laksala
Sea Street, Galle
State-initiated department store with an impressive selection in particular of traditional crafts (batiks, basketwork, wood carvings) at very inexpensive (fixed) prices.

WHERE TO STAY/ WHERE TO EAT

▶ Luxury

① *Amangalla*
Church Street
Tel. 091 / 223 33 88
Fax 091 / 223 33 55, amanresorts.com
Stylish accommodation within the Dutch fort: the Amangalla is in the former, carefully restored New Oriental Hotel, for more than 140 years the best address in Galle. Today it's one of the most expensive hotels on the island; a night in the Garden House

Modern design in the luxury resort The Fortress

costs around 700 US dollars. But there are double rooms for less around 400 US dollars.

② *Galle Fort Hotel*
28, Church Street, Galle Fort
Tel. 091 /223 28 70
Fax 091 / 223 29 39
www.galleforthotel.com
13 rooms, restaurant, bar, pool, health facilities
New hotel under German management in the 300-year-old house of an old-established merchant family. Individual atmosphere, excellent yet inexpensive restaurant open to non-guests.

③ *The Fort Printers*
39, Pedlar Street
Tel. 091 / 224 79 77
Fax 091 / 224 79 76
www.thefortprinters.com
5 rooms, restaurant, pool
Following the trend to convert ancient buildings into modern hotels, this establishment was set up inside the Dutch Fort. There used to be a printing press here; today there are just five stylish rooms with all conveniences. Parts of the interior still recall the printing-press days.

④ *The Fortress*
Matara Road, Kogolla Beach, PO Box 126
Tel. 091 / 438 09 09
Fax 091 / 438 03 38
www.thefortress.lk
49 rooms and suites, pool, restaurant, tea-room, health facilities, ayurveda, fitness studio, yoga pavilion, watersports centre, diving school, wedding chapel, library and much more besides.
Brand new luxury refuge close to Galle with every desirable feature. The architecture of the resort is based on that of the Dutch forts. It is located right on the south coast. Behind the walls, guests will find elaborately designed gardens and waterscapes, quite apart from the hotel. Here you are spoilt with things you never knew existed.

Baedeker recommendation

► Luxury
⑤ *Light House*
Dadella (at the northern exit to the city)
Tel. 091 / 222 37 44, Fax 091 / 273 40 21
www.jetwinghotels.com
60 rooms, 3 themed suites, 2 restaurants, coffee shop, bar, health facilities, pool, private beach
The best address in Galle, the staircase leading to the reception desk is an experience in itself. Very comfortable rooms, first-class cuisine.

► Mid-range
⑥ *Closenberg*
11, Closenberg Road, Magalle
Tel. 091 / 222 43 13
Fax 091 / 222 22 41
www.closenburghotel.com
20 rooms (including four suites), restaurant, bar, very nice garden
Legendary stylish establishment dating from 1860 on a tongue of land; the rooms are furnished in the colonial style with many fine antiques.

► Budget
⑦ *The Lady Hill*
29, Upper Dickson Road
Tel. 091 /224 43 22
Fax 091 / 223 48 55
www.ladyhills.com
20 rooms, restaurant, pool, bar
From the rooftop bar there is possibly the best view of Galle and the sea. The rooms are friendly and comfortable.

Galle Map

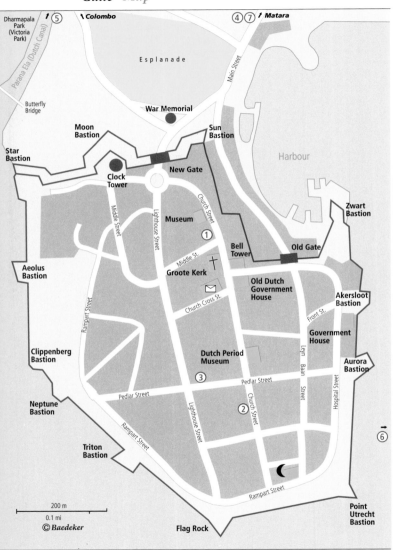

Dharmapala Park (Victoria Park) ⑤

↑ Colombo

④⑦ ∕ Matara

Parana Ela (Dutch Canal)

Esplanade

Butterfly Bridge

War Memorial

Moon Bastion

Sun Bastion

Star Bastion

Harbour

Clock Tower

New Gate

Middle Street

Lighthouse Street

Museum ①

Church Street

Bell Tower

Old Gate

Zwart Bastion

Aeolus Bastion

Middle St.

Groote Kerk

Old Dutch Government House

Akersloot Bastion

Church Cross St.

Front St.

Government House

Clippenberg Bastion

Rampart Street

Dutch Period Museum ③

Leyn Baan Street

Aurora Bastion

Pedlar Street

Church Street

②

Hospital Street

Neptune Bastion

Pedlar Street

Lighthouse Street

Rampart Street

⑥

Triton Bastion

Rampart Street

200 m

0.1 mi

© Baedeker

Flag Rock

Point Utrecht Bastion

Where to stay
① Amangalla
② Galle Fort Hotel
③ The Fort Printers

④ The Fortress
⑤ Light House
⑥ Closenberg
⑦ The Lady Hill

There are wonderful views from the ramparts around the fort

the harbour bay by a stretch of grass known as the Esplanade. The Butterfly Bridge, dating from Dutch times, and the Main Street connect Fort and Pettah with Kaluwella.

The ramparts of the fortifications, a **popular promenade**, follow the line of the shore and on the landward side separate the peninsula from the hinterland. Their total length is about 4km/2.5mi, including the second rampart, which the Dutch built to reinforce the first. The ramparts have eleven bastions, of which the Star, Moon and Sun Bastions secured the fort to the landward side.

The Fort is entered today by the New Gate constructed by the British in 1873. They also built the Clock Tower. The Moon Bastion on the Esplanade stands on the remains of the Portuguese fort, the Conceyçao, while the Star Bastion stands on the remains of the St Antonia fort, also built by the Portuguese. To the west are the Aeolus, Clippenburg, Neptune (on which the signal station once stood) and Triton bastions, built in around 1730. There used to be a windmills here. On the cliffs known as Vlagge Klipp and Flag Rock at the southern tip there were once a Portuguese bastion and a lighthouse.

New Gate

The new lighthouse stands on Point Utrecht Bastion, while nearby looms the former Powder Tower with an inscription that records

Bastions

that it was completed in 1782. The next bastions are Autors Bastion and Akersloot Bastion, named after General Coster's birthplace. During the Dutch colonial period there is said to have been an underground passage between Akersloot and Zwart Bastions (the latter now housing the police station). Zwart Bastion (Black Bastion) is probably the oldest of all the fortifications; the remains of the Portuguese Santa Cruz fort, dating from 1580, can still be seen. Here incoming ships used to be inspected and let into the harbour through a grid, which still exists.

From 1669 and 1873, the old gate formed the only entrance to the city. The relief on the outside of the gate shows the coat-of-arms of King George III of Great Britain (reigned 1760–1820), while that on the inside shows that of the Dutch Vereenigde Oostindische Compagnie, flanked by two lions, surmounted by a cockerel, and below, the date 1669 in Roman numerals. The Sun Bastion was built in 1667 and forms the northern boundary of the harbour. Between it and Zwart Bastion there used to be two more forts, Vismark Bastion diagonally opposite the New Oriental Hotel (today the luxury Amangalla Hotel) and Commadement Bastion. The street names are English translations of the Dutch names. Any walk through the district will pass numerous former Dutch administrative buildings, one Dutch and two English churches, a Buddhist temple and the former residences of wealthy English merchants, built in the typical Dutch style (recognizable by the broad verandas).

> ### ! *Baedeker* TIP
>
> **Jewellery, antiques, crafts**
> The little Historical Museum at 31–39 Leyn Baan Street is worth a visit. It is in one of the oldest buildings in Fort district, which was constructed true to the style of the old mansions and dates from about 1680. The varied collection of jewellery, antiques and crafts is worth seeing (opening times: Tue – Sun 9am – 4pm).

Government House The old Government House near the old gate (Queen's House), today the headquarters of the company Walker, Son & Co., was once the residence of the Dutch governor of Galle, and then of the British administrator. Above the entrance is a stone plaque with the cockerel and the date 1683.

Churches Of the old Dutch church of 1640 nothing now remains. In fact no one is quite sure exactly where it stood. The present **Dutch church** in Church Street, completed in 1755, was endowed by Gertuyda Adriana de Grand in gratitude for having given birth to a daughter after years of childless marriage. The church has two fine Baroque gables. The floor inside, paved with grave slabs, is worth seeing. Opposite the church is an older bell-tower (1701)).

Somewhat further along Church Street is the Anglican **All Saints' Church**, built in 1871, with epitaphs from British colonial days. Further still are the Arab College, and, near the sea-front, the mosque.

In Light House Street is the Methodist church, dating from 1894, while at the intersection of Rampatt/Great Modera Baystreet is the Sri Sudharmalaya Buddhist temple.

Other sights

North-west of the Forts, on the other side of Dharmapala Park, is the district of Kaluwella (black town), the **native quarter** (as opposed to Fort, the white, or European, quarter). Right by the grounds of the Town Hall on Calvary Hill is the Roman Catholic cathedral of St Mary, built in 1874.

Kaluwella (district)

To the east of the harbour is the Pettah, the **bazaar quarter** of Galle. With a bit of luck you might find some pretty craft items.

Pettah

In the Kerkhof, a Dutch cemetery near the market, are the graves of Dutch officials and officers. The gate bears the inscription »Memento mori« (Remember You Will Die) and the date 1786. From this date this cemetery presumably replaced the two older ones inside the Fort.

Intact residential quarter from the time of the Dutch

Surroundings of Galle

Kogalla At the milestone with the inscription 83, south of Galle, a road turns off the left towards the Kathaluwa Temple, about 3km/2mi further on. Its interior walls are covered with paintings by four 18th-century artists. They depict, arranged in friezes, scenes from the Jataka, dancers, and a group of musicians dressed in Western costumes. The style is provincial, and the depiction of the human figures somewhat clumsy. The plants and animals are by contrast more lively. What is remarkable, though, is the delight in story-telling which had evidently gripped the artists, and the relatively subtle coloration.

? DID YOU KNOW ...?

■ ...that a legend from the Ramayana is connected with the Rhumassala Kanda, a huge overgrown rock on the Watering Point? When Lakshmani, the loyal brother of Prince Rama, was wounded in battle, Rama sent the monkey god Hanuman to the Himalayas to get a particular medicinal herb. However Hanuman forgot its name and brought a whole rock that was overgrown with all sorts of plants, and it is now lying here.

Typical of this region is **surf-angling**, which can be seen on the way from Ahangama, a few kilometres to the east of Kogalla. The fishermen sit on pillars about 5m/17ft high driven into the sea-bed. From there they cast their lines. As serious attempts to catch anything are only made in the early morning, or maybe in the evening just about, those anglers who can be observed in the daytime or who sit around on the shore are doing it for the tourists, in other words they are hoping for a tip.

Gal Oya National Park

D–E 7

Province: Eastern/Uva   **Altitude:** 7–30m/25–100ft

Gal Oya National Park is 256sq km/100sq mi in extent, making it Sri Lanka's fourth-largest. The hilly landscape, dominated by high grass and trees, is criss-crossed by waterways, while the horizon is marked by the bizarre outlines of rocks and mountains.

Vedda homeland The area has always been considered the tribal homeland of the Vedda, of whom there are still several hundred living here. The National Park is one result of the damming of the Gal Oya to create the huge Lake Senanayake, Sri Lanka's largest lake, natural or artificial. It was the focus of an ambitious development project which has brought the region a certain prosperity. Since the end of the civil war, access to the park is unrestricted.

▶ VISITING GAL OYA NATIONAL PARK

GETTING THERE

By car:
from Colombo via Kandy and
Mahiyangana – Maha Oya – Ampara
– Inginiyangala (app. 290km/180mi)
or via Ratnapura – Wellawaya –
Siyambalanduwa – Inginiyala (app.
320km/200mi)

WHERE TO STAY

In the east of the National Park there
are some state-run bungalows and a
campsite. The Safari Inn Hotel close
to the entrance can also be recommended. Otherwise the nearest places
to stay are in ▶Ampara.

What to see in the Gal Oya National Park

The Senanayake Dam, built with American support, is 1200m/
1300yd long and 90m/300ft high. Its construction created the reservoir of the same name, some 90sq km/35sq mi in area; it commemorates the first Prime Minister of Sri Lanka, then called Ceylon, Don
Stephen Senanayake.
The whole project includes a number of other, albeit much smaller,
reservoirs, among them the Ekgal Aru, the Jayanthi Wewa and the
Namal Oya Wewa, along with some rivers and canals in the valley of
the Gal Oya. The economic development gave rise to a few small factories on the fringe of the National Park, while additional inhabitants
were also enticed into the area.

Senanayake Dam

The main entrance to the nature conservation area is a few kilometres to the west of ▶Ampara, where Jeeps can be hired. Like all of
Sri Lanka's national parks, it may only be explored on land by Jeep
in the company of a ranger, while **leaving the vehicle inside the park
is strictly forbidden**. However it is also possible to explore the park
by boat (information at the main entrance).
The Gal Oya National Park is primarily the home of numerous wild
elephants, but there are also deer (including the white-spotted chital), a few leopards and, allegedly, some bears, which are, it must be
said, rarely seen. The banks of the waterways are a paradise for numerous birds. Occasionally crocodiles can also be seen.

*Nature
conservation
area*

Inside and outside the National Park there are a few caves which
were originally occupied by the Vedda. For example in the Danigala
mountains at a height of more than 610m/2000ft and near Makara
(also a good place to observe wild elephants). Ratugala, 32km/20mi
north of Inginiyagala, is home to a small **tribe of Vedda**, who live in
the jungle in fairly primitive conditions. In Gonagala there are some
caves with rock paintings, which presumably date from the 3rd or
8th century, the remains of a dagoba and a moonstone.

Vedda caves

Toucans live hidden in the tree tops in Gal Oya Park.
Their large beaks are striking.

Westminster Abbey (mountain) On the south-east edge of the National Park is the rocky summit of the 558m/1830ft mountain known as Westminster Abbey, from where there is a magnificent view. It was given its unusual name by British seafarers, who, sailing along the coast, were reminded of the silhouette of the Abbey in London. At the foot of the rock is another Vedda cave.

Giritale

Province: North Central   **Altitude:** app. 105m/340ft

One of Sri Lanka's oldest reservoirs, which was restored at the start of the 20th century, forms the focus of one of the most interesting nature conservation areas on the island. The landscape is also extraordinarily attractive, with jungle alternating with open grassland.

What to see in Giritale

Minneriya reservoir The Minneriya reservoir with an area of app. 1800 hectares or 4500 acres was created in AD 275 by King Maha Sena, taking its water from the Elahera canal dating from a century earlier. In 1903 the reservoir was renovated, having silted up, and connected by a 140km/ 90mi extension of the Elahera canal to the Kandul and Kantale reservoirs further to the north.

The small Giritale reservoir is also connected to the canal network; like the other reservoirs, it too provides for adequate irrigation for the local agriculture.

Giritale reservoir

Impenetrable jungle and open grasslands characterize the Giritale Minneriya Sanctuary a few kilometres from Giritale. It is home to not only a few wild elephants, but also leopards, which are however rarely seen. There is a better chance of observing the diverse local birdlife. No fewer than 39 species have been counted on a single walk through the sanctuary, including the white-throated kingfisher, various paddybirds, the Sri Lankan brown fish-owl, the Indian oriole and the koel, a grey-spotted cuckoo species. A **boat trip on the Minneriya reservoir** is a good idea, as it will provide a sighting of a large

✱ Giritale Minneriya Sanctuary

Water buffalo bathing in Minneriya Reservoir

● VISITING GIRITALE

GETTING THERE

By car:
from Habarane to Minneriya (20km/12mi), from there to Giritale (12km/8mi); from Polonnaruwa to Giritale (10km/6mi)

By train:
the Minneriya and Hingurakgoda stations on the line from Gal Oya to Batticaloa are each app. 6km/4mi from Giritale).

By bus:
good services from Habarana, Polonnaruwa and Minneriya

WHERE TO STAY

► **Luxury**
The Deer Park Hotel
Reservation in Colombo:
04, Hunupitiya Road
Colombo 2
Tel. 01 / 44 88 50, 44 88 48, 44 71 53
Fax 01 / 44 88 49
80 rooms, restaurant, bar, pool
Hotel built in the style of a lodge not far from the historical sites of Anuradhapura, Polonnaruwa and Mihintale. Very nice, comfortable rooms

number of birds. On the edge of the sanctuary there are a few sizable teak plantations planted ny the government as part of a re-afforestation programme.

Hambantota

D 9

Province: Southern
Population: 12,000

Altitude: 7m/25ft

Hambantota, a centre for obtaining sea-salt and, since the tsunami, once again a lively fishing port, is located in the dry zone of the south coast on a splendidly curving bay. Typical of the region are the undemanding palmyra palms which have been planted in an attempt to secure the shifting dunes.

Tsunami damage

In addition to the Singhalese, this place is home to many Malays, who are adherents of Islam. They are said to have given the place its name: hambans (little boat) and tota (harbour) are words in Malay. Hambantota is also a good starting point for trips through the ►Yala National Park. Hambantota was not just damaged by the tsunami: almost the whole place was washed away. At the Sunday market alone, which was in progress at the time, more than 5,000 people lost their lives. Although the government of Sri Lanka has singled out the Hambantota region as a model for speedy and unbureaucratic reconstruction and made funds available for 6,223 houses, signs of the devastation are still obvious.

▶ VISITING HAMBANTOTA

GETTING THERE

By car:
Via the A 2 from Colombo (240km/150mi), Galle (122km/75mi) and Matara (77km/49mi)
By bus:
good services from Galle

**WHERE TO STAY /
WHERE TO EAT**

► **Budget**
Oasis Ayurveda Beach Resort
Tel. 047 222 64 50 Fax 047 222 06 52
www.oasis-ayurveda.com

40 rooms, 2 restaurants, bar, pool, gym, tennis, squash, yoga
The Oasis was the first hotel in Hambantota to be reconstructed and receive guests after the tsunami. It lies right next to an extensive, almost deserted beach, in the middle of a 5 hectare/12.5 acre garden, next to a pretty lake, and the site is very quiet. The complex is in two parts, one being reserved for guests who have not booked any extras. Spa guests can have an ayurveda buffet or medically prescribed meals.

Hambantota harbour was already known to Greek seafarers, and it was through them that the Alexandrian geographer Ptolemy heard about it. On his map he called it Dionysii. The Malays who currently inhabit Hambantota are for the most part descendants of Malay soldiers recruited by the British and, earlier, by the Dutch. **History**

What to see in Hambantota

Even after the tsunami, Hambantota is an important fishing port. The market is particularly busy in the morning when the boats land their catches. **Fish market**

From the attractively located lake Karagan Lewaya immediately to the west of Hambantota there is, in good weather, a view reaching as far as ►Adam's Peak, the pass of ►Haputale and the seven mountain peaks of ►Kataragama. **Karagan Lewaya (lake)**

Surroundings of Hambantota

Some 11km/7mi west of Hambantota, shortly before the mouth of the Walawe Ganga, is the little town of Ambalantota. Here there are the sparse remains of an old Dutch fort, an old Rest House (now a police station), the Girihandu Vihara and an Archaeological Museum. The Girihandu Vihara contains an important limestone relief in the style of the Indian Andhra art (roughly mid 1st century BC to 2nd century AD). It depicts a standing Buddha with several theatrical images of figures paying homage to him and offering gifts. The work was probably carried out by an Indian artist. The Archaeological Mu- **Ambalantota** seum has on display finds from the area, which was settled very early on, including the 1.8m/6ft tall, finely carved statue of a bodhisattva dating from the 7th/8th century (opening times: Sat – Thur 9am–5pm; admission charge).

Kunandaka Lena Cave

From Ambalantota a road leads to the Ridiyagama reservoir in the middle of the jungle, created between 1928 and 1932. Nearby is the Kunandaka Lena Cave (also known as Karambagalle), in which were discovered **the oldest paintings in Sri Lanka** . As the monk Buddhagosam reported in the 5th century, a hermit monk had lived there for twelve years without knowing about the paintings on the ceiling. It was not until pilgrim monks came to visit him that they were pointed out to him. The paintings were done in red paint on a white ground, and they depict the head of a bodhisattva and the bust of an apsara (heavenly virgin) emerging from the clouds, who in her turn is handing a flower to the bodhisattva.

Hatton · Dikoya

C 8

| **Province:** Central | **Altitude:** 1340m/4400ft |

The little town of Dikoya, picturesquely situated between hills thick with tea-bushes, has long since grown together with the neighbouring town of Hatton.

Major tea-growing region

At heights of between 1200 and 1600m (4000 and 5000ft), this part of the Central Highlands, known as Upper Glenn, grows the best tea in Sri Lanka. It is also the largest single tea-growing region on the island. Not far from Hatton is the source of the Mahaweli Ganga, at 332km/206mi Sri Lanka's longest river, which starts its journey by winding around the high mountains first to the west, then east, and then north, reaching the sea at Mutur near Trincomalee. The town is a good starting point for climbing ►Adam's Peak.

What to see in Hatton and Dikoya

✶✶ Landscape

The landscape around Hatton is a sight in itself: rolling hills, on which it doesn't just look as if every square metre is covered in tea-bushes, dense green forests and the backdrop of magnificent mountains. A stay or a visit is recommended especially between December and March, when there is hardly any rain and the air is pleasantly fresh.

✶ Tea factories

A visit to a tea factory is an interesting experience, usually taking about half an hour, during which visitors will find out a great deal about the processing of the leaves and about the different varieties.

▶ VISITING HATTON · DIKOYA

GETTING THERE

By car:
from Colombo via Avissawella on the A7 (135km/85mi); from Nuwara Eliya via the A7 (48km/30mi); from Kandy via the A5 to Ginigathena, then on the A7 (72km/45mi)

By train:
the station is on the Highland Line.

By bus:
good services from all the places named above

WHERE TO STAY

In Hatton there are two reasonably comfortable guesthouses, one being the Ajantha Guest House, tel.: 051 2222337.

Among the properties than can be visited are the Mount Vernon Estate and Court Lodge Estate near Dambulla and Talawakelle, and the Tea Research Institute in St. Combs Estate; **no booking necessary**. In most tea factories the tour ends with a freshly brewed cup of tea. Even so, visitors should remember the poor conditions in which the countless, mostly Tamil tea-pluckers live and work. Their work is hard, while their pay is very low. Not surprisingly, there is considerable potential for social tension.

✳ Hikkaduwa

B 9

Province: Southern   **Altitude:** 5–36m/18–130ft

For many years, Hikkaduwa has been a famous bathing resort on the southwest coast of Sri Lanka, known throughout the world for its beautiful beaches. The much praised coral reefs however have been seriously damaged by both human and environmental influences. Even so, Hikkaduwa has lost little of its popularity, and the hospitality of the inhabitants continues to be its greatest capital.

Auch Hikkaduwa was badly hit by the tsunami, almost all the hotels along the coast were seriously damaged. All have since reopened, however, and the proprietors have made the best of the situation by upgrading their rooms. In the low season, Hikkaduwa looks almost deserted, but even at this time bathing is possible in some places.

Tsunami damage

What to see in Hikkaduwa

Although the coral gardens near the coast have been placed under protection orders, they are no longer the preferred goal of divers and snorkellers. However the variety of the marine life is still consider-

✳
Coral reefs

▶ VISITING HIKKADUWA

GETTING THERE

By car:
from Colombo via the A 2 (98km/ 60mi); from Galle via the A 2 (19km/ 12mi)
By train:
Hikkaduwa is a station on the line from Colombo to Matara
By bus:
good services from Colombo and Galle

BEACHES

Hikkaduwa's beaches are regarded as the best surfing beaches in Sri Lanka. Surfers from all over the world gather here between November and April, experts are attracted in particular to the southern end of the coral reef. In Hikkaduwa there are a few shops that hire out boards. The water is also good for swimming, but not if you like to bathe alone.

MARKT

Above Hikkaduwa station a Sunday Market takes place every week, to which farmers and merchants come from the surrounding region.

WHERE TO EAT

▶ Inexpensive
Restaurant Refresh
384, Galle Road
Tel. 075 / 45 81 08 - 9
Comprehensive menu, a lot of fresh fish straight from the sea. Cosy atmosphere, but a little more pricey than average

▶ Budget
Abbas Restaurant
7, Waulagoda Road
Tel. 091 / 227 71 10
Daily 9am – 10pm
A good place for railway fans, the train goes right past the restaurant. Apart from that, the place has the best steaks in town and good coffee. And the trains aren't so very frequent.

WHERE TO STAY

▶ Luxury
Amaya Reef Resort & Spa
400 Galle Road
Hikkaduwa
Tel. 091 / 438 32 44
Fax 091 / 438 32 43
www.amayaresorts.com
54 rooms, restaurant, bar, pool
Very comfortable hotel with tastefully furnished, modern rooms. Dignified atmosphere, at the moment probably the best hotel in Hikkaduwa

▶ Mid-range
Corel Garden
Galle Road
Tel. (in Colombo) 01 / 232 08 62
Fax 01 / 243 90 46
coral@keells.com
150 rooms, restaurant, coffee shop, bar, pool, tennis, squash, water sports, gym
Large hotel on a tongue of land, popular with an international public for many years. Modern rooms

Corel Sands Hotel / Blue Coral
326, Galle Road
Tel. 091 / 227 75 13, 227 74 36
Fax 091 / 438 32 25
www.coralsandshotel.com
75 rooms, restaurant, bar, 2 pools, water sports
After some damage following the tsunami, this beach-side hotel has been rebuilt and modernized at the same time. The same proprietor now owns the neighbouring Blue Coral Hotel, and guests of either can use the facilities in both. Attentive service, clean rooms

▶ Budget
The Plantation Villa Hotel
Baddegama Road, Baddegama
Tel. / Fax 091 / 924 05
Those who want to get away from the
hustle and bustle of Hikkaduwa, but
still want to be near the beaches, will
find what they want in this little hotel
in the hinterland of Hikkaduwa. Good
restaurant with local specialities; regular cooking course

In Dodanduwa: Oriental Rest
54, Galle Road
E-mail: info@oriental-rest.de
www.oriental-rest.de/english.html
6 rooms, restaurant
Small, inexpensive guest-house with
pretty rooms. Very nice garden right
by the beach. Helpful owner.

Baedeker recommendation

▶ Mid-range
Ayurveda-Centrum
Lawrence Hill Paradise
47, Waulagoda Middle Road
Tel. 091 / 227 50 74
Fax 091 / 438 32 99
http://en.ayurvedakurlaub.de
14 rooms, ayurveda restaurant, pool
In this hotel, located in a wonderful 1.2
hectare / 3 acre garden on a hill above
Hikkaduwa, all the guests have come for the
ayurveda. For those seeking rest and
relaxation, this is the place, and the beach
isn't far either. All ayurveda services are
included in the price.

Ayurveda hotel in the middle of a lovely garden: Lawrence Hill Paradise

able, including numerous fish species, molluscs, etc., which can also be observed on **trips in the glass-bottomed boat**. Beyond the coral banks there are also large fish such as barracuda and Moray eels, as well as turtles. The worldwide phenomenon of coral bleach has not spared the coral reefs of Hikkaduwa.

Landscape The landscape around Hikkaduwa is not only marked by wide and fairly well looked after beaches, but also by a hinterland covered by a broad variety of vegetation. To the north of the town centre there is a large lagoon, with boat trips on offer.

Sinigama Vihara Some 2km/1.5mi from Hikkaduwa bus station is Sinigama Vihara temple, which can only be reached via a wooden walkway. It is one of two temples in Sri Lanka where people who have been robbed can pray for the return of their property. In the temple there is a special oil which can be ignited at home, whereupon the thief will be beset by disease, accident or some other unpleasant fate. In order to avoid worse, he then gives himself up.

The best attractions of Hikkaduwa are to be found under water

Surroundings of Hikkaduwa

The present Buddhist temple of Purana Totagama Raja Maha Vihara in Telwatta, a small town to the north of Hikkaduwa, was built in 1805, but goes back to an earlier foundation. At the start of the 15th century this was the home of Sri Lanka's most famous poet Sri Ranula, before King Parakrama Bahu II summoned him to his court in Kotte. The Makara arch at the entrance is regarded as one of the most beautiful of the Kandy period. The figure of the god Amora with arrows tipped with flowers is unique of its kind. This motif seems to have been borrowed from European art. The murals inside depict Jataka scenes from the life of the Buddha.

Telwatta

Baedeker TIP

Promenading on the Only Path

The monastery on Polgasduwa accepts male visitors only wishing to spend a few days learning about the teaching of the Buddha. In order to ensure undisturbed meditation and study of the scriptures, the island can only be visited with a written invitation (www.metta.lk/temples/ih/Info.htm#english).

The fishing village of **Dodanduwa** is picturesquely located on the magnificent Lake Ratgama, formed by the Ratgama Oya, on which there are a number of luxuriantly vegetated islets. Cinnamon bushes grow in the immediate surroundings. The villagers are known for their strict Buddhism. The tsunami caused considerable damage in places here.

The temple of Kumarankanda Raja Maha Vihara in the middle of the village has some very fine murals and a footprint of the Buddha. Also of note are various statues of gods.

◄ Kumarankanda Raja Maha Vihara

About 1km/1100yd further on stands the temple of Sailabima Aramaya, reached by a long stone staircase. The murals tell of Buddha's birth and depict other scenes from his life. This was the site of Sri Lanka's first school for the sons of Buddhist laymen, as well as a college for the monastic community.

◄ Sailabima Aramaya

The island of Polgasduwa in Lake Ratgama, which is served by boats from the lakeside, has become quite famous. In 1911, a 33-year-old German by the name of Anton Gneth – his monastic name was Nyanantiloka, and later he was honoured with the name of Mahathara (i. e. Eldest) – founded a **Buddhist monastery.** He and the other German monks were deported during World War I and not allowed to return until 1926. By then the little monastery was in ruins and everything had to be rebuilt. Gneth, or rather Nyanantiloka, made a name for himself as the author of numerous commentaries and as the translator of parts of the Pali canon, including the Visuddhi Magga (Path of Purity) and Anguttara Nikaya (Discourses of the Buddha). He spent the last four years of his life with his pupil Nyanaponika in the latter's forest cell near Kandy, dying in Colombo in 1957 in the wake of an operation; he was accorded a state funeral.

Polgasduwa (island)

Excursions

Within easy reach of Hikkaduwa by bus or train there are a number of worthwhile excursion destinations, e. g. ►Galle and further south ►Matara or ►Kalutara and ►Ambalangoda to the north.

✶ ✶ Horton Plains

C 8

Province: Central   **Altitude:** app. 2150m/7000ft

The lonesome highlands of Horton Plains –Sri Lanka's most elevated plateau – are covered with grass and scrub, and are a popular destination for ramblers, as well as being a pleasant place to stay in the hot months. The area takes its name from Sir R. W. Horton, who was the British governor of Sri Lanka from 1831 to 1837. The Horton Plains are a National Park, as they are home to the last remaining tropical cloud forests, which are deemed worthy of protection.

Rambling on Horton Plains

A hike across the Horton Plains is one of the most memorable experiences that Sri Lanka has to offer the nature-lover. Hikers should set out early, because at this time of day there are still good views over the pristine landscape and bizarre vegetation; by 11am – especially at World's End – there are often dense fog banks. It must be said that the fauna at this altitude is not particularly diverse, consisting at best of a few species of birds.

The Horton Plains are criss-crossed by a **well signposted network of footpaths**, which ramblers are not allowed to leave (stout footwear is needed, the paths are slippery!). To get there, an off-road vehicle is advisable, but these can be hired in all of the nearby centres. There is an admission charge for the National Park itself. The Horton Plains are bounded to the north by Totapola, at 2359m/7739ft the third-highest mountain in Sri Lanka (reckon on about 2 hours for the ascent).

✶ ✶ World's End

A walk across the undulating grasslands and areas with subtropical vegetation leads to two **viewpoints**, Big World's End and Little World's End. At the former, the cliff wall drops almost 1000m/3300ft steeply into the valley, and the latter is also impressive, though here the drop is only (!) 600m/2000ft.

Baker's Falls

A magnificent walk, (but one that'll bring you out in sweat at any time of the year) leads after about half and hour to Baker's Falls, a wild and romantic cascade from a pool at the top, with large tree ferns and rhododendrons growing around the pool at the bottom. The falls were named after Sir Samuel Baker, a famous British explorer.

▶ VISITING HORTON PLAINS

GETTING THERE

By car:
from the west via Talawakelle (A 7), Agrapatana and Diyagama Estate; from the north via Nuwara Eliya or Hakgala. The Horton Plains are app. 170km/110mi from Colombo.

By train:
the nearest stations are in Pattipola and Ohiya (bozj about 11km/7mi away).

WHERE TO STAY

There is unfortunately no accommodation in the designated Horton Plains conservation area. The best base for a visit is ▶Nuwara Eliya.

Jaffna

A/B 2

Province: Northern
Population: 146,000

Altitude: 2–7m/7–25ft

Even in the past, the Jaffna peninsula saw few visitors. With the outbreak of the civil war in 1983, the tourist trade, such as it was, virtually collapsed. Even now that the civil war has ended, Jaffna is not (yet) a tourist destination of any significance. The town was town badly damaged in the fighting, most historic buildings of importance were destroyed. It will also be years before there is any accommodation that could be recommended.

Almost all the native Singhalese have been driven out and their houses burned down. The town of Jaffna will certainly be marked for years to come by the destruction caused by the ethnic conflict. However, the continuity of the Dravidian culture with its roots in south India had already been broken when the colonial masters destroyed the old temples and palace buildings.

Marked by war

Even so, the landscape of the peninsula offers a surprisingly marked contrast with the rest of the country. It is barren, and dominated by undemanding vegetation. The irrigation of the agricultural areas is not effected through reservoirs and canals, as it is just a few dozen kilometres further south, but by the use of wells. Nonetheless, numerous small fields bear witness to the hard work of the local people, who have succeeded, in spite of all the obstacles nature has placed in their way, in getting the soil to bring forth some fruit at least. The people, small and very dark-skinned Tamils, have been settled here since time immemorial; they are hospitable and friendly. Most of

Barren landscape

▶ VISITING JAFFNA

GETTING THERE

By car:
from Colombo via Anuradhapura
(A 6, A 10, A 28, A 20), then via the
A 14 to Mannar and from there via the
A 32 to Jaffna. There are numerous
checkpoints on the way.
By train:
currently there is no rail connection
between Colombo and Jaffna, though
one is expected to be restored in the
foreseeable future.

WHERE TO STAY
Apart from a few guesthouses offering
basic conveniences, there is still no
accommodation in Jaffna that can be
recommended.

them /following the expulsion of the Singhalese, there are now only about 60,000 inhabitants) live packed together in Jaffna town, and are adherents of Hinduism.

History Not much is known about the historical development of this part of the island. It is likely that in the first half of the 13th century a Tamil adventurer (maybe a king's son) from southern India set up a principality on the Jaffna principality, whose capital was called Nallur. Marco Polo, who visited this city in 1292, reports that the principality was ruled by a king named Sandernaz, who owed tribute to no other king. The Rajavali chronicle reports that in the 14th century, King Arya Chakravarti was the most powerful ruler in Ceylon, because the two other kings, Vikrama Bahu II in Gampola and Alakeshvara in Rayigama, paid tribute to him. When King Alakeshvara, who had established a new, heavily fortified royal city in Kotte, not far from Colombo, refused to pay, Arya Chakravarti marched south. He took Chilaw, Negombo and Colombo, but was repulsed from Kotte, thus bringing to an end the payment of tribute to the ruler in the north. In the first half of the 15th century, the kingdom of Arya Chakravarti in Jaffna was subordinated to the powerful Vijayanagara kingdom in southern India. In about 1450, however, the Singhalese king Parakrama Bahu IV succeeded in reconquering the north of Ceylon and united it with his own kingdom. He enfeoffed the victorious general Prince Sapumal with the peninsula. In 1477 Arya Chakravarti invaded Jaffna once more, however, and prised it away from the Singhalese kingdom, which was in any case falling apart. Until 1619 the rulers of Jaffna held out against the Portuguese, but in 1621 they were forced to surrender after the last of them was executed. In 1658 rule passed from the Portuguese to the Dutch, and in 1796 to the British. During the whole period of colonial rule Jaffna was a target of intolerant missionary attempts. The Portuguese introduced Roman Catholicism, but the Catholics in their turn fell victim to the Dutch, who sought to establish their own Reformed Church.

Even after the end of the civil war, Jaffna is not (yet) a travel destination of any importance. The city was too seriously damaged by the military conflict, and most of the historic buildings of significance were destroyed. It will also be years before it is possible to recommend any accommodation.

Kalutara

A 8

Province: Western
Population: 38,000

Altitude: 3m/10ft

Kalutara lies on both sides of the mouth of the Kalu Ganga, which is 300m/330yd wide at this point. A bridge connects the two halves of the town, which is a centre of the rubber trade and home to basket and mat weavers.

In 1042, the south Indian prince Vikrama Pandya, who ruled the Ruhuna kingdom, moved his seat of government to Kalutara, as he feared attack by the Chola kings, who at this time ruled in Polonnaruwa. But just one year later he was murdered by a prince from northern India, who then established himself as ruler of the Ruhuna kingdom. In the early 13th century, many people moved from the heartland of the kingdom to the south, and southwest. In order to secure them a living, King Parakrama Bahu II had coconut palms planted on the coast. In 1655 the town fell to the Dutch. They built a fort, extended and strengthened the fortifications already built by the Portuguese, and turned Kalutara into an important trading centre. 1797 saw the arrival of the British, who, preferring Colombo, did not enlarge Kalutara any further.

History

What to see in Kalutara

The striking landmark of the town is the admittedly relatively modern dagoba. It differs from the traditional dagoba in that its interior is hollow, and can be accessed.

★
Dagoba

Opposite the dagoba is the little temple complex of Gangatilake Vihara. The buildings are also relatively modern and from the point of view of cultural history, of little significance. On the roadside is a small shrine, where Buddhist motorists stop to make an offering of a few coins to ensure a safe onward journey.

In the hinterland of Kalutara there are extensive **rubber plantations**. 31km/20mi to the east of the town is the Rubber Research Institute, specializing in new methods of production.; it tests its ideas with the owners of smallholdings in the area.

Surroundings of Kalutara

► VISITING KALUTARA

GETTING THERE

By car:
from Colombo on the A 2 or, taking a more interesting route through the interior via Bandagarama (52km/ 30mi); from Bentota on the A 2 (22km/12mi)

By train:
Kalutara is a station on the line from Colombo to Matara

By bus:
good services from Colombo and from the bathing resorts further to the south

**WHERE TO STAY /
WHERE TO EAT**

► **Mid-range**
Kani Lanka Resort & Spa
St Sebastian's Road, Katukurunda,

Kalutara
Tel. 034 / 42 80 801, fax 034 / 222 65 30
www.kanilanka.com
105 rooms, restaurant, pool, health facilities
Very comfortable hotel situated on a tongue of land.

► **Budget**
Lily Beach Hotel Restaurant & Inn
123/12, Abrew Road
Kalutara North
Tel. / Fax 034 / 222 21 59
lilyrest@sltnet.lk
5 rooms, restaurant. Close to the beach, four of the five rooms have a splendid sea view. The proprietors are famous for their delicious Sri Lankan cuisine, with sea-foods (lobster!) being a speciality. Good value for money.

★ ★ Kandy

C 7

Province: Central
Population: app. 110,000

Altitude: 490–504m/1600–1650ft

Kandy, the »most beautiful city ion the island« and the heart of Sri Lanka, lies in undulating, forested hill country. The pride of the city is the Temple of the Tooth, but the idyllic late in the middle of town and the world-famous Botanical Garden are also something to write home about.

Intellectual and religious centre

Kandy is very conscious of the historic role which it played as the last capital of the Singhalese kingdom and seat of the last Singhalese king (Raja Sinha II). Today the town is the intellectual and religious centre of Sri Lanka, a result not least of the fact that Buddhists, Hindus, Moors and Christians co-exist here in peace. The university, founded in 1835, is the country's largest by far. The inhabitants of Kandy like to see themselves as Sri Lanka's elite, as the mere description **»Kandyans«** indicates. The name Kandy, incidentally, is short for »Kanda-uda-pas-rata«, which means »kingdom in the mountains«.

15th century	Viceroy Vikrama Bahu makes Galle his capital and builds a palace.
16th/17th centuries	The kingdom of Kandy is the centre of resistance to the Portuguese invaders.
1636	Treaty of Protection with the Dutch against the Portuguese
1760 – 1766	Struggle against the Dutch protectors
1815	The British become the colonial masters in Kandy; the Singhalese kingdom is abolished.

Kandy was long protected from the colonial invaders not only by the hills, marshes and the mighty Mahaweli Ganga, which forms a loop to the north of the city, but also by the climate, which is conducive to malaria. Until 1815, when the British finally succeeded in taking possession of the city, Kandy was the last residue of the Singhalese kingdom.

History of the city

As temple inscriptions in the area prove, the Kandy region was already settled in the 5th century. It was only at the end of the 15th century, however, that the viceroy Vikrama Bahu (1447–1511), hitherto resident in Gampoha, in his search for a secure location, made this then insignificant place his **capital** and had a palace built. During this period the central royal house was based in Kotte, not far from Colombo. In 1518 the Portuguese started their conquest of the island. But while the king of Kotte joined forces with the Portuguese in the hope of gaining political advantage, a **resistance movement**, formed under his brother Mayadunne, the king in Sitavka, which was carried on by his son, the future King Raja Sinha I (1582–1592). Kandy was ruled at this time by a prince named Karalliyadde Bandara, who was defeated by Raja Sinha I in 1582, and forced to flee with his daughter Dona Catherina to Trincomalee. But Raja Sinha I was unable to hold Kandy, and in 1588 he was deposed. In 1592, with the help of the Portuguese, the Singhalese Don Juan, who had converted to Christianity, became king of Kandy. But his conversion was short-lived as he immediately announced his return to Buddhism, taking the name Vimela Dharma Suriya I. This was seen by the Portuguese as a provocation, and in revenge they occupied Kandy briefly, looting it in the process. Dharma Suriya I soon succeeded, however, in defeating the Portuguese occupation forces left behind in the city, whereupon he continued to rule undisturbed until 1604.

The reign of his successor King Raja Sinha II (1605–1687) was also dominated by conflict with the colonists. In 1606 he formed an alliance with the Dutch, who had landed in Sri Lanka, with a view to expelling the Portuguese. The Dutch for their part had no intention of helping the king, as soon became clear. They used the non-payment of alleged war debts as an excuse to take a number of coastal towns, from which they had previously expelled the Portuguese, as a lien. In other areas too there were continual disputes, especially in respect of the cinnamon trade and the introduction of a new system of taxation, but ultimately the lords of Kandy always came out on top.

Resistance to the colonial government

From 1739 Kandy was ruled by the Tamil Nayakkar dynasty, whose kings however were for the most part not Hindus, but Buddhists. Under Sri Vijaya Raja Sinha (1739–1747) the Christians were expelled from Kandy. The most important ruler was Kirti Sri Raja Sinha (1747–1778), who initiated a movement of religious renewal, leading his kingdom into a cultural heyday. In spite of treaty obligations to the Dutch, he entered into secret negotiations with the British with the aim of expelling the Dutch from Sri Lanka. The British however were not interested in making concessions, and in 1795 began to conquer the island for themselves, declaring it a crown colony in 1802. Only the kingdom of Kandy managed to escape their clutches, at least until 1815. It was only the third military campaign (since 1802) which secured the British final victory. The king was captured and taken to south India, where he died in 1832. In the Convention of Kandy (1815) the last remains of the kingdom were also declared a crown colony, and Colombo became the capital. Until independence in 1948, however, Kandy remained the centre of the anti-colonial resistance.

? DID YOU KNOW …?

■ …that the city of Kandy has had a number of Singhalese names, such as Maha Nuwara (Great City)? It has also been called Kanda Uda (Country in the Mountains); the Portuguese turned this into Candia. The present name dates from the period of British colonial rule.

What to see in Kandy

Kiri Muhuda (lake)

The long artificial lake which gives Kandy much of its charm was created between 1810 and 1812 in the reign of the last king of Kandy from a modest pond which had been maintained as a home for the sacred terrapins. The masonry embankment was commissioned by the British governor in 1875 on the occasion of a visit by the Prince of Wales; it resembles the decorative walls of the Temple of the Tooth. On the lakeside, not far from the entrance to the temple precinct, stands a pretty pavilion, which once served the royal dynasty. Today it houses a public library and the tourist information office. There are now only few remains of the pleasure palaces which once stood on the island in the lake. On the bridge not far from the entrance to the Temple of the Tooth is a **place where boats can be hired**, but a walk around the lake is also rewarding (app. 4.5km/ 3mi).

Kandy, now the island's third-largest city, →
is considered the most beautiful of the old royal cities

Kandy Map

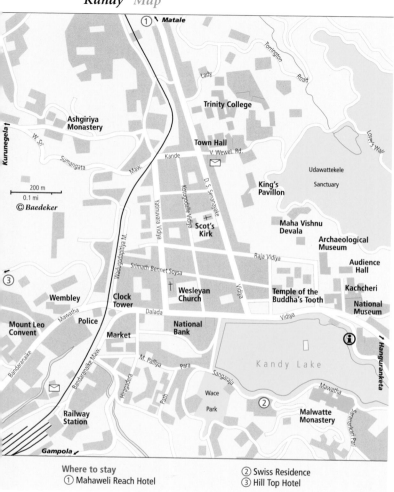

Where to stay
① Mahaweli Reach Hotel

② Swiss Residence
③ Hill Top Hotel

Malwatta Vihara (temple) The Malwatta Vihara on the south bank of Lake Kandy, founded in the second half of the 18th century by King Kirti Sri Raja Sinha, is one of the leading Buddhist monasteries in Sri Lanka. The senior monk is the highest dignitary of all the monasteries in the south of the country and co-protector of the tooth relic. The temple itself consists of two parts. The interesting monks' residence can be reached via a ramp which leads up a slight elevation. By agreement with one of the residents, it is possible to view the buildings (but don't forget to take your shoes off!). The buildings form three sides of quadrangle, in the middle of which is a hall supported on wooden columns. With their labyrinthine corridors, through which gutters run, and their tiny cells, they are an interesting example of Sri Lankan domestic architecture.

The second part of the complex is reached by steps leading from the lakeside road. The most interesting building here is the image house. On the eastern side of the lower floor are very lively stone sculptures, while the walls of the upper storey are covered in pictures painted in the Kandy style. The main hall contains statues of the Buddha, Vishnu and Saman, as well as those of various benefactors, including that of King Kirti Sri. Of particular note is the fact that the Bot, the actual shrine, is, as in Thailand, surrounded by stones (Semas). The explanation for this arrangement, which is found nowhere else in Sri Lanka is simple: King Kirti Sri brought Thai monks to the island, who here created an imitation of the Buddhist architecture of their homeland. Above the southwest shore of the lake is one of the most desirable residential quarters in town with buildings dating from the British colonial period.

✱ A walk through the city centre

The city centre with its crowded shops and restaurants is bordered to the south and east by two roads: D. S. Senanayake Vidiya (which eventually leads to Katugastota) and Dalada Vidiya, which goes to Peradeniya. The two roads meet at the Queen's Hotel. This is **Kandy's most lively quarter**, which is why it is particularly worth strolling around here for an hour or so. Many of the largely 19th-century buildings still have something of the charm of the Victorian age. There are a number of Christian churches here, as well as two mosques. As for temples, one famous one is the Kataragama Devale, dedicated to several Hindu deities. Vishnu and Ganesha in particular are venerated here, but most of all the god of war, Skanda. The tower over the entrance, with its numerous figures, is most impressive. It symbolizes the Hindu pantheon.

Highlights Kandy

Kiri Muhuda
A short evening boat trip on Kandy Lake is a romantic experience.
▶ page 264

Dalalada Maligawa
The Temple of the Tooth is the most important Buddhist shrine in Sri Lanka.
▶ page 268

Peradeniya Botanical Garden
A natural landscape of incredible luxuriance and colour
▶ page 275

Huna Falls
Amazingly beautiful watery landscape in the vicinity of Kandy
▶ page 281

▶ VISITING KANDY

AUSKUNFT
Travel Information Centre
Headmans Lodge
13, Deva Veediya, Kandy
Tel. 081 / 222 26 61

GETTING THERE
By car:
from Colombo via the A 1 (116km/ 72mi); from Kurunegala via the A 10(42km/25mi); from Dambulla via the A 9 (72km/45mi) and from Nuwara Eliya via the A 5 (77km/48mi)
By train:
the nearest station is Peradeniya on the line from Colombo to Matale.
By bus:
good bus services from all the above-named places.

WHERE TO STAY/ WHERE TO EAT
▶ **Luxury**
① *Mahaweli Reach Hotel*
35, P.B.A.Weerakoon Mawatha
Tel. 081 / 447 27 27, fax 081 / 221 28 54
www.mahaweli.com

114 rooms, restaurants, bar, pool
Somwhat away from the city centre, this hotel overlooks the Mahaweli Ganga, Sri Lanka's longest river. The rooms are spacious, the restaurant is famous. Very attractive garden.

▶ **Mid-range**
② *Swiss Residence*
23, Bahirawakanda
Tel. 011 / 58 73 305, fax 011 / 23 72 336
www.jetwing.net
40 rooms, restaurant, bar, pool
Well maintained, individual hotel on the outskirts of Kandy with comfortable rooms and attentive service.

▶ **Budget**
③ *Hill Top Hotel*
200/21 Bahirawakanda, Peradeniya Road
Tel. 074 / 74 44 41, fax 074 / 43 37 55
www.aitkenspencehotels.com
82 rooms, restaurant, bar, pool
The location in the hills above Kandy is impressive, the rooms are nicely furnished.

Market Hall
On no account should a visit to the Market Hall at the western end of Dalada Vidiya be missed, as it has a larger range of goods on offer than anywhere else in Kandy. The best time to go is the morning.

National Museum of Kandy ☉
The museum occupies part of the former royal palace that was reserved to the queen. On display are jewellery, textiles, weapons, ritual objects and ivory carvings dating from the 17th to the 19th century (opening times: Sun – Thur 9am–5pm; admission charge).

✸ ✸ Dalada Maligawa (Temple of the Tooth)

History of the Tooth
The history of Kandy is – like that of all the royal cities in Sri Lanka – closely linked to the history of the holy tooth relic, which, admittedly, has gathered its fair share of legends. After the solemn cremation of the Buddha's remains in Kushinagara (northern India) in 483

BC a number of unburnt fragments of bone, including a collar bone, were found in the ashes, and also four teeth. One of the teeth was presented to the king of Kalinga in southern India, where it was venerated for 800 years. When the Buddhist faith disappeared from India, the relic was at risk of being stolen by Hindu kings and possible destroyed. One legend has it that

the tooth had resisted all attempts by the Panda king to destroy it, and was even raised on a lotus blossom back to the surface of a pond into which it had been thrown. The Buddhist nun Hemamala, daughter of King Guhasiwa, brought the Tooth – concealed in her hair – to Sri Lanka in AD 313. King Sirimeghavana had a special temple built for it in his palace precinct, and in the succeeding years the Tooth was taken annually in a solemn procession to the Abhayagiri monastery, where it could be venerated by all the faithful.

In the political turmoil of the late 10th century, when Anuradhapura had to be abandoned as capital, **the great migration of the relic** began, although it continued to enjoy the particular attention of the kings. Finally its possession came to be the most important bargaining point for any claimant to the throne. It passed through the principality of Ruhuna (in the south of the island), and then, among other places, Kotmale, the Beligala rocks, Dambadeniya and eventually to Yapahuwa, where it was stolen and taken back to India by the Pandyas, who had stormed the fortress towards the end of the 13th century. By negotiation, King Parakrama Bahu II managed to get the Tooth back, however, and he had it taken to Polonnaruwa. After that it was in Kurunegala and in Gampola, where allegedly it was kidnapped and taken to China, like the Singhalese king himself. King Alakesvara is said to have got it back again, because it can be proved to have been present at the coronation of Parakrama Bahu VI in Rayigama in 1412. From there, the Tooth was taken to the new capital of Kotte, where it fell into the hands of the Portuguese at the end of the 16th century. They are said to have taken it to their Indian colony of Goa and destroyed it. In order to legitimize himself as king, however, Vimela Dharma Suriya I, who seized power in Kandy in 1592, needed the Holy Tooth. So he spread a rumour that the Portuguese had only destroyed a copy, and that he possessed the original. The people decided to believe the king. Since then, the Tooth in Kandy has been regarded as the holiest Buddhist relic in Sri Lanka.

Opening times

The Temple is accessible all day long, but the shrine, a two-storey wooden structure in the inner courtyard, is only opened for the religious ceremonies (puja) at 5.30am, 9.30am and 6.30pm. These occasions are announced by loud gong-beats and drum-rolls.

The Dalada Maligawa, the »Temple of the Tooth«, stands within the former palace precinct. Nothing now remains of the earliest buildings put up to house the holy relic. The oldest extant part is the inner building, which dates from the reign of King Kirti Sri Raja Sinha (1747–1778). The present appearance of the whole complex dates from 1803 under the last king of Kandy, Sri Vikrama Raja Sinha (1798–1815), who had the conduits laid out and ordered the construction, using European architectural forms, of the massive entrance pavilion, the decorative exterior walls and the dominant octagonal front building with its ambulatory.

Temple complex

Visitors enter the temple complex from Palace Square, having passed through a number of **security checks** introduced since the attack. A first noteworthy feature is the staircase with its fice steps, two of which are flanked by elephant reliefs carved in the exterior walls. They come from the palace of King Sri Vira Marendra Sinha (1707–1739) in Kundalase and reflect, in their expressiveness and rich decor, the typical sculptural style

> **! Baedeker TIP**
>
> **To Kandy by train**
> The train ride to Kandy from Colombo is one of the most memorable experiences a railway fan could hope to ask for. It takes about eight hours, and the journey of 180km/112mi climbs 2000m/6600ft. The stretch is full of hairpin bends (including the unique Demodera loop) and no fewer than 47 tunnels, a masterpiece of railway engineering.

of the Kandy period. The two decorative columns above the reliefs are gifts from Burma. The semicircular, richly ornamented **moonstone** is workmanlike, but does not match the quality of the moonstone in ►Anuradhapura. Another moonstone only appears to follow the patterns, thus for example the lions and wild geese do not face the central point, the lotus, but are looking at the approaching beholder. In the moat, which is crossed by means of a stone bridge, live terrapins, regarded as sacred. A relief opposite the temple gate depicts the goddess Lakshmi with two elephants.

Also worthy of note are a few gates and doorposts on the lower floor richly decorated with sculpted reliefs. They show male and female guardians, a Makara gate-arch, the wheel of teaching set in motion by the Buddha, lions, lotus blossoms, and much more besides.

In the interior courtyard stands the actual shrine, which is also the oldest part of the temple. It is a two-storey, richly decorated building, built entirely of wood. The columns and rafters have carvings of extraordinary beauty. A staircase leads to the upper storey, from which a corridor leads to a door studded with silver and decorated with mother-of-pearl and ivory inlays. Behind the door is the holy of holies, the Tooth. The reliquary consists of seven dagoba-shaped golden containers or karanduwas fitting into one another, and studded with pearls and precious stones.

← *This beautiful temple complex is home to the centre of Buddhist faith in Sri Lanka*

DALADA MALIGAWA

* * The Temple of the Tooth in Kandy houses the island's most treasured relic, one of Buddha's canine teeth. The relic has been moved several times over the centuries. Now in the temple in Kandy, it still fascinates the followers of the enlightened Buddha. Every year in July or August, during the eleven-day Kandy Perahera, it is carried through the town on a magnificently adorned elephant.

⏱ Open (reliquary casket):
5.30am, 9.30am and 6.30pm

① Moat
To get to the temple cross the stone bridge over the moat, which is full of fish and turtles. The moat was built by Kandy's last king, Sri Vikrama Rajasinha (1798–1815).

② Architecture
The foundations for the current building were laid in 1706. Its angled tiled roof is one of the typical elements of »Kandyan architecture«. The octagonal tower-like extension was added only at the beginning of the 19th century. It was built so the

Large mounds of flowers pile up in the Temple of the Tooth as they are offered as sacrificial gifts by believers

sacred tooth could be presented to the people from its balustrade. Today it houses an extensive library with valuable palm-leaf manuscripts.

③ Place of worship
The place of worship with several Buddha statues that have been donated by Buddhists from all around the world is located on the ground floor.

④ Reliquary room
On the first floor, in the Udamale, behind a door decorated with ivory teeth that is opened to the accompaniment of drumming during times of worship is an approx. 1m/3ft reliquary casket in the shape of a dagoba. It contains six further caskets one within the other, all of which are richly ornamented with gems. The innermost one contains the venerated relic, Gautama Buddha's right upper canine.

The wooden pillars and the other woodwork in the Temple of the Tooth are decorated with exceptionally beautiful carvings

the sanctum are ree times a day sitors who come imes stay in the meditation hall.

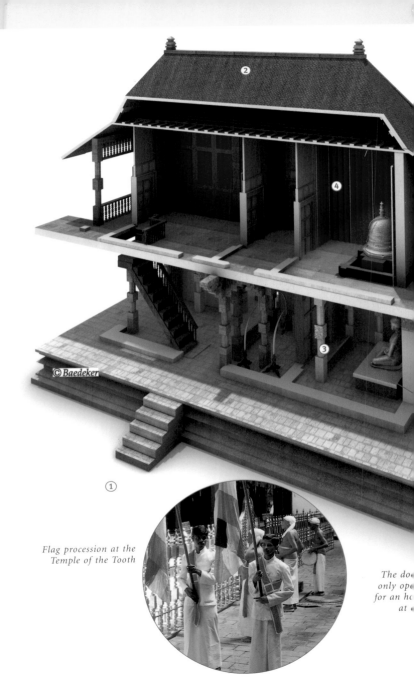

①

②

③

④

Flag procession at the Temple of the Tooth

*The do⋯
only op⋯
for an h⋯
at ⋯*

© Baedeker

The most precious container, the last, is of ivory, and holds the sacred relic, the Holy Tooth, which is 5cm/2in long and 1.5cm/0.7in in diameter. It is, however, only displayed at special ceremonies that take place every four years. Apart from the **original relic**, which lies on a lotus blossom, it is also possible to see a copy which is taken on procession through Kandy once a year at the Esala Perahera, the solemn festival lasting several days. The seven containers are lockable, the keys being in the possession of the high priest of the Malwatte and Asgiriya monasteries, who also take it in turns to officiate at the religious ceremonies in the temple.

Octagon The way to the Octagon leads past a room containing several statues of the Buddha dating from various eras. The Octagon itself was erected for the royal family; a throne used to stand here, from which the ruler could watch the Perahera and present the relic. By means of a trapdoor the king could get into a tunnel that led directly to his pleasure palace on the islet in Lake Kandy.

Sermon Hall The three-storey Sermon Hall, an impressive structure richly decorated with sculptures, which also served as a residential building for the monks, rounds off the temple complex to the east. On the second floor is a small museum; among the exhibits is a wooden model of the Temple of the Tooth and a copy of the Buddha's footprint on ►Adam's Peak. Smaller buildings to the side link the Sermon Hall to the Halls of Veneration.

Audience Hall To the east of these is the former Audience Hall of the kings of Kandy, which stands on a tiered plinth. It was started as early as 1784, but not finished until the reign of the last king. The carvings on the columns and rafters are worth seeing; they were only completed under British rule in 1820. In 1815 the Convention (in reality more a surrender) between the Kingdom of Kandy and the British was signed here, declaring the last Singhalese kingdom on the island to be a British colony. Today the hall houses the Kandy supreme court.

Hall of Columns To the north, the temple precinct is adjoined by the Hall of Columns, erected in 1803. The rafters are extravagantly decorated with carvings, in particular flower motifs.

Archaeological Museum Further to the north are the remains of the old royal palace, which in colonial times was the residence of the deputy governor in Kandy. Today it houses an archaeological museum. The collection includes mainly items from the Kandy period (opening times: Sat – Thur 9am – 5pm; admission charge).

National Museum The graceful building to the south of the Audience Hall, built to Dutch plans in 1765, now houses the National Museum of Kandy.

The collection is worth seeing, and includes the golden crown of King Raja Sinha II, precious ivory and wood carvings, ritual oil lamps, lifesize wooden figures with the typical Kandy costume, and palm-leaf manuscripts. Also worthy of note are the engravings with views of 19th-century Kandy, and maps of Ceylon (opening times: Wed–Mon 9am–5pm; admission charge, but all-in tickets are available for the cultural triangle).

Natha Devale (temple)

To the north-west of the Temple of the Tooth is the 14th-century Natha Devale, the city's oldest religious building. Here the rulers of the Singhalese kingdom were presented with the sword, the sign of their office. The Hindu deity Natha is, incidentally, the city's patron. The most noteworthy feature inside the Devale is the sculpture of a recumbent Buddha.

Pattini Devale (temple)

Not far from the Natha Devale is the Pattini Devale, which is dedicated to the goddess Pattini, a deity of Mahayana Buddhism. She embodies purity and helps to protect man and beast alike from epidemics and other diseases. There are very few depictions of her on the island, another being in the National Museum in ► Colombo. It was King Gaja Bahu (112–134) who introduced the Pattini cult to Sri Lanka, staging an annual festival in honour of the goddess, in order to guarantee rain and thus prosperity in the kingdom.

? DID YOU KNOW …?

■ …that on 26 January 1998 a member of the Tamil Tigers detonated 250kg/550lb of explosives outside the temple complex? This attack left its mark on the whole country. Not only were eight people killed, but the temple too suffered serious damage. As if by a miracle, the most sacred area was hardly affected.

Udawattakele Sanctuary

It must be pretty **unique worldwide** to find a nature reserve in the middle of a city. But there is one in Kandy, where immediately above the Temple of the Tooth there is the Udawattakele Sanctuary, originally a royal hunting ground. Some of the footpaths through the sanctuary still bear the names of the wives of British governors and senior colonial officials. There are many different birds, butterflies and monkeys to be seen here.

Surroundings of Kandy

✶✶ Peradeniya Botanical Garden

The Peradeniya Botanical Garden is one of the most beautiful and comprehensive in south or south-east Asia. Almost every species of Asian tropical plant is to be found here, as well as some from the temperate zones. The garden, 80 hectares/200 acres in extent, is surrounded on three sides by the River Mahaweli Ganga, whose bed here is horseshoe-shaped.
The history of the garden goes back to 1371, when King Vikrama Bahu II had a palace built here in the midst of a pleasure garden. King

Kirti Sri Raja Sinha (1747 – 1781) made it his royal garden, and his successor Raja Sinha II also had a residence here.

Today's Botanical Garden was set up in 1821 by the Englishman Alexander Moon, and it was opened to the public in 1824. Moon, though, died the following year, and for years the garden was neglected, until it was re-instated and enlarged by George Gardner in 1844. The worldwide fame enjoyed by the Botanical Garden today, however, is largely due to G. H. K. Thwaites, the director of the Garden from 1849 to 1857, who further enlarged it and added a large number of tropical plants.

There is a small admission charge to the Botanical Garden. Also, for an additional charge, it is possible to drive around it. (Opening times: daily 8am – 7pm).

Tour of the Garden ▶

Even before entering, visitors will be met on the right by a row of *Amherstia nobilis* from Burma and the Malaysian peninsula, also known as the **»Queen of Flowering Trees «**. On the other side are two fine Rambong rubber trees from Assam, which were planted in 1914. On the triangular lawn opposite the entrance is a splendid mahogany and on either side of the entrance is a royal poinciana or Flame of the Forest from Madagascar.

The Botanical Garden is a gem of landscape gardening

Botanical Garden Map

1 Main Entrance
2 Spice Garden
3 Hibiscus bushes
4 Giant bamboo
5 Palm tree garden
6 Herb garden
7 Study garden

8 Pine grove
9 Herbarium,
   plant museum
10 Succulents house
11 Orchid house
12 Orchid greenhouses
13 Java almond trees

14 Palm avenue
15 Flower garden
16 Tropical ferns
17 Aqai palm avenue
18 Cook's pine avenue
19 King palm avenue

© Baedeker

Memorial trees

The part of the garden commemorating prominent visitors to Sri Lanka is worthy of note. Each has had a tree planted in his or her honour, with a sign at its foot giving the name of the person and the species of tree.

Next to the entrance is the **Spice Garden** with an almost-180-year-old nutmeg tree, as well as cinnamon trees, ginger, cardamom, cloves, vanilla and pepper. Following Lake Drive, visitors will come to the Cajuput rubber tree, and then the Upas tree from Java, whose bark contains a poison that was used for arrows or blowpipe darts. Not far on is the Burmese giant bamboo, the world's tallest bamboo: it reaches a height of 40m/140ft and a diameter of 24cm/10in. Turning left into South Drive, the next feature is the lake, covered in **water lilies and lotus blossoms** and set in gently undulating landscape. On its banks grow various water plants, including papyrus from Egypt.

The hill path to the left crosses the northern part of the **Palm Garden** with betel-nut or areka palms, whose fruit and leaves are rolled up and chewed in many parts of Asia on account of their mildly intoxicating effect. Further on are kitul or toddy palms, whose nectar is used to make the arrack which is very popular on the island. In addition there are specimens of the aqai, royal and sealing-wax palms, as well as the native Sri Lankan nibong palm. To the left of the path are three talipot palms, at 25m/85ft the tallest of all palm species. Their huge fan-shaped leaves are used to create palm-leaf manuscripts (olas). There follows a further **Herb Garden** with numerous medicinal herbs, and then a study garden with an experimental breeding station.

Following Lake Drive, the visitor will see various trees native to Sri Lanka (for example the Ceylon screw pine, the sandalwood tree, and several mahoganies). From the corner of River Drive/Jonville Drive there is a fine view over the large lawn with Gannoruwa Hill in the background. The focus is a particularly beautiful specimen, planted in 1861, of *Ficus benjamina* (weeping fig) with a magnificently spreading crown. To the north of the lawn there is a **herbarium**. Where Jonville Drive meets Monument Road, there is a male specimen of the famous Coco de Mer, which otherwise only grows on the Seychelles.

The road from the lake to the north leads to the **orchid house** with numerous splendid specimens from all over the world. Continuing along River Drive northwards, you will come to the avenue of açaí palms, which was planted in 1905, followed by an arboretum with a number of interesting trees. Before coming to the suspension bridge over the Mahaweli Ganga, watch out for the numerous specimens of native trees and shrubs. The return route to the starting point passes an avenue of stone pines named after Thomas Cook, and the avenue of royal palms.

The monastery of Gadaladeniya is about 6km/4mi to the west of Peradeniya. It was built as long ago as 1344 on a low rock ridge. Architecturally, the Vihara is a combination of a Buddhist image building
and a Hindu devale: the main shrine has a hall and another building
with a secondary temple in front of it. The way the cornices on the
latter and on the main building are structured shows strong Dravidian influences. The secondary temple has a dagoba-like top to its
roof, while the main shrine has an octagonal sikhara. Once past the
pillar lined entrance, visitors will see the bronze statue of a standing
Buddha inside.

The complex includes a further temple, the Vijayotpaya. It has a cruciform ground-plan, and niches occupied with Buddha figures. Here
a Burmese influence is evident.

✷ Gadaladeniya Vihara

The bright, white building of the Lankatilaka monastery can be seen from far away

Lankatilaka Vihara

About 2km/1.5mi south of Gadaladeniyais the monastery of Lankatilaka, which was also built during the Gampola period in the 14th century.

Inscriptions in the ancient Singhalese language report on the building of the temple, whose construction, reminiscent of the Burmese architecture of Pagan and its **exposed location on a rounded rock** make it one of the most beautiful examples of Ceylonese architecture. 172 steps carved into the rock lead up to the building, but the strenuous climb is rewarded by a splendid view over the rice fields and the wooded hilly countryside. The rectangular central shrine is surrounded by a building with halls projecting at each of the points of the compass, producing a cross-shaped ground-plan. The façade is very finely structured with cornices, projections and recesses, and decorated with attractive elephant statues. The building was originally of four storeys, but when the two top ones collapsed, they were replaced by a tiled roof supported by solid timber rafters.

Inside there is a colossal statue of a seated Buddha, flanked by two further Buddha figures. Characteristic of the time when they were carved (14th century) are the folds of the garments, falling in regular wavy lines. The painting at the rear imitates architecture, while to either side there are paintings of lions and mythical beasts. Also worthy of attention are the walls and ceiling of the anteroom; their attractive paintings were, however, subject to major restoration during the Kandy period.

Embekke Devale

To the south of the Lankatilaka Vihara is the Embekke Devale, the third temple from the Gampola period; it too dates from the 14th century and is dedicated to the Hindu god of war Skanda. It differs

Skilfully joined beams in Embekke Devale

from the previous temples in having **highly elaborate wood carvings**, which were enjoying a heyday at the this period. The open hall of the drummers (Dig-Ge) is particularly attractive, its 32 wooden pillars and also the rafters being full of highly varied carvings. Among other things, one can recognize wild geese, a double-headed eagle, wrestlers, dancers, soldiers and much more, in graceful, flowing movement. Another noteworthy feature is the structure of the rafters, designed to achieve an optical effect. The 26 struts unfold from a single point towards visitors as they enter. This building was probably once used, at least some of the time, as the audience chamber of the kings of Gampoha; it is thought that it was brought here by one of the Kandy kings and restored. The shrine contains the painted statue of a seated Buddha.

Kandy Highlands

Gampola, the »holy city on the river« (Siripura Ganga), is an attractive place in the Kandy Highlands (20km/12mi from Kandy) with pretty houses and gardens along either side of the Mahaweli Ganga. As **the rulers' residence** and centre of art during its heyday, Gampola enjoyed a few years of splendour.

In 1344 King Ghuvanaike Bahu IV (1341 – 1351) moved the capital of his realm here, while his bother, King Parakrama Bahu V, resided in in ► Dedigama. Vikrama Bahu III (1357 – c1374), and also Alakeshvara, king of Rayigama and Kotte, was required to pay tribute to the king of Jaffna. The next king in Gampola (Bhuvanaike Bahu V) succeeded in annihilating the forces of the king of Jaffna at the battle of ► Matale. There are two versions of what happened next: according to one, Vira Bahu II ascended the throne in 1391 or 1392, while according to the other seven regents ruled successively until 1412. The sixth of these was Vira Alakeshvara, who in 1399 was forced to flee to India, but later returned and made himself king. In 1411 he and his family were captured by the Chinese general Cheng Ho and taken to China. There his trail went cold. Cheng Ho had put in Sri Lanka with some of his ships on his second expedition, according at least to Chinese chronicles, in order to take the Holy Tooth to China.

Of the palace and temples of the kings who resided here, **there are only a few sparse remains**. A good impression of the buildings of this period can be got from the Lankatilaka Vihara and the temple of Gadaladeniya (► Kandy). Gampola is home to many Muslims and Hindus apart from the Buddhists. A Hindu temple in the centre is worth seeing, withs its high roof covered with hundreds of statues of Hindu deities.

4km/2mi south of Gampola on the road to Nawalapitiya is the Niyamgapaya Vihara, whose stepped base with figurative sculptures and attractively carved door jambs date from the Gampola period. The superstructure was added later, however.

Gampola

◄ Niyamgapaya Vihara

★
Hunas Falls

The pleasantly cool climate, the beauty of the gently undulating landscape and the comfortable Hunas Falls Hotel, situated in a picturesque location on a hillside in the middle of a garden fill of flowers, are the **major attractions of this region**.

The water from the Hunas Falls collects in a small lake next to the hotel, where one can also fish for trout. Even non-residents should take the opportunity to stroll through the pretty gardens (including a kitchen garden with herbs and fruit).

In the surroundings you will also find cinnamon, cardamom, nutmeg, clove and tea plantations, while to the east are the Matale mountains with their highest peak, the 1862m/6109ft Knuckles massif.

Hanguranketa

Hanguranketa (28km/18mi from Kandy), in the 17th century the place of refuge for the Singhalese king Raja Sinha II, also lies in the enchanted Kandy Highlands near the deep Great Valley. In the surroundings maize, vegetables and above all tobacco are grown, as well as rice on elaborately laid-out terraces. It was around Hanguranketa, incidentally, that the first coffee bushes on Sri Lanka were planted.

An uprising in Kandy forced King Raja Sinha II to flee the capital in 1864 and hand over the throne to his son, still a minor. He sought shelter in Hanguranketa, and when he was able to return to Kandy once more, he had a kind of summer palace built in the place of his exile, and it was here that he spent most of his time from then on. Even so, it is said, he was very suspicious of all his compatriots, but even more so of strangers who tried to approach him. So by night he had drums beaten and trumpets blown in order to show people that he was on his guard. He himself would wander through the palace in disguise, watching his bodyguards, in case there were a traitor among them. He occupied the inhabitants of the town by getting them to divide a large hill in two, and to build a canal and embankments, in order to fill the valley with water. He scared off Europeans with wild animals, which he kept in the garden. The Englishman Robert Knox, who was his prisoner at the time, in his book **»A Historical Relation of Ceylon«**, provides a lively description of life at court. During the fighting with the British and the uprising of 1817, the town was badly damaged.

✱ Buddhist Temple

The Buddhist temple in the city was built in 1830. Typical of the post-Kandy era is the moonstone. decorated with floral elements, unusual by contrast is the stupa. In one room of the Vihara various ritual brass lamps can be seen; these have donated by the faithful. The library contains one of the most comprehensive collections of palm-leaf manuscripts (olas) anywhere. Wall paintings depict the Perahera, the great festive procession in Kandy, in which the monks from this monastery also take part.

Vishnu temple ►

Not far from the Buddhist temple is a Hindu shrine dedicated to the god Vishnu, which would be unremarkable but for two **costly cloths from the 17th century**. These were donated by King Raja Sinha II. They depict scenes from his battle against the Portuguese, which he won. On one picture a regiment of Moors mounted on camels can be seen, the only such picture in Sri Lanka. If you ask a monk nicely, he will be pleased to show you the cloths.

✱ Remains of the Royal Palace ►

One important feature is a 17th-century door-frame carved out of a single rock, with finely worked relief sculptures, that was taken from the former royal palace. The motifs are bird-like mythical creatures and ornamental foliage, a crowned female figure, makaras and a band of lotus blossoms. The entrance is guarded by lions and stags. In 1885 a large stash of jewels was discovered here.

The two Hindu temples dedicated to the god Vishnu and the goddess Pattini were built during the Kandy period. Apart from the usual decorations, there is nothing much to see.

◄ Hindu temples

The monastery of Alu Vihara (►Matale), famous not least because of its history, is also worth a visit. Also easily accessible from Kandy is the well-known Pinawela elephant orphanage (►Kegalla). A journey through the magnificent mountain landscape leads to the ►Hunnas Falls.

Other places to go

Kataragama

Province: Uva   **Altitude:** app. 16m/60ft

Kataragama, the most sacred place on the island for Hindus Insel, lies at the foot of Kataragama Peak (424m/1391ft) and on the crystal-clear Menik Ganga, the »river of jewels«, and next to the Yala National Park. At the full moon at the end of July or beginning of August, thousands of pilgrims visit what is otherwise a dreamy place for the feast of Esala Perahera, filling it with life.

The history of the place goes back to the 3rd century BC. This is said to have been the headquarters of the Kshatriya warrior caste invited by King Devanampiya Tissa to Anuradhapura to plant a cutting of the Bodhi. Later, in 181 BC, King Duttha Gamani, before moving from his principality if Ruhuna to Anuradhapura, is said to have visited the temple in Kataragama in order ask the war-god Skanda to liberate the town from the Chola.

History

? DID YOU KNOW ...?

- ...that the war-god Skanda is known to Buddhists as Kataragama? And since all Hindus also venerate the Buddha, they turn also to him with their supplications, and regard Kataragama as a holy site. They also believe that the Buddha meditated here on his third visit to Sri Lanka.

According to the legend, Skanda, the second son of Shiva and Parvati, who lived on the mountain of the gods, Kailasa, in Tibet, heard of the beauty of the chief's daughter Valamma, and decided that she must be his. Disguised as a beggar, he confessed his love to her on the Menik Ganga, and asked her to marry him. Valamma, though, was outraged, and rejected him. Then Skanda's brother Ganesha appeared in the form of a wild elephant, and scared the girl so much that she fell into the arms of the alleged rescuer, and said yes after all. Skanda then transformed himself into a shining hero and took her to Kataragama Peak.

★ ★
Kataragama
Perahera

Every year, on the occasion of the full moon that takes place at the end of July or the beginning of August, thousands of Hindus and Buddhists gather in Kataragama to take part in the rites and processions of the well-known Esala Perahera. The **festivities** last for nine days, getting more lively all the time, before culminating magnificently on the last night. All the ceremonies begin with a ritual bath in the Menik Ganga. After further ritual acts, the actual procession begins, with richly decorated elephants, one of which carries the reliquary. This procession is repeated every evening, becoming noisier and more magnificent all the time. The climax comes on the last evening, when the faithful flagellate themselves or fall into a trance and walk barefoot over glowing embers.

What to see in Kataragama

★
Maha Devale

The holiest temple in Kataragama, the Maha Devale, is a white, square and rather unassuming building. It stands in the middle of a park at the end of a large palace on the banks of the Menik Ganga, surrounded by a wall decorated with elephants and peacocks (the latter being the creature on which Skanda rides). Since the precinct has been declared a »Sacred Zone«, snack bars and the like have had to

The pilgrim festival of Kataragama is always very colourful

⏵ VISITING KATARAGAMA

GETTING THERE

By car:
from Colombo via Ratnapura and
Timbolketiya, from here either by the
southern route (A 18) via Ambalantota and Tissamaharama or the
northern route from Tissamaharama
(app. 290km/175mi). From Tissamaharama it's about 16km/10mi.
By train:
The nearest station is Matara (terminus of the line from Colombo), from
there bus connections (about 4
hours).

WHERE TO STAY

▶ **Mid-range**
Rosen Renaissance Hotel
Tel. 047 / 360 30-2
Fax 047 / 360 33
www.kataragama.org/rosen-hotel.htm
52 rooms, restaurant, bar, pool
New 4-star hotel in the middle of
splendid landscape and not far from
the centre of Kataragama. The rooms
are well furnished and equipped.

move out. The only stalls are those selling offerings. The entrance
gate, facing east, is decorated with carvings. The interior of the
shrine is surprisingly plain, without even a picture of the god. In the
sanctuary, to which only the priests have access, is a container whose
contents, maybe a relic, are unknown. Flowers and fruits are presented to it, and the oil-lamps have been kept alight since time immemorial. Clearly nothing has ever been changed here, as under-
scored by the timelessness of this holy place. **The temple comes to
life during the daily prayer sessions** at 4.30am, 10.30am and
6.30pm, when believers gather before the shrine of their chief god.
These are the best times to visit, as the heartfelt prayers of the pilgrims create a special atmosphere.

Next to the Maha Devale, other sights include the Ganesha temple
dedicated to the elephant god, and a shrine dedicated to Vishnu,
each of which holds a statue of Buddha, Vishnu and Skanda. At the
other end of the square is the no less plain mosque and the graves of
two Muslim saints. The older of the two is the destination for a pilgrimage by Sri Lanka's Muslims, because it contains the mortal remains of Jabbar Ali Sha, a pious man who lived in Kataragama at the
end of the 19th century. The Kiri Vihara (milk dagoba), a large, bluish-white structure, dates back to the 3rd century BC, though it was
renovated in the 1980s and given a crystal pinnacle with a gold setting. Buddhist pilgrims make offerings of flowers and coconuts here,
before moving on to the Maha Devale. To the right in front of the
dagoba is a small museum. The bodhi tree nearby is said to have
been planted by King Devanampiya Tissa in person; it is allegedly
more than 2200 years old. Near the tree is the little Pattini temple,
where women pray for fertility.

Kegalle

Province: Sabaragamuwa
Population: 18,000

Altitude: 124 m/407ft

Kegalle, a bustling town in the middle of a productive rice-growing region, is situated at the foot of the rugged Hill Country around Kandy, which is covered in lavish vegetation. In addition to rice there are also tea and rubber plantations here. The famous elephant orphanage is nearby.

✳ ✳ Elephant Orphanage in Pinawela

The internationally famous Elephant Orphanage in Pinawela is government-funded, making it **unique in the world**. This place, not far from the Maha Oya riverbank, is home to around 75 elephants of all ages, who for whatever reason are enjoying special protection by humans (▶ Baedeker Special p. 286).

Baedeker TIP

When Babies are Given the Bottle
The best time to visit the orphanage is when the few-month-old elephants are given the bottle. This has to be done five times a day, but only the feeding times of 9.15am and 1.15pm are open to visitors. The bath in Maha Oya is also a much-photographed event (daily 10am – noon and 2pm – 5pm, admission charge).

The Elephant Orphanage is situated 35 km/20mi west of Kandy, approx. 8 km/5mi north of Kegalle and 85 km/53mi north of Colombo. It is easy to get to by car or bus (from Colombo via Ambepussa and Kegalle on the A 1; from Kurunegalla first via the A 6 to Polgahawela, then on the A 19 to Kegalle and onwards on the A 1 to Udamulla. From Kandy take the A 1 to Udamulla (in Udamulla the orphanage is signposted). Every tour operator and many taxi drivers offer trips to Pinawela.

Beligela A few kilometres west of Kegalle is Beligela, the **former residence** of King Parakrama Bahu's cousin and feudal vassal Prince Gajabahu II (1132 – 1153), who defeated the king in their battle for power and who also probably killed him. Nothing is left of Gajabahu's palace. All that has remained is the temple, which was expanded and beautified by later kings. Of the good stonework, a finely worked moonstone is particularly remarkable.

Temple ruins On the two peaks of the nearby Beligala rock are the ruins of several temples, including that of the sacred tooth relic, which is now in ▶Kandy. It was built under King Vijaya Bahu III during the first half of the 13th century.

▶ VISITING KEGALLE

GETTING THERE

By car:
from Colombo on the A 1 (77 km/
48mi); from Kandy on the A 1
(39 km/24mi)
By rail:
the closest stations are Polgahawela
and Rambukkana (both approx.
12 km/7mi away).
By bus:
good bus services from Colombo and
Kandy

WHERE TO STAY

▶ **Mid-range**
Ralidiya Hotel
Opposite the Elephant Orphanage
Tel. 035 / 226532 1, 226 406 9
Fax 035 / 226 406 9
www.ralidiyahotel.com
Recommended hotel with well fur-
nished rooms. Quite busy during the
day because of the many coaches.

Kelaniya

A 8

Province: Western **Altitude:** 5 m/16ft

**Kelaniya, in a loop of Kelani Ganga just a few kilometres from Co-
lombo, feels like a tranquil garden town. This changes once a year
when the first full moon of the new year is celebrated and thousands of pilgrims flood into the town. The temple is considered
one of the most sacred Buddhist sites in Sri Lanka and is also the
seat of a significant Buddhist university.**

The Mahavamsa chronicle reports that Buddha himself visited the **History**
temple dedicated to the god Vibushana (Rama) here that already existed in the 5th century before he took a giant step, touching
Adam's Peak leaving a footprint behind and returning to India
through the air. The temple complex probably started out as a dagoba around which King Yatala Tissa had a town built in the 3rd
century. It seems a monastery also already existed at this time because according to legends there were confrontations between one
of the subsequent kings and a member of the community of monks.
The king is said to have done him a great injustice, whereupon the
sea flooded large parts of his kingdom including the town of Kelaniya. In order to pacify the sea the king is said to have put out his
daughter in a golden boat that finally made landfall in the southwest
near Kirinda. The sea was satisfied with the apparent sacrifice and
retreated again.

AN ORPHANAGE FOR ELEPHANTS

A century ago, when Sri Lanka was home to around 12,000 elephants living in the wild, survival was no problem, not even for injured animals. Even when the father or mother was gone the herd looked after the young.

This changed when people started taking possession of the wild elephants' places of refuge. Forests were cut down, roads were built. These roads often cut through the trails the elephants had known and used for many centuries. A further reason was ruthless poaching and the hunt for precious ivory, an activity that colonial rulers were particularly enthusiastic about.

Is the Elephant Orphanage in Pinawela there to soothe the country's own bad conscience or is it just a welcome opportunity to get in the tourists? Probably a bit of both, but it must also be said that the government is seemingly really interested in the continued existence of these lovable animals.

Feeding time

It is just after nine in the morning. The elephant keepers are dissolving a particularly nutritious milk powder in large buckets filled with water. As if it could not wait any longer, a small elephant nudges the keeper gently to the side with its trunk. It does not take long to prepare the expensive **special food**, and the feeding of the little elephant can begin. It is the second meal of the day because the elephant calf was already given

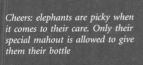
Cheers: elephants are picky when it comes to their care. Only their special mahout is allowed to give them their bottle

A lively trio bathing in the morning

around eight litres of milk early in the morning. For dessert it devours a fresh green bundle of sugar cane and a few leaves. This all costs money, the keeper says. But this project is largely funded by the state, and through global advertising the state also ensures that Pinawela is a fixture on every tourist itinerary. In addition the local traders make a good living from selling T-shirts with elephant prints, and stools covered in elephant skin.

The larger elephants can take care of themselves. An adult bull eats around **250 kilograms** a day. Here in the orphanage the food is served almost ready to eat. Since nothing that grows in the area is really palatable to the elephants, it has to be brought in by lorry.

Bathtime

Next it is time for a refreshing bath. One after the other the animals make their way to the river. There is a mahout next to every elephant. The **mahout** is the elephant driver, the most important person in the life of a tamed elephant. From time to time the mahout pulls his elephant in the

desired direction with a hook, which the elephants bear without complaining. A short while later the elephants are joyfully rolling around in the muddy brown water of the Maha Oya, where the mahouts scrub their skin while dozens of visitors take pictures, which does not seem to irritate the elephants in the slightest.

Working?

From this perspective these elephants have a much better life than the approximately 500 working elephants used in Sri Lanka in agriculture and forestry. They are indispensable helpers in the dense jungle, as they are quite capable of carrying teak trunks weighing several tons.

The elephants of Pinawela do not have to do any exhausting work. Since they cannot simply be released into the wild, where they would no longer be accepted by other elephants, they will have to spend their entire lives in the orphanage. However, a very pleasant job awaits one or two of them: some will be chosen to be magnificent **parade elephants** during the great perahera of Kandy.

Historically, it seems that Tamil invaders destroyed the town as well as the temple and monastery several times. King Vijaya Bahu III (1232–1236) of Dambadeniya had the temple rebuilt and a new town constructed. The temple was partially destroyed by the Portuguese in the 16th century, then later rebuilt again and expanded under the Dutch.

★ ★
Raja Maha Vihara

The temple complex is not far from the centre of Kelaniya in park-like grounds; stairs lead up to the temple terrace. In front of it is the magnificent white entrance gate that dates back to the Dutch period. The European influence is unmistakable. The nicely curved exterior lines that end in spirals are reminiscent of the Baroque, while the typically Ceylonese Makara Thorana (Makara arch) has been much altered from its original form. The Dutch did not go so far as to use actual European ornamentation. They used traditional motifs such as lions, deities, lotus blossoms and the vase of abundance.

The low building to the right behind the entrance gate houses a small Hindu temple. Behind it is the gleaming white dagoba that was built in the classical form. Its oldest parts probably date back to before Christ. It is said to **house a throne studded with gemstones** on which Buddha allegedly sat during his visit to Kelaniya. The oldest parts of the vihara or image gallery date back to the 13th century, but it was only given its architectural appearance in the typical Kandyan style in the 19th century. The characteristic features of this style are the double-stepped roof, the octagon surrounded by pillars at the rear, as well as the likewise octagonal pillars perforated by rectangles in the atria.

Moonstone ▶

A fairly recent moonstone, but designed in line with the old order, forms the threshold to the stairs. The steps depict reliefs of dwarfs and the balustrade has the shape of an elephant whose trunk is rolled up in a spiral. The exterior walls are covered in friezes. They show elephants with geese and dwarfs between them; it is a remarkable fact that none of them are alike. Further animal sculptures decorate the lower section of the pedestal. The door frames and panels carved of wood and with artistic reliefs in the individual panels are particularly beautiful.

Temple interior ▶

The main room to the right is the oldest part of the temple. The other rooms were added much more recently. It houses the 13 m/42 ft figure of a recumbent Buddha. The wall paintings reveal a clear European influence in their vitality as well as in the coloration and luminosity. Between the pictures, which mainly depict scenes from the Jataka, there are dancers, musicians and flower motifs. One of

▶ VISITING KELANIYA

GETTING THERE

By car:
from Colombo towards Kandy
(12 km/7mi)
By bus:
Good, regular connections from
Colombo

WHERE TO STAY

► **Budget**
Sarasa Hotel
937, Kandy Road
Wedamulla
Tel. 02 / 291 04 60
Fax 02 / 291 54 26
19 rooms, restaurant
Simple but well cared for hotel

these pictures deserves special attention, because it shows the nun Hemamala bringing Buddha's sacred tooth to Sri Lanka (according to legend she hid it in her hair). The ceiling of the main room is painted in interesting geometrical patterns.

One important feature outside is the magnificent bodhi tree, which stands on a structured terrace. Throughout the day Buddhists can be seen here walking around the terrace with containers filled with water with which they sprinkle the tree while they mutter prayers. The pools in front of the main entrance of the temple, in which **ritual cleansing** takes place, were only built recently.

Bodhi tree

The remaining buildings in the temple grounds are part of the Buddhist university that was founded in 1958. It is known by the name Vidyalankara. and developed from a school, founded by Buddhist monks, for the reforming and deepening of Buddha's teachings.

Buddhist university

Kurunegala

B 7

Province: North Western
Population: 30,000

Altitude: 85 m/279ft

The rugged rocks on the outskirts of Kurunegala, including the 330 m/1083ft »Elephant Rock«, the idyllic Batalagoda Reservoir and several cultural attractions in the surrounding area make this town particularly appealing.

Between 1293 and 1326, during the reigns of kings Bhuvanaika Bahu II and Parakrama Bahu IV, who felt the capital of ►Polonnaruwa had become too unsafe as it was constantly being threatened by the Tamils, Kurunegala was the capital of the Singhalese kingdom. The

History

▶ VISITING KURUNEGALA

GETTING THERE

By car:
from Colombo on the A 1 to Ambepussa, then on the A 6 (133 km/83mi); from Kandy on the A 10 (42 km/26mi)

By rail:
station on the line from Colombo to Jaffna

By bus:
good bus services from Colombo and Kandy

**WHERE TO STAY /
WHERE TO EAT**

▶ Budget

Diya Dahara Hotel
7, Northlake Road
Tel. 037 / 222 34 52
Fax 037 / 222 00 92
The best rooms are in the hotel's newly built wing. The rooms are comfortable and inexpensive and many of them have lovely views of the lake. The adjoining restaurant is recommended.

The Ranthaliya Resthouse
South Lake Road
Tel. 037 / 222 22 98
This guest house is basic and only has a modest level of comfort, but the rooms are clean and the good restaurant serves tasty local dishes.

kings built a palace and a temple for the sacred tooth relic here (▶Kandy). It was also during this period that Marco Polo (▶Famous People) visited the city.

After the death of King Vijaya Bahu V his sons argued about who should ascend the throne. The usurper Vasthimi Kumareya, whose mother was a Muslim concubine, was the first to seize the throne, while the younger rightful son retreated to the country. After some time he was sought out, however, since his brother showed excessive favouritism towards the Muslim subjects. After his coronation he moved to Dambadeniya with the justification that Kurunegala had been desecrated by a half-Muslim king. Kurunegala subsequently lost its importance.

What to see in Kurunegala

wn on the lake Nothing remains of the royal residence and the temple. They probably once stood on the site of the present-day market, which always has a large variety of different fruits on offer. **Many jewellers** with engraved goods line the streets. The very nice Lake Batalagoda with its countless water lilies all around the edge was probably created by King Bhuvanaike Bahu II as a water reservoir; on its western shore is a pretty rest house which has been extended into a small hotel.

Above the town are some very strangely shaped rocks named after animals: Elephant Rock (Etagala) and Tortoise Rock (Ibbagala); Elephant Rock is the highest at 330 m/1083ft. In addition there are Goat Rock and Crocodile Rock as well as several other smaller ones.

Rocks of Kurunegala

The views of the densely forested mountain landscape and the reservoir are particularly stunning from Elephant Rock and Tortoise Rock, where Ibbagala Vihara is a **worthwhile destination** as it has some Buddha statues and a highly venerated footprint of Buddha to offer.

Around Kurunegala

Around 20 km/12mi northeast of Kurunegala there is a temple, situated on a rocky outcrop, known as Silver Temple; 200 steps lead up to it. King Duttha Gamani is said to have founded it in around 100 BC out of gratitude for the vein of silver he discovered here. The current buildings date from the 18th century when King Kirti Sri Raja Sinha had the monastery refurbished. It is known for its extensive collection of old palmleaf manuscripts kept in the library. The richly carved doors decorated with ivory inlays are also remarkable. The motifs have been taken from the world of mythology: in addition to tendrils and lotus blossoms there are a dancing-girl and lions as well as a vase of abundance, from whose foliage female deities appear. **The works are of exceptional refinement**. A peculiarity is the altar, which was a gift from a Dutch governor. The Delft tiles that adorn the altar depict Christian scenes.

✱ Silver Temple

Around 23 km/14mi north of Kurunegala is the hermitage of Arankale, an interesting ruin in a beautiful, tranquil forest (access via Ibbagamuwa, turn left behind the town towards Kumbukwewa, when the road forks take the left-hand road). At the start of the 1st century the sage Maliydeva retreated here with his monks. The complex can be accessed via a cobbled **meditation path** lined by high metrosideros trees. The path arrives at a **meditation circle** surrounded by tall, carved stones. Stone columns lying around are the only visible remains of the monastic complex, which was probably built in the 6th century. Believers from the villages place their food donations for the monks on the tables made of carved stone that stand in a nearby clearing.

✱ Arankale (hermitage)

Dambadeniya Dambadeniya is around 92 km/57mi from Colombo south of Kurunegala. For a few years, during the confusions of the Chola reign in the 13th century, the town was considered the Singhalese capital during the resistance to the Tamils in the actual capital of Polonnaruwa. Vijaya Bahu III, the nominal king from 1232 to 1236, based himself in Dambadeniya, but it was only his son who managed to liberate Polonnaruwa again. The town later fell once more into insignificance. Some ruins survive of the period when Dambadeniya was the capital, but they are hard to verify.

✳
Sri Wijaya Sundarama Raja Maha Vihara Parts of the Sri Wijaya Sundarama Raja Maha Vihara temple, which is protected by a large rock, date back to the 13th century. The unusual shape of the dagoba is also striking. It bears a rectangular roof and also possesses an atrium. The guard stones flanking the staircase up to the two-storey statue house are also unusual; they depict scenes from the Jataka, the stories of Buddha's past lives. The left-hand one shows a seated Buddha at the centre, above and below him battle scenes, while the right-hand one also depicts battle scenes and an elephant which is evidently stamping on the victims. The atrium to the image gallery is adorned by a pretty roof in the Kandyan style. The fan-like timberwork deserves particular attention. The exterior and interior walls of the upper floor, which is reached via a narrow stairway, are decorated with good wall paintings (those on the external walls were not completed). On the right-hand wall is a depiction of Vishnu clad in a Buddhist robe; he is leading a number of worshipping monks.

The large image gallery from more recent times houses the statue of a recumbent Buddha. Opposite the entrance a path goes through paddy fields to a rock on which a citadel once stood.

Mahiyangana (Alutnuvara)

Province: Uva   **Altitude:** approx. 223 m/732ft

The now small town whose dagoba becomes the destination of many Buddhist pilgrims once a year during the September full moon is situated in magnificent scenery on Mahaweli Ganga at the foot of the Central Highlands.

History Mahiyangana was inhabited long before the time of Christ and in the 17th century it was still a flourishing town, not least because several European missions reached Kandy from Batticaloa via the Mahawli Ganga, which is navigable as far as Mahiyangana. There are still some Vedda settlements around Mahiyangana; the Vedda are Sri Lanka's aboriginal inhabitants. They enjoy special government protection, which is also why they cannot be visited.

▶ VISITING MAHIYANGANA

GETTING THERE

By car:
from Kandy on the A 26 (74 km/
46 mi), from Badulla on the A 8 to
Waywatta, then on the A 26 to
Mahiyangana

By rail:
from Colombo to Kandy (several
connections a day), then on by bus

or a rental vehicle

By bus:
daily bus services from Kandy, Batticaloa and Badulla

WHERE TO STAY

The closest accommodation is in
▶Kandy, in Mahiyangana itself there
are no recommended places to stay.

✦ ✦ Mahiyangana Dagoba

The chronicle of the Mahavamsa, which is filled with many a legend, **Surrounded by**
reports that Buddha visited a town called Mahanaga (or Maha Na- **park-like**
gara, which means »big town«) nine months after his enlightenment **landscape**
in order to convince the Yakshas, Sri Lanka's legendary daemonic
aboriginal inhabitants who gathered here from time to time, of his
teachings. He is said to have achieved this by **performing several
miracles**. The most impressive event, as recorded by the chronicle, is
that Buddha flew off through the air after his sermon. According to
the historical tradition it was Mahanaga, a brother of King Devanampiya Tissa (250 – 210 BC) and founder of Magama, the old capital of
the kingdom of Ruhuna (now an abandoned place in the dense jungle), who had the dagoba built. A curl of hair dedicated by the enlightened one to the Yakshas was the first relic of this dagoba. It was
placed in a gem-encrusted urn and was the reason why the dagoba
was built. To this day it is one of the most important Buddhist places
of worship in Sri Lanka.

To get to the dagoba there are two options; either via the 2000 steps **Temple comple**
of the pilgrim's path or via a narrow road. The dagoba's 2.2 m/7 ft
door surround is adorned with Buddhist symbols (sun, lotus blossom and hare); these depictions refer to a story in the Jataka in
which Buddha's previous lives, of which there are more than 500, are
described. The moonstone is decorated with a band of elephants and
horses as well as a closed lotus bud.

During restoration works in the early 1950s a reliquary chamber **Reliquary**
with a square floor plan was uncovered; it was probably only built **chamber**
during the restoration of the 11th century. The niches at the cardinal points of the four walls house one or more likenesses of Buddha
in the Indian Amaravati or Pala style. The stone, box-shaped con-

tainer in the middle of the room, which has an edge length of 1.22 1.33yd and a height of only 1.1 m/3 ft 6 in, contained two relics, small dagobas made of copper with a golden tip as well as coins and flowers made of gold leaf. Four bronze figures of people on horseback, armed with sword and shield, accompanied by a woman stood as if on guard at the sides of the stone container. The other objects in the chamber (including iron tridents as a symbol of Shiva, golden banners, copper containers and lamps, bowls with coins as well as semi-precious and precious stones) were set up symmetrically around the stone container. The walls were covered with paintings of which only fragments survive. These were carefully removed and, just like the other objects, taken to the national museum of ▶Anuradhapura.

Matale

C7

Province: Central
Population: 37,000

Altitude: approx. 470 m/1542ft

Matale, a progressive town in the central region, is at the heart of a large plantation region where natural rubber, cinnamon, pepper, chillis, tea, rice and vegetables are cultivated. The necessary conditions allowing such different crops to flourish are created by the humid tropical climate in the lowlands surrounded on all sides by mountain ranges, except for in the north.

What to see in Matale

Fort Macdowall Above Saxton Park at the centre of Matale are the remains of Fort Macdowall. It was built by the British at the start of the 19th century during the war against the kings of Kandy.

The Hindu temple situated on the main road through Matale, Sri Muthumariamman Thevasthaman, is a must-see for its lavish, colourful statues, but it is unremarkable as an example of sacred architecture.

✳ ✳ Aluvihara (rock temple)

Historically significant Situated in a rugged rocky landscape, Aluvihara is one of the most significant sites for Buddhism in Sri Lanka. Even though not much remains from the monastery's great heyday it is still worth visiting for the famous rock temple alone. The ability of the Singhalese to incorporate buildings harmoniously into the landscape also becomes remarkably clear here.

The monastery, which can be accessed from the road by two stone stairways, both with around 50 steps, was founded by Wattagamini

▶ VISITING MATALE

GETTING THERE

By car:
from Kandy on the A 9 (24 km/15mi), from Dambulla on the A 9 (48 km/30mi), from Kurunegala via Kandy (59 km/37mi), via Ibbagamuwa (43 km/27mi)

By rail:
Matale is the last stop on the line from Kandy.

By bus:
there are many direct connections every day from Kandy

▶ Visiting the Temple

The rock temple of Aluvihara is 30 km/20mi north of Kandy and only 3 km/2mi north of the district capital of Matale, which is also the location of the nearest railway station. From there the temple complex can be reached by taxi.

WHERE TO STAY

Baedeker recommendation

Holiday home near Ovilla
In the Valley of the Knuckle Mountains
Tel. 056 / 406 26 62
Fax 056 / 405 28 48
2 rooms
Situated in a wide valley and surrounded by the magnificent mountain landscape of Matale is this holiday home, which was only built in 2003. It has very comfortable rooms (a double room and a single room). The owner does not just offer pleasant ayurveda treatments but also excursions to the surrounding area. The holiday home also has wheelchair access, which is a rarity in Sri Lanka.

Abhaya in the 1st century BC. **It is almost jammed in between splintered granite rocks**; the best overview of the entire complex can be had by climbing a further steep slope and looking down from the dagoba above the actual temple.

Beside the lower dagoba is a hall carved out of the rock containing paintings and statues depicting the enlightened one in the typical poses (meditating, teaching and resting). Other caves contain the monks' living quarters. King Walagam Bahu is said to have stayed in one of the caves. He fled the capital Anuradhapura from the Tamils in around 103 BC.

The rock temple of Aluvihara obtained its great significance in 80 BC when around 500 Buddhist monks from all around the world met here to write down Buddha's teachings, which had previously been handed down orally, on palm leaves (olas). This is when the canon of scriptures known as Tripitaka (= three baskets) was written down in Pali, the sacred language of Buddhism. In these three baskets (Vinayapitaka, Suttapitaka and Abhidammapitaka) Buddha's teachings have been summarized. Together with the comments written down by the monks they are still used as the guideline for recitations.

In a small museum nearby monks demonstrate the art of writing on palm leaves. The fact that they are true masters of this art benefits them now because during the war between the British and the kings of Kandy in 1646 a large number of the valuable manuscripts were destroyed. The reconstruction work is are still going on. To this day new insights of the Buddhist religion from all around the world are written down in this traditional manner.

Around Matale

Around 15 km/9mi east of Matale are the ►Hunas Falls, set in beautiful mountainous landscape.

Hunas Falls

Nalanda (23 km/14mi from Matale) is still in the area dominated by the extensive plantations that begin north of Kandy. The crops cultivated here include cocoa, rubber, vegetables and rice. Beyond this are is a mountain region still partially covered in dense jungle.

Nalanda

In the first half of the 12th century Nalanda was briefly the residence of the Ruhuna princes and later King Parakrama Bahu I, who went to battle from here against Gaja Bahu III from Polonnaruwa. However, he was only able to rule after Gaja Bahu's death in 1153.

The Nalanda Gedige around 1 km/0.6mi east of the town is one of the earliest stone buildings in Sri Lanka. It is dated to the 8th or 9th century. The architectural style and the still extant sculptures reveal it to have been alternately a Buddhist and a Brahman temple; its monks followed Mahayana Buddhism. The shape of the temple with its arched roof and horseshoe-shaped gable, a recurring motif of Buddhist temple architecture certainly taken over from Hindu models, strongly exhibits the influence of the southern Indian architecture of the Pallava period (approx. 625 – 800). Other details such as the stair design with moonstone and the Makara balustrade as well as the dancing dwarfs come from the Buddhist architectural canon.

★
◄ Nalanda Gedige

> ! **Baedeker TIP**
>
> ### Sri Lanka's spices...
>
> All around Matale there are many spice gardens, some of which are also open to the public. One is along the road to Kandy for example. It is definitely worth stopping at. Watch how spices are cultivated, harvested and processed. Of course the spices can also be bought here.

Remarkable sculptures were found in the temple and the surrounding area. Now they are exhibited in the temple. Amongst them are a guard stone with a snake temple under the seven-headed shield of Naga, a four-armed Ganesha as well as several small sculptures in erotic positions. This latter kind of sculpture is mainly found in southern India. The admission charge to the temple is included in the collective ticket for the Cultural Triangle.

← *Dignified and introspective: Buddha statue in Aluvihara*

Nalanda Wewa (reservoir) ► The way to Wahakotte, 15 km/9mi north of the town, goes past the picturesquely situated Nalanda Wewa, one of Sri Lanka's many artificial lakes. On its shores many different bird species can be seen.

Ataragollawa ► Near Ataragollawa, 21 km/13mi from Nalanda (A 9 to Naula, then turn right) and situated amongst ruins is the relatively well preserved 12 m/40 ft statue of a recumbent Buddha from the 9th/10th century. Near Elahera, 8 km/5mi further east, there were once high-yielding gemstone mines, which have, however, been exhausted. The Elahera

Elahera Canal ► Canal, created by Vasabha (67 – 111), the first ruler of the Lambakanna dynasty, was initially 50 km/30mi long but in the 6th century it was lengthened by 100 km/60mi and formed a significant part of the complex irrigation system that also includes Amban Ganga and the reservoirs of Minneriya and Giritale.

✴ ✴ Matara

C 10

Province: Southern
Population: 43,000

Altitude: 7 m/23ft

Matara is situated on a wide bay in the island's far south. This is where Nilwala Ganga, coming from the mountains, flows into the sea and this is also where the railway line from Colombo ends. The hinterland was once a large spice garden. Today visitors will still find cinnamon and tea plantations as well as citronella fields. The town is somewhat remote and so it has maintained some of its charm from days gone by despite the damage caused by the tsunami.

History Between 1518 and 1656 the Portuguese occupied Matara several times, but it was only the Dutch who built two forts between 1656 and 1796. When the Kandyan king Kirti Sri Raja Sinha (1747 – 1781) tried to seize power over some of the Dutch territory, the Dutch retaliated by stopping salt deliveries to Kandy. The king reacted by moving south with his troops and conquering Matara. However, in 1765, after the Dutch had entered Kandy, he had to withdraw his troops again and make peace with them as well as hand over the entire southern strip of coastline to them.

Dutch coat of arms on the bastion in Matara

● VISITING MATARA

GETTING THERE

By car:
from Galle on the A 2 (41 km/25mi);
from Hambantota on the A 2 (70 km/43mi)
By rail:
terminus of the line from Colombo
By bus:
good services from Galle

**WHERE TO STAY/
WHERE TO EAT**

► **Budget**
Isolabella House
Veherahenawatta, Nilwella-Dickwella
Tel. 777 / 45 07 22
www.ayurveda-isolabella.de
Carla and Flavio Barattini are the
owners, Italians as their names sug-

gest. This small guesthouse is situated
between Matara and Tangalle. It has
good rooms at inexpensive prices and
when Flavio cooks he serves up more
than just pizza.

Guesthouse with a nice pool: Isobella House

✱ ✱ Dutch Fort

The star-shaped fort complex was built by the Dutch governor van
Eck in 1763. The monumental entrance gate bears his name as well
as the Dutch coat of arms and the year 1770, the year of its completion. The fort now houses **a small museum** whose collection is a
smorgasbord of items that cannot necessarily be connected to Matara
(however, the many aerial photographs of Sri Lanka's archaeological
excavation sites are noteworthy). The buildings within the larger fort
near the coast is now used by the government and administration
(Matara is the district capital). Not far away is the obligatory clock
tower. This one dates back to the Dutch period. A causeway connects
the mainland to the small island of Chula Lanka, whose now abandoned monastery was founded by a Thai monk.

Around Matara

Just over a kilometre west of Matara is one of Sri Lanka's nicest
swimming beaches: the small bay of Polhena. Offshore there are nice,
but partially plundered coral reefs.

✱
Beach of Polhena

Not far from here is Dondra Head, the southernmost point of the island of Sri Lanka (►Dondra).

Dondra Head

Medirigiriya

C5

Province: Northern Central   **Altitude:** 155 m/509ft

Medirigiriya, now a fairly forlorn place in the middle of some magnificent landscape not far from Polonnaruwa, possessed a significant temple from very early on. The well preserved ruins have great significance for the artistic development in Sri Lanka.

✳ ✳ Vatadage of Medirigiriya

Complex
As is reported in the Mahavamsa chronicle, Kanittha Tissa (approx. 164–192) had a Uposatha hall built in Mandalagiri Vihara, as the place was called at the time. In the second half of the 7th century King Agabodhi began building the Vatadage (round temple). According to an inscription a hospital was added to the monastery complex in the 9th century. At this time a number of villages in the surrounding area were also part of the monastic complex. King Nissanka Malla had the Vatadage restored at the end of the 12th century; he also commissioned four statues of sitting Buddhas, which face the four staircases.

As in ► Anuradhapura the temple complex of Medirigiriya fell into ruin over time. It was only in 1934 that archaeologists from Colombo started paying attention to the complex, which by then was completely overgrown by the jungle. It was not until 1941 that restoration work began, which was completed in 1955.

Alongside the Vatadage of Polonnaruwa the one in Medirigiriya is **the most significant example of this temple type in Sri Lanka**. It stands on a granite rock that has steps leading up it.

Dagoba
At the centre of the round temple is a dagoba with a diameter of approx. 8 m/27 ft; at its core it is around 800 years older than the rest of the structure. At the four cardinal points, opposite the entrances, are the statues of Buddha, but only the eastern one is in its pristine state. The other three statues were put together from remains that were found within the complex. However, the facial features and postures are still very impressive.

On the terrace laid out on irregularly worked granite and limestone blocks stand octagonal stone pillars with remarkably beautiful capitals. They are arranged in three concentric circles and vary in height: the 16 pillars of the innermost circle have a height of 5.18 m/17ft, the 20 of the second circle 4.88 m/16ft and the 32 of the outer circle only 2.74 m/9ft; they are incorporated in a surrounding balustrade. Between the second and third circles of pillars is a brick wall with gaps at the four cardinal points; apart from a few remains in the southwest it has disappeared. It and the columns once supported the wooden roof.

▶ VISITING MEDIRIGIRIYA

GETTING THERE

By car:
from Polonnaruwa on the A 11 to Giritale, then turn right towards Hingurakgoda, from there travel northbound (approx. 30 km/20mi)
By rail:
from Polonnaruwa to Hingurakgoda, transfer here and carry on by taxi

WHERE TO STAY

Unfortunately there is no recommendable accommodation in Medirigiriya and the surrounding area. It is better to continue on to ►Polonnaruwa.

The gallery terrace is paved with granite slabs. The 5.20 m/17ft pedestal is made of brick and stands on a natural rock.
The entrance to the Vatadage is in the north. Visitors walk through a 2.75 m/9ft gate to get to the 27 steps that lead up to an almost square platform. The moonstones in front of the four stairways leading up to the temple proper are unadorned.

Statue house, bodhi tree

from the Pilimage (statue house) northwest of the Vatadage the foundations of a number of square stone pillars without capitals still survive, as do three colossal statues of standing Buddhas.
The pedestal of the bodhi tree enclosure, richly adorned with lion reliefs, was made towards the end of the Anuradhapura period (10th century). Amongst the remains of the hospital a vat carved from a monolith is of note. It was probably made in the 9th or 10th century and was most likely used to store cooked rice until it was time to hand it out to the monks and patients.

✹ ✹ Mihintale

C 5

Province: Northern Central   **Altitude:** approx. 309 m/1014ft

The Buddhist monastery of Mihintale is situated on Mount Missaka. It is one of the island's oldest and is considered the »cradle of Buddhism« in Sri Lanka. Mihintale attracts hundreds of pilgrims every day and on the day of the June full moon it is visited by tens of thousands of people to celebrate the Poson Poya festival.

History

The monastery of Mihintale owes its construction to the monk Mahinda, who was sent out by King Ashoka to spread the teachings of the enlightened Buddha in Sri Lanka. He found a keen listener in King Devanampiya Tissa, who soon declared Buddhism the state re-

▶ VISITING MIHINTALE

GETTING THERE

By car:
from Anuradhapura, A 9 (15 km);
from Kandy on the A 9 (138 km/86mi)
By bus:
Good connections from
Anuradhapura.

WHERE TO STAY

There is currently only a modest
guesthouse in Mihintale but it is not
far to ▶Giritale and its recommended
hotels.

ligion. That was in 250 BC, shortly after the king had ascended the throne. Mahina lived for a long time as a hermit in Mihintale, proclaiming Buddha's teachings. He also founded a Sangha, one of the first Buddhist communities. King Tissa had a large monastery and dagobas for several relics built on the hill near Mahinda's hermitage. Despite the confusions of the centuries Mihintale never fell into ruin. All of the rulers were interested in preserving the buildings and renovating them when necessary.

Monastery Complex of Mihintale

Old hospital from the town of Mihintale the A 9 goes to the ruins of the monastery complex. To the left of the road are the remains of the old hospital, whose foundations and pillars still allow visitors to make out the individual rooms. The **practical arrangement** of the wards is remarkable. They were easy to reach from an interior hallway. The stone tub that was carved from a granite block was presumably used for healing baths and the big millstone for grinding medicinal herbs.

Indikatuseya and Katuseya Dagoba Somewhat further along on the same side of the road are the ruins of the Indikatuseya and Katuseya Dagobas (8th century). The base of the dagobas is impressive. It consists of a rounded ledge of carved stone. Its configuration is also remarkable. The stairway up to the stumps of some pillars, all that remains of a building, is decorated by attractive guard stones.

Remains of a vatadage Shortly before starting the climb up the stone stairs notice the remains of a temple on the left-hand side. It resembles the Mahasena palace in Anuradhapura in its composition, but here it has the shape of a round structure, which is reminiscent of the vatadage temple type.

Stairway The monumental stairway that leads to the top of the hill presumably dates back to the monastery's founding days. It was carved out of the granite rocks and consists of four flights with a total of 1840 steps, which are lined by magnificently flowering frangipani trees.

from the first landing a narrower stairway leads up to a plateau on which the Kantaka Chaitya Dagoba rises up. It was named after the horse on which Buddha is said to have left the parental court and forsworn the lavish lifestyle. According to the legend the horse died of grief. The dagoba was probably built in the 2nd century BC and was 30 m/100ft tall; today it is in ruins. The circumference of its well preserved base is 130 m/426 ft; its three parts are typical of the early Singhalese dagobas. The four vahalkadas (altars) with very nice sculptural ornamentation, largely from the 1st century AD, are quite striking. They boast finely chiselled edges, friezes consisting of elephants, wild geese and extremely lively depictions of dwarfs. The left stele of the eastern vahalkada has ornaments of plants, an elephant, a peacock with its young and a vase of abundance with two birds. On the stone altar in front of the vahalkadas offerings were made during ritual acts. On the right side of the eastern Vahalkada is the torso of a female figure, on the southern one the relief sculpture of the snake king Muchalinda in human form. They are believed to be the earliest pieces of sculpture in Sri Lanka.

Kantaka Chaitya Dagoba

Mihintale *Map*

In the area around Kantaka Chaitya there are more than 60 living-caves in the rocks and under rocky slopes. They were inhabited during the time of the first community of monks (3rd century BC). Some still have visible inscriptions in the Brahmi script.

Monks' living-caves

Returning to the main stairs and climbing up higher visitors will reach the second section of the stairs and the remains of a monastery that was probably built in the 9th century. The remains of an aqueduct, supported by high stone pillars, are of interest, as is a large and a smaller stone basin, which was presumably used to store donated food, but possibly also to store herbs for making medicines. The ruins of a large building, probably the image gallery, include two vertical monoliths, probably from the 10th century. They bear inscrip-

Remains of a monastery

tions providing insight about the rules in place at the time: »Nobody who has taken life may live near this hill.« Other inscriptions explain the instructions for taking care of the sick as well as the tasks of the temple servants.

Sinha Pokuna (lion pond) A path to the right of the main stairs goes to the lion pond (Sinha Pokuna) with **one of Sri Lanka's best animal sculptures**. It depicts a lion through whose mouth the water once flowed into the pool. The finely chiselled pool surrounding is classically austere: a frieze on the outside with very attractive reliefs of animals and dancers and in the upper surround individual reliefs of figures.

Naga Pokuna (snake pond) Continue up the main stairs, which now start becoming narrower. At some point a path turns off to the right and climbs up steeply to Naga Pokuna (snake pond). The pool is almost 40m/130 ft long and has been carved from the rock. The bas relief of a five-headed naga that has been carved into the rock is quite impressive.

Ambasthala Dagoba The main stairs now lead to Ambasthala Dagoba (mango tree dagoba) surrounded by high coconut palms; it was built in the first quarter of the 1st century AD. The reliquary chamber within contains

View from the peak of Sila rock

some of the mortal remains of the monk Mahinda. Of the complex, built in the style of a vatadage, most of the pillars arranged in two concentric circles still survive and some of them have lovely capitals. A modern building with an octagonal floor plan to the south of the dagoba marks the spot where Mahinda and the king first met.

Opposite the entrance to the Ambastala Dagoba a path leads down to the spot known as Mahinda's bed. It is a cave with a carved, flat stone on which the monk is said to have slept and meditated. **Mahinda's bed**

Up steep steps carved into the rock visitors will get to Sila Rock, from where the **view** of the jungle, Mahakandarawa Wewa (a reservoir) and Anuradhapura in the west is magnificent. **Sila Rock**

On the opposite hill to the left of the small pond is the small rock temple of Mahinda Vihara, which contains a modern depiction of the encounter between the monk and the king. **Mahinda Vihara**

The peak of Mount Missaka is adorned by the gleaming-white 21 m/ 69ft Maha Seya Dagoba from the 10th century, which is visible far and wide. It has the typically Sri Lankan bubble shape. One of its relics is a hair from Buddha's head. The nearby Hindu temple is consecrated to Shiva, Parvati and Ganesha. **Maha Seya Dagoba**

Monaragala

D 8

Province: Uva   **Altitude:** approx. 74 m/243ft

Monaragala is situated in the fertile lowlands of Kumbukkan Oya, which irrigates the paddy fields and allows countless rubber trees to flourish. To the north the foothills of the Uva's mountains rise up and to the south the jungle becomes denser.

While the town itself does not have any sights of its own to offer it is a good base for visiting several ruins in the area.

Around Monaragala

Only a few kilometres east of the town is Galebadda, a fortified former residence of the kings of Ruhuna. It was probably built during the first half of the 12th century. The ruins allow the floor plan of the complex to be made out quite clearly; the actual palace was located within the walled citadel along with some other buildings. The citadel only had one entrance. A high wall secured the complex. Queen Sugala of Ruhua, who resisted the new king Parakrama Bahu I of Polonnaruwa, was in possession of the sacred tooth relic, the king- **Galebadda**

⏵ VISITING MONARAGALA

GETTING THERE
By car:
from Wellawaya on the A 4 (34 km/
21mi); from Hambantota on the A 2

to Wellawaya, then turn right on to
the A 4 to Monaragala
By bus:
good service from Hambantota

---

dom's emblem. When Parakrama Bahu I came to Udundora the queen had fled, but his troops still managed to find her and take possession of the relic.

Dambegoda Vihara
Near Maligavila, 15 km/9mi south of Monaragala, are the ruins of Dambegoda Vihara. It possesses a colossal statue of Buddha, which is now on the ground. It was originally 12 m/39ft tall and 3 m/10ft wide at the shoulders, and presumably once stood in a large image gallery made of brick, but none of it survives. The corresponding lotus-shaped pedestal with a 4 m/13ft diameter, a moonstone composed of several pieces and a guard stele with the relief of a Naga king in the elegant Tribhanga pose are further remarkable features. It is thought all of these works were made in the 6th or 7th century.

aves in the area
The area south of the road between Wellawaye and Monaragla is rich in caves and many of them were likely to have been **inhabited in prehistoric times**. The large cave of Budugalge was a sacred Buddhist site and contains several interesting sculptures of Buddha (including a fairly large recumbent Buddha). To get to the cave turn south in Kumbukkana near Buttala, then drive approx. 8 km/5mi further. From here it is a walk of around 1.5 km/1mi. A long stone stairway leads up to the cave.

⋆ Negombo

A 7

Province: Western
Population: 123,000

Altitude: 5 m/16ft

Negombo, one of Sri Lanka's best-known seaside resorts, is so appealing because of its geographical location at the end of a lagoon with countless little islands and pretty bays.

History
Negombo is currently the island's fifth-largest town. It was founded by Arab traders. In the 16th century the Portuguese created a centre of their cinnamon trade here and fortified the town. In around the middle of the 17th century the Dutch took over Negombo and built

a canal, which, together with the southern section, connects Colombo with Chilaw and Puttalam. It is still in use today. In 1796 the British occupied the town, which the Dutch had abandoned, and demolished many of the fortifications.

What to see in Negombo

The old town centre with its narrow, winding streets is now a **lively shopping district** with a large fruit and vegetable market under a huge banyan tree. This market and the fish auction hall, when the fishermen arrive with their catch (the high seas fishermen as early as 4am, the coastal fishermen only in the afternoon at around 3pm), are particularly lively.

★
Town Centre

Only the eastern main gate with the year 1678 at the southern end of Main Street and parts of two bastions still survive of the fortifications from the time the Dutch were here.

Dutch fort

In the old town of Negombo there are a large number of Catholic churches, some of which have beautifully ornamented façades. There is an old Dutch church near the canal, which dates back to the Dutch period; the steep roof that comes down low to the ground and the small belfry that acts as a ridge turret are characteristic features.

Catholic churche

The canal, built during the Dutch period, is used by padda-boats to transport vegetables, fruit, coconuts and other goods, even today. The canal, which once had a length of around 120 km/75mi and connected Colombo with Puttalam, played an important role at the start of the 19th century as a way of supplying the people with food. Taking a tranquil **trip in a padda boat** is highly recommended. Several of the boat owners offer them (information: Muthurajawela Boat Center, 2/14 Pamunugama Road, Delathura).

> **? DID YOU KNOW ...?**
>
> ■ For a long time Negombo was a centre of Jesuit missionary activity and even today a large percentage of the inhabitants are Roman Catholics. That is one reason why a Passiontide play is performed here, or, more specifically in Duwa near Negombo, which is unique in Sri Lanka. The highlight of the celebrations are a re-enacted Way of the Cross, a puppet theatre and of course a large market.

This small museum is dedicated to Walisinghe Harischandra, a national hero who lived in Sri Lanka in the 19th century. His achievements consisted of him showing the people of Sri Lanka the value of their own cultural identity during a time in which the Western lifestyle was threatening to push out their centuries-old way of life. Several pieces of furniture and other items from Harischandra's personal effects are worth seeing (open: Sat – Wed 9am – 5pm; the museum is closed on public holidays; admission charge).

Walisinghe Harischandra Museum

🕐

◉ VISITING NEGOMBO

GETTING THERE
By car:
from Colombo on the A 3 (38 km/ 24mi) towards Katunayake Airport (a more attractive and only marginally longer route runs along the lagoon).
By rail:
station on the route from Colombo to the north
By bus:
good services from Colombo

WHERE TO EAT
► **Inexpensive**
Seahorse Palace
27, Silvester Road
Tel. 031 / 227 52 11
Excellent fish dishes as well as international cuisine

WHERE TO STAY / WHERE TO EAT
► **Luxury**
Brown's Beach Hotel
175, Lewis Place
Tel. 031 / 55 55 000
Fax 031 / 224 87 05-72

www.aitkenspencehotels.com/browns
140 rooms, 2 restaurants, bar, nightclub, pool, tennis, squash
Hotel rich in tradition with comfortable rooms. The wide sandy beach is right in front of the hotel.

Blue Oceanic / Royal Oceanic
Lewis Place
Tel. 011 / 587 330 11
Fax 011 / 237 23 36
104 rooms, 2 restaurants and bars, coffee shop, pool, tennis, squash, private diving station
Old-established hotel with very well looked-after and comfortable rooms right on the beach

► **Budget**
Lagoon View Rest House
Corner of St Joseph Street / Main Street
Tel. / Fax 031 / 531 02 50
This guesthouse, with very nice rooms, is not on the beach of Negombo, but on the big lagoon.

Around Negombo

Gampaha

The city of Gampaha is one of Sri Lanka's nicest garden cities. The Botanical Garden of Henarathgoda is the oldest in the country and thanks to the scientific laboratory it is of great significance. There are large pineapple plantations and coconut palm groves in the vicinity.

✳
Henerathgoda Botanical Garden

The very attractive Botanical Garden of Gampaha (2 km/1mi north of the city) emerged from an experimental field for plants. It now encompasses an area of 14ha/35acres and is home to around 1500 tropical and subtropical plant species. This is where the first rubber tree outside of Brazil was planted and this is also where Sri Lanka's natural-rubber industry, still a significant factor in the country's economy, began. In 1876 the Englishman Henry Wickham smuggled several cuttings or seeds from a rubber tree growing in the wild in the Amazon region to England. Since they did not really flourish in the conditions there they were brought to Henerathgoda, where they can still be admired today.

Amongst the garden's other plants a collection of various palm species (including several specimens of the coco-de-mer tree from the Seychelles), rubber bushes from Malaysia and the chaulmoogra tree, which is allegedly the source of an effective medicine for treating leprosy, deserve special mention (open: daily 9am–6pm, admission charge).

> ! **Baedeker** TIP
>
> **The Versatile Nut**
> The Madampe Coconut Research Institute north of Colombo is worth a visit. The people working here are researching all of the products that can be made from the palm and its nut.

Rock temple of Varana

East of Gampaha (straight on at the intersection with the A 1, turn left after approx. 6 km/4mi) is the early Buddhist rock temple of Varana with remains of wall paintings and a Buddha statue chiselled from the rock. The caves, none of which are very deep, are located on three different levels. Some have eaves up to 15 m/49ft high. One of the inscriptions presumably dates back to the 3rd century BC when the temple caves were founded. From the top of the rock the wonderful view is reward enough for the somewhat laborious climb up a trail.

Tomb of Solomon Bandaranaike

On the A 1 towards Nittambuwa, just a few kilometres beyond Yakkala on the left-hand side is the tomb of Solomon Bandaranaike (►Famous People), who was assassinated in 1959; it is a classically beautiful complex. The area belonged to his father, a senior official under British colonial rule. He built a comfortable house in the English colonial style here. The tomb itself is situated under a magnificent white fig tree.

✳ Nuwara Eliya

C 8

Province: Central
Population: approx. 26,000

Altitude: approx. 1880m/ 6170ft – 2000 m/6570ft

Nuwara Eliya, the »city above the clouds«, is situated in the middle of the mountains of Uva, in a hollow formed by Sri Lanka's three highest mountains. As a result of its mild climate Sri Lanka's highest town is a popular place of refuge for the people from the hot and humid southwest during the hot season. Temperatures here rarely exceed 25 °C/77°F and the air is dry and fresh.

Nuwara Eliya Map

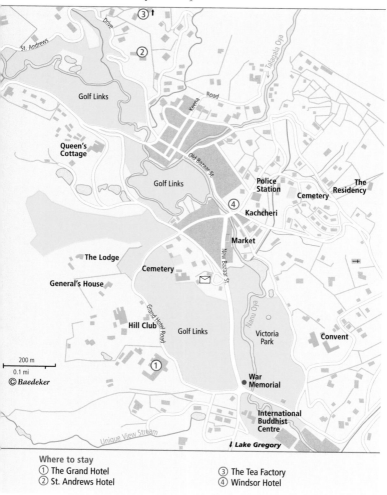

St. Andrews
Drive
③
②
Golf Links
Keena Road
Talagala Oya
Queen's Cottage
Old Bazaar St.
Golf Links
Police Station
Cemetery
The Residency
④ Kachcheri
Market
The Lodge
Cemetery
General's House
New Bazaar St.
Namu Oya
Grand Hotel Road
Hill Club
Golf Links
Victoria Park
Convent
200 m
0.1 mi
© Baedeker
①
War Memorial
International Buddhist Centre
Unique View Stream
Lake Gregory

Where to stay
① The Grand Hotel
② St. Andrews Hotel
③ The Tea Factory
④ Windsor Hotel

Very British The town clearly bears the signature of the British, who fashioned the houses and gardens according to their ideas: large lawns, golf courses and villas in the country-house style that were usually inhabited by tea planters at the time. Tea plantations still dominate the appearance of the fantastic mountain landscape all around. In the town the English flair and the atmosphere of a spa in the mountains still survive today.

Well-tended park, British colonial style: a guesthouse in Nuwara Eliya

In the Indian epic Ramayana the mountains around Nuwara Eliya play a role as one of the residences of the giant king Ravana. He is said to have abducted the princess Sita, the wife of the hero Rama, to this place. The town's history becomes more tangible and verifiable during the time of the British, who started coming here to hunt in around 1820 (preferably elephants and leopards; almost exclusively by giving chase) and in around 1825 they set up a rest home for their officers. The British governor Sir Edward Barnes had the first sur-faced road built in 1828 and in 1846 Sir Samuel Baker built many houses in the town. In 1875 the first horse race took place in Nuwara Eliya. Horse racing was prohibited when the British left, but these days it is allowed again (however, betting is still not permitted). In 1889 an 18-hole golf course was added.

Nuwara Eliya was also always important to Sri Lanka from an eco-nomic perspective. After the coffee bushes became infested by coffee rust, the Scotsman James Taylor began with the first experiments to naturalize tea from Assam in India in the mountains of Sri Lanka in 1867. He was successful, because **to this day the best tea of Sri Lan-ka is grown here**; it is known as Broken Orange Pekoe, a highland tea.

⏵ VISITING NUWARA ELIYA

GETTING THERE

By car:
from Colombo via Kotte, Kaduwela, Hanwella, Avissawella, Hatton (180 km/110mi); from Kandy via Gampola, Pussellawa and Ramboda (77 km/48mi); from Badulla on the A 5 (56 km/35mi)

By rail:
the nearest station is in Nanu Oya on the line between Colombo and Badulla (8 km/5mi away).

By bus:
good services connections from Colombo, Kandy and Badulla

WHERE TO STAY/ WHERE TO EAT

▶ **Mid-range**

① *The Grand Hotel*
Tel. 052 / 222 28 81-7
Fax 052 / 222 22 64-5
www.tangerinehotels.com
156 rooms, restaurant, coffee shop, 3 bars
Very British – all the way down to afternoon tea: for anyone wishing to travel in the footsteps of the British colonial rulers in Sri Lanka the Grand Hotel must be the first choice. The recent addition on the other hand is timeless and modern.

② *St. Andrews Hotel*
10, St. Andrews Drive
Tel. 052 / 222 30 31
Fax 052 / 222 31 53
www.jetwinghotels.com
52 rooms, restaurant, bar
Tudor-style manor house with a British atmosphere. Tea can be enjoyed in the afternoons while sitting out in the splendid garden at cast-iron tables or in the evenings by the open fire. You sleep under heavy canopies. The 18-hole golf course is a stone's throw away.

Baedeker recommendation

③ *The Tea Factory*
Kandapola
Tel. 052 / 222 96 00
Fax 052 / 222 96 06
www.aitkenspenceholidays.com
57 rooms, restaurant, bar
This lovely hotel was set up in a tea factory built in around 1930. It is worth a visit for its fantastic view of Sri Lanka's mountains alone. During the refurbishments large parts of the tea factory's interior were kept and the hotel still has a tea plantation.

▶ **Budget**

④ *Windsor Hotel*
P.O. Box 01
Tel. 052 / 222 25 54
Fax 052 / 222 28 89
Email: windsor@lanka.ccom.lk
50 rooms, restaurant, bar
Hotel built in the colonial style with cosy rooms and a lot of atmosphere

British influence: St. Andrews Hotel

What to see in Nuwara Eliya

Some of the buildings enlivening the parks and gardens are of the purest and most beautiful British colonial style. The post office with a pretty clock tower, the Anglican Holy Trinity Church and the war memorial are all of note. Victoria Park with its large lawn and tall trees, the Nanu Oya river and the idyllically situated ponds are all lovely places to go for walks.

Townscape

What is now the Grand Hotel, a spacious timber-framed country house, was built by governor Barnes to be his home. The building has lost some of its former glory, which also attracted celebrities. Nevertheless it is one of the top addresses in Nuwara Eliya. Heavy red curtains in the communal areas, massive leather suites and magnificent chandeliers hanging from the ceilings are still an expression of the supposedly English way of life.

✱ **Grand Hotel**

The Hill Club, a further symbol of the English way of life, was founded in 1876 by a British plantation owner called Waring, who employed 15,000 workers on his 20ha/50 acre plantation. The seventh generation of Warings handed the plantations and the Hill Club over to a successor in 1972. Although he is from Sri Lanka he made sure that the British atmosphere has stayed alive until today. The attractive stone building with timber framing was built in the Tudor style and is, strictly speaking, only open to members. However, visitors are welcome and there are said to be members who also rent out their rooms to guests during their absence. Just enquire at the reception.

✱ **Hill Club**

Around Nuwara Eliya

Nuwara Eliya is an **excellent base for trips** to Sri Lanka's unique mountain landscape. The work on the tea plantations can be observed just a few kilometres out of town and many of the tea factories are open to visitors.

✱✱ **Mountains and Tea Plantations**

Take the A 5 to Hakgala Botanical Garden, situated around 10 km southeast of Nuwara Eliya. It is one of three botanical gardens in Sri Lanka. The grounds go back to a coffee plantation; it was subsequently used to grow cinchona trees to obtain quinine against malaria and tea was also grown here. In 1861 William Nock created a model garden in which he experimented with plants from temperate climates. This allowed a **wonderful park landscape with lotus ponds, old trees and an orchid house** to develop over the years. From the summer house at an altitude of 1646 m/5400ft there is a magnificent view over the mountains to the peaks of Namunkula (open: daily 8am – 6pm; admission charge). Right beside the botanical garden is Hakgala Nature Reserve, which is still home to a few specimens of the rare big Purple-faced Leaf Monkey.

✱ **Hakgala Sanctuary Botanical Gardens**

Drive from Nuwara Eliya to Kandy

A drive from Nuwara Eliya to ►Kandy is one of the most scenic experiences in Sri Lanka. The road leaves the town and climbs steeply to Ramboda Pass at 1996 m/6549ft, passing the falls of the same name, which plummet from 100 m/330ft.

✶✶ Polonnaruwa

C/D 6

Province: North Central   **Altitude:** approx. 110 m/360ft

Polonnaruwa, for a long time protected by dense jungle, was the second capital of the Singhalese kingdom. One of the most important rulers, Parakrama Bahu I (1153 – 1186) shaped its appearance with magnificent buildings, bringing about a significant style of Singhalese art.

Polonnaruwa town centre is located on the eastern shores of Lake Parakrama Samudra

AD 993	The administration is moved from Anuradhapura to Polonnaruwa.
1055	Polonnaruwa is made the capital.
1153–1186	Under the reign of King Parakrama Bahu I the town experienced a golden age.
1196–1215	Constant decline owing to quarrels over the succession; destruction of Polonnaruwa
19th century	The city is rediscovered by archaeologists and in 1935 opened up to visitors.

History

It is not entirely clear when the site of present-day Polonnaruwa was first settled, but there are indications that people were first here in the 4th century AD, but maybe earlier. The further history of Polonnaruwa is inseparable from that of ► Anuradhapura. When the Cholas attacked and sacked the city in 993, and lodged themselves deep inside Singhalese territory, they designated it as their capital. Until 1073 they ruled Sri Lanka from here, the island having become no more than a province of their powerful south Indian kingdom. It was only King Vijaya Bahu I, a prince of the Ruhuna kingdom which had established itself in the south of the island, who managed to reconquer Anuradhapura and drive the Chola from Sri Lanka. But he too retained Polonnaruwa as his capital. Various kings reigned here until 1235, one of the most important being Parakrama Bahu I, who ascended the throne in 1153 and is still regarded as the unifier of the kingdom. He was followed by King Nissanka Malla, before the Kalinga prince Magha attacked with a strong Malay army and subdued the Singhalese kingdom. A number of sub-kingdoms formed in revolt against these foreign rulers.

While King Parakrama Bahu II succeed once more in regaining and reuniting much of the kingdom, his residence was in ► Dambadeniya to the south. It was the first capital in a series of others, in a period today referred to as the Period of Short-lived Kingdoms. Polonnaruwa stepped into the limelight once again when King Parakrama Bahu III took over the government, but his successor moved their capital to the south; the city fell into oblivion and was overgrown by the jungle. It was only in 1890 that public attention was aroused by reports of British colonial officials concerning the remains of a magnificent city in the jungle. A few years later excavations started, and in 1935 visitors were allowed on the site for the first time. For some years now UNESCO has contributed financially to the archaeological work, which is far from complete. Even so, the ruined city has been declared a World Heritage Site.

What to see in Polonnaruwa

Most of the sights in Polonnaruwa can be accessed by good paths, **Roads** and there are even some roads that can be driven along. The ruins

▶ VISITING POLONNARUWA

GETTING THERE

By car:
from Dambulla via the A 6 to Habar-ana, then via the A 11 (68 km/45 mi); from Anuradhapura via the A 13 to Marandankawala, then via the A 11 (101 km/65 mi)
By rail:
good services from Dambulla and Habarana
By bus:
Several good services a day from the abovementioned towns.

WHERE TO EAT

▶ **Moderate**
① *ACME Transit Hotel*
90, Polonnaruwa Road
Tel. 066 / 700 16
6am – 11pm
On the drive between Anuradhapura and Polonnaruwa a good place to take a break is this small restaurant. Excellent Sri Lankan cuisine, pretty garden. Eight basic rooms (with air-conditioning) are also rented out.

WHERE TO STAY

▶ **Mid-range**
① *The Village*
Habarana
Tel. 066 / 227 00 47
Fax 066 / 227 00 46
www.johnkeellshotels.com
106 cottages, restaurant, bar, pool, excursions
Ideally situated hotel halfway between Anuradhapura and Polonnaruwa with very comfortable rooms in the cottage style.

are not so extensive as those of Anuradhapura, but it is still worth exploring them with a vehicle. Because of the continuing excavations, though, temporary road closures are always a possibility, and new finds may not yet be accessible.

Outside of the town walls

Parakrama Samudra (lake) The fortified centre of town is situated on the eastern shore of the 18 sq km/7 sq mi artificial lake Parakrama Samudra. It is named after King Parakrama Bahu I, who had it made in order to heighten the yield of the paddy fields of the surrounding area by irrigating them with the lake's water. After Polonnaruwa's decline the lake also silted up. It was only enlarged this century and is now fulfilling its original function again. There were once two summerhouses, or secondary palaces, on Parakrama Samudra, which could only be reached by

Polonnaruwa *Map*

boat when the lake was filled with water. Now a walkway leads to the one closer to the main palace. However, only a few broken pillars still remain.

At the western end of the dam that borders the reservoir is a statue carved from the rock that may be a depiction of **King Parakrama Bahu I** but possibly someone else. The sculpture's satisfied facial expression is if anything evidence of the former assumption because the king truly could be satisfied with the economic success his reservoir effected. To protect the statue from the weather it has unfortunately been covered in an unattractive sheet metal roof.

In the south, outside of the former town walls, is **Potgul Vihara**, a monastery in which the holy scriptures were kept. It presumably dates back to the time before Parakrama Bahu; surviving ruins include a mandapa (prayer pavilion) and a round building with a circumference of 48 m/52yd on a rectangular base. According to an inscription it was built upon the request of Chandravati, the second wife of Parakrama Bahu I. It is likely that dagobas once stood at the four corners. In front of the round building in the east is a small hall and this is also where the only recognizable entrance is. In front of the 4.5 m15ft bricks walls are façades that still have faint traces of artistic paintings. Next to the two long sides of the platform as well as on the east side there are still remains of two similar structures, which are all reminiscent of the temple architecture of Cambodia.

Where to eat
① ACME Transit Hotel
Where to stay
① The Village

Highlights Polonnaruwa

Palace of King Parakrama Bahu I
Magnificent colossal building that once boasted 1000 sumptuously furnished rooms
► page 321

Gal Pota (Stone Book)
The heroic deeds of a king written in stone
► page 324

Rankot Vihara Dagoba
The largest dagoba in Polonnaruwa
► page 327

Rock Temple Gal Vihara
The four monumental statues in the former monastic complex are masterpieces of Sri Lankan sculpture.
► page 328

Just a few metres away the remains of the old town wall can be made out. At one point it was 5m/16ft thick and equally high. Not far from here is the former **palace of King Nissanka Malla**, probably a very modest two-storey building with thick brick walls. According to the historical facts the king had this palace built in a great hurry in just seven months since it could not be expected of him to have to live in the residence of a predecessor. At the same time as the palace Nissanka Malla had a council hall built, an elongated, rectangular pillared hall that is accessed by a few steps in the northeast. Some of the pillars have now fallen over but they used to support a wooden roof. The pillars, square at the bottom and octagonal in the middle with simple, square capitals, are monolithic. At the bases of many pillars the names of ministers as well as other dignitaries have been recorded. According to an inscription a 1.8 m/6ft stone lion, the kingdom's symbol, once bore the king's throne. The sculpture's design shows abstracting tendencies, but the animal seems as dignified as it does fearsome.

Inner town centre

Urban fortifications　The town's fortifications probably date back to the year 1037, but were significantly developed later on under Parakrama Bahu I. The wall complex consisted of three rings and had 14 entrance gates. The place grounds encompassed an area of around 10ha/25 acres and was surrounded by a high wall as well as, in some places, by moats. The main entrance is in the north.

★ ★
Palace of King Parakrama Bahu I　The palace grounds and the main courtyard in the east are surrounded by a gallery. The palace of King Parakrama Bahu I itself, a massive brick structure, had a square floor plan of 46 m/50yd by 46m/50yd. It contained a spacious atrium (31 m/34yd x 13 m/14yd) whose ceiling was once supported by wooden columns whose stone

pedestals still survive. Adjoining the atrium were two further halls with remarkably thick walls. A gallery surrounding the building was divided into 40 rooms that were inter-connected and open to the outside. In the south a staircase leads up to the upper floors; according to the chronicle Culavamsa, there are supposed to have been seven of them. The beginnings of two storeys can still be made out on the high, magnificent ruins. The Culavamsa says the palace possessed more than 1000 magnificently furnished rooms.

Somewhat further to the east is the council hall, a building with nicely designed features and a square floor plan. It too was built by Parakrama Bahu. However, it underwent several subsequent changes and may also have been expanded. The hall has been built on a substructure with three steps, which is supported by a terrace. Between finely sculpted cornices three relief friezes surround the structure. On the lower base, separated from each other by the pilasters, are some very lifelike elephants (hence also the name Elephant Hall) as well as lions with a threateningly raised paw and wide open mouth

✳ **Council hall**

Sculptures of animated elephants and lions adorn the council hall

on the central frieze. The top frieze depicts Ganas, the fat dwarfs who are bringers of good fortune. They are dancing, singing and running and all of them have different facial expressions.

In the north a grand stone staircase leads up to the hall in two sections. The entrance is made of a beautiful moonstone. The four balustrades have been fashioned from bold makara arches. At the top two magnificent lion sculptures flank the entrance to the hall. The hall's stone pillars, of which there are four rows of twelve each, most of which are still standing, are richly decorated with sculptures. This is where the king held his council with his ministers and religious dignitaries.

Within the citadel are the remains of various ancillary buildings (picture galleries, theatre, baths etc.).

Kumara okana (Royal Bath)

from the southeast corner of the king's palace two steps lead up to the royal bath (Kumara okana) outside of the citadel. It was commissioned by Parakrama Bahu I and had a square outline with rectangular projections. In addition to basin made of finely chiselled stones the exemplary manner in which the water was brought in and treated is remarkable. It was brought to the bath by underground pipes from Parakrama Samudra, but before it flowed into the pool through the two makaras protruding from the wall it was filtered (the device for this was discovered by coincidence). To the south of the bath are the remains of a pavilion, including a stairway with a moon tone and a makara balustrade as well as lion gateways.

Baedeker TIP

A Rest for the Feet

Those who like cycling and do not mind bumpy roads have the option of exploring the extensive grounds by bicycle. Some hotels on the lake hire out bikes for around 200 rupees a day.

Within the Quadrangle

The Quadrangle, thus named by the British, is actually called Dalada Maluwa and is a closed-off compound. There are several buildings on a terrace, of which some temporarily housed the sacred tooth.

Thuparama (Statue House)

The building known as Thuparama is probably the oldest building in Polonnaruwa. It was likely built at the end of the 11th century, meaning either during the time of the Chola period or definitely no later than during the early days of King Vijaya Bahu's reign. It survives almost complete. However, not much is known about its history or significance. It was possibly built to function as a Buddhist Patimaghara (statue house). It is a massive rectangular brick vault, above which a square tower base with flat crests rises up. The façade is structured by both horizontal features (cornices and ornamental friezes) and verticalm richly sculpted pilasters. Only fragments re-

Polonnaruwa Quadrangle *Map*

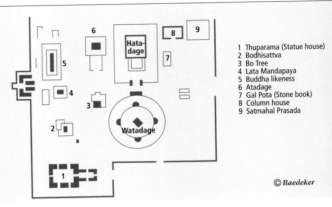

1 Thuparama (Statue house)
2 Bodhisattva
3 Bo Tree
4 Lata Mandapaya
5 Buddha likeness
6 Atadage
7 Gal Pota (Stone book)
8 Column house
9 Satmahal Prasada

© Baedeker

main of the once monumental Buddha statue in its interior. Several other statues of Buddha have been partially restored. A 3 m/10ft brick statue is particularly impressive. It was once covered in stucco. Although it is not known when it was made the way in which it was shaped and its lines suggest it was made at around the same time as the Gal Vihara group.

The vatadage, a round temple with stupa, most likely dates back to the pre-Polonnaruwa period but was extended by King Parakrama Bahu I and later beautified and restored by Nissanka Malla. It is one of the most elegant and well designed buildings of its kind in Sri Lanka. The round temple stands on an equally round terrace 36 m/39 yd in diameter and a wide ambulatory. The centre is formed by a small dagoba surrounded by two rows of columns (that once supported a high ceiling), a high brick wall and a further row of columns as well as a stone balustrade. The pedestal is surrounded by two friezes with finely sculpted lions and dwarfs. At the four cardinal points stairways with moonstones at their bases and makara balustrades lead up to the Buddha statues in the samadhi posture (one statue is severely damaged) at the entrances. They show the typical characteristics of the Polonnaruwa period: the smooth gown with no folds, the hair that sits like a cap, and the strip of garment over the left shoulder. The facial expression comes across as regal and introspective. The surrounding walkway is ornamented with stone slabs oriented towards the centre of the circle. The rectangular atrium in the north, whose pillars may once have supported a wooden roof, was probably only added by King Nissanka Malla.

★
Vatadage
(Round Temple)

A highly unusual building that stands out from Sri Lanka's other religious structures is Satmahal Prasada, which means »**seven-storey**

Satmahal
Prasada

The watadage of Polonnaruwa was once one of the most elegant buildings in the sacred complex

building«. It is a pyramidal brick building that had at one point been rendered. In its appearance it is closely related to similar structures in Thailand and Burma (such as to the Wat Kukut in Lamphun/Thailand). Although the suggestion that it was a donation by Siamese or Burmese monks who were guests at the monastery of Polonnaruwa cannot be proved, this suggestion nonetheless seems the most probable. The niches of the individual »storeys« were once filled with statues of Buddha, of which some are still partially extant. On one side a small staircase leads up to a chamber which may have housed a relic in the past.

Gal Pota (Stone Book) Not very far away is Gol Pota, the »stone book«. It is an 8 m/27 ft long, 1.25 m/4 ft wide and 60 cm/24 in high monolith, which, according to a section of the extensive inscription, was brought here from Mihintale or Sigiriya. In 72 lines divided into three fields, King Nissanka Malla describes his achievements for the kingdom and for Buddhism as well as his building activities. On the stone's front end is a remarkable relief sculpture depicting Lakshmi the goddess of good fortune between two elephants who form a vase of abundance with their trunks. The group is framed by wild geese.

Gatekeeper's hut On the Quadrangle's east and west sides there are stone structures that may have served as gatekeeper's huts.

Nissanka Malla had the Hatadage (also known as Daladage) built for
the sacred tooth relic. It was surrounded by a high brick wall. Hatadage means **»house of the 60 relics«**, but also »the house built in 60
days«. Daladage means »house of the tooth relic«. The wall forms a
rectangle measuring approx. 36 m/39 yd by 27.5 m/30 yd; the entrance is on the south side. The atrium in the north bears inscriptions in which the king once again boasts about his deeds and
achievements. A staircase leads up to the upper, wooden storey, in
which the tooth relic was once housed. In front of the entrance is a
moonstone, whose shape resembles a semi-oval, but whose visual depictions seem somewhat mannered. In the interior of the cella, between stone pillars, there are three statues of a standing Buddha on
lotus pedestals.

✷ **Hatadage**

Atadage means **»house of the eight relics«**. This building was constructed during the reign of King Vijaya Bahu I in the second half
of the 11th century and later served as a model for the abovementioned Hatadage built by King Nassanka Malla. It too consisted
of several storeys, or certainly at least two. Here too the second
storey was reserved for the tooth relic. Many stone images richly
ornamented with reliefs still survive; some of the motifs include
the vase of abundance, from which a liana is growing, forming
medallions that contain figurative scenes. Also of note are the door
frames adorned with reliefs and the very nice statue of a standing
Buddha.

✷ **Atadage**

Not far away is Nissanka Malla Mandapa, a place of worship for the
sacred tooth relic surrounded by a simple stone wall. The eight stone
pillars modelled on budding lotus stems are both unique and highly
graceful. They appear to simply grow out of the terrace; the capitals
form a lotus bud. At their centre is a miniature dagoba with an frieze
of worshippers on the pedestal. The shrine was built under Nissanka
Malla and is evidence of a pleasure in ornamentation that enjoyed a
heyday during his reign.

Mandapa (place of worship)

Outside of the Quadrangle

Leave the Quadrangle in the north and turn eastwards. This is the location of the Pabulu Vihara (coral shrine), a kind of stepped dagoba
donated by a wife of Parakrama Bahu I. It has been kept very simple,
though unfortunately it is dilapidated, and stands on a terrace. The
complex was surrounded by a stone wall (prakara). Steps lead up to
the first and second circular terrace. A carved rock was probably
used as a flower altar.

Around the dagoba there are six small stone huts that house statues
of Buddha and bodhisattvas; some of them appear to have come
from Anuradhapura. In one of the statue huts the brick core of the
sculpture of a recumbent Buddha can still be made out.

Shiva Devale (Hindu temple)

The Shiva Devale is the only monument that can be placed with certainty in the time of Chola rule in Polonnaruwa. It is really very modest, built entirely of stone and still in quite a good state. The proportions are elegant and harmonious, the structure austere. At the entrance there are two sculptures of the bull Nandi, Shiva's vehicle, which are remarkable. In its interior is a lingam, the symbol of Shiva, the god of fertility. An inscription reveals the temple's old name (Vanavan Madevi Isvarmudaiyar).

Vishnu Devale (Hindu temple)

Not far from the fortified town's north gate are the ruins of Vishnu Devale, which dates back to the 13th century. Only the substructure made from carved stones is still extant, the structure above that was presumably made of bricks is severely weathered. It houses a statue of Vishnu in a bad state of repair.

Ganadevi Kovil (Hindu temple)

Opposite are the ruins of the Ganadevi Kovil that once housed a lingam.

Manik Vihara

Outside of the town's fortifications near the north gate is the Manik Vihara, a brick dagoba with a high rectangular terrace made of bricks. The platform is surrounded by a remarkably well preserved lion frieze. The animals are depicted from the front on terracotta slabs in such an **exaggeratedly terrifying** manner that they almost seem like caricatures. One of two nice stone stairs flanked by guard stones leads up to the terrace; a door fame put together from carved stones is also still extant.

Shiva Devale (Hindu temple)

Along the northbound road on the left-hand side is a further Shiva Divale. Its ruins were restored in the 1980s by the Archaeological Department. The temple consists of an atrium and a cella as well as a two-part side room in the same order. The main cella contains a round yoni and the lower part of a lingam, while the cella of the adjoining building contains a brick pedestal for a statue that is no longer present. The door posts at the entrance to the cella reveal that the door was not even full height. A round stone on which the door must have turned has been reinstated.

Rankot Vihara (Ruvanveli Dagoba)

The Rankot Vihara (also known as Ruvanveli Dagoba) has a height of 55 m/180 ft and a diameter of 56 m/185 ft, making it the largest complete dagoba in Polonnaruwa. The massive structure is surrounded by several statue houses and was only restored a few years ago. The many inscriptions reveal the dagoba was built by King Nissanka Malla. It is remarkable that limestone mortar was applied in layers at intervals of of approx. 3 m/10 ft; this was probably done to balance out irregularities in the structure. On the lotus frieze on the lower terrace there are traces of earlier painting. At the entrance to the temple complex is a stone seat whose inscription states that Nissanka Malla oversaw the building works from here.

The Gopalabatta, a flat rock to the east of the road, has four caves on its eastern side that were, according to a Brahmi inscription, already inhabited by reclusive monks in the 5th century. During the Polonnaruwa period they were probably part of a monastery. In one of the caves the remains of a Buddha statue were found; it was possibly once an image gallery.

Gopalabatta rock

The complex known as Alahana Parivena (cremation monastery) has an assembly hall for monks (Baddhasima Prasada), a statue house (Lankatilaka) and the Kiri Vihara (milk dagoba) as well as a cremation site for the deceased members of the royal family and the monks. It is likely that he mounds dotted around the area all contain small dagobas with the ashes of members of the royal family. Excavations have also uncovered the foundations walls of the monks' quarters. At the upper end of the complex are two caves containing magnificent Buddha statues.

Alahana Parivena

The ruins of the Lankatilaka is quite remarkable. It was once used as a statue house. It contains the torso of a Buddha statue that must have once been around 13 m/43 ft tall; it is quite striking. The richly structured façade is also interesting, giving beholders the feeling it is part of a multi-storey building, but this is an illusion because the interior is actually relatively small, not least because of the incredible thickness of the walls. Opposite the entrance to the Lankatilaka are the stone pillars of a mandapa, decorated with lotus blossoms, in which drummers and other musicians come together for the ceremonies.

Lankatilaka (statue house)

The Kiri Vihara, also called the milk dagoba after the gleaming white plaster made of crushed shells, was presumably donated by Suhadda, one of Parakrama Bahu I's wives. The simple 24 m/80 ft structure in classical form is adorned with mouldings on the base and thus seems light and elegant. By the way, the dagoba has never been renovated: when it was freed from the invading jungle the bluish-white plaster was almost completely intact.

✽ Kiri Vihara

✽ ✽ Rock temple Gal Vihara

Following the road further northwards, visitors will find the most significant attraction of Polonnaruwa, the rock temple Gal Vihara. Its actual name is Uttarama, but the term »Black Rock« is also customary. In the chronicle Culavamsa it is written that this temple was commissioned by King Parakrama Bahu I.
The four monumental Buddha statues carved from the rock that are now outside were most likely once housed in three imposing statue houses of which only fragments of the walls remain. The sculptures are amongst the **masterpieces** of Singhalese stonemasonry.
The largest statue is the recumbent Buddha, measuring 14.1 m/46 ft. The staggered feet indicate that this is a statue of the enlightened one

»Black Rock«

who has entered Nirvana. The facial expression is clearly detached, the body is relaxed and yet the head and body have maintained their archaically charismatic force. Using the most basic means the sculptor achieved the **highest degree of effect**; by using curving lines (such as on the waist and hips) or by making the creases in the gown wavy he softened the statue's austerity.

The meaning of the 6.93 m/23 ft statue next to its head still has not been determined with certainty. It is possible the statue is of Ananda, Buddha's favourite disciple, because he was present when the enlightened one entered Nirvana. However, Ananda is usually depicted standing at Buddha's feet, and so it could be that it is Mahinda, the monk who brought Buddhism to Sri Lanka (but he was not present at Buddha's death). The posture with folded arms and the hands ly-

The Gal Vihara in Polonnaruwa is famous for its uniquely beautiful Buddha statues

ing on the upper arms is quite unusual and completely outside the usual iconographic framework. Many art historians consider this statue as the **artistically most valuable** of the four.
A grotto carved out of the rock contains a 1.5 m/5 ft statue of a sitting Buddha whose high throne is adorned with lion reliefs, pilasters and flower ornaments. The statue, enclosed at the back by a makara arch, gets its quality from its simplicity. The fourth statue, a statue of Buddha meditating, is around 5 m/16 ft in height and is leaning against a rock wall richly adorned with makara arches. The artist placed a kind of halo around Buddha's head and the throne is decorated with a lion frieze.

King Parakrama Bahu I had the Demala Maha Seya Dagoba, the Great Tamil Dagoba, built, presumably by Tamils who had been captured and brought to Sri Lanka during his military campaigns in southern India. It may have been designed to be the formidable dagoba of Polonnaruwa, a suggestion supported by the magnificent base measuring 165 m/180 yd in diameter. It is uncertain what it may have looked like because everything that can be seen today dates back to more recent times, although older parts were incorporated.

✷ **Demala Maha Seya Dagoba**

Somewhat further north on the left-hand side of the road is the lotus bath, made of finely carved stone in the shape of a lotus blossom. The application of the symbolic shape of the lotus to baths is **typical of the pleasure in ornamentation** peculiar to the Polonnaruwa period. It is thought that there must have once been seven other baths like it in the surrounding area. The complex once belonged to the Jetavana monastery founded under Parakrama Bahu I.

Lotus bath

The Tivanka Pilimage, the statue house of the Jetavane monastery, is the northernmost building of the historical Polonnaruwa. It got its name from a likeness known as a tivanka, the image of a standing Buddha, for which it was built by Parakrama Bahu I. The brick building with its powerful walls is still somewhat larger than Lankatilaka and the façades are more richly adorned with stucco reliefs. There was once a passageway in the wall of the front hall that leads up to the upper storeys. The entire building shows very strong southern Indian influences.

✷ **Tivanka Pilimag (statue house)**

However, the statue house is famous for its **remains of wall paintings**, which unfortunately only survive in fragments, but probably once covered all the walls. They presumably date back to the late 12th / early 13th century, and, using the format of continuous narrative, they depict scenes from the life of Buddha and scenes from the

! Baedeker TIP

Elephant Safari

There are now several organizers (such as Samagi Villa Safari) offering jungle trips to the area around Polonnaruwa where you can go and watch elephant herds. Such a safari takes around six hours and is tiring but very exciting.

Jataka (Buddha's past lives). In most images the graphic aspect is foremost but some also try to bring across mood and atmosphere.
The 8 m/26 ft statue of a standing Buddha in the interior is impressive. It is, however, missing its head, which weathered and fell off over the years.

Around Polonnaruwa

Nayipena Vihara

One could be forgiven for thinking Nayipena Vihara was a Buddhist temple but it was not. It was only called Vihara after an exceptionally beautiful stucco relief of a many-hooded, many-headed cobra under the rubble of a collapsed roof. It is thought more likely to have been a Vishnu Devale, i.e. a Hindu temple. The sanctum still contains the pedestal but the corresponding statue has not yet been found.

Shiva Devale (Hindu temple)

The Shiva Devale is larger than the Nayipena Vihara described above but it has a similar layout. It had six consecutive rooms requiring worshippers to make their way through four rooms first. It is only in the fifth room that they were able to show reverence to the likenesses or symbols of the deities that stood in the sixth room. Now it is home to a nicely made, restored lingam.

★
Rock monastery of Dimbulagala

Around 15 km/9mi southeast of Polonnaruwa is the 334 m/1096 ft mountain Gunner's Coin, which, as the **natural rock fort** Dhumarakkha Pabbata, played a role in the very early history of the Anuradhapura kings. Climbing up to the rock monastery of Dimbulagala is not without its dangers and it is definitely hard work. However, this effort is rewarded by some very nice paintings from the 6th century that Queen Sundari, the daughter-in-law of King Parakrama Bahu I, commissioned for the decoration of the caves.

Pottuvil

E 8

Province: Uva   **Altitude:** 7 m/23ft

The small town of Pottuvil, which is only really known to insiders, gets less praise for its attractions than it does for its proximity to the excellent beaches along the east coast and particularly for its outstanding surfing opportunities. Arugam Bay is the epitome of heaven for surfers.

What to see in the area

tsunami damage

At exactly 9.04am the tsunami hit the island of Sri Lanka, destroying almost all of the towns and villages along the east coast. The damage is still visible in some places and many of the roads are still in a pro-

⏵ VISITING POTTUVIL

GETTING THERE

By car:
from Colombo on the A 2 to Pan-adura, continue on the A 8 to Ratna-pura and from there on the A 4 to Pottuvil (approx. 322 km/206 mi)
By rail:
from Colombo go all the way to the terminus Matara, then take a bus to Wellawaya. The bus from Wellawaya to Pottuvil unfortunately only runs twice a day.

WHERE TO STAY

▶ Budget
Stardust Beach Hotel
Arugam Bay
Tel. / Fax 063 / 224 81 91
www.arugambay.com
Very nice guesthouse under Danish management and a popular place to stay with surfers from around the world. The rooms are either spacious doubles in a new building or cabanas right on the beach.

visional state. Nevertheless many businesses working in tourism have opened again even though most of the hotels are operating on a reduced room number.

In the face of all the adversity several **international surfing championships** have since taken place here again, because Arugam Bay is still one of the world's top ten surfing destinations.

Arugam Bay

Quite a few small hotels and restaurants have sprung up along the beaches. Often natural materials were used in their construction. The »Tri Star Beach Hotel«, which used to have the best rooms and the only pool on the bay, has been reopened in its old form and has been extended by a new wing right by the beach. In addition the opening of several new comfortable bungalow complexes such as »Bombardi Resort« and »Royal Garden Beach Hotel«, the likes of which are still unusual in this region, is imminent.

Puttalam

A 5

Province: North Western
Population: 41,000

Altitude: 3 m/10 ft

Puttalam is situated in Sri Lanka's northwest on a wide lagoon that stretches north for around 60 km/37 mi and finds its way to the open sea through Dutch Bay, which is dotted with several large islands.

Many of the town's inhabitants are Christians: the Catholic church St Anne on the headland that protects the lagoon is an important pil-

Christian pilgrimage destination

grimage destination for all Christians in Sri Lanka. The main economic activities here are fishing and obtaining salt from the seawater. In earlier days Arabian seafarers and merchants used this place as a base for their activities. Pearl fishing is also of significance. The location, at the edge of the region affected by the civil war, prevented any further economic developments in recent years.

What to see in Puttalam

Shaped by fishing Puttalam is a typical fishing town and one of the island's most important. It is interesting to watch the bustling fishermen at the harbour, in the market hall (where the catch is auctioned off) and in the streets lined by stalls selling dried fish.

Salt fields The salt fields reach as far as Palavi, 6 km/4 mi south of Puttalam. More than a fifth of Sri Lanka's salt requirements are obtained here from sea water that is evaporated by the sun, leaving the salt behind.

ovely headland The approx. 60 km/37 mi headland opposite Puttalam that separates the lagoon from the sea is particularly attractive. It is covered in sand dunes and coconut palms.

Around Puttalam

✱
Talawila Near Talawila, approx. 24 km/15 mi northwest of Puttalam on the abovementioned headland, is the large St Anne's Church, the destination of many pilgrims every year on 26 July. The church itself does not have any particular features of interest.

Kalpitiya The town of Kalpitiya further north on the lagoon is inhabited by Moors, the descendants of the Arabian seafarers. In medieval times it was an important port. The Portuguese built a fort at this strategically favourable location, which was later expanded by the Dutch. It is in a good state of repair, as is a church dating from the Dutch period.

Wilpattu National Park Around 33 km/20 mi north of Puttalam is one of the entrances to Wilpattu National Park that is one of Sri Lanka's biggest with an area of around 1300 sq km/500 sq mi. According to reports the national park that once stood out for its great diversity in its animal life has been **badly battered** by the military activities of LTTE and the Singhalese military. It was only in 2005 that the national park was opened to visitors again. The numbers are still remarkable. It is home to Sri Lanka's largest leopard population as well as to many other animals (elephants, bears, monkeys etc.). However, during the civil war many animals looked for new territories. The villus, large water pans filled by rain water that dry out completely during dry spells, are typical of the landscape here.

▶ VISITING PUTTALAM

GETTING THERE

By car:
from Colombo on the A 3 (134 km/83mi); from Anuradhapura on the A 12 (79 km/49 mi); from Kurunegala on the A 10 (88 km/55 mi)

By rail:
Puttalam is currently the terminus on the line between Colombo and Jaffna

By bus:
good services from all the above-mentioned towns

TOURS

Sunway Holidays
Main office: Sunway House

25, Kimbulapitiya Road, Negombo
Tel. 031 / 223 82 82 or 531 25 55
Fax 031 / 223 81 82
www.sunwayholidays.lk
The organizer offers well-guided tours to Wilpattu National Park with an overnight stay in basic accommodation.

WHERE TO STAY

There are several basic places to stay in Wilpattu National Park that can be booked through various tour operators. More comfortable accommodation is available in ►Anuradhapura.

✴ Ratnapura

B 8

Province: Sabaragamuwa
Population: 47 000

Altitude: 27 m/89 ft

Ratnapura, the »city of gems«, is surrounded by mountains and is itself situated on hills in the wet, hot and humid valley of Kalu Ganga. It is also the capital of Sabaragamuwa Province. The name of the province is keeping the town's legendary name alive (Sabaragama = village of the barbarians).

Even the Greeks, Arabs and Chinese valued Ratnapura's wealth in gemstones more than 2000 years ago. These days the town and the surrounding area are inhabited by many Thais working in the jewellery trade. It is not known when the town at the base of the highlands was founded; it already existed during the time of King Parakrama Bahu I (1153 – 1186), who promoted the search for gemstones here. During the Kandy period collecting gemstones was reserved for the kings. Now the state controls this enterprise.

Gemstone Mec

What to see in Ratnapura

There are still some remains of the British Fort. From here and from other locations in the town the view of Sri Lanka's sacred mountain, ►Adam's Peak, which is only around 30 km/20mi, is very good.

Fort

CITY OF GEMS

All around Ratnapura there are many holes in the fields. At first glance they are difficult to spot, not least because most of them are covered in a roof of rice straw. And then there are the rivers of the surrounding area that flow down from the nearby mountains, carrying sand and stones with them. What will one day adorn elegant fingers is found under the ground and in the rivers: sapphires, rubies, aquamarines and topazes. However, there are no diamonds on Sri Lanka.

It is hard physical work to obtain what is so sought after all around the world, says Ahmed. Ahmed is a Moor, a descendant of the Arab merchants who arrived in Sri Lanka in the 8th century. Soon after their arrival they discovered gems at the foot of Adam's Peak. Ratnapura has been considered the city of gems ever since. Nowhere else on the island is the search for gems more fruitful than here. There are only two ways on Sri Lanka to get rich quick, or fairly quick: either by searching for gemstones or by trading in them. Ahmed has opted for the latter because it is by far the easier option – except in the case of discoveries that create a stir such as

the legendary »Blue Bell of Asia«, which weighed an impressive 400 carats and was not meant for just anyone. Just anyone would not have been able to afford it, and so it was bought by the British royal family.

Hard-won

The methods of obtaining gemstones have remained unchanged since olden days. First a special pick-axe and spade are used to dig a square hole that is then extended to a shaft of up to 15m/50ft. When the hole is deep enough a scantily clad worker, either hanging on a rope or on a small wooden platform, is lowered and then digs a horizontal gallery. Using small

The gem dealers can supply almost everything: rubies, sapphires, topaz, amethysts, aquamarines, tourmalines, cymophanes (cat's eyes) and garnets

Soon these stones will be processed into pieces of jewellery

spades the workers scrape together the clay earth by the light of candles or petroleum lamps. The candles do more than just provide light. They are also indicators of the air's oxygen content. Whatever the workers scratch off from the gallery walls deep below ground is tipped into a flat woven basket that is then transported back along the gallery and lifted out of the hole with ropes.

The payoff for all the hard work

The workers above are already waiting for the basket and its contents. They carry it to the side, and one worker picks up a hose while the other switches on the diesel generator. The water gushes into the basket under very high pressure, getting smaller and sometimes larger stones out of the earth. With an expert eye and routine movement one of the workers separates the worthless stones from the precious ones. Often all they find are small **moonstones** or **aquamarines**. Anything that looks as if it may be valuable is taken to Ratnapura. Here the buyers come into play. They assess the stones' quality and calculate a price, which is frequently arbitrary. There are no uniform prices, which is why many do not agree to the first price they hear.

Export and processing

Every year gemstones worth around 65 million US dollars are exported from Sri Lanka to countries around the world. This is the official figure. It is hard to say what leaves the island by less regulated routes. This does happen of course, even though prospecting is under state control.

A large proportion of the gems goes to countries that have expertise in **manufacturing jewellery**, such as Thailand, where gems from Sri Lanka are sought-after raw materials for tasteful items in line with Western tastes. However, the government in Colombo has spent years trying to establish jewellery making on the island itself. Young, talented people are sent overseas to learn the art of the correct cut and suitable mount. But they also acquire knowledge and techniques that are actually frowned upon: sapphires that only have a low purity grade are heated in a special process, giving them a bluish hue that does not exist in nature. Such stones are popular, even though they lose their blue tint again after a few years. Of course there are also some talented jewellers on the island who have set up shop on their own initiative. They often market their creative work directly to tourists and also make items to order.

► VISITING RATNAPURA

GETTING THERE

By car:
from Colombo on the A 4 via Avissawella (102 km/63 mi) or via Panadura on the A 1, then onwards on the A 8 (98 km/60 mi); from Hambantota on the A 2 to Nonagama, then on the A 18 (124 km/77 mi); from Wellawaya on the A 4 (120 km/75 mi)

By rail:
station on the line from Colombo to Opanayake

By bus:
good services from all the towns listed above

WHERE TO EAT

There are some restaurants serving Sri Lankan cuisine in the town centre around the clock tower.

► Moderate
Jade Restaurant
Senanayake Road
Inexpensive and authentic Chinese and Thai cuisine – this place is often frequented by gemstone wholesale buyers.

WHERE TO STAY

► Mid-range
Ratnaloka Tour Inn
Kosagala, Kahandama

Tel. 045 / 223 00 17
Fax 045 / 222 24 55
53 rooms, restaurant, pool
Hotel somewhat outside of town, well equipped. Most rooms have lovely views of tea plantations and the surrounding landscape.

► Budget
Rain Forest Lodge Deniyaya
Temple Road, Deniyaya
Tel. 07 77 / 06 81 28-9
Guesthouse with only three rooms but a fabulous location in the middle of some impressive scenery. The owner offers full board (without alcoholic beverages) and also organizes trips into the rainforest.

► Luxury / Mid-range
Rainforest Edge
Balawatukanda, Waddagala
Tel. 045 / 225 59 12
Fax 045 / 225 59 13
www.rainforestedge.com
This hotel, which blends nicely into its surroundings, is situated on a hill on the edge of Sinharaja Rain Forest. It has very nice rooms with lovely rainforest views. Adjoining ayurveda centre.

Maha Saman Devale
Outside of town, above Kalu Ganga, is the Maha Saman Devale temple, which is visited by Hindu and Buddhist pilgrims every year. The temple is consecrated to the god Saman, the protector of Sri Lanka. The temple district is surrounded by a wall. In the forecourt are the remains of a Portuguese church from the 16th century. The archway leading into the temple complex also has Portuguese elements. Every year in July/Aug an impressive Perahera takes place here, which lasts several days.

A gigantic tree in Siharaja rainforest

The area rich in gems, the Ratnapura Trench, encompasses an area of approx. 8000 ha/19,800 acres between the rivers Kalu Ganga and Amban Ganga. The gravel layer that formed during the post-glacial period was later covered by a layer of silt. Gemstone mines are particularly numerous near the eastbound road to Pelmadulla and the hard physical work can also be observed from close up. The search for gemstones (►Baedeker Special p. 332) takes place under the control of government inspectors, but every worker is given a bonus when a valuable find is made. They are also allowed to keep every gem they find in an area declared to have been exhausted. Trading with gemstones was mainly in the hands of the Moors, except during the colonial period. The Moors once again own many of the jewellery shops that are thick on the ground here.

✳ **Gemstone Mine of Ratnapura**

Ratnapura's National Museum was founded in 1946 and contains a small but good collection of gems and precious stones. Boards explain the history of gemstone mining and the museum also has a model of a gem mine as well as different finds from the town's history (Colombo Road, open: Sat – Thu 9am – 5pm).

✳ **National Museum of Ratnapura**
🕐

The drive from Pelmadulla in a southwesterly direction is very attractive. The road makes its way through the last surviving area of tropical rainforest that seems almost pristine. As part of the Sinharaja Rain Forest Reserve it is not just under protection, it is also a UNESCO World Heritage Site. Strictly speaking this approx. 130 sq km/50 sq mi area may only be accessed by scientists, but some hotels offer **guided tours** on the only trail that goes through the national park. The rainforest is home to many animal species as well as several endemic bird species.

✳ ✳ **Sinharaja Rain Forest Reserve (rain forest)**

★ ★ Sigiriya

Province: Central   **Altitude of the fort:** 363m/1190ft

The mighty rock of Sigiriya rises up 200 m/984 ft from a plain surrounded by forests and lakes. As if the sight of it alone were not fascinating enough the rock also has a (now derelict) fort on its summit plateau as well as the most famous wall paintings of Sri Lanka, the »cloud maidens of Sigiriya«, in a gallery beside the fort. The entire complex is now protected as a UNESCO World Heritage Site.

Lion's Mouth The name Sigiriya developed in the 5th century during the reign of King Kaayapa: »giri« means mouth or also rock, »sinha« or »singha« means lion and refers to the front of a lion that has been carved from the rock and through whose mouth is the base of the stairs (in the past they were nothing but small steps carved into the rock) that leads up to the peak.

Stronghold The Culavamsa chronicle contains a legend concerning King Kassyapa I, who moved his seat of government here in the 5th century. It takes place around the rock of Sigiriya, but particularly around the fort on its summit plateau. He was the elder of two sons of King Datthu Sena (459 – 477); his mother was one of the king's concubines who came from a lower-class background, while Mogallana, the younger brother, was born to the king's marriage with his main wife and queen. Upon the instigation of Migara, the army general and Datthu Sena's son-in-law, Kassyapa, imprisoned his father in the year 477, seizing the throne, while Mogallana fled to India. Meanwhile Migara was skilled at convincing Kassyapa that his father possessed great treasures that were not intended for him but for his brother Mogallana. As a result Kassyapa had his father tortured so he would reveal the treasure's location. Duttha Sena finally led his extramarital son and Migara to Kala Reservoir, jumped in, bathed and said: »This, friends, is all the treasure I have!« Kassyapa was so angry about this that he decided to kill his father. He had him shackled naked and walled up alive.

Kassyapa I now began to fear the revenge of his brother who had fled to India and so he moved from Anuradhapura to the rock of Sigiriya after having a powerful stronghold built there. Mogallana indeed returned with a great army in 495. For reasons that remain inexplicable to this day, Kassyapa left his fort and faced the battle. However, when it was became obvious he was defeated he used a knife to take his own life. Mogallana became king in Anuradhapura. He handed over the rock fort of Sigiriya to his priests. It soon fell into oblivion however, and was only rediscovered in 1811 by the British major H.

Forbes. In 1894 restoration works got under way.
The rock of Sigiriya contains caves that were already inhabited very much earlier in around the 2nd century BC, probably by reclusive monks.

★
Royal Gardens

On the east and west sides of the base of the rock there are two rectangular spaces covering an area of approx. 40 ha / 100 acres, which are surrounded by a wall and a moat. The western section is fortified by two further walls with moats.
The main entrance is to the west and upon entering visitors will first get to the Royal Gardens, which are laid out in such a manner that the axis points straight at the rock. The landscape designer(s) incorporated the existing boulders into their plans. There are two ponds respectively on either side of the path, each surrounded by a rectangular brick wall. The water was brought here from the lake via underground pipes. Between mounds surrounded by oval moats on which the remnants of some buildings can be made out, the path leads to an octagonal pond surrounded by a brick wall. The rock in the pond has indentations above the water's surface; these indentations were probably used to place oil lamps in.

To get to the rock fort visitors walk through the extensive gardens

Sigiriya *Map*

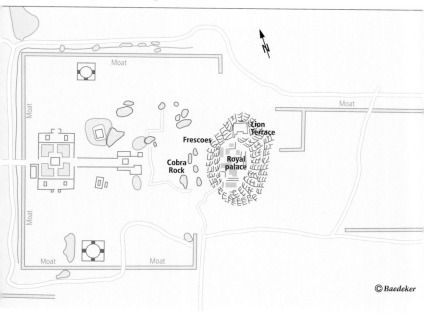

Moat

N

Moat

Lion Terrace

Frescoes

Cobra Rock

Royal palace

Moat

Moat

Moat

Moat

© *Baedeker*

★ ★
Rock Fort of
Sigiriya

A number of large rocks form a natural boundary between the Royal Gardens and the inner complex; they also form the first of several terraces at different heights on the main rock. Here too the remains of past construction can be made out in some places but their purpose is still being puzzled over today.

Rock caves

The rocks of the western terrace house a total of 23 caves. Seven of them bear Brahmi inscriptions from the 2nd century BC–2nd century AD in their interior. It emerges from them that they served religious purposes, presumably as homes for the monks, long before Kassyapa had his palace built here. Some other caves on the other hand contain paintings with depictions of women dating from Kassyapa's reign, which makes it likely that the king may have had a large number of monks from Anuradhapura brought here, who then lived in these caves.

On the first terrace the remains of a dagoba can still be made out. The Deranyagala cave on the terrace above also contains paintings. In the northwest of this cave the narrow paths led to a brick staircase that was only discovered in 1958 and allowed the rock to be ascended from the west. Further routes up the rock can be found in the north and south. However, the southern route could not be restored anymore and a portion of it was replaced by a new staircase.

► VISITING SIGIRIYA

GETTING THERE

By car:
from Dambulla on the A 6 to Inama-luwa, then turn right (19 km/12 mi); from Polonnaruwa
on the A 11 to Habarana, then turn left, turn left again after around 4 km/2.5 mi and left again after another 4 km/2.5 mi (55 km/34 mi); from Anuradhapura on the A 13 to Mar-adankadawala, then turn left and continue on the A 11 to
Habarana (carry on as described above, 67 km/42 mi)
By rail:
the closest train station is in Habarana (19 km/12mi).

WHERE TO STAY

Baedeker recommendation

► **Mid-range**
Sigiriya Village
Reservations in Colombo:
Colombo Fort Hotels Ltd.
53 1/1, Sir Baron Jayatilleke Mawatha
Colombo 01
Tel. 011 / 238 16 44 und 238 16 45
Fax 011 / 238 16 45
www.sigiriyavillage.lk
120 rooms, restaurant, pool
Very nicely situated hotel with views of the rock of Sigiriya. Cottage-style rooms

Cobra's Rock

This staircase goes up to Cobra's Rock, which bears this name because of its astonishing resemblance to an upright cobra. Under a stone rain gutter at the entrance to a cave there is a Brahmi inscription from the 2nd century BC that reads: »The Cave of Chief Nagu-li«. Inside it are the remnants of wall paintings (including floral motifs).

Cistern Rock

The path leads up to Cistern Rock, which got its name because of its shape, which is broken in two. The fallen section contains a throne carved into the rock as well as further seating. The terrace presumably had Sri Lanka's first audience hall. A cave below the rock contains the remnants of some wall paintings.

Mirror Gallery

The main access to the peak is a 145 m/159 yd gallery that runs along the west side of the rock at a height of 15 m/50 ft. The first 19 m/21 yd form what is known as the Mirror Gallery, because the paintings that were once on the rock wall used to be reflected on the smooth surface of the ochre wall opposite. This wall is covered with many, still well preserved inscriptions (graffiti) that were carved by visitors between the 7th–12th centuries with metal styli. Around 700 of them have been translated and published by the Singhalese archaeologist Paranavitana; some poetically praise the beauty of the women in the paintings, others the uniqueness of the royal palace on the rock of Sigiriya as well as the achievements of its builder.

ROCK FORT OF SIGIRIYA

✱ ✱ From the middle of the jungle rises a bizarre gneiss rock. Along with the luxurious gardens leading up to it, this rock once formed a courtly paradise. Architecturally speaking it is incomparable; it could almost be called a wonder of the world. Even today magnificent artistic work can be seen in the remains.

🕐 Opening times:
8am – 5pm

① **Water garden**
Visitors can still picture the magnificence and exquisite beauty of this place when they set eyes on the many remains of pools, pavilions, fountains and ponds. They were all fed by an ingenious canal system. The four L-shaped pools once surrounded a pavilion. The pools themselves are likely to have served as baths, because they had smooth walls and steps.

② **Rock garden**
Picturesque rocks adorn this area. Along its winding paths visitors will also find the cave of the cobra's hood, the preacher's rock and also an old monastic complex with a dagoba and bodhi tree.

③ **Terrace garden**
The rock garden leads to the terrace garden. Several terraces are situated one above the other here, connected by brick stairs. They lead up to the rock's entrance area, the Lion Gate.

④ **Lion Gate**
Today the huge paws are all that is left of the colossal lion that once took up the entire front of the mountain.

⑤ **Royal palace on the summit plateau**
The complex and floor plan of the 1.2 ha/3-acre palace can still be seen very clearly. The inner palace lay to the west, the outer one to the east, while the palace gardens were located to the south. They were laid out around a rock pool that was used as a reservoir.

⑥ **Sigiriya Wewa reservoir**
Old inscriptions have revealed that this lake used to possess clear water with colourful water lilies floating on it. It fed the complexes in the water garden through an ingenious system of underground channels, which possessed control valves, circular pipes and filters. The water was collected through channels cut into the rock, which gathered the run-off.

Taking a breather on the way up to the summit plateau

Wall paintings The gallery with Sri Lanka's most famous wall paintings was once not just protected by a projecting rock wall but additionally by a wooden roof. This is the only explanation of how these pictures have survived the centuries. An iron spiral staircase that was in a London underground station until the 1930s and then brought here leads up to the paintings 12 m/39 ft above the Mirror Gallery.

The paintings depict 19 women of the utmost grace and perfection; only fragments survive of another. Some archaeologists are of the opinion there must have been quite a lot more paintings, a hypothesis that is strengthened by further paint residue in other locations. Even though none of them have been restored, those that visitors can see depict some fair-skinned women (presumably mistresses) as well as some dark-skinned women (»gold-skinned«, as they are called in the graffiti), who presumably represent servants. At first glance they appear to be bare-breasted, but upon closer inspection a thin top can be made out and the dark-skinned maidens are also wearing a rudimentary brassiere. Almost all of them are holding flowers in their slender, expressive hands. One dark-skinned maiden is serving petals and fruit, while another is holding what appears to be a jewellery box. The head-dresses of all of the maidens is particularly ornate. It is interesting that the girls can only be seen from the hips up, while the lower part of their bodies disappear in the implied clouds (which has earned them their common name »**cloud maidens of Sigiriya**«). Maybe they are not human but mythical creatures.

The paintings are not frescoes in the proper sense. They were made using natural pigments to produce red, yellow, green, white and black, which were then applied to the rock surface that had been pre-treated with three layers. Their lines are very masterful, but of course the name of the artist who created them is unknown. Although in many of the details the paintings show a resemblance to the paintings in the famous caves of Ajanta in the modern state of Maharashtra in India, they still differ in significant ways and demonstrate a certain originality in Sri Lanka's art.

> ! **Baedeker TIP**
>
> **National Museum of Sigiriya**
> After descending it is worth visiting the archaeological museum south of the surrounding wall. It contains Buddha statues, guard steles and the limestone statue of a queen or goddess amongst other things. Further valuable finds were however brought to the National Museum in Colombo (open: daily 8.30am – 6pm).

Climbing up to the summit plateau from the mirror gallery a path leads along the rock to the Lion Plateau. Between the magnificent paws carved from the rock a staircase secured by brick walls and then an iron staircase lead up to the summit plateau (it helps to have a good head for heights). It is also advisable to climb up to the summit plateau in the morning because there are hornets' nests on the rock walls below the stairs and at times their inhabitants can react quite aggressively.

Up on the summit visitors will now reach the citadel that was once surrounded by a wall that in turn appeared to be a continuation of the rock. Below the main rock, from which the view of the jungle and Sigiriya Wewa (reservoir) is magnificent, there are some impressive boulders in the northern section. In them there are further caves. The largest is 12 m/13 yd long and contains the remains of a brick wall. Carry on northwards through the two boulders to get to a black rock whose surface is covered in many square holes. It is likely they once contained wooden columns that supported a further roof. Three wide seats, one above the other, are carved into the rock. Maybe King Kassyapa once sat on the uppermost one as he saw his half-brother's army that ultimately brought about his death, albeit indirectly.

The significance of the buildings that once stood on the summit plateau has not yet been solved with absolute certainty. In any case, only their foundation walls remain and it requires a fair amount of imagination to interpret their former purpose. However, the masterful achievement of those who built the fort is quite evident; it must be borne in mind that all the construction materials had to be brought up to the summit plateau.

Protected under a projecting rock the images of the Cloud Maidens have survived. It is not yet known who exactly they depict.

Tangalla

C 9

Province: Southern   **Altitude:** 5 m/16ft

Tangalla was valued as a seaport by the Dutch and the British alike. It is situated in the very arid zone of the island's south. The beautiful, palm-lined bathing beaches with their fine sand are very well known.

What to see in Tangalla and around

Reconstruction

Until the tsunami hit several houses from the Dutch colonial power has survived, but the town was largely flooded.

★ ★
Blow Hole
(crevice)

Between Tangalla and Dickwella there is a very special natural phenomenon, the Blow Hole. It is said there are only six such places in the world. It is not clear how the water fountains of up to 25 m/82 ft are formed; it is believed, however, that the water of the incoming

During the monsoon (end Mayend July) the natural spectacle of the blow hole is at its most impressive

► VISITING TANGALLA

GETTING THERE

By car:
from Galle on the A 2 (75 km/47 mi);
from Hambantota on the A 2 (43 km/
27 mi)
By rail:
the closest train station is in Matara
(terminus of the line from Colombo).
By bus:
good services from Galle and Matara
as well as Hambantota

WHERE TO STAY / WHERE TO EAT

► Luxury
Amanwella
Bodhi Mawatha, Wella Wathuara
Tel. 094 / 472 24 13 33
Fax 094 / 472 24 13 34
www.amanwella.com
30 suites, restaurant, bar, pool
Aman means something like peace in
Sanskrit, while Wella is the Sinhala
word for beach. This luxury hotel has
both to offer. This level of luxury has
its price. The Amanwella is one of the
island's most expensive hotels. Those
who stay in the Garden House will
pay around US$1700. However, less
expensive options are also available. A
double room costs around US$300.

► Mid-range
Tangalla Bay Hotel
Hambantota Road, Pallikkuduwa
Tel. / Fax 047 / 403 46
166 rooms, restaurant, bar, pool
This hotel is built on a rock spur and
because of this the tsunami did not
cause much damage. The hotel and its
wonderful beach were soon able to
open again. Well kept rooms

► Budget
Sunrise Beach Cottages
M.M. Santha
Tel. 077 / 7537 33
Fax 077 / 607 97 26
Basic but clean bungalows right on
the sea with a magnificent sandy
beach. Restaurant

Eva Lanka
Tangalla
Tel / Fax 047 / 224 09 40-1
www.eva.lk
23 rooms, restaurant, pool
The owner is Italian and when he
does the cooking the result is very
delicious. Very tastefully furnished
rooms. Gorgeous beach!

waves gets in under the rocks and is then pushed upwards through a
crevice. This creates a lot of negative pressure, causing the water to
shoot up into the air.
To get to the Blow Hole turn off the A 2 at milestone 117 into a narrow track to the sea and follow the signs.

Around 16 km/10mi north of Tangalla is the 91 m/300 ft black rock
Mulkirigala (access from Wiraketiya or Beliatta). It contains several
caves that were used as homes by monks. A cave temple with several
statues of Buddha, including the sculpture of a 10.5 m/35 ft recumbent Buddha, was built during the reign of King Duttha Gamanai

Mulkirigala R

(161 – 137 BC) or possibly by his brother. The wall paintings in the Pihala Vihara date back to the 19th century; they recount episodes from Buddha's past lives in a naïve narrative manner. The monastery, one of the oldest in Sri Lanka, houses an extensive collection of books and manuscripts. In 1826 the English scholar and government official George Turnour and the monk Galle found parts of the Mahavamsa chronicle, which was written in Pali.

Tissamaharama

D 9

Province: Southern   **Altitude:** 30 m/98ft

Tissamaharama, as the capital of the former kingdom of Ruhuna, has a rich past. However, many treasures in the expansive area of ruins still have not been uncovered. The nearby Yala National Park is a paradise for animals and as a result it attracts many thousands of visitors.

History | Mahanaga, one of King Devanampiya Tissa's (260 – 210 BC) younger brothers, is thought to be the town's founder. He called it Mahagam or Magama. Mahanaga had to flee from the capital Anuradhapura because the queen, who was very popular with the people, was out to kill him. During this time the Kshattriya dynasty (who had presumably come here from India and were members of the warrior caste of the same name) ruled the region from Kataragama, 16 km/ 10 mi further north. Between them and Mahanaga there were some bellicose confrontations initially, but later they made a peace that was subsequently sealed by marriage.

Later Kavana Tissa, one of Mahanaga's great-grandsons, married the daughter of the ruler of Kelaniya and added more territory to the kingdom of Ruhuna. As a result the kings of Ruhuna controlled the entire south of the island. At this time the Tamils who had come from southern India were already governing in Anuradhapura under King Elara (approx. 204 – 161 BC). Prince Duttha Gamani of Ruhuna, one of King Tissa's sons, gathered an army, moved to Anuradhapura with it and killed Elara in a duel. After his victory he ascended the throne and governed from 161–137 BC as a splendid king in Anuradhapura.

During the subsequent period the Singhalese kings often sought refuge in the kingdom of Ruhuna to act against invaders from southern India. One of them was King Vijaya Bahu I, who managed to oust the Chola rulers from the island in 1070. However, some of the kings of Ruhuna also turned against the kings of the north, mainly to secure their area of influence in the south. Tissamaharama played an important role for a good 2000 years of the island's history, but then the town lost much of its importance.

▶ VISITING TISSAMAHARAMA

GETTING THERE

By car:
from Hambantota on the A 2 to Wirawila, then turn right and right again after around 6 km/3.5 mi (32 km/20 mi); from Wellawaya on the A 2, bear left when the road forks at Wirawala reservoir (66 km/41 mi)

WHERE TO STAY

▶ **Mid-range**
Rest House
Tissamaharama
Tel. 047 / 372 99
Good base for visits to Yala National Park. People hiring out Jeeps and licensed national park guides can always be found outside the hotel.

What to see in Tissamaharama

The ingenious irrigation system is quite remarkable. It was created by the early rulers of Ruhuna. It consists of several reservoirs (wewas) fed by the nearby rivers Kirindi Oya and Menik Ganga. This system transformed the originally bare region into a **flourishing landscape**. It made it possible to grow large quantities of rice, helping the kings to become very rich. The system fell into ruin or silted up over the years and were only repaired in the 20th century. Since then people have been settling here again.

Irrigation syste[m]

Several magnificent monolithic pillars still remain of the old royal palace on a hill to the east of town. They probably supported a multi-storey building (maybe made of wood). The building is likely to have been constructed in the 2nd century.

Old royal palac[e]

The Yatala Dagoba was built in the 2nd century BC. The attached monastic complex contained inscriptions dating back to the time before Christ as well as to the 7th and 8th centuries. The dagoba is named after one of Mahanaga's sons who was born here.
During restoration works significant finds were discovered, such as the head of a Buddha statue made of limestone, the sculpture of a standing Buddha as well as a statue that probably depicts King Kavanna Tissa. The statue of a Buddha with crossed arms is quite remarkable; such a pose is quite unusual in Sri Lanka. A further feature of note is the 80 cm/31 in stele with a depiction of seven male figures who have not been identified. The figure in the middle is standing under three parasols, making it likely that this is a depiction of a ruler and his retinue.

✱
Yatala
Dagoba

To the south of town are the ruins of Chandagiri Vihara with inscriptions on a large octagonal stone that presumably date back to the period between the 1st century BC and the 1st century AD.

Chandagiri
Vihara

Tissamaharama Vihara The Chandagiri Vihara, founded in around 160 BC under King Ka-kavanna Tissa, always used to be a meeting place for all monks living south of Mahaweli Ganga at the start of the rainy season. They meditated here and sought instruction from the monastery's resident monks. According to the chronicle 363 monk's cells existed here in the 9th century. The dagoba, which was also built during the time the monastery was founded, is, at 60 m/197 ft, probably the tallest that ever existed in the kingdom of Ruhuna.

ruins on the road to Kirinda The road to Kirina, a fishing port 13 km/8 mi south of Tissamaharama, is lined by ancient ruins, most of which are still awaiting restoration. Kirinda was once a significant port for Tissamaharama and was probably also known to Greek seafarers. Just outside town a road turns off to Palatupana, the starting point for a visit to ▶Yala National Park.

Trincomalee

D 4

Province: Eastern   **Altitude:** 7 m/23ft

Trincomalee, because of its sheltered location, has been considered a preferred location of trade and industry for many centuries. A large harbour, one of the world's most beautiful natural harbours, played a major role in this. The city in the northeast of Sri Lanka also played a role in tourism, less because of any particular sites than because of the magnificent beaches.

Peninsula Trincomalee is situated on a very elongated peninsula that is hardly wider than a kilometre. Towards the northeast a headland projects into the open sea. This was the location of Fort Frederick. The actual city is situated on both sides for about 2 km/1 mi. There are several small islands just off the coast, such as Pigeon Island, **which has a very attractive coral reef**. Not far from Trincomalee near Mutur the Mahaweli Ganga, Sri Lanka's longest river, flows into the Indian Ocean after flowing across country for 332 km/206 mi.

Occasional Area of Tension

Because of the confrontations it can be very difficult at times to visit Trincomalee and the surrounding area. Anyone still wanting to travel to Trincomalee should get information from the tourist offices in Colombo about the current situation before setting off.

Tamil character According to estimates Trincomalee is home to around 360,000 people and recently to Singhalese people again too. The vast majority of the population, though, is made up by Tamils and Moors. In and around Trinco, as the city is usually called, the tsunami caused severe damage and thousands of people died or were injured and tens of thousands of families were rendered homeless.

Little is known about the early history of the city, which is called Gokanna in the chronicle. Tamils from India settled here more than 2000 years ago. They called the town Thirukonamalai (sacred sun hill). Ptolemy mentioned Trincomalee as the »harbour of Helios«; Egyptian and Greek seafarers had told him about it. King Dhutta Sena (276–303), it is recorded in the Mahavamsa chronicle, had all Hindu temples in Gokanna destroyed. In the 8th century Muslim settlers arrived.

In 1592 King Vimela Dharma Suriya I fled Kandy from the Portuguese and came here. In order to expel the Portuguese from the island, King Senerat allowed the Dutch in 1612 to build a fort in Kottiyar (near Trincomalee); however, it was taken by the Portuguese shortly after it was completed. In the years that followed the French, Dutch and British fought over this area. The British finally managed to take Fort Frederick under General James Stuart in 1795. To protect the entrance to the inner harbour they built the less well fortified Fort Ostenburg. From the 19th century until Sri Lanka's independence Trincomalee was used by the British as a naval port from which they controlled the Indian Ocean. In 1905 the fortifications of Fort Frederick were razed to the ground and in 1942 a Japanese aerial attack on the British fleet destroyed the little that was left.

A paradise in the middle of the zone formerly affected by the civil war: Pigeon Island near Trincomalee

The harbour of Trincomalee had its heyday in the 17th and 18th centuries when sailing ships were still crossing the oceans. After the harbour of Colombo was developed Trincomalee increasingly lost its importance.

What to see in Trincomalee

Temples There are several Hindu temples in Trincomalee; however, they all date back to more recent times, which is why they are of little art-historical value. On Dockyard Road Kadakarai Temple and Mudu-gayan Kovil are still worth visiting because of their extensively orna-mented entrance towers.

Fort The fort of Trincomalee on the town's north side was built by the Portuguese. Some of the stones they used came from the Hindu temple that was destroyed here, which was considered degrading by the Hindus. The Portuguese extended the fort in 1656. Today it has re-stricted public access because it is mainly used by the military. Within the fort is the former residence of the Duke of Wellington, who came here in 1792 to recover from an illness he had caught during a military campaign against Tipu Sultan in southern India. There is a magnificent old bodhi tree in the garden. The tame deer and stags belong to the Koneswaram Temple on Swami Rock at the end of the headland the fort stands on.

Around Trincomalee

★
Pigeon Island Only around ten minutes by boat from Trincomalee is the small cor-al island of Pigeon Island. Every imaginable water sport can be in-dulged in here, but the colourful coral reef makes diving and snor-kelling particularly interesting.

 VISITING TRINCOMALEE

GETTING THERE

By car:
from Colombo on the A 1 and then the A 6
By rail:
from Colombo via Kurunegala, Dambulla and Habarana (approx. 7 hrs.)
By bus:
from Colombo via Maho and Galoya (approx. 8 hrs.)

WHERE TO STAY

▶ **Mid-range**
Club Oceanic
Uppuveli, approx. 12 km/7 mi outside of Trincomalee
Tel. / Fax 026 / 223 07
www.johnkeellshotels.com
56 rooms, restaurant, bar, pool, pri-vate beach, diving school
The hotel was renovated because of the tsunami; it is situated on a long, wide sandy beach. Many water sports facilities; great for families.

Near the small town of Kanniyai, a few miles northwest of Trinco-malee on the A 12, there are seven hot springs whose creation is associated with a legend from the Ramayana: after the king's son Rama had freed his wife Sita from the clutches of the giant Ravana, the giant was so enraged about this that he rammed his spear into the ground. As a result the Earth cried seven hot tears that are still worshipped here at the seven hot springs by believers.

✴
Hot Springs near Kanniyai

Weligama

B 10

Province: Southern   **Altitude:** 5 m/16ft

The small fishing village of Weligama (the name means »village in the sand«) possessed an important seaport for many centuries but it lost its significance at the latest when the port facilities in Colombo were extended.

The construction of a road to shorten the distance between Galle and Matara has also cost the town much of its original charm. Nevertheless there are still some nicely situated beaches with high coconut palm trees and fine sand here. Several hotels and guesthouses were flooded by the tsunami, but all of them have reopened again.

What to see in Weligama

The 3.5 km/2mi bay framed by red laterite rock resembles the landscape of Galle and was also used as a seaport. Today only fishing boats come here. There are **two small islands** in the bay, Taprobane (Greek: copper island; one of the names the entire island of Sri Lanka held in earlier times) and Parei Duwa (pigeon island). Taprobane is only 1 ha/2.5 acres in size and was once in the possession of the French Comte de Nouny, who had a magnificent villa and a tropical garden set up here. The house was later inhabited by the American author and composer Paul Bowles; now it is a fine hotel.

Bay

? DID YOU KNOW ...?

■ ...that according to legend the first coconut to be washed ashore in Sri Lanka arrived on the island near Weligama? When exactly this took place and where it came from is not known, but it was an event of lasting importance: coconut palms and coconuts have been the island's economic backbone for many years. Even today no other fruit is used so intensively in Sri Lanka as coconuts.

Near to the railway crossing is the Hindu Natha Devale with a colossal relief sculpture; it is believed to have been made either in the 6th or the 11th century. It is located in a niche in the rock wall and was

Statue of King Kustha Raja

▶ VISITING WELIGAMA

GETTING THERE

By car:
from Galle on the A 2 (26 km/16 mi);
from Matara on the A 2 (16 km/10 mi)

By rail:
station on the train line between Colombo and Matara

By bus:
good services from Galle and Matara.

WHERE TO STAY

▶ Mid-range

Taprobane Island
Tel. 091 / 438 02 75
Fax 091 / 222 26 24
www.taprobaneisland.com
13 rooms, restaurant, bar, pool and private beach
This very dignified hotel is situated on a small island and has rooms in various price categories; the luxurious beach houses are the most expensive. It is also possible to hire the entire island.

▶ Budget

Bay Beach Hotel Weligama
Kapparatota
Tel. / Fax 041 / 502 01
www.baybeachhotel.com
60 rooms, pool, private beach, PADI diving school
Mid-range hotel with plenty of comfortable rooms. Nice pool.

worked from the stone. It has not yet been determined whether the magnificently clad figure wearing a crown and a bracelet is the bodhisattva Avalokitesvara or the bodhisattva Samantabhadra (the god Saman). The legend says Kushta Raja, the leper king, came to Weligama to cure his sickness by drinking the juice of the royal palm for three months.

★ ★ Yala National Park (Ruhuna National Park)

Province: Uva   **Area:** South Coast

Yala National Park was founded in around 1900; it is the best-known of Sri Lanka's national parks, even though it may not necessarily be home to the most species. Nevertheless is it well worth visiting, since many other parks in the north and east only have limited access for visitors.

Only partially accessible

Yala National Park covers an area of approx. 1300 sq km / 500 sq mi and is structured into a western and eastern section (the latter has been given Strict Nature Reserve status and may only be visited with special permission).

Despite the sparse vegetation typical of Sri Lanka's south, Yala National Park is a refuge for all kinds of animals. Wild elephants live here just as peacefully as crocodiles, sambar and chital deer, flamingos, peacocks, tortoises, buffaloes, jackals, leopards and allegedly also some sloth bears. The flora resembles a savannah: low bushes, only few trees and shallow lakes with mangroves. The dead trees that can be found in some of the lakes and make ideal resting places for the many representatives of the local bird world are quite impressive. From November to April these birds are joined by many bird species from India and western Asia, who come here to overwinter.

Flora and fauna

On its southeastern side the park borders on the sea; the strip of coastline is even more attractive because of its **lovely sandy beach** (one of the few places where rangers give visitors« permission to leave the vehicle and go swimming).

A drive through the park is best early in the morning or in the afternoon because most animals try to escape the noon sun, making them harder to find.

Kumana Bird Sanctuary is **part of Yala National Park** and entering it requires a permit. It is home to a particularly diverse bird world, including many species of water fowl, along with hornbills, herons, pelicans, eagles and more. This is also a good place to encounter water buffalo, stags, wild pigs and reptiles.

Kumana Bird Sanctuary

 VISITING YALA NATIONAL PARK

GETTING THERE

By car:
from Hambantota on the A2 to Tissamaharama, carry on from there by Jeep to the main entrance
By rail:
the closest train station is in Matara (terminus of the line between Colombo and the South). Carry on from there by bus or taxi.

TOURS

The park is open every day from 6am6pm, the main entrance, Palaputana Gate, is around 20 km/12mi east of Tissamaharama, where drivers are always waiting, offering their services. The park may only be accessed by vehicles accompanied by a ranger. It is not permitted to drive into the park in a private vehicle. Getting out of the car is strictly prohibited unless the ranger says otherwise in specific locations. In addition to the park's admission charge visitors will have to pay for the vehicle as well as for the ranger.

WHERE TO STAY

► **Mid-range**
Yala Safari Game Lodge
P.O. Box 1, Tissamaharama
Tel. / fax 047 / 380 15
The comfortable »Yala Village Resort«, by far the best hotel on the edge of Yala National Park, managed to survive the tsunami more or less unscathed. Only the villas on the beach were flooded but they have been rebuilt. The hotel will find Jeeps and licensed rangers for guests.

★★ Yapahuwa

Province: North Western

Height of the rock fort: 92 m/ 280 ft

Yapahuwa is neither a town nor a village, it is rather what remains of an imposing 12th century rock fort that rises up abruptly by 92 m/280 ft from the wilderness. The complex is a similarly bold and magnificent creation as the residence of ► Sigiriya, designed with perspective and architectural symbolism in mind.

History Brahmi inscriptions in some of the plentiful caves prove that Buddhist hermits lived here, at least in the 2nd century AD. The kings of Sri Lanka appear to have only noticed the strategic location of this place in the 13th century; if they did so earlier no records survive. When the Kalinga prince Magha was the king of Sri Lanka

In a remote location in the jungle: the rock fort of Yapahuwa

▶ VISITING YAPAHUWA

GETTING THERE

By car:
from Kurunegala on the A 10 to Padeniya, then continue on the A 28 and turn right at Maho. It is possible to walk from Maho (a pleasant walk), otherwise take a taxi. The bus only goes the first 3 km/2 mi to the turning to Yapahuwa.

By rail:
Maho is a railway junction where the lines from Colombo to Trincomalee and Jaffna meet.

WHERE TO STAY

In Maho, around 4 km/2.5mi from Yapahuwa, there is a resthouse with basic rooms. Better accommodation is available in Kurunegala.

(1215 1236) resistance groups formed in several parts of the country. One of them occupied the rock that was named after their leader Subha (Yapahuwa is the Sinhala word for Subhagiri or Subhapatta). This group developed it into a defensive complex because they were able to observe the rebels' movements in the south. King Bhuvanaike Bahu I put an army together from here for his brother Vijaya Bahu II, who had been the kingdom's administrator since 1262. This army achieved a victory against the Malay king Sri Dharamaraja from Ligor near Yapahuwa. In 1272, after his brother had been murdered in Dambadeniya, Bhuvanaike Bahu fled with his wife to Yapahuwa; it was only when he was proclaimed king several months later that he chose the secure mountain fort to be his residence and the capital of his kingdom. As a symbol of his power he also possessed the **holy tooth**. His reign was marked by battles against the southern Indian Pandya under Arya Chakravarti and against enemies in his own country who were after the throne. Chinese coins found in Yapahuwa suggest that Bhuvanaike Bahu I maintained friendly relations to China and may have even asked the Chinese for help (**Marco Polo** for example reports that a party had come to Yapahuwa from the Mongol ruler Kublai Khan, who had conquered China).

When Bhuvanaike Bahu I died in 1284 it was also the end of the short golden age of Yapahuwa. The Pandyas even managed to conquer the fort and gain possession of the sacred tooth relic. King Parakrama Bahu II (1287 1293) however successfully negotiated to have it returned to Sri Lanka.

The Portuguese also knew of the existence of the old fort of Yapahuwa, while the Dutch probably did not. When an officer of the British army set up camp nearby he discovered the impressive complex. First excavations were undertaken in 1888.

Rock Fort Yapahuwa

Complex
Two parallel walls surround the southern section of the rock at a distance of 100 m/110 yd. The outer wall, 14 m/45 ft thick and 4.5 m/14 ft high consists of piled up earth covered in brick walls and stone blocks at the base. There is a 13 m/40 ft wide ditch on the outside of the 900 m/990 yd long wall, in which there are three gates. The main gate is opposite the palace access in the southwest. Remains of the buildings between the two walls are very scarce.

The lower town was located behind the inner wall. The temple at the eastern access was built by a monk from Nettipologama in the 18th century; King Kirti Sri Raja Singha from Kandy is said to have acquiesced to its construction. Inside is a column that was found within the complex bearing an old inscription that testifies to this.

> ### Baedeker TIP
>
> **Visiting the Caves**
> The caves are normally closed but they are still used by monks living here for their devotions and so it is possible to visit them on request.

Cave temple
Somewhat further to the northeast is a cave temple with paintings from the 18th century (Kandyan period). Amongst other things they depict **Buddha's 24 visions**, the seven weeks after his enlightenment and his first sermon. The painting on the ceiling is equally remarkable. The two Buddha figures are depicted in the same unusual pose (arms crossed) as the Ananda statue in Polonnaruwa. The statues in the cave temple were probably made at the end of the 18th century, maybe even later. The bodhi tree that belongs to the temple was probably only planted in the 19th century.

Somewhat further north is another cave with an interesting roof, around 15 m/50 ft above ground. At the southern end of the interior a 7.5 x 3.6 m (25 x 12 ft) walled area was created, presumably for a Vihara. The temple also contains a large stone throne.

Mandapa
Near the stairs to the palace are the remains of a building that housed 52 columns. The bases are still present. It is called the Mandapa or also Ambassador's Pavilion because it may have served as a guesthouse for foreign emissaries.

Stairs
The most impressive feat to be admired in Yapahuwa today is the monumental staircase that is richly structured and adorned with lively sculptures in the upper section. It is the **expression of a strong desire for display** and of a strength that builds on legitimation as well as a sense of religious and political mission.

This palace access consists of six stairway sections and the landings in between. The lower section of this staircase is unadorned. After a landing measuring 7.5 m/25 ft in width, the upper section begins, ornamented with magnificent sculptures. This section reaches its har-

monious completion in an impressive gate decorated with many figures, including sculptures of lions of outstanding quality.

On either side of the entrance were windows artistically carved from
granite; they are **unique in all of Sri Lanka**. One has survived and is
now in the small archaeological museum in the lower town. It consists of 45 touching circular shapes; each circle contains a figure
(lion, elephant, swan, dwarf, dancer) cut out in the silhouette manner.

Also richly adorned is the makara arch above the window openings,
below which is a scenic depiction: the goddess Lakshmi is sitting, legs
crossed, holding a lotus in each hand, as she is being bathed by two
elephants who are cupping containers with their trunks. The palace
proper, a brick building with an area of 432 sq m/516 sq yd, was evidently very modest, which, by the way, also led to the conclusion
that it may not have been a palace but a temple for the sacred tooth
relic. On the other hand it was also assumed that after the construction of the magnificent stairs events occurred that no longer permitted further buildings to be constructed.

Glossary of Religious and Cultural Terms

Abhaya mudra gesture of protection (made by Buddha statues)
Anuradha Indian deity (god of light)
Apsara female spirit
Avalokiteshvara bodhisattva in Mahayana Buddhism
Avatara incarnation of a deity
Ayurveda traditional, holistic natural medicine in Sri Lanka and India
Bikkhu Buddhist monk
Bikkhuni Buddhist nun
Bohdi tree a tree considered sacred since Siddharta Gautama reached enlightenment while sitting under such a tree (scientific name: Ficus religiosa)
Bodhigara temple where a ▶bodhi tree is worshipped
Bodhi-maluwa terrace for a ▶bodhi tree
Bodhisattva a person who is believed to be closest to ▶nirvana, but who remains on earth to show other people the right path
Brahma creator of the world and the supreme deity of Hinduism; one of the three ▶Trimurti
Brahman the world soul
Buddha Siddharta Gautama, creator of Buddhism
Castes term for the different social classes
Chaitya originally an early Buddhist burial mound that over time developed into a temple with a wide central nave and two narrow side aisles
Chakra disc, emblem of the god ▶Vishnu, also »wheel of law«, which was first set in motion by ▶Buddha
Chattra a parasol, an honorary royal symbol, also used to crown a ▶stupa or ▶dagoba
Cella central room of a Buddhist temple
Chulavamsa continuation of the ▶Mahavamsa
Dagoba sacred Buddhist building, developed from a burial or reliquary hill into a pagoda
Daladaga house of the sacred tooth relic (such as in Kandy and Polonnaruwa)
Devale Hindu temple
Devi female Hindu deity, original form of Parvati, Kali etc.
Dharamsala accommodation for pilgrims
Dharma Buddha's teachings, cosmic order
Diphavamsa chronicle of events on the island of Sri Lanka
Dravida style southern Indian architectural style
Enlightenment the insight obtained by ▶Buddha about how human suffering can be overcome
Gana goblin in ▶Shiva's retinue
Ganesha ▶Shiva's vehicle, also seen as his son
Garuda sun bird, also ▶Vishnu's vehicle
Guard stele panel with figurative depictions in front of the entrance to a temple
Gupta style northern Indian architectural style, named after the Gupta dynasty

Hanuman monkey god from the ►Ramayana

Hinayana also ►Theravada; Buddhist teaching of the »low vehicle«; in contrast to ►Mahayana Buddhism, humans can only reach the state of enlightenment through their own power

Hinduism one of the world's four main religions with around 900 million followers

Incarnation »to be made flesh«; term for the rebirth of the souls in a human or animal body

Jataka the previous lives of ►Buddha (there are said to have been more than 500 existences in different guises)

Kailasa sacred Hindu mountain in Tibet

Kali terrifying manifestation of ►Devi

Kantaka Chaitya ►Siddharta Gautama's (►Buddha's) horse on which he is said to have left his parental palace

Karma »action«; the sum of all the mental and physical actions that are the basis for the current existence

Kataragama another name for the god of war, ►Skanda

Ketumala flame of enlightenment (decoration on top of the heads of many Buddha statues)

Kovil small Hindu temple that is not reserved for any specific deity (as opposed to ►Devale)

Krishna eighth manifestation of the god ►Vishnu (is often depicted as a shepherd)

Kshattriya Indian warrior caste

Lakshmi female Hindu deity of affluence and beauty and ►Vishnu's wife

Lingam phallic symbol of the god ►Vishnu

Lohapasada »bronze palace«; a building decorated with or covered in metal

Mahabharata greatest epic of classical Indian literature

Mahapali alms house, this is where the poor were given their food by the monks

Mahavamsa old chronicle of the Singhalese kingdom from the 6th century

Mahayana Buddhist teaching of the »high vehicle«; it says that every human being can reach the desired state of enlightenment and thus ►nirvana, and ►Buddha and ►bodhisattvas can aid them in this (as opposed to ►Hinayana)

Maheshvara name of the god ►Shiva

Mahinda Indian monk who brought Buddhism to Sri Lanka

Mahout elephant driver

Makara architectural element in the form of a dragon (such as at the entrances to temples)

Mandapa prayer room for a relic

Meru according to Hinduism the mountain on which the gods of the Hindu ►pantheon live

Moonstone semi-circular stone in front of temple entrances, symbol of the threshold between the material and the spiritual world (not to be confused with the semi-precious gem also called moonstone)

Moors descendants of Arab seafarers and merchants who still live on Sri Lanka today

Muchalinda a Hindu deity of the underworld (snake god, who covered Buddha as he meditated by fanning out his seven heads)

mudra gesture or pose of Buddhist iconography

Naga Hindu deity of the underworld, depicted as a snake-like being with a human torso

Nirvana term from Buddhist teaching; »blowing out«; nirvana is the condition when a human being escapes the cycle of birth life – death – rebirth for good

Ola Buddhist texts written on palm leaves; the leaves of the talipot and Palmyra palms are used

Pantheon according to Hindu belief, the term for the entirety of their gods

Paria »untouchable«; term for a person who does not belong to any ►caste and is considered impure (»untouchable«) as a result

Parvati Hindu deity

Patimaghara picture house, part of the temple complex

Perahera Buddhist procession (also pilgrimage)

Pilimage statue house, part of the temple complex

Poya festival that takes place on the full moon of every month

Prakara stone fence around a temple

Prakriti term for the primordial matter from which the world is made

Prasada prayer hall in a temple complex

Puja Hindu ceremony in a temple

Purnagheta vase of abundance, a very popular image on Sri Lanka: symbol of the inexhaustible wealth of Buddhist teaching

Raja term for rulers

Ramayana classical Indian epic

Ravana king in the Indian epic ►Ramayana

Samahera Buddhist novice monk

Sangha Buddhist community of monks

Sanskrit the sacred language of ►Hinduism

Sarasvati female Hindu deity of science and wife of ►Brahma

Sari a gown for women, usually artistically woven, that is wrapped around the body several times

Sarong a simple gown for men worn around the lower part of the body

Shiva destroyer of the world, one of the three ►Trimurti

Shivalinga phallic symbol of the god ►Shiva

Siddharta civil name of the historical ►Buddha

Sikhara tower-like addition above the entrance to a Hindu temple

Singh(a) Indian: »lion«

Sita princess from the Indian epic ►Ramayana who is abducted by ►Ravana and brought to Sri Lanka

Skanda Hindu deity of war

Sri added to a name to mean »sacred«

Sri Pada symbolic and thus larger-than-lifesize footprint of ►Buddha (for example on Adam's Peak)

Stupa Thai and Burmese form of the dagoba

Sutren the literal tradition of ►Buddha's teachings

Tamil Eelam »land of the Tamils«; term for the independent republic desired by the Tamils living in the north of Sri Lanka

Tamil Tigers Militant wing of the LTTE whose members were also willing to commit suicide attacks

Theravada also ►Hinayana; Buddhist teaching that in contrast to ►Mahayana Buddhism also claims to be the pure, unadulterated teaching

Thorani Hindu deity (deity of the earth)

Toddy palm sap; after toddy is distilled it becomes arrack

Trinity term for the three highest deities of ►Hinduism (►Brahma, ►Shiva and ►Vishnu)

Tripitaka the »threefold basket«, sacred manuscript cycle in which Buddha's teachings are summed up; the Tripitaka consist of three baskets (Vibaya-pitaka, Suttapitaka and Abhidhammapitala), which together with the commentaries written down by monks are used as the basis of recitations

Upasaka lay followers of the Buddhist teaching

Ushnisha snail-shaped plaited curl of hair as a symbol of a ►Buddha's enlightenment or omniscience

Vahalkada altar on which the sacrificial items were placed during ritual acts

Vahana the vehicle of a deity

Vatadage ►watadage

Vedda »the hunters«, Sri Lanka's aboriginal population

Vedas »science«; the earliest Hindu texts

Vihara Buddhist monastery, term for the temple complex

Vishnu preserver of the world, a member of the ►trinity

Watadage round, roofed temple building

Wedda ►Vedda

Wewa artificial reservoir

Yaksha »daemons«, terrifying creatures that stand at the entrances to temples to frighten evil spirits and keep them away

Yama Hindu god of death

Yoni indentation carved into the stone in which the ►lingam was placed

INDEX

a

Abhayagiri Dagoba **196**
accommodation **108**
Adam's Bridge **19**
Adam's Peak **182**
administration **40**
administrative structure **41**
airport **109**
Alahana Parivena **325**
Alutnuvara **292**
Aluvihara, rock temple **294**
Ambalangoda **184**
Ambalantota **249**
Ampara **187**
animal watching **149**
animism **96**
antiques **111**
Anuradhapura **188, 331**
Arankale (hermitage) **291**
Archaeological Museum, Anuradhapura **192**
areas of tension **142**
art periods **73**
asana-ghara **81**
Atadage **323**
Aukana **201**
Aukana, Buddha statue **201**
Avissawella **202**

b

Backhaus, Ralph **191**
Baker's Falls **256**
Balangaloda culture **58**
Bandaranaike, Sirimavo **101**
Bandaranaike, Solomon **101**
Bandarawela **204**
banks **139**
Basawak Kulam **192**
batik **96**
Batticaloa **205**
Battuta, Ibn **102**
beaches **112**
bears **28**
belief in spirits **96**
Beligela **284**
Bell, H. **191**
Bentota **208**
Beruwala **210**
Bharati, Subramanya **132**
bicycles **155**

Big World's End **256**
Bikkhu **50**
Bikkhuni **50**
birds **27**
Blow Hole **344**
Bodhi tree **82**
bodhisattvas **73**
botanical gardens **32**
Brahma **53**
Brahman temples **82**
Brahmanism **52**
Brahmins **39**
Bridge on the River Kwai **203**
Buddha's postures **86**
Buddha Shakyami **86**
Buddha's footprint **183**
Buddhism **47**
Buddhist temples **79**
Buddhist university, Kelanyia **289**
Buduruvagala, rock statues **235**
Bulan Kulam **192**
Burgher people **34**
buses **155**
butterflies **27**

c

camping **109**
canoeing **150**
caste system **39**
casting out spirits **97**
cave temples **82**
Central Highlands **20**
Ceylon Tamils **34**
Chandagiri Vihara **347348**
chetiya-ghara **80**
Chilaw **212**
children **112**
Christianity **54**
civil war **67**
classical art **73**
Cloud Maidens **90**
coconuts **45**
coffee cultivation **44**
Colombo **213**
Colombo Plan **42, 66**
Colombo: Bandaranaike Memorial Conference Hall **225**
Colombo: Beira Lake **224**
Colombo: Burgher district **223**
Colombo: Cabinet Offices **220**
Colombo: Christ Church **223**

Colombo: Cinnamon Garden **225**
Colombo: Clock Tower **219**
Colombo: Dehiwala **226**
Colombo: docks **223**
Colombo: Dutch Period Museum **222**
Colombo: Fort **219**
Colombo: Galle Face Green **224**
Colombo: Galle Face Hotel **224**
Colombo: Grand Oriental Hotel **220**
Colombo: Hulftsdorp **222**
Colombo: Jami Ul-Afar Jumma Mosque **222**
Colombo: Kotte **215**
Colombo: Laksala department store **220**
Colombo: Miller's department store **220**
Colombo: Mount Lavinia **225, 227**
Colombo: National Museum **225**
Colombo: Old Parliament Building **219**
Colombo: Pettah **220**
Colombo: Prime Minister's Residence **220**
Colombo: Samudrah House **224**
Colombo: Santa Lucia Church **223**
Colombo: Sri Jayawardanapura **215**
Colombo: St **223**
Colombo: St Peter's Garrison Church **220**
Colombo: Supreme Court **223**
Colombo: traders and market quarter **220**
Colombo: Wolfendahl Church **223**
Colombo: Zoological Garden **226**
Colombo: Temple of the Hindu goddess Kali **221**
Colombo: Temple of the War God Skanda **222**
Colombo: Town Hall **225**
Colombo: Viharamahadevi Park **225**
colonial period **78**
colonization **43, 61**
Commonwealth of Nations **42**

communications **144**
compulsory military service **42**
cookshops **121**
corals **31**
cosmology **53**
cricket **149**
crocodiles **28**
customs **96**

dagoba **79**
Dalada Maligawa **197**
Dambadeniya **292**
Dambegoda Vihara **306**
Dambulla **91, 227**
Dambulla, cave temples **227**
dance **93**
Dedigama **233**
deities **52**
Demala Maha Seya
   Dagoba **327**
demons **97**
depictions of Buddha **84**
Digayapi **187**
Dikoya **250**
Dimbulagala, rock
   monastery **328**
Dipavamsa **9192**
diplomatic representations **131**
diving **151**
diving schools **152**
Dodanduwa **255**
domesticated animals **31**
Dondra Head **299**
Dowa Temple **235**
drink **118**
drinks **123**
drugs **113**
Dutch fort, Batticaloa **207**
Dutch Fort, Matara **299**
Dutch fort, Negombo **307**

eating habits **120**
economy **32, 42**
education **35**
Elahera Canal **298**
electricity **113**
Elephant Orphanage **29**
Elephant Orphanage in
   Pinawela **284**
elephants **29**

elevations **21**
Ella **234**
Embekke Devale **278**
emergency **113**
energy **46**
entry and exit regulations **111**
environmental protection **31**
eternal cycle **53**
etiquette and customs **114**
exchange rates **138**

fauna **22, 27**
festivals **115**
fishing **46**
flora **22**
flying foxes **27**
flying time **109**
food **118**
foreign policy **42**
forestry **46**
forms of government **40**
Fort Macdowall **294**
fruit **122**

Gadaladeniya Vihara **277**
Gal Oya Development
   Scheme **187**
Gal Oya National Park **244**
Gal Pota (Stone Book) **322**
Gal Vihara **325**
Galapatha Raja Maha
   Vihara **208**
Galebadda **305**
Galle **236**
Galle: churches **242**
Galle: Fort **237**
Galle: Government House **242**
Galle: Kaluwella **243**
Galle: Pettah **243**
Gampola **279**
Ganadevi Kovil (Hindu
   temple) **324**
gecko **28**
gemstone mines **335**
gemstone workshops **210**
gemstones **46, 148**
geological configuration **19**
getting there **109**
Girihandu Vihara **249**
Giritale **246**

Giritale Minneriya
   Sanctuary **247**
Giritale reservoir **247**
golf **150**
Gondwana **19**
Gopalabatta rock **325**
Goyigama **40**

Hakgala Botanical Garden **313**
Hamangala Caves **188**
Hambantota **248**
hand positions **87**
handicrafts **95**
Hanguranketa **280**
Haputale Pass **204**
Hatadage **323**
Hatton **250**
health **126**
help for disabled travellers **156**
Henerathgoda Botanical
   Garden **308**
hiking **150**
Hikkaduwa **251**
Hinayana Buddhism **48**
Hindu temple, Chilaw **212**
Hinduism **52**
holidays **115**
Horton Plains **256**
hotels **108**
Hunas Falls **279**
hydropower **46**

immunizations **111**
Indian Tamils **34**
Indikatuseya and Katuseya
   Dagoba **302**
industry **46**
information **130**
irrigation system **22**
Islam **53**
Istripura, caves **204**
Isurumuniya Vihara (rock
   monastery) **198**

Jaffna **257**
Jaffna lowlands **21**
Jayawardene, Junius **104**
Jetavanarama Dagoba **197**

k

Kachimalai Mosque **210**
Kalpitiya **330**
Kalutara **259**
Kandy **260**
Kandy Dances **93**
Kandy Highlands **279**
Kandy period **77**
Kandy: Archaeological Museum **272**
Kandy: Dalada Maligawa **266**
Kandy: Kandy Lake **262**
Kandy: Malwatta Vihara (temple) **264**
Kandy: Market Hall **266**
Kandy: Natha Devale (temple) **273**
Kandy: National Museum **266, 272**
Kandy: Pattini Devale (temple) **273**
Kandy: residential quarter **265**
Kandy: Temple of the Tooth **266**
Kandy: Udawattakele Sanctuary **273**
Kanniyai, hot springs **351**
Karagan Lewaya (lake) **249**
Karava **40**
Kataragama **53, 281**
Kataragama, Perahera **282**
Kegalle **284**
Kelaniya **285**
Kiri Vihara **325**
Kitulgala **203**
Kogalla **244**
kolam maduwa **95**
Kotte period **77**
Kovias **39**
Kshatriyas **39**
Kumara okana (royal bath) **320**
Kumarankanda Raja Maha Vihara **255**
Kurandaka Lena Cave **250**
Kurunegala **289**
Kuttam Pokuna (pools) **196**

l

Lady Manning Bridge **207**
landscapes **19**
language **132**
Lankarama Dagoba **196**
Lankatilaka (statue house) **325**
Lankatilaka Vihara **278**
Laurasia **19**
leopards **28**
Liberation Tigers of Tamil Eelam (LTTE) **35**
Liberations Tigers of Tamil Eelam **67**
literature **91, 135**
Little World's End **256**
logging **23**
Lohapasada **84, 192**
lotus bath **327**

m

magazines **137**
Maha Devale **282**
Maha Seya Dagoba **305**
Mahabharata **92**
Mahavamsa **91**
Mahaweli Ganga **22, 250**
Mahaweli Project **22**
Mahayana Buddhism **48**
Mahinda's bed **305**
MahindaVihara **305**
Mahiyangana **292**
mail delivery times **144**
Malayadi Temple **188**
Manik Vihara **324**
Marawila **213**
marine fauna **31**
mask carving **95**
Mask Museum **185**
masked plays **95**
masks, carved **185**
Matale **294**
Matara **298**
measures **156**
media **137**
Medirigiriya **300**
metalwork **96**
Mihintale **301**
Mihintale, monastery complex **302**
mining **46**
Minneriya reservoir **246**
Mirisavati Dagoba **191**
modes of transport **154**
Monaragala **305**
monastic community **51**
monastic order **51**
money **138**

monkeys **27**
monks **50**
monsoon **159**
moonstone **80**
moonstone, Queen's Pavilion **196**
Moors **34**
motorbikes **156**
mountain biking **150**
mountain rainforests **23**
Mulkirigala **345**
music **93, 94**

n

Nalanda **297**
Nalanda Wewa (reservoir) **298**
Namunkula **313**
Nataraja **88**
national coat of arms **40**
national emblems **40**
national parks **31, 139**
nationalization **66**
nature conservation **31**
Navamdama **40**
Nayipena Vihara **328**
Negombo **306**
Nevalas **39**
newspapers **137**
Nillakgama, excavations **200**
Nissanka Malla Mandapa **323**
Niyamgapaya Vihara **279**
no swimming **112**
nudism **112**
Nuwara Eliya **309**

o

official language **132**
official name **40**
old hospital, Mihintale **302**
opposition **42**

p

painting **89**
Palace of King Nissanka Malla **318**
Palace of King Parakrama Bahu **318**
Pallas **39**
Pandukabhaya, King **189**
Parakramabahu **22**
parliament **40**

patima-ghara **81**
Peradeniya, Botancal Garden **273**
personal safety **142**
photography **146**
pickpockets **142**
Pigeon Island **348**
Pinawela **284**
Polgasduwa (island) **255**
Polhena **299**
political parties **42**
politics **32**
Polo, Marco **103**
Polonnaruwa **314**
Polonnaruwa period **75**
population **32**
post **144**
post offices **144**
Potgul Vihara **317**
Pottuvil **328**
Premadasa, Ranasinghe **104**
prices **145**
prime minister **40**
prostitution **146**
provinces **41**
Pujavis **39**
Punkhagama (dagoba) **233**
Purana Totagama Raja Maha Vihara **255**
Puttalam **329**

q

Quadrangle **320**

r

rafting **150**
rainforest **22**
Rajavali-Chronik **258**
Ramayana **92**
Ranamasu Uyana (Royal Gardens) **198**
Ranjangane, ruins **200**
Rankot Vihara **324**
Ratna Prasada (Jewel Palace) **196**
Ratnapura **331**
Ravana Ella waterfall **235**
rebirth **53**
religion **47**
rest houses **108**
restaurants **121**
rice cultivation **44**

Ridiyagama-Stausee **250**
rivers **21**
rock fort Yapahuwa **356**
rock fort, Sigiriya **338**
rubber **45**
rubber plantations **259**
Ruhunu National Park **31**
Ruwanweli Dagoba **194**

s

Sabaragamuwa **187**
Sailabima Aramaya **255**
sailing **150**
salt fields **330**
Samadhi Buddha **196**
Samahera **50**
Samsara **53**
Sangha **51**
Sanskrit **132**
Sasseruwa, Buddha statue **201**
Satmahal Prasada **321**
schools **35**
secular architecture **84**
Senanayake Dam **245**
Senanayake, Don Stephen **104**
Senanayake, Dudley Shelton **104**
Shiva **53, 88**
Shiva Devale (Hindu temple) **328**
Shiva Devale (Hindu temple) **324**
shopping **147**
Shudras **39**
Siddharta Gautama **102**
Siddhartha Gautama **47**
Sigiriya **336**
Sila Rock **305**
Silver Temple, Kurunegala **291**
Singhalese **32**
Singing Fishes **207**
Sinhala **132**
Sinharaja Rain Forest Reserve **335**
Sinigama Vihara **254**
Sitavka **202**
slash-and-burn **22**
snake species **28**
snorkelling **151**
society **32**
southeastern lowlands **21**
southwestern part of the island **19**

spells **99**
spices **149**
spirits **97**
sport **149**
sports trip operators **152**
Sri Lanka Freedom Party (SLFP) **42**
Sri Maha Bodhi **192**
Sri Wijaya Sundarama Raja Maha Vihara **292**
stamps **144**
state **40**
state president **40**
stupa house **80**
Sunandaramaya Mahavihara **187**
surf-anglers **244**
surface configuration **19**
surfing **150**

t

taboos **114**
Tamil **132**
Tamil people **34**
Tamil United Liberation Front (TULF) **35, 42, 67**
Tangalla **344**
taxis **155**
tea **149**
tea cultivation **44**
tea factories **204, 250**
teak **23**
temple architecture **79**
tennis **150**
Theravada **48**
thovil **97**
three-wheeler **155**
Thuparama **81**
Thuparama (statue house) **320**
Thuparama-Dagoba **195**
time **153**
Tinapitiya, Lake **213**
tips **115**
Tissamaharama **346**
Tivanka Pilimage (statue house) **327**
tourism **46**
trade unions **42**
train **154**
transport **153**
travel documents **110**
travel insurance **112**
Trimurti **52**

Trincomalee **348**
turtles **28**

u

Underwater world,
 Hikkaduwa **251**
United National Party (UNP) **42**
Uposatha-ghara **81**
urban fortifications **318**

v

vaccinations **127**
Vaishyas 39
Varana, rock temple **309**
Varanasi (Benares) **81**
vatadage **80**
Vedda **58**

Vedda caves **245**
Vedism **52**
Velalla **39**
Velli-duraya caste **40**
Victoria Dam **22**
Vijithapura **201**
visa **110**
Vishnu **52**
Vishnu Devale (Hindu
 temple) **324**
visitor numbers **47**
visual arts **84**

w

Walisinghe Harischandra
 Museum **307**
water sports **150**
websites **131**

weights **156**
welfare system **35**
western monasteries,
 Anuradhapura **199**
Westminster Abbey
 (mountain) **246**
wewas **22**
when to go **157**
Wilpattu National Park **32, 330**
World's End **256**

y

Yala National Park **31**
Yala Nationalpark (Ruhuna
 National Park) **352**
Yapahuwa **354**
youth accommodation **109**

PHOTO CREDITS

LIST OF MAPS AND ILLUSTRATIONS

Highlights **3**
National Parks **33**
Sri Lanka **41**
Foreign Rulers on Sri Lanka **63**
Climate **158**
Tours **163**
Tour 1 **167**
Tour 2 **173**
Tour 3 **176**
Tour 4 **178**
Anuradhapura **193**
Colombo **216**

Colombo Fort **219**
Cave Temple of Dambulla (3D) **231**
Galle **240**
Kandy **264**
Kandy, Botanical Garden **275**
Mihintale **303**
Nuwara Eliya **310**
Polonaruwa **317**
Polonaruwa Quadrangle **321**
Sigiriya **338**
Rock Fort of Sigiriya (3D) **341**

PUBLISHER'S INFORMATION

Illustrations etc: 155 illustrations, 23 maps and diagrams, one large map
Text: Heiner F. Gstaltmayr, Anita Rolf; with contributions by Gabriele Gaßmann, Karen Schreitmüller, Reinhard Zakrzewski
Editing: Baedeker editorial team (John Sykes)
Translation: Michael Scuffil
Cartography: Christoph Gallus, Hohberg; Franz Huber, Munich; MAIRDUMONT/Falk Verlag, Ostfildern (city plan)
3D illustrations: jangled nerves, Stuttgart
Design: independent Medien-Design, Munich; Kathrin Schemel

Editor-in-chief: Rainer Eisenschmid, Baedeker Ostfildern

1st edition 2011

Based on Baedeker Allianz Reiseführer »Sri Lanka« 4. Auflage 2010

Copyright: Karl Baedeker Verlag, Ostfildern
Publication rights: MAIRDUMONT GmbH & Co; Ostfildern

Printed in China

BAEDEKER GUIDE BOOKS AT A GLANCE
Guiding the World since 1827

- Andalusia
- Australia
- Austria
- Bali
- Barcelona
- Berlin
- Brazil
- Budapest
- Cape Town • Garden Route
- China
- Cologne
- Dresden
- Dubai
- Egypt
- Florence
- Florida
- France
- Gran Canaria
- Greek Islands
- Greece
- Iceland
- India
- Ireland
- Italian Lakes
- Italy
- Japan
- London
- Madeira
- Mexico
- Morocco
- Naples • Capri • Amalfi Coast
- New York
- New Zealand
- Norway
- Paris
- Portugal
- Prague
- Rome
- South Africa
- Spain
- Thailand
- Turkish Coast
- Tuscany
- Venice
- Vienna
- Vietnam

DEAR READER,

We would like to thank you for choosing this Baedeker travel guide. It will be a reliable companion on your travels and will not disappoint you.
This book describes the major sights, of course, but it also recommends hotels in the luxury and budget categories, and includes tips about where to eat or go shopping and much more, helping to make your trip an enjoyable experience. Our authors ensure the quality of this information by making regular journeys to Sri Lanka and putting all their know-how into this book.

Nevertheless, experience shows us that it is impossible to rule out errors and changes made after the book goes to press, for which Baedeker accepts no liability. Please send us your criticisms, corrections and suggestions for improvement: we appreciate your contribution. Contact us by post or e-mail, or phone us:

▶ **Verlag Karl Baedeker GmbH**
   Editorial department
   Postfach 3162
   73751 Ostfildern
   Germany
   Tel. 49-711-4502-262, fax -343
   www.baedeker.com
   www.baedeker.co.uk
   E-Mail: baedeker@mairdumont.com